Keyboard Music
before 1700

ROUTLEDGE STUDIES IN MUSICAL GENRES
R. Larry Todd, General Editor

Keyboard Music before 1700, 2nd edition
Alexander Silbiger, Editor

Eighteenth-Century Keyboard Music, 2nd edition
Robert L. Marshall, Editor

Nineteenth-Century Piano Music, 2nd edition
R. Larry Todd, Editor

Nineteenth-Century Chamber Music
Stephen E. Hefling, Editor

Twentieth-Century Chamber Music, 2nd edition
James McCalla

Keyboard Music before 1700

ROUTLEDGE STUDIES
IN MUSICAL GENRES

EDITED BY

Alexander Silbiger

Routledge

New York and London

Published in 2004 by
Routledge
29 West 35th Street
New York, NY 10001
www.routledge-ny.com

Published in Great Britain by
Routledge
11 New Fetter Lane
London EC4P 4EE

10 9 8 7 6 5 4 3 2 1

Library of Congress Cataloging-in-Publication Data

Keyboard music before 1700 / edited by Alexander Silbiger.—2nd ed.
    p. cm. — (Routledge studies in musical genres)
  Includes biblographical references and index.
  ISBN 0-415-96891-7
  1. Keyboard instrument music—History and criticism.
I. Silbiger, Alexander, 1935– II. Series.
ML549.K49 2003
786'.09—dc21   2003047162

Contents

Preface

To the Second Edition

The first edition of *Keyboard Music before 1700*, now out of print, was well received and adopted as a textbook or reference at several institutions. It clearly responded to a need for a readable and yet informative survey of the early keyboard literature, and nothing has appeared since to take its place. Thus we are pleased to present a new edition that incorporates the scholarship of the last few years, updates the bibliographies of editions and literature, and adds a newly written chapter on performance practice.

Notwithstanding the predictions of prophets of doom (who always seem to be with us), interest in early keyboard music continues to be vigorous and healthy, and the few years that separate our two editions have brought an impressive number of new publications. The production of critical editions has been especially remarkable, with important new editions of works of Blow, Buxtehude, Cornet, Kerll, La Barre, Merulo, Philips, Scheidemann, and Scheidt; in addition, new collected works of major composers such as Chambonnières, D'Anglebert, Frescobaldi, Kuhnau, and Bernardo Pasquini and first editions of the important Bauyn and Oldham manuscripts are on the way. Each of the *Guides to Literature and Editions* following the individual chapters has been emended to incorporate these new publications, and the bibliographies include a total of approximately 100 new items under Literature and 40 new items under Editions.

The most substantial and, we hope, most welcome addition is an entire new chapter on performance practice. When planning the original edition we decided that since performance practices differed so much from one region to the next, it would make the most sense to treat the topic within the context of each chapter. However, particularly in response to the frequent use of this book in educational settings, we became convinced that there would be merit to including a systematic general introduction to the topic. Although to the experienced harpsichordist and organist much of what is presented in this chapter will be familiar, we hope that in at least a few areas we have presented fresh perspectives. Also, since in recent years the study of performance practice has been subject to a certain amount of criticism, we thought it might be useful to sketch briefly how the interest in this topic came about and what useful purpose it continues to serve.

We have taken the opportunity to correct any errors that had come to our attention, the number of which was gratifyingly small. Several musical examples were reset to correct misprints discovered in their original versions. We owe thanks to John Mayrose for help with the preparation of these examples, to Timothy Dickey for his assistance with updating the text, to Robert Parkins for his comments on the new chapter, and to Bruce Haynes for commenting on the section on pitch. Finally, we wish to express our gratitude to Richard Carlin of Routledge for his enthusiasm and support for reissuing the series of which this book forms part.

Alexander Silbiger
March 28, 2003

Preface
To the First Edition

This is the first in a set of four volumes that offer a guide to the rich literature of Western keyboard music. Several differences from the other volumes deserve mention here. Our volume covers a much longer time span—longer, in fact, than the three other volumes combined. That difference amounts to more than just chronological range; although all music before 1700 is often labeled "early," the stylistic and conceptual distance between a late fourteenth-century keyboard dance like those in the Robertsbridge fragment and a late seventeenth-century prelude and fugue like those by Buxtehude is hardly less than the distance between a Buxtehude prelude and fugue and a Stockhausen Klavierstück. The scope of our volume was enlarged further by the decision to include the literatures of both stringed keyboard instruments and organ rather than restrict ourselves, as do the later volumes, to stringed keyboard music. That decision was almost unavoidable because for much of the period before 1700 keyboard music does not divide neatly into harpsichord, clavichord, and organ repertories. The parting of the ways between the two literatures became irrevocable only with the acceptance of the piano as the principal stringed keyboard instrument, not so much because of its capacity for dynamic nuance—which had always been within the clavichord's power—as because of the increasing importance of the sustaining pedal as a basic element of its technique.

Other differences resulted from the nature of the early repertory. Among sixteenth- and seventeenth-century composers too few figures stand out sufficiently with respect to the character and distinctness of their work to make a division into individual chapters on each a sensible organizational choice, as it was, for instance, for nineteenth-century composers. One could perhaps imagine an entire chapter on Cabezón, on Byrd, or on Frescobaldi, but whom to pick among the multiple creative talents flourishing in France under Louis XIV, or for that matter among their contemporaries in England and Germany, without doing serious injustice to the many important artists thus ignored? On the other hand, national traditions remained remarkably distinctive throughout the period, more so than during the later eighteenth and much of the nineteenth centuries. This distinctiveness extended from characteristic styles and genres to notation, instruments, and performance practices. Thus a division into chapters by national tradition seemed the preferable structure for organizing our material. It should go without saying that our chapter titles do not refer to political entities (which in some cases did not even exist yet) but to regions united by a common culture and language. In this context we should also assure our readers that generalizations made about certain national traits and tendencies do not refer to innate characteristics of the people born within each region, but rather to common aspects of their culture. The individual treatment of each region does risk drawing attention away from those aspects of the early repertory that are shared by the national traditions and also from the sometimes fruitful cross-pollinations among them; we have therefore in chapter 1 included a brief overview of the entire European scene, noting both similarities and differences among respective literatures.[1]

Two further differences from the repertories covered in the other volumes must be addressed here—differences that are not intrinsic, but concern the relationship of today's audiences to the music, specifically, their comparative unfamiliarity with the early repertory and with its context. Keyboard music written after 1700 is regularly performed and widely heard, or to be more precise, a canon of works from this period is regularly performed and widely heard. Restricted as that canon may be, its familiarity also makes it easy to relate to less frequently played music from the period. But for keyboard music before 1700, no such canon currently exists; at best we are in the early stages of the formation of one. Until a few decades ago the main interest in this repertory was historical rather than artistic, largely motivated by the desire to trace the antecedents of J. S. Bach. Specific pieces were valued for having paved the way, provided models, or even anticipated compositions of his rather than for their own merits; Willi Apel refers to Bach's works as "that singular corpus to which everything that precedes seems to point, for which all earlier works seem as mere preparation" (1972, xiv). But studying Froberger, for instance, for the way he foreshadowed Bach has the effect of placing Bach between us and Froberger, thus obscuring the earlier composer from our view; it turns him into a historical artifact. (This does not mean that we should disregard historical connections, but merely that we should be mindful of time's arrow; no problem arises when we study Bach for how he reinterpreted Froberger, or Froberger for how he reinterpreted Frescobaldi.) Many previous studies of the early keyboard repertory, including Apel's monumental survey, have been strongly affected by using Bach and other later masters as points of reference, not only in the treatment of individual composers but, even more important, in the views on various genres and their histories—an issue to which we shall return in chapter 1.[2] In this book we have tried to avoid such a perspective, hoping as much as possible to view the seventeenth century directly from our own time, unmediated by the intervening centuries.

Perhaps even more unfamiliar than the early repertories are the cultures that produced them. When entering any foreign territory, a lack of sensitivity to different customs and conventions may lead to misunderstandings and misinterpretations. Similarly, without some knowledge of what purpose this music served, where and on what it was played, how it was notated, and how the notation related to what was performed, much of it may appear strange, clumsy, and even dull. Thus, before plunging into discussions of the music, we must consider, more so perhaps than in volumes dealing with later periods, its contexts, sources, notation, genres, performance practices, and instruments—in short, its "musicological" aspects. We have tried to keep the intrusion of those topics to a minimum, treating them only to the extent necessary. The culture and habits of the early keyboard players are a worthy topic for another book, and the story of their instruments would hardly receive justice by anything less, but the primary goal of this volume is to provide a guide to their preserved compositions for the benefit of present-day musicians and music lovers.

We also must warn our readers not to expect an encyclopedic survey of the keyboard literature before 1700 along the lines of Apel 1972. Rather than providing a continuous narrative of the development of keyboard music in each region—a narrative that is largely mythical—we have selected the composers and pieces that we believe still have most to offer in terms of artistic interest and value. Historical significance, although of some consideration, generally took second place in the selection process. Inevitably, our judgment on what to include and what to omit, what to emphasize and what to skim past, will not please everyone, but that is in the nature of a book of this sort.

For certain compositions the question arises as to whether or not they should be regarded as keyboard music. Our criterion for inclusion was the working definition: any music that appears to have been scored to be directly playable on a keyboard. In principle this includes open score and tablature arrangements of songs or vocal polyphony if there are signs that, beyond the act of transcription, an effort was made to adapt the works to keyboard. Music published in separate parts for individual voices also is occasionally advertised as suitable for keyboard (e.g., the Venetian publication *Musica nova accommodate per cantar et sonar sopra organi et altri strumenti* [1540]), but, as is evident from compositions that survive in both keyboard and ensemble versions, a keyboard rendition would entail more than simply playing all the voices as written; therefore, works of that type have been left out of consideration. For works notated in open score the situation is more ambiguous; many of those were in fact intended primarily for performance at the keyboard and are discussed here as such. Finally, although we are well aware that the preserved specimens of keyboard music present only a minute fraction of the music that was played and heard (the rest either being lost or, more often, never written down) and that what survives may be neither typical nor necessarily the best of what was heard, we have made the still-existing compositions our sole concern and not entered into speculations about the nature of the vanished repertory.

Readers will note some differences in approach and organization among the chapters. In part this reflects differences among the national traditions, in part preferences of the individual authors. The Italian and Spanish chapters include extensive coverage of the sixteenth century, treated scantily in the French chapter, but that accords with the comparative size and interest of the surviving repertory. We hope that any inconsistencies resulting from the authors' individual approaches will be found a small price to pay for the special expertise that each brings to his contribution.

Every chapter concludes with a Guide to Literature and Editions, a Bibliography (subdivided into Editions and Literature), and a list of Manuscript Short Titles (except for chapter 4). Again, no attempt was made at comprehensiveness, and emphasis was placed on recent literature, preferably in English; the reader is referred to the bibliographies in Apel 1972 and NG 1980 for additional earlier items. Similarly, the editions singled out for listing are those each chapter author considered most reliable as well as most accessible.

Alexander Silbiger

ACKNOWLEDGMENTS

The authors wish to thank the following individuals for providing assistance, information, or comments: for chapter 1, Robert Parkins, Kathy Silbiger, and Peter Williams; for chapter 2, Candace Bailey, John Caldwell, Mark Greengrass, Curtis Price, Richard Turbet, and Peter Williams; for chapter 3, David Fuller, Robert Gallagher, Elisabeth Gallat-Morin, Arthur Lawrence, David Ledbetter, and Lenora McCroskey; for chapter 4, Jenifer Griesbach; and for general editorial assistance, Isabel Bélance, Gary Boye, John Michael Cooper, Camille Crittenden, Boyd Gibson, and Charles Youmans.

We also want to express our appreciation to Jonathan Wiener, Jane Andrassi, and other members of the staff of Schirmer Books for their expert assistance and their patience and understanding. Finally, we wish to pay special tribute to Maribeth Anderson Payne, former editor in chief, who conceived and initiated this series of volumes on keyboard music.

NOTE ON CITATIONS

Secondary literature is cited according to the author-date system; full citations are given in the literature bibliographies for each chapter. Editions usually are cited by composer and/or (in the case of anthologies) title, sometimes with the addition of the name of the editor or date of publication; full citations appear in the edition bibliographies. Manuscripts are cited by short titles; at the end of most bibliographies a list of manuscript short titles is provided that gives their full RISM sigla. Sigla for series publications used only within a chapter are explained in their bibliography entries. The following are used throughout the volume:

Apel 1972   Apel, Willi. *The History of Keyboard Music to 1700.* Bloomington, IN, 1972

NG 1980   *The New Grove Dictionary of Music and Musicians.* General Editor, Stanley Sadie. London, 1980

NG 2001   *The New Grove Dictionary of Music and Musicians.* Edited by Stanley Sadie; executive editor, John Tyrell. London, 2001

CEKM   *Corpus of Early Keyboard Music.* General Editors, Willi Apel, John Caldwell. American Institute of Musicology, 1963–

SCKM   *17th Century Keyboard Music; Sources Central to the Keyboard Art of the Baroque.* General Editor, Alexander Silbiger. New York, 1987–89

Notes

1. A further danger of our division into national chapters is that it might slight the contributions of smaller nations such as Poland and the Scandinavian countries. The surviving repertory of each of those countries is, however, comparatively small, and they have contributed few keyboard figures of more than regional significance.

2. Apel 1972. Surprisingly, Apel seems to have been aware of this trap (p. xiv), but nevertheless stepped into it again and again. Although his book supposedly deals with keyboard music before 1700, the "Bach" entry in the index gives 219 page references—on the average, one mention of his name every fourth page; furthermore, he is brought into the discussions of 54 different composers and 19 different genres!

Contributors

ALAN BROWN is Reader in Music at the University of Sheffield, England. Among his publications are two volumes of *The Byrd Edition* (the *Cantiones Sacrae* of 1589 and 1591) and a volume of *Elizabethan Keyboard Music* in the series *Musica Britannica*. Together with Richard Turbet he co-edited *Byrd Studies*.

JOHN BUTT is Gardiner Professor of Music at the University of Glasgow. His publications include *Bach Interpretation, Bach–Mass in B Minor, Music Education and the Art of Performance in the German Baroque*, and *Playing with History*. He has made eleven solo recordings on organ and harpsichord, including works of Bach, Elgar, Frescobaldi, Kuhnau, Pachelbel, and Telemann.

BRUCE GUSTAFSON is Professor of Music at Franklin & Marshall College. He is the author of *French Harpsichord Music of the Seventeenth Century* and co-author of *A Catalogue of French Harpsichord Music, 1699-1780*. He has published editions of music by Jaques Hardel, La Barre, Étienne Richard, and Jean-François Tapray, and is the author of numerous articles about French keyboard music.

ROBERT JUDD is Executive Director of the American Musicological Society and Adjunct Professor of Music at the University of Pennsylvania. He has published numerous editions of Italian instrumental and keyboard music including works by Andrea Gabrieli, Girolamo Cavazzoni, Giovanni Girolamo Kapsberger, Claudio Merulo, and Adrian Willaert.

ROBERT PARKINS is Associate Professor of the Practice of Music and University Organist at Duke University. A specialist in early Iberian keyboard literature, he has published articles in journals both in the USA and abroad. His recordings of Iberian keyboard music on organ and harpsichord are available on the Calcante, Gothic, Musical Heritage Society, and Naxos labels.

ALEXANDER SILBIGER, Professor Emeritus of Music at Duke University, is the author of Italian *Manuscript Sources of Seventeenth-Century Keyboard Music* and general editor of *Frescobaldi Studies* and of *Seventeenth Century Keyboard Music* (a set of facsimiles in 28 volumes). He has prepared editions of madrigals by Nicola Vicentino and of sacred concertos by Matthias Weckmann, and published numerous articles on music from the sixteenth to the eighteenth centuries.

CHAPTER ONE

Introduction: the First Centuries of European Keyboard Music

Alexander Silbiger

With the introduction of a keyboard, musicians lost direct contact with the source of their music. A mechanism, sometimes elementary, sometimes formidably complex, was interposed between vibrating strings or air columns and their own bodies. Yet this device proved to be a tool of unprecedented power, allowing a single individual to harness music's full harmony, whether for private solace or for the spiritual uplift of a multitude. Few of the instrument's qualities were as consequential as the ability of each of the player's hands to produce music by itself. The two hands could be like two players, both emerging from one, and easily merged back into one. This effect determined much of keyboard music's special character as well as the forms of notation; the early history of keyboard music can be seen as a history of the exploration and exploitation of this two-handed potential.

Simultaneous negotiation of both hands was, and continues to be, a chief challenge to those seeking to master the keyboard; whereas players of a single line can channel their musicality into realizing the line's expressive content, players of multiple lines must also manage the interplay and balance among several voices. It is no wonder that keyboard playing would become a nearly indispensable auxiliary skill for all musicians attempting to grasp and manipulate the complex textures of music of later centuries, and that so many composers would come from the ranks of masters of that skill. The addition of a pedal board would eventually enhance the instrument's power further, without changing its fundamental nature. Finally, the arrangement of the keys according to ascending pitches almost naturally led to polarized roles for the hands, with a division of labor between treble and bass, or melody and accompaniment, and may very well have facilitated the rise of those conceptions so crucial to music's further development.

Although an instrument functioning in principle like an organ was already known in ancient Greece and Rome (ancient texts credit its invention to an Alexandrian engineer, Ctesibius, in the third century B.C.), we have no evidence of instruments with keyboards sufficiently similar to their modern counterparts to permit real polyphonic playing much before the late fourteenth century (which is not to say that such instruments could not have existed somewhat earlier). From that period survive concrete reports on organs and their use, parts of actual instruments, and clear depictions of organists with both hands on the keyboard. The harpsichord and clavichord also seem to have entered the musical world around this time; a document from 1397 credits the invention of the former to a Viennese physician, Hermann Poll, who called his device a *clavicembalum*.

It probably is no coincidence that the first samples of notated keyboard music date from this period.[1] More surprising is the wide geographic distribution of these early specimens, which come from England, the Netherlands, Italy, and Germany; the urge to record keyboard solos on parchment or paper evidently was not confined to any one part of Europe. On the other hand, the varieties of notational forms, which laid the foundations for long-lived regional traditions, suggest that these forms did not emanate from a central source but represent local solutions to the problem of capturing keyboard music on the page. How to take full advantage of the possibilities offered by these new, or newly improved, instruments, and how to notate the results, would by no means have been obvious, and the surviving evidence provides no more than occasional hints of the story of its accomplishment.

Notation

Musical culture had been solidly based on musicians performing single lines, and polyphony was created by the collaboration of several such performers. Coordination of their parts had become much facilitated by the comparatively recent system of mensural notation. This system primarily served singers, who had been the main practitioners of polyphony; pitch notation relied on solmization practice, and thus was relative. When it was realized that on a keyboard more than one voice could be performed, the obvious thing to try would have been the simultaneous rendition of two independent voices, one by each hand, although there also may have been experimentation with drones and parallel organum.[2] Thus it comes as no surprise that the earliest surviving keyboard pieces have mostly two-voice textures, with each voice notated quite distinctly. Even adaptations of three-part songs tend to retain only two of the voices, usually cantus and tenor (or sometimes cantus and a composite of the two lower voices). At most an occasional sustained sonority is filled in with a third note. Elaborate diminutions in the upper voice suggest a well-developed right-hand technique, but no such demands were yet made of the left hand. Because of the two-part texture and the slow-moving lower voice, some of these pieces may sound a bit thin and static to modern ears, although one cannot help admiring the dazzling diminutions, particularly those of the Faenza Codex.[3] During the second half of the fifteenth century a third voice finally makes its entry in Germany, with partial reliance on the pedal; however, judging by the surviving examples, the playing of full-voiced polyphonic or chordal textures had to wait for the next century.

The surviving specimens of keyboard music from before c. 1500 are few. A rough count nets some 25 manuscripts ranging from fragments preserved in book bindings to the quite substantial Faenza and Buxheim Codices.[4] It is a minor miracle that these manuscripts exist at all, since solo keyboard playing during this period, and indeed, for much of the time covered by this book, largely proceeded without the aid of written music. (Pianists still tend to perform in public without scores.) Some awareness of how the music was notated should be of interest even to players who approach this repertory mostly through modern editions, and might in fact help them interpret what they see.

Two fundamentally different approaches are encountered in the early sources. The first is called old German organ (or keyboard) tablature because it was used mostly in the Germanic regions, although it may not have originated there, since early examples exist from England (Robertsbridge fragment, c. 1360) and Italy (Bologna fragment, c. 1480; see Ill. 1.1).[5] In principle it consists of a single staff on which the upper line for the right hand is notated more or less as if it were a vocal part; the pitches of the lower lines for the left hand are placed immediately below, and are represented by letters with, in the later sources, the addition of rhythmic symbols (usually in the form of little strokes and flags); see also Illustrations 4.1 and 4.2. The origin of this curious but long-lived practice (until c. 1570) can be imagined as follows. In fourteenth-century polyphonic songs each voice was notated by itself on a different part of the same page (so-called "choirbook" format). Someone trying out a song on a keyboard would need to look simultaneously at two different parts of the page or, more realistically, to memorize part of one voice while reading another. The tablature notation may have started when, as a memory aid, people began indicating with letters a lower part underneath the highest part.

The second method, called Italian keyboard tablature or *intavolatura* (although variants of the same idea were used in France, England, and

ILLUSTRATION 1.1. "Tabula et intavolature del canto de organo," Bologna fragment, late fifteenth century (*I-Bu* MS 596.HH. 2⁴, f. 2). Reproduced by courtesy of the Biblioteca universitaria di Bologna.

eventually even in Germany), employs two parallel staves that indicate the lines for the right and left hand with (again, more or less) vocal notation. Thus, it closely resembles modern keyboard notation, although we will note a few differences of which one should be aware when preparing editions or performing from a facsimile. The assignment of each of the two staves to a different hand was to remain part of the Italian tablature tradition through the seventeenth century. Illustration 1.2 shows one of the earliest examples, stemming from the northern Netherlands, with the typically active right hand and slowly moving left hand.[6] Each hand is occasionally asked to play two keys simultaneously (e.g., penultimate measure of the second system). Characteristic of Italian tablature and contributing to its modern appearance are the bar lines, not usually seen in vocal notation of the time. In fact, the staff notations used in both the early German tablatures for the right hand and the early Italian tablatures for both hands differed in several respects from the contemporary mensural notation; we shall come back to these differences, which concern especially the notation of time values and accidentals and usually can be related to the different orientations of singers and keyboard players.

In Germany the asymmetric, right-hand-privileging tablature was abandoned in the late sixteenth century, not, as had happened elsewhere, by giving the left hand its own staff, but by extending the letter notation to the right hand. The resulting so-called new German organ tablature remained in common use throughout the seventeenth century, with occasional competition from the *partitura* system and, increasingly, from staff notation. The tablature's layout tended to be polyphonic, with each voice represented by a row of letters above which were placed the durational signs; see Illustration 4.4. Although this system does not provide a suggestive graphic representation of musical events comparable to that of staff notation, it does offer several advantages that may account for its long survival. Writing staff notation has always been a laborious process, requiring a special skill and wasteful of precious paper; to print a complex keyboard score in a manner that really does it justice called for the even rarer skill of engraving it on a copper plate (for examples, see Ills. 5.10 and 5.12). Copying a score in new German tablature was quick and used up relatively little paper; it could be printed quite economically by combining a limited number of set type pieces (see Ill. 4.4). This tablature also was probably easier to learn to play from (provided one knew one's alphabet), since there was a direct connection between each letter and each key, and no clefs to worry about. On the other hand, a player had to take in two distinct symbols for the pitch and duration of each note, or eight symbols altogether for a four-part chord, which does seem rather cumbersome.

From the fifteenth to the eighteenth centuries Italian tablature developed more or less smoothly to modern notational practice. To avoid

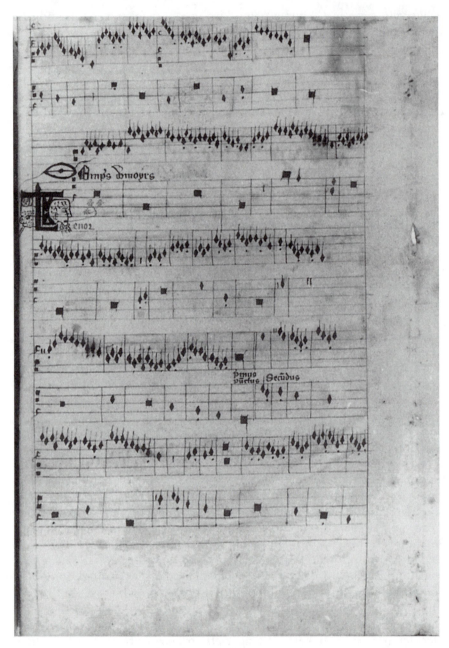

ILLUSTRATION 1.2. "Empris domoyrs," Groningen fragment, late fourteenth century (*NL-G* Inc. 70v). Reproduced by courtesy of the University Library, Groningen.

ledger lines staves often had more than five lines—commonly six for the treble staff and seven or eight for the bass staff. A more important difference, often still noticeable in modern editions of the tablatures, is that the original notation indicates what should be played, but makes no effort to show the underlying voice leading by rests, direction of stems, double stems, or division between staves.[7]

When contrapuntal voicing was of prime concern in keyboard compositions, Italian composers could avail themselves of *partitura* notation or open score, usually in four voices. It was especially favored for pieces in the polyphonic style like ricercars and fantasies, but also was sometimes used—at least in Naples—for other types of works, such as toccatas, dances, and variations. A fringe benefit that may account for some instances of its use was that printers had a much easier time printing the individual voice staves than the complex textures represented on the staves of tablature notation, particularly when printing from movable type. Thus, both pedagogical benefits and economy may be responsible for the occasional use of partitura almost everywhere in Europe (see, e.g., Ills. 4.7, 4.9, and 6.4).

Outside Italy and Germany we have no evidence of a continuous tradition of notating keyboard music before the sixteenth century. In England and France a two-stave system similar to Italy's came into use, although the approaches were different in each country. The English seemed to have looked on their keyboard scores as an attempt to accommodate several voices on two staves rather than as a tablature, and they carried over several elements of mensural notation, although until the later seventeenth century they did prefer six-line staves. When there are more than two voices, an attempt is made to preserve each voice's horizontal integrity (sometimes a middle voice is written entirely with black notes to distinguish it from the other voices; see Ill. 2.2), whereas there is little concern with the vertical alignment of simultaneous pitches (Ills. 2.2 to 2.5 provide various other samples of English notation).

There are so few French keyboard sources from before the seventeenth century that it would be dangerous to regard their idiosyncracies as representative of a French tradition. Like the later French sources they possess one characteristic that would be universally adopted in keyboard notation from the eighteenth century onward: the use of two five-line staves. In fact, except for the frequent use of soprano clef in the upper staff and baritone clef in the lower one (and in some cases the heavy overgrowth of ornament signs), most early French keyboard scores can be read with little difficulty by present-day players (see Ills. 3.2 and 3.3, the latter showing the peculiarly French nonmetric notation of the *préludes non-mensurés*, discussed in chapter 3).

Sixteenth- and seventeenth-century Spanish sources show notational systems similar in principle to new German tablature, except that numbers were used rather than letters (see Ill. 6.5), and we have already noted instances of the use of *partitura*. Eventually, however, two-staff notation gained the upper hand.

It may seem curious that distinct national forms of keyboard notation (and other instrumental notation such as lute tablature) persisted during a time when vocal notation everywhere had become more or less standardized.[8] The difference may have had to do with the rather limited circulation of keyboard music compared with the much wider dissemination of much of the vocal repertoire. For example, the masses and motets of Josquin and other Franco-Netherlandish composers, the subsequent madrigals of the Italians, and the chansons of the French were regarded as works of music that existed in permanent, notated forms and were copied, studied, and performed throughout Europe. On the other hand, keyboard music in a sense existed only in performance, and a player recorded a piece on paper mostly for himself or for his pupils— a situation that began to change as more keyboard pieces were published, although for a long while even those served primarily as "lessons."

ACCIDENTALS

All types of tablatures differ from mensural notation in their method of indicating chromatic alterations. To a singer an accidental meant a hexachord shift,[9] or a temporary transposition, but for a keyboard player it was merely a mechanical instruction to play the adjacent raised key. In German tablatures accidentals were indicated by the attachments of little hooks (to either note or letter) that always signified a sharp (e.g., E flat would be shown as a raised D), except for B flat, which was written as B (and B natural as H); many sixteenth-century Italian tablatures used dots rather than flat or sharp signs. Of greater consequence to the modern player is the matter of "musica ficta" (used here in the modern sense of editorially added chromatic alterations rather than in the original sense of pitches outside the Guidonian system). In vocal notation accidentals were often omitted, either because they were self-evident or because they were left as options for the singers. In tablatures that practice was less common (although by no means nonexistent), surely because it must have appeared pointless to tell a player to press, say, the F key when the F-sharp key was intended. Nevertheless, particularly in scores with staff notation, the accidentals were treated quite casually. During this period the degree inflection of a particular pitch was not so crucial for the musical meaning of a passage as it would become in later centuries. In Beethoven it makes all the difference whether a given chord is major or minor, but in Byrd no more than momentary color may be at stake.

A further distinction from later notation is that in early keyboard scores an accidental applies only to the note that immediately follows, and not, as is customary today, to the remainder of the measure (a principle clearly tied to the later notion of key). Thus, at least in theory, accidentals are repeated as needed, and when they are absent the note should not be altered. In practice they were often omitted, leaving it for the modern editor or player to decide whether or not the omission was deliberate or the result of carelessness. A further complication is that in some scores an accidental also applied to repeated pitches but in others it did not, so that in the case, say, of two Cs with a sharp before the first one, the editor (or often the player) must determine if both are to be played as C sharp or if a chromatic descent C sharp−C was intended. The moral is that players should not necessarily follow the accidentals prescribed in either original texts or modern editions, but be ready to alter them in any way that gives a more musically satisfying result. To be sure, what is musically satisfying to our ears might not have been so back in the seventeenth century; we may, for example, be conditioned to prefer a more "tonal" to a more "modal" version. Nonetheless, by increasing our familiarity with the music of the period, we can hope to educate our ears sufficiently to arrive at a reasonable approximation (teaching us, for instance, that the more "tonal" solution is indeed more likely to be the right one!).

METER AND NOTE VALUES

Differences from mensural notation in the indication of meter and note values depend on the type of tablature. In English and Italian scores the most striking difference is the addition of bar lines, never seen in single-line ensemble parts; their insertion sometimes affected notes meant to continue beyond the measure.[10] The same note shapes and values were used as in contemporary mensural notation (but no ligatures); thus in scores before c. 1600, and often thereafter, the half note rather than the quarter note represents the basic beat in duple time, and bar lines tend to appear every four half notes (although in many scores their placement is somewhat irregular). Because of this, certain mid-twentieth-century editions (e.g., volumes in the *Musica Britannica* series) halved note values, with even further reductions for triple meter, but the policy has become less widely practiced. Reduction of note values, often by a factor of four, remains common in music transcribed from letter and number tablatures; as a result, modern editions from tablature often have a rather black appearance, with what looks like measures in $\frac{2}{4}$ meter (although equivalent to $\frac{4}{2}$!). The reason for such drastic reduction of the original note values is undoubtedly the deceptive appearances of the duration signs in these tablatures; a quarter note, for example (after c. 1480), is represented by a flag with two beams, thus resembling a sixteenth note. The resemblance is even more misleading in old German tablature, in which the note shapes on the staff often resemble mensural note values that are four times smaller; this can be seen very clearly in Illustration 1.3, from an example in Sebastian Virdung's *Musica getutscht*

ILLUSTRATION 1.3. Sebastian Virdung, "Heylige, onbefleckte," upper voice, in mensural notation and, underneath, in tablature (*Musica getutscht* [1511], ff. J1, 2v).

(1511) on how to transcribe a vocal composition into tablature (the example also illustrates several of the other differences between mensural and tablature notation).

One legacy of the mensural system increasingly prevalent in the late sixteenth and early seventeenth centuries is a bewildering variety of meter signatures, including Cs with dots, backward Cs, circles with and without slashes, often in combination with various numerical ratios, and sometimes followed by peculiar-looking note shapes like black whole notes or white eighth notes. In theory these symbols convey something about tempo or rhythmic relationships, but all too often they were used with little consistency, and it is no longer possible to recover precisely what the composer had in mind. If in such cases the editor does not provide a plausible interpretation, a bit of experimentation may be called for. At some transition points a precise proportion, for example 3:2, will work perfectly; at other times it is better to keep the pulse constant, or to follow one's instinctive inclinations. A sometimes useful rule of thumb is: the shorter the note values, the faster the tempo; but a second good rule is to disregard that first rule when it doesn't give good results.

The Early Repertory

As long as keyboard players were limited to single lines, they probably were satisfied with a repertory of chant melodies, popular songs, and dance tunes shared with other musicians. One imagines them decorating their melodies with increasingly elaborate divisions as the keyboards became more responsive and flexible. When they began exploring two-handed playing, their only existing model would have been polyphonic ensemble music; adaptations of popular ensemble pieces make up a substantial segment of the earliest surviving repertory. For some time such pieces outweighed in number the first of what might be considered autonomous keyboard works: cantus firmus settings of liturgical chants (with the chant in long note values in the left hand) and, eventually, pieces not based on an existing song but on a church mode or psalm-tone formula, with titles like prelude, preambulum, intonation, or ricercar.

Present-day musicians may feel frustrated by the absence in this early repertory of a substantial body of original keyboard compositions comparable to the sonatas, suites, and character pieces bequeathed by the great masters of later times. That now so-familiar and much-loved concert repertory is, however, by no means typical of what was commonly played and published; workaday keyboard fare has always consisted predominantly of arrangements of popular songs and arias. Many such settings are simple to the point of being skeletal, although occasionally a Byrd or a Liszt would make his virtuoso fantasies on these tunes available to less gifted players. Keyboard adaptations of famous ensemble pieces, from sixteenth-century canzonas to nineteenth-century symphonies, have always been in demand, and, naturally, the need for technical exercises and other educational materials has remained constant through the centuries. Today, if one visits one of the increasingly rare music stores that actually sell "sheet music" (rather than just CDs or synthesizers), one finds a similar selection of pop and jazz standards, old Broadway and current MTV hits in easy, unadorned settings, piano method books, church hymn collections, an occasional transcription of a Duke Ellington or a Thelonious Monk solo, and just maybe a volume of Bach inventions or Chopin nocturnes. The earliest keyboard repertory was in many ways very similar.

The popular songs were often French; from the Machaut ballades in the Faenza Codex to the ubiquitous Lully arrangements of two and a half centuries later, French imports made their way into the keyboard books of England, Germany, Italy, and Spain along with favorite native songs and dances. A lot of pieces were copied out for teaching purposes, which, since playing and composing were not yet entirely separate activities, could include models for improvisation (e.g., on a liturgical chant or dance bass) as often as finger exercises. Most precious are what look like recorded improvisations of master performers, as found, for example, in the early fifteenth-century Faenza codex or, a century later, in the ricercars of Marc' Antonio Cavazzoni—witnesses to the high levels of artistic and technical attainment of an unwritten tradition.

Not until approximately the middle of the sixteenth century do we see the creation of sets of carefully crafted compositions that were committed to paper, copied, published, admired, and remembered. Among the earliest of such collections are those of Girolamo Cavazzoni published beginning in 1543 (in 1672 Lorenzo Penna still recommended them to students, along with the works of Luzzaschi, Merulo, and Frescobaldi[11]). In 1567 Merulo projected the publication of a dozen volumes, mostly of his own compositions and intabulations, although only a few volumes were realized. Meanwhile, in Spain Antonio de Cabezón was creating an œuvre impressive for its size and variety as well as for the musical weight of its content. Before long these composers were joined by Byrd in England, Sweelinck in the Netherlands, and others elsewhere. Each contributed a memorable body of original works that signaled the transformation of keyboard music from an ephemeral, improvised art form to one with a growing repertory of substantial compositions to be preserved and treasured by successive generations.

There is no doubt that these are the works that will continue to attract the widest interest from musicians and their audiences. Still, whoever takes the trouble to explore the large quantities of unpretentious song settings, dance variations, liturgical service music, and pedagogical material that continued to be produced (mostly by obscure or anonymous figures) will be rewarded by many a gem of unusual charm. The lines between the two repertories are not always so sharply drawn; several major composers have contributed attractive little pieces for near-beginners as well as arrangements of famous chansons and madrigals or variations on well-known airs and dances. Among those arrangements and variations are some of their most technically demanding and artistically imaginative compositions—works that deserve comparison with the improvisations by the great jazz masters of our own century.

Genres and Their Contexts

As with most music from the more remote past, it is generally difficult to find precise answers to the questions that might help to set a given piece in its historical frame—questions such as why was it composed, where and when was it performed, what purpose was it meant to serve? Most pieces were probably not written for monetary gain, at least not directly. Composers rarely earned a substantial part of their income from writing keyboard pieces; most made their living by performing, supplemented with some teaching. The circulation and publication of a musician's works might of course enhance his (or, in extremely rare instances, her) reputation and thus contribute indirectly to his position and earnings, but for the most part it was a sideline to his professional activities. The nature of those activities was likely to determine the character of his compositional work for keyboard.

ORGAN MUSIC

The "bread and butter" for most keyboard players was undoubtedly playing the organ at religious services, whether in small parish churches, major cathedrals, monasteries, or princely chapels. Among the notable exceptions were Sweelinck, whose duties at the Amsterdam Oude Kerk included public recitals but no participation in the Calvinist services (restricted to unaccompanied psalmody), and Chambonnières, who probably was unique among the early keyboard composers in playing the harpsichord exclusively during his professional life. For the majority, though, the need to supply varied and attractive music throughout the church year was ever present, and although they undoubtedly met this need for the most part by improvisation, almost all have left us examples—presumably notated for less gifted organists or as models for their pupils—of how they responded. The repertory includes pieces with specific liturgical designations, such as mass and hymn versets and pieces *per l'elevazione*, but also many other types of pieces that could serve at various moments of the service, from prelude to postlude; even plainsong and chorale settings were probably not limited to the songs' liturgical contexts.

HARPSICHORD MUSIC

Solo harpsichord playing more likely took place in connection with the court appointments and engagements that many of these musicians enjoyed in addition to their organ posts (harpsichords were occasionally used in churches, but, one suspects, largely for continuo). The details are rarely recorded (e.g., in 1520 Marc' Antonio Cavazzoni is listed in the personal payroll of Pope Leo X for playing the *gravicembalo*; see Jeppesen 1960, 1:80), but probably ranged from very private performances for one or a few family members to providing entertainment for such formal occasions as a state visit. The visits of musicians themselves to foreign courts, alone or in the entourage of a legation, would have been especially important for mutual exposures to the styles of visitors and hosts (and may of course have involved performances on both organ and harpsichord); notable among such visits are those of Cabezón to England (1554–55), of Bernardo Pasquini to France (1664), and especially of Froberger to several European capitals.

As with the church services, these artists did not need written music for their court performances, although some may have liked to work out more complex compositions on paper; most music that circulated in manuscript or print probably served students and collectors. Many pieces no doubt reflected the improvisations with which the artists diverted their patrons—improvisations that might have included warmups of arpeggiations and scales, variations on favorite airs, cantus firmus settings, and fugal fantasies on given themes. To associate various genres with more specific venues or occasions is generally not possible; in fact, there is an entire category of pieces like preludes, toccatas, fantasies, ricercars, and tientos that could fit any function, sacred or secular, that were suitable to any time or place, and playable on whatever type of keyboard instrument was appropriate to the occasion, even if originally conceived for a different type.

Scholars have worked hard to try to define the differences among these genres in terms of their structural organization, since form has been such an important factor in their understanding of later genres. However, the distinctions that seemed to have mattered most were those of mood and character. Among the Italian types the ricercar was serious and dignified, whereas the canzona was tuneful and lighthearted and the capriccio playful and witty. The toccata moved back and forth between moods of hesitation and determination, reflecting its preludial roots. Other nationalities were more limited in their choice of titles, with the Spanish at the other extreme calling almost everything a tiento, but that uniform label conceals a diversity of content scarcely less than that of Italy's manifold genres.

IMITATIVE GENRES

It would be a mistake to lump together all the canzonas, capriccios, fantasias, ricercars, and tientos as early, not yet fully developed varieties of fugue, and to evaluate them according to the strictness of their counterpoint and consistency of their subject(s). During the eighteenth century the fugue became an exceptional sort of piece associated with learning and antiquity, but in our period imitation was part of the normal home-and-garden style of serious music and by itself did not define a genre. Thus, in the English fancy the primary agenda was, as the title suggests, display of the artist's fantasy, not the rigorous working out of one or more subjects in imitation; the occasional interjection of homophonic and even dancelike episodes or allusions to popular tunes is a natural consequence of that conception. Furthermore, these largely imitative pieces do not show a progressive evolution toward the monothematic fugue; monothematicism is a feature present in some very early examples and missing in some very late ones. The earlier ricercars, fantasies, and tientos often use neither a single subject nor a set of markedly contrasting subjects, but rather a progression of ideas that appear almost to evolve from each other. The prevailing aesthetic, particularly in the earlier examples, is one of continuous flow and cohesion rather than of overall unity embracing a clearly articulated structure.

DANCES

Dances always have been part of the solo keyboard repertory, even though we do not know how much the keyboard instruments actually were used to accompany dancing. The remarkable estampies in the Robertsbridge fragment somewhat resemble a set of monophonic instrumental pieces from the same time (in London 29987) and may represent models for adapting such single-line pieces to the keyboard by splitting the line between the two hands, accompanying it in parallel octaves, sixth, or fifths, or adding a slow-moving bass. Most fifteenth-century players did not, however, consider dance music worth putting on parchment or paper, and most of the largely anonymous keyboard dances from the sixteenth century, whether from England, France, Germany, or Italy, are rather simple settings of popular dance tunes and basses, with one hand (usually the right) either playing the tune or stereotypical divisions, and the other hand providing an accompaniment, often with parallel block chords. In 1593 Girolamo Diruta still wrote with barely concealed contempt about the differences between playing dances and playing "serious music" (Diruta 1984, 54), although by that time composers like Byrd had already begun to create dance music for the keyboard that was as "serious" and artfully made as any other genre.

Several of the earliest serious dance compositions, whether the pavans of Byrd in England or the galliards of Trabaci in Naples, also exist in versions for instrumental ensemble. It could be that when composers wanted to move beyond keyboard dances that were merely harmonizations of popular tunes, they began by adapting ensemble dances, and for some time continued to conceive their keyboard dance compositions initially as four–voice polyphonic settings. This might explain why so many late sixteenth- and early seventeenth-century dances, including those of Byrd, Trabaci, Scheidt, and even Andrea Gabrieli's Passamezzo—his sole contribution to this repertory—are so heavily contrapuntal.

A new approach to writing original and idiomatic dance music for keyboard was introduced by Frescobaldi; his dances, particularly the correntes, capture the lightness and bounce of popular dance music, yet are impeccably crafted, often with hints of polyphonic voicing. His inspiration may have come from both the well-developed stylized dance repertory of the lute and the music of the fiddle-playing dance masters. Dance music is always driven by fashion and exoticism (with, of course, more than a hint of eroticism); Frescobaldi turned his back on the pavans and passamezzos that dominated much of the earlier dance repertory, and in addition to the corrente (probably of French lineage) and the balletto (a form of allemande or German dance), he promoted the passacaglia and the ciaccona (chaconne), of Spanish and New World origins respectively. In his last publications he began to combine his short dance pieces into little cycles, favoring the sequence balletto-corrente-passacaglie.

The idea of combining different dance types was hardly new; pairs of musically related pavans and galliards, for example, had been enjoying great popularity in England. The practice was to assume even greater importance for the next generations. Frescobaldi's student Froberger joined the Spanish sarabande and the English gigue to the German allemande and the French courante, and thus is often credited with laying the foundations of the classical dance suite. Because of the scarcity of French harpsichord music from before 1650, we are not certain to what extent he actually provided the lead or—more likely—followed already existing French conventions. It is, however, beyond question that during the later part of the century France provided the models of dance music for the rest of Europe, including new favorites like the minuet that trickled down from the court of Louis XIV. With the inspiration of those models, the English, Germans, and Italians all created their own traditions of keyboard dances, thus contributing to the rich and diverse Baroque repertory.

We shall close with an instructive example that illustrates the flow of keyboard music across national boundaries during the middle of the seventeenth century, and the regional accents acquired by the foreign imports. Example 1.1 shows the beginning of a courante attributed to a Monsieur de la Barre—probably Pierre Chabanceau de la Barre (1592–1656), organist and *maître joueur d'épinette* (master player of the spinet) at the French court. The piece, perhaps because of its haunting melody, seems to have enjoyed international popularity; copies survive in seven manuscripts from England, Germany, Italy, and the Netherlands. Since in one manuscript it appears twice, there actually are eight versions, no two of which are identical. Example 1.1 presents the first strain of the versions in manuscripts from (a) England, (b) Germany, (c) Italy, and (d) the Netherlands.[12] Except for converting the examples to five-line staves with treble and bass clefs, we have preserved as much as possible the features of the original notations, including all ornament signs, rests, key and time signatures, and, in (a), the black whole notes (equivalent to half notes).

Beginning with the end of phrase, we observe that the F-major chord in mm. 7–8 in the English and German versions is embellished by nearly continuous arpeggiation, whereas in the other two versions it is left comparatively plain. Does this mean that English and German harpsichordists were more fond of prolonging final chords in this fashion than their Dutch and Italian colleagues? A similar question can be asked about the ornamentation. The English and Dutch versions are richly

EXAMPLE 1.1. La Barre, *Courante*

(a) English version

(b) German version

(c) Italian version

(d) Netherlandish version

supplied with pairs of diagonal strokes—the ubiquitous English ornament signs that presumably prescribe some form of trill or mordent (about the precise meaning we are still guessing; see p. 48.)[13] But why are there no ornament signs at all in the Italian version; did Italian harpsichordists not decorate their playing with trills and other flourishes? We know from many contemporary sources that Italians were as fond of trills as anyone else, but that they considered such matters as where to add ornaments or how to arpeggiate a chord mere interpretive details best left to the performer. The opposite extreme to this laxity is shown in m. 6 in the German version, where an entire trill is meticulously spelled out note by note. Written-out trills appear again several times later in the piece; perhaps this characteristic cadential figure was still enough of a novelty in Germany for the copyist to think it safer to write it out rather than indicate it by a sign. In general, the spelling out of details was as much a tradition in Germany (with Bach as the classical example) as was their omission in Italy.

Other interesting differences among these and the other versions do not become evident until one looks at the entire piece. For example, in all but the Dutch version the courante is followed by a characteristically French *double,* a variation, mostly of the treble voice, in flowing eighth notes. The *double* is more or less the same in all versions and thus forms part of the piece. One question facing the player is whether one should first play the plain versions, with repeats of both strains, and then the *double,* again with repeats (i.e., A:‖:B, A′:‖:B′), or whether one could substitute the double strains for the repeats (AA′BB′), a more economical format more in tune with modern lifestyles. The manuscripts suggest that both methods were practiced, at least outside France. Our Italian version clearly shows the A and B strains with repeats, followed by the two *double* strains with their repeats; the English version has A going directly into A′, followed by B and then B′, all without repeats. The German version is the only one to include a second variation, with eighth-note divisions in the bass; its strains serve as written-out repeats for the *double,* and thus the resulting scheme is A :‖: B :‖ A′ A″ B′ B″.

No version of this courante exists in the hand of the composer or in any other French manuscript or publication. What the lost original was really like, and which of the surviving versions would have been closest to it, are questions that cannot be answered; even in Paris it may not have existed in any fixed form but perhaps was played differently at different times, whether by the composer or by anyone else (see p. 125). To try to arrive at some kind of synthetic version based on the "best" readings would seem to be a futile exercise. Each of the surviving versions must at one time have been the basis of a performance somewhere in Europe and today could be legitimately played as such.

The moral of our exercise is that, notwithstanding the impression given by erudite scholarly editions, most early keyboard music (and most other kinds of early music for that matter) does not really exist in any kind of definitive version. Except for the comparatively rare cases in which pieces have been preserved in autographs, or in manuscripts or editions prepared under the composer's supervision,[14] the text we know probably differs in many details from the composer's original conception. Our example also suggests that any copy of a piece from a place far from where it was composed very likely picked up flavors and accents from its new home. But rather than lament this unalterable situation, we should rejoice in the large amount of music that somehow has survived the onslaught of time, and remember that each score represents a musician's idea of how a certain piece of music should sound. With knowledge and imagination we can bring these scores back to life and thus enhance our pleasure and, one hopes, that of our listeners.

Guide to Literature and Editions

Williams 1993 offers a comprehensive treatment of the early history of the organ (to c. 1250) and how it became associated with the Christian church, with many provocative new ideas. A recent reference on several aspects of early keyboard instruments, music, and practices within the larger musical and social context of fifteenth-century Europe is Strohm 1993, in particular pp. 74–75, 90–93, and 367–74. On seventeenth-century music in general, Bianconi 1987 makes fascinating reading despite its (quite deliberate) privileging of Italy and its (equally deliberate) marginalizing of instrumental music.

For keyboard music, Apel 1972 remains indispensable, even though it must be used with caution. For its time the book was an admirable accomplishment, but Apel's perspective on music history has become rather antiquated. In addition to the tendency to evaluate composers and their works as links in an evolutionary chain leading toward J. S. Bach, we should mention his excessive emphases on the value of originality—with the consequent devaluing of intabulations as "arrangements"—and on the formal aspects of compositions, such as his attempts to identify the "toccata forms" of Merulo or Frescobaldi, even though for genre definitions in pre-1700 music, textures and cultural (or affective) associations may be more important than structural schemes.

Handy surveys on the instruments and their history are Williams and Owen 1988 on the organ and Ripin and colleagues 1989 on other keyboard instruments. An annotated list of the sources of keyboard music (to c. 1660) can be found in Caldwell 2001. There is no good general study on early keyboard notation. As an introduction, Apel 1961 is still serviceable, although his transcription policies are outdated; see also Rastall 1982. On the significance of various tablature notations, see Silbiger 1991; interesting interpretations of early printed formats, particularly with reference to Italy and Spain, can be found in Judd 1989. On reading from original notation, see SCKM, 1: vii–ix and Silbiger 1994; on modern editions of early keyboard music in general, see Silbiger 1989 (note in particular 186–88 on accidentals). A valuable source on performance practice and many other aspects of early keyboard music is Williams 1989.

Many of the earliest keyboard pieces and fragments (before c. 1500) are included in CEKM, 1, although the edition is not always satisfactory; Sanders and colleagues 1986, 149–57, gives better versions of some of the Robertsbridge numbers. Editions of most of the other earliest pieces can be found only in various musicological studies, including Cattin 1964–77, Nadás 1985 (203–06), Daalen and Harrison 1984, Wolf 1919/1963 (254–55), and Ziino 1981. Strohm 1993, 368 (n. 317) lists recent reports on additional German sources. For music after c. 1450, see the Guide to Literature and Editions concluding each chapter.

Notes

1. See the Guide to Literature and Editions at the end of this chapter.

2. Such techniques are still reflected in the estampies of the late fourteenth-century Robertsbridge fragment; see CEKM, 1: 1–3. Williams (1993, 43–44) presents further thoughts on early modes of polyphony that might have been enabled by the keyboard.

3. See p. 247. Of course, the possibility that players sometimes added a third voice, for instance by turning a six into a six-three chord or adding a fifth to an octave (in accordance with the polyphonic style of the period), cannot be excluded.

4. In recent years some people have argued that the Faenza Codex was intended for two lutes rather than for keyboard, and a debate on this issue has ensued; see p. 306, n.2. We shall regard it here as keyboard music. It is reasonable to assume that in Italy, as elsewhere, some music for keyboard instruments was written down, and on the basis of later sources from Italy and elsewhere, one would predict that with regard to repertory, style, and notation such music would resemble Faenza. It is not clear that an equally strong case (essentially the "if it quacks like a duck . . ." argument) could be made for lute duets.

5. On the Robertsbridge fragment, see Strohm 1993, 83–84; on the Bologna fragment 596, see Fallows 1977, 18–28.

6. For later examples of Italian tablature, see Illustrations 5. 10 and 5.12.

7. For more on this point, see Silbiger 1991.

8. As late as the early fifteenth century there were still significant differences among the vocal notations of France, Italy, and Germany.

9. Singers read their parts using the solinization technique, that is, according to the syllables of a movable hexachord ut, re, mi, fa, sol, la, with a semitone between mi and fa. A flat signified the placement of fa, a sharp or natural the placement of mi.

10. Ties, although not unknown, were often omitted, and continuation across a bar line was handled by a variety of means (not always understood by modern editors): a note was repeated, a prolonging dot was placed in the following measure, or the note was simply cut off at the bar line.

11. Quoted in Judd 1989, 201.

12. The manuscripts are cited, along with modern editions, in Gustafson 1979, 2:21–22. The sources for Example 1. 1 are (a) *F-Pn* Rès. 1185, No. 44; (b) *G-Bds* Lynar A 1, No. 65; *(c) I-Rvat* Fondo Chigi, MS Q.IV.24, No. 13; (d) *NL*Uim MS q. 1, No.22. Modern editions of several of these and other versions are given in

Gustafson 1999, 12–17.

13. The triple stroke in Example 1. 1 a is much rarer; is it a prolonged trill, as in Example 1. 1b?

14. Among the few surviving autographs of keyboard music from before 1700 are the beautiful dedication volumes prepared by Froberger for the Austrian emperors (although the flamboyant captions were contributed by a professional artist); among manuscripts prepared under a composer's supervision and including his corrections and annotations is William Byrd's My Ladye Nevells Booke; and among editions prepared by a composer are the series of volumes of Frescobaldi's keyboard works published during his life time. By comparison, hardly any of Sweelinck's keyboard compositions survive in a source that even stems from the Netherlands, and one can only speculate how close the many English and German manuscript copies of his music are to what he actually wrote.

Bibliography

Apel, Willi. *The Notation of Polyphonic Music, 900–1600.* Cambridge MA, 1961.
Bianconi, Lorenzo. *Music in the Seventeenth Century.* Trans. David Bryant. Cambridge, 1987.
Broude, Romald, "Composition, Performance, and Text in Solo Music of the French Baroque." *Text* 15 (2002): 19–49
Caldwell, John. "Sources of Keyboard Music to 1660." In NG 2001, 24: 19–39.
Cattin, Giulio. "Ricerche sulla musica a Santa Giustina di Padua all'inizio del Quattrocento. 1. Il copista Rolando da Casale, nuovi frammenti musicali dell'Archivio di Stato." *Annales Musicologiques* 7 (1964–77): 17–41.
Daalen, Maria van, and Frank L. Harrison. "Two Keyboard Intabulations of the Late Fourteenth Century." *Tijdschrift van de Vereniging voor Nederlandse Muziekgeschiedenis* 34 (1984): 97–108.
Diruta, Girolamo. *The Transylvanian (Il Transilvano). 2 vols.* Ed. Murray C. Bradshaw and Edward J. Soehnlen. Henryville, 1984.
Edler, Arnfried. *Gattungen der Musik für Tasteninstrumente,* Teil 1, Von den Anfängen bis 1750. Handbuch der musikalischen Gattungen, 7. Laaber, 1997.
Fallows, David "Fifteenth-Century Tablatures for Plucked Instruments: A Summary, a Revision, and a Suggestion." *The Lute Society Journal* 19 (1977): 7–33.
Gustafson, Bruce and R. Peter Wolf, eds. *Harpsichord Music Associated with the Name La Barre.* The Art of Keyboard, 4. New York, 1999.
Jeppesen, Knud. *Die italienische Orgelmusik am Anfang des Cinquecento.* 2d edition. 2 vols. Copenhagen, 1960.
Judd, Robert Floyd. "The Use of Notational Formats at the Keyboard." Ph.D. dissertation, University of Oxford, 1989.
Marshall, Kimberly. *Iconographical Evidence for the Late-Medieval Organ in French, Flemish and English Manuscripts.* 2 vols. New York, 1989.
Nadás, John Louis. "The Transmission of Trecento Secular Polyphony: Manuscript Production and Scribal Practices in Italy at the End of the Middle Ages." Ph.D. dissertation, New York University, 1985.

Rastall, Richard. *The Notation of Western Music: An Introduction.* New York, 1982.

Ripin, Edwin, et al. *Early Keyboard Instruments.* The New Grove Musical Instruments Series. New York, 1989.

Sanders, Ernest H., et al. *Polyphonic Music of the Fourteenth Century.* Vol. 17. Monaco, 1986.

Silbiger, Alexander. "In Defense of Facsimiles." *Historical Performance* 7 (1994): 101–04.

———. "Is the Italian Keyboard Intavolatura a Tablature?" *Recercare* 3 (1991): 81–103.

———. "Reviews [Review essay on early keyboard editions]." *Journal of the American Musicological Society* 42 (1989): 172–88.

Strohm, Reinhard. *The Rise of European Music 1380–1500.* Cambridge, 1993.

Thistlethwaite, Nicholas and Geoffrey Webber, eds. *The Cambridge Companion to the Organ.* Cambridge, U.K., 1998.

Williams, Peter. "Keyboards." In *Performance Practice,* ed. Howard M. Brown and Stanley Sadie 2: 20–43. New York, 1989.

———. *The Organ in Western Culture, 750–1250.* Cambridge, 1993.

———. and Barbara Owen. *Organ.* The New Grove Musical Instruments Series. New York, 1988.

Wolf, Johannes. *Handbuch der Notationskunde.* Vol 2. Leipzig, 1919. Reprint. 1963.

Ziino, Agostino. "Un antico 'Kyrie' a due voci per strumento a tastiera." *Nuova rivista musicale italiana* 15 (1981): 628– 33.

Manuscript Short Titles

Bologna fragment	*I-BU* MS 596. HH. 2[4]
Buxheim Codex	*D-Mbs* Cim. 352b
Faenza Codex	*I-FZc* MS 117
Groningen fragment	*NL-G* Inc. 70
London 29987	*GB-Lbl* Add. 29987
My Ladye Nevells Booke	*GB* private collection
Robertsbridge (fragment)	*GB-Lbl* Add. 28550

CHAPTER TWO

England

Alan Brown

Even the most concise survey of Western musical history will make some reference to the virginalists, that school of English keyboard composers who flourished in the late Elizabethan and Jacobean eras.' The largest source to preserve their music, the Fitzwilliam Virginal Book, is one of the best known of all musical manuscripts. It has been available in a modern edition for more than a century and was the basis for Charles van den Borren's pioneering study (1912). Hardly less familiar is the earliest substantial manuscript of virginal music, My Ladye Nevells Booke (hereafter Nevell), dated 1591 and devoted to music by William Byrd. Byrd, who excelled not only in keyboard writing but in virtually every genre cultivated by the Elizabethans, will be the focus of special attention in this chapter. He played a vital role in developing the forms and characteristic textures of the virginalists. Nevertheless, his younger contemporaries, among whom John Bull and Orlando Gibbons are prominent, did not simply imitate him. Each brought a distinctive personality to the art of keyboard composition.

Needless to say, the virginalists do not tell the whole story of English keyboard music before 1700. Thomas Tallis in the sixteenth century and Henry Purcell in the seventeenth (to name but two) may have been active primarily in other fields, but they produced finely crafted keyboard works that can be appreciated for their own merits and not merely as representing particular genres or anticipating later developments.

Inevitably, keyboard music was affected by the political factors that had such profound effects on English life in general. In particular, the turbulent middle years of both the sixteenth and the seventeenth centuries took their toll. The English Reformation instigated by Henry VIII (r. 1509-47) signaled the end of an important school of liturgical organ composition, and in the period of the Civil War and Commonwealth

(1642–60) organs were again silenced and in many instances destroyed. But these setbacks were reversed at other times and for English music as a whole a much more positive picture emerges in the years of Elizabeth I (r. 1558–1603) and James I (1603–25), and—after the Restoration of the monarchy—Charles II (1660–85).

To a large extent the history of English keyboard music is the history of keyboard music in London. Most of the composers whose work we shall be considering served as organists of the Chapel Royal, or were otherwise involved with the royal music; some were organists of Westminster Abbey or St. Paul's Cathedral. All of the seventeenth-century printed sources of English keyboard music were issued in London. Some composers, however, were also associated with provincial cities: Byrd began his career in Lincoln, Bull in Hereford, and Thomas Tomkins ended his in Worcester. In the mid-seventeenth century Oxford was a center of some importance, as the fine collection of keyboard manuscripts in the Library of Christ Church bears witness.

The Background

Chronological accounts of European keyboard music invariably begin with an English source, the so-called Robertsbridge fragment from the late fourteenth century, already touched on in chapter 1. The six pieces therein (two incomplete) may perhaps have been copied by an English scribe, but the music itself is almost certainly of continental provenance.

From fifteenth-century England it is likely that no keyboard music survives at all, and no instruments are extant. However, there is ample evidence for the use of organs during this century, in records of payments to organ builders and technicians in various parts of the country. Probably most fifteenth-century church organs were modest in scale; if they possessed more than one rank (set of pipes) there was no mechanism for bringing them into play separately, so variations in volume or tone quality would not have possible. It was not uncommon for a church or cathedral to possess two or more organs—one, for example, on the main choir screen and another in the Lady Chapel—so that wherever services took place an organ would be available. The role of the organist was to participate in the liturgy by playing sections of plainsong that would otherwise have been sung. This practice presumably arose partly in order to provide variety and partly to give some relief to the singers. The earliest unambiguous reference to *alternatim* performance, that is, the alternation of choir and organ in the performance of a plainsong, dates from 1396 and concerns a Te Deum sung "alternantibus organis" at the reception of a new abbot at St. Albans (Harrison 1963, 206). It is not known whether on that occasion the organ played only the plainsong notes, or something more elaborate, but during the fifteenth century the addition of counterpoints to the plainsong melody (no doubt improvised at first), and the decoration of the plainsong line itself, must have become regular features. The earliest surviving English liturgical organ music, from the early sixteenth century, shows these procedures at a fairly sophisticated level of development.

Information about organs in the sixteenth century is somewhat more abundant; records of payments include details of a kind lacking in earlier times. For example, at the Church of St. Lawrence, Reading, in 1513 "xjd" (11 pence) was paid for two locks, "one for the stopps and the other for the keyes." This is apparently the earliest reference to stops; as the word implies, these were used to shut off certain ranks of the organ, but the term soon acquired its modern meaning of a register of pipes that can be brought into play.

A famous document of 1519 is the contract between the organ builder Anthony Duddyngton and the churchwardens of All Hallows, Barking (by the Tower), London, for

> a pair of organs . . . of double C-fa-ut that is to say xxvii plain keys, and the principal to contain the length of v foot, so following with Bassus called Diapason to the same, containing length of x foot or more: and to be double principals throughout the said instrument . . . with as few stops as may be convenient. [spelling modernized]

The phrase "pair of organs" does not mean two instruments or even two manuals. The term appears to derive via French from the Latin *par organorum*—a set of matching pipes. "Double C-fa-ut" is the C below the bass stave and in conjunction with "xxvii plain keys" implies a compass of 27 naturals from C to a″ (the black notes being understood). The organ was to contain principal and diapason ranks, the former sounding an octave above the latter. Other aspects of the instrument remain ambiguous. The given pipe lengths of five and ten feet may or may not imply that the pitch was a major third or so below our present standard, and the meaning of "double principals" is obscure. It could refer to two ranks of pipes (e.g., one stopped, and one open) or to a small chorus of stops whose lowest component sounded at 4′ pitch, extending down to "double C-fa-ut."

In 1526 John Howe and John Clymmowe undertook to build an organ at Holy Trinity, Coventry, with "vii stops and xxvii pleyn keyes." Here again, a keyboard running from C to a″ is probable. This compass is sufficient for all extant English liturgical organ music.

An unusually informative source is the inventory of musical instruments belonging to Henry VIII, made in 1547. The list includes more than 60 instruments held in the King's different houses, the majority being at Westminster under the care of Philip van Wilder, Henry's

"Keeper of the Instruments." There are double and single regals, double and single virginals, and just two clavichords relegated to the list of "Instruments of Soundrie Kindes" (clavichords seem to have been more common in the previous century). The "double" instruments had a more extended bass range (probably to C, as opposed to c or G). The regal was a small chamber organ, no doubt similar to the smaller instruments used in churches. The inventory gives details of the pipework for several of the regals (though not precise specifications); typically they had three or four ranks, including pipes of wood, tin, or brass, the regal (reed) stop itself, and often a "Cimball" (perhaps a small two-rank mixture). Sometimes a rank of pipes was divided, although exactly where is not stated. One of the largest instruments was "A paire of double Regalles with viii halfe stoppes and one hole stoppe of pipes." This division would enable the player to use different tone colors in the upper and lower registers of the single manual instrument.

Following the Reformation and during the reign of Elizabeth the organ suffered a period of neglect; many churches allowed their instruments to fall into disrepair, and there is little evidence even of the building or use of house organs. In the early years of the seventeenth century there was a revival, in which an important part was played by Thomas Dallam. Complete specifications survive for a number of his instruments, some of which have two manuals. The organ he built at Worcester Cathedral in 1613–14 has often been quoted as a typical example:

> Great: 2 open diapasons (8′); 2 principals (4′); one twelfth ($2\frac{2}{3}$′); 2 fifteenths (2′); one recorder (stopped) (8′?)
> "Chaire Organ" (Choir): one [stopped] diapason (8′); one principal (4′); one flute (4′?); one fifteenth (2′); one twenty-second (1′)

For the Great diapasons the explanation is added "CC fa ut a pipe of 10 foot long," which confirms a compass descending to C and suggests a pitch (once again) about a major third below that of today.

Organs built after the disruptions of the midcentury were similar in essential respects to those of Dallam, although the manual compass would often be extended down to G_1. There were still no pedals. A two-manual organ commissioned from Robert Taunton for Wells Cathedral in 1662 had a very similar layout to the previous example:

> Great: 2 open diapasons (8′); one stopped diapason (8′); 2 principals (4′); one twelfth ($2\frac{2}{3}$′); one twenty-second (1′); one recorder (8′?)
> Chaire Organ: One stopped diapason (8′); one flute (4′?); one principal (4′); 2 fifteenths (2′); one twenty-second (1′)

English organ building in the late seventeenth century was dominated by "Father" Bernard Smith and Renatus Harris. Both of them added a third manual ("echo organ") to their largest instruments from the 1680s onward.

The 1547 inventory describes a large number of "Virginals." In modern usage the term usually refers to the small rectangular instrument with strings running parallel to the keyboard, but in the sixteenth century it was applied to any type of harpsichord. No doubt some of Henry's instruments were of the rectangular type, but his collection also included "longe Virginalles made harpe fasshion," which suggests the characteristic harpsichord shape with the strings lying at right angles to the keyboard. Henry's stringed keyboard instruments were almost certainly imported from Northern Italy or the Low Countries. Van Wilder himself was a Netherlander, and Dionysius Memo, a keyboard virtuoso from Venice, played at court in 1517.

We know tantalizingly little about the instruments that the virginalists had at their disposal. Almost certainly, the majority were still imported. A sixteenth-century Italian virginal, said to have belonged to Queen Elizabeth, is in the Victoria and Albert Museum, London. Its compass, originally C/E (short octave) to f′″, is standard for Italian virginals of this century—but not in agreement with that which suffices for the music of Byrd and most of his immediate successors (C, D, E to a″). Harpsichords and virginals by members of the Ruckers family of Antwerp certainly found their way to England in Byrd's time. The most common Ruckers instrument was the single-manual harpsichord with 8¢ and 4¢ stops, and a compass of C/E (short octave) to c′″. The Ruckers virginals normally had the same compass and one 8′rank. Russell mentions nearly 20 instrument makers resident in England in the sixteenth century whose names appear in various records, but of their work only one example survives. It is a combined organ and harpsichord, dated 1579, by L. Theeuwes, a Netherlander who had settled in London by 1568. Its keyboard ran from C to c′″, with a chromatic bottom octave, and the harpsichord had three registers, 8′, 8′, 4′.

The importation of foreign instruments continued at least until 1637, when Charles I ordered a large double-manual harpsichord from the Ruckers workshop. However, about 20 rectangular virginals by English makers survive from the years 1641 to 1679 (see, e.g., Ill. 2. 1). They are all of the type with the keyboard left of center, which meant that the string was plucked near the left-hand bridge, giving a bright tone. English harpsichords from before 1700 are extremely rare. One example, made by Charles Haward in London in 1683, has two 8′stops and may originally have had a lute stop. Haward also made "bentside" spinets. In the last quarter of the seventeenth century the spinet replaced the virginal as the standard small domestic keyboard instrument. It had a single set of strings, running at about 35° to the keyboard; the normal compass was G_1/B_1 (short octave) to c′″or d′″, which is suitable for most of the keyboard music by Restoration composers.

ILLUSTRATION 2. 1. Virginal by James White, made in London and dated 1656. The compass is G_1/B_1 (short octave) to c'''. The instrument is seen here in a contemporary setting at the Museum of London. Reproduced by kind permission of the Museum of London.

The Two Sixteenth-Century Traditions

No keyboard music was printed in England before the seventeenth century. Manuscripts are our only sources; however, English keyboard manuscripts earlier than Nevell are scarce. Many must have been lost in the religious upheavals of the midcentury. Those that do survive represent two traditions, sacred and secular; Byrd drew on both in forming his own keyboard style. The most important source for liturgical organ music is London 29996. The three relevant layers of this composite manuscript (ff. 6–48; ff. 49–67; ff. 158–178′) were probably all compiled before 1559, the date when the Catholic rite finally ceased to be the official one in England. The hymn settings on ff. 158–178′ are arranged liturgically, beginning with Advent and continuing as far as the first Sunday in Lent. The largest of the purely secular sources is the so-called Dublin Virginal Manuscript of c. 1570. This book did not originate in Ireland; rather, the one composer named, "mastyre taylere," can probably be identified as John Taylor, who was organist of Westminster Abbey in 1562–70. A third source, the Mulliner Book, copied by Thomas Mulliner in London,

EXAMPLE 2.1. Grounds in Hornpipes by Aston and Byrd

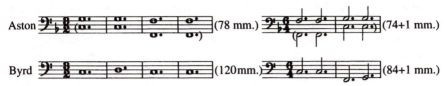

c. 1560–75, contains a miscellany of music probably compiled for the use of choirboys (see Flynn 1993). About half the pieces are plainsong settings, although not in any particular liturgical order; among the rest are keyboard transcriptions of anthems and of secular and sacred songs, and a few examples of what appear to be idiomatic harpsichord works.

At least one earlier manuscript survives to give us some idea of the kind of music played by the professional harpsichordists at Henry VIII's court. It is Royal App. 58, dating from c. 1520–40, with its three famous pieces in idiomatic keyboard style: "A hornepype" by Hugh Aston and the anonymous "My lady careys dompe" and "The short mesure off my lady wynkfylds rownde." All three use a melody-and-accompaniment texture with broken chord figurations in the left hand. The most extended piece is Aston's Hornpipe, which could well have been the direct model for Byrd's piece of the same name (MB 27/39).[2] Both works have a first section with a 4-measure ground (if barred in $\frac{3}{2}$ meter) and a second section with a 2-measure ground (if barred in compound duple time). Example 2.1 shows, in their simplest form, the grounds used in the two pieces. Aston's ground is essentially in the tenor, often supported by the bass notes shown in brackets in the example. It begins on the supertonic, but from m. 23 onward new right-hand figurations tend to begin on the tonic measures, anticipating the pattern of the second section. Example 2.2 shows a few measures on either side of the change of meter. The seamless join here is typical of Aston's sustained melodic line, which often bridges the statements of the ground.

The other two pieces have more obvious connections with the court: Sir Nicholas Carew (d. 1539) was Henry's "Master of the Horse" and Sir Richard Wingfield (d. 1525) his ambassador to France. The "dump" is again based on a ground—a simple alternation of G (tonic)

EXAMPLE 2.2. Aston, Hornpipe, mm. 77–80

and D (dominant). The opening right-hand melody has a resemblance to the "Western Wynde" tune that must have been well known at court. The haunting third piece does not employ a ground, though only three chords are used. It achieves its effect by a flexible melody cast in nine- and ten-measure phrases and by the use of chords of the flattened seventh (B flat in a C-major context).

These three idiomatic pieces could well have been played on the regal as well as on the virginal, and the same is true of six short dances that follow them in Royal App. 58: "The empororse pavyn" (in triple time), "A galyarde," "The kyngs pavyn" (in another ink has been added "King henry the viij^th pavyn"), "The crocke," "The kyngs ma[s]cke," "A galyard." All are in three parts, but they appear to be keyboard reductions of four-part consorts with one part (alto or tenor) omitted. (The third dance is found as a four-part pavan in continental printed sources of 1559 and 1571.) Peter Holman has reconstructed these pieces for recorder quartet or other instruments.[3] Their significance from the point of view of the development of keyboard music is that they are early examples of consort dances adapted for keyboard performance—a process that recurred later in the century, and soon led to the composition of original pavans, galliards, and other dances for keyboard.

A companion volume to Royal App. 58 is Royal App. 56, probably the earliest source to preserve English liturgical organ music. This is the English equivalent to several continental repertories of plainsong-based music by Cavazzoni, Cabezón, Schlick, and others. In English settings, the chant selected as a cantus firmus is normally carried by one voice in a texture with a fixed number of voices, and it will be used in its entirety without intervening rests. Nearly always each note of the chant is given equal value. The cantus firmus may be presented plainly in breves or semibreves, but more often it is decorated to a greater or lesser extent by a process referred to by Morley as "breaking the plainsong" (1597/1971, 96; 1597/1952, 178). The process is illustrated in Examples 2.4 and 2.8 below. Breaking of the plainsong is particularly common in two-part textures, with the cantus firmus in the lower voice. The result has the character of a free duet in which hints of imitation may occur. In three- and four-voice settings, such imitations as are present are usually the province of the descanting (i.e., non–cantus firmus) voices.

The surviving repertory is almost equally divided between music for the Mass and music for the Office services such as Matins and Vespers. Two works merit the title "Organ Mass"—a setting of the Ordinary by Philip ap Rhys and a Mass Proper for Easter Day by Thomas Preston. Both are designed for *alternatim* performance and both are incompletely preserved. More than a dozen settings survive of the Offertory *Felix namque*. The organ polyphony normally begins at the word "namque," leaving the opening word to be sung by the choir; the concluding "Alleluia" is also rarely set. For the Office, hymn settings predominate.

Polyphony is usually provided for two, three, or four verses, and it is clear that *alternatim* performance was again envisaged. Four settings of the Te Deum, by Avery Burton, John Redford (two), and John Blitheman, all provide polyphony for the odd-numbered verses only. Royal App. 56 includes among its miscellaneous contents the chants for the even-numbered verses of the Te Deum, no doubt intended for use in conjunction with organ verses.

The organ music in Royal App. 56, all anonymous, is somewhat idiosyncratic. For instance, there are two settings of *Felix namque,* of which the first (EECM 10/10) has an opening section (up to "Maria" in the chant) in quintuple time, each plainsong note having the value breve plus minim; the cantus firmus begins in the alto but at note (m.) 13 switches to soprano, where it remains for the rest of the piece. The second section is in triple rhythm (still quite unusual in the context of this repertory), the chant notes being written as semibreve plus minim, but various proportions are soon introduced (2 against 3, 4 against 3, 8 against 3) and the final measures exploit a $\frac{3}{2}:\frac{6}{4}$ cross-rhythm. This piece is well worth playing, and not just for its unusual features; it is a vigorous work and its well-paced rhythmic changes will certainly hold a listener's attention. The second *Felix namque* in Royal App. 56 (EECM 10/11), in triple time throughout, is apparently an organ duet. The plainsong is written out at the end of the piece (beginning on d′) and, as John Caldwell has suggested (1973, 24), it is most effective if supplied by a second player an octave higher than written.[4]

The principal sources for English liturgical organ music, as mentioned above, are London 29996 and the Mulliner Book. The only composer named in both is John Redford, organist of St. Paul's Cathedral, who died in 1547. Music by Thomas Preston appears only in London 29996; the Mulliner Book is a valuable source for Tallis and Blitheman.

Redford was a resourceful composer, though he preferred to write in two or three parts rather than four. Several of his pieces have a written compass an octave higher than usual, c to g‴; the effect would have been achieved by playing an octave lower and using only the principal (4′) rank (i.e., in early sixteenth-century terms, "stopping" the diapason rank). Redford's name was also associated with a particular technique of plainsong setting; the heading "with a meane" occurs often in the Mulliner Book (see Ill. 2.2), and the seventeenth-century source for his hymn *O quam glorifica* describes it as "A very good vers called redfordes meane." The meane style involved a widely spaced three-part texture with the cantus firmus normally in the bass and the middle part divided between the hands; often the voices are quasi-canonic, with entries at the octave (in Ex. 2.3 the lowest voice is based on the "faburden" of the chant[5]—in effect, a melody whose notes lay a fifth or a third below those of the chant). Byrd, who seems to have been able to absorb any musical influence that came his way, was doubtless acquainted with this style of

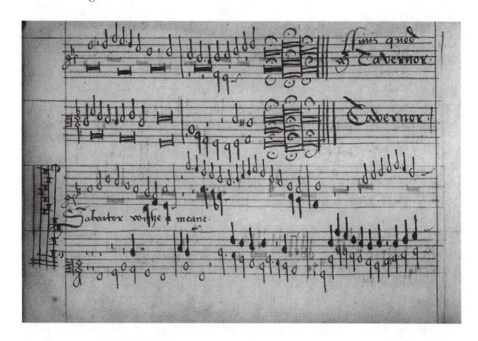

ILLUSTRATION 2.2. The Mulliner Book (London 30513), f. 42v. The end of the In Nomine from Taverner's mass *Gloria tibi Trinitas* in a keyboard arrangement, and the beginning of Redford's *Salvator [mundi] with a meane*. Black notation is used in the former to identify the plainsong cantus firmus, and in the latter to distinguish the middle ("meane") voice. Reproduced by kind permission of the British Library.

keyboard writing, as it occurs prominently in his mainly three-part Fantasia in C (MB 27/27).

One of the outstanding works in the entire liturgical organ repertory is Blitheman's setting of the hymn *Eterne rerum conditor* (Mulliner, Nos. 49–52). The four verses, respectively a 2, a 3, a 4, and a 3, explore a range of techniques and moods. Verse I "breaks" the plainsong to produce an evenly flowing imitative dialogue (Ex. 2.4); verse 2 treats an accompanying figure almost as an ostinato, whereas in verse 3, with the

EXAMPLE 2.3. Redford, *Salvator [mundi] with a meane* (Mulliner, No. 36)

EXAMPLE 2.4. Blitheman, *Eterne rerum conditor*, verse 1

slightly decorated plainsong in the tenor, the top part has five phrases of varying length, all beginning differently but together forming a beautifully shaped melody. (This verse carries the legend "Melos suave," which Edward Lowinsky (1953) has interpreted as an indication of the tremulant stop on the organ.) In verse 4 the hymn melody finally surfaces unadorned, accompanied by a lively left-hand duet.

Tallis's three settings of the antiphon *Clarifica me Pater* (Mulliner, Nos. 99, 101, 104) have great dignity and may well be played as a group, notwithstanding that all of them are in four parts with the plainsong in the same tenor position. Against the tenor the other voices weave short imitative figures, "maintaining the point" (Morley's phrase) for the duration of each piece. Example 2.5 shows approximately the first half of the second *Clarifica me Pater*. As the six-note motive unfolds the music is articulated by what might be called "passing cadences": plagal on D (mm. 3–4), perfect on G (m. 8) and, one sequential step lower, on F (mm. 10–11). In all three *Clarifica* settings the rise and fall of the top voice is carefully judged, and the music can be comprehended by player and listener as a single span—not an easy achievement for the composer in this form, where the foundation is a series of single notes to be "got through."

The difficulties inherent in the genre are of course liable to become more evident in longer pieces, and this can be illustrated in some examples by Thomas Preston. London 29996 contains a group of seven *Felix namque* settings by Preston (EECM 10/13–19), all in four parts. The first

EXAMPLE 2.5. Tallis, *Clarifica me Pater II*

four settings have the chant in breves, respectively in treble, bass, alto, and tenor. In each piece Preston employs a succession of imitative figures against the cantus firmus, but these lack distinctive character, and in spite of the cadences that occur at various points, the music conveys no strong sense of structure. Preston's antiphon *Beatus Laurentius* (EECM 6/5) has a similar layout. It starts well, with the first imitative point derived from the opening of the cantus firmus (Ex. 2.6), but it soon becomes apparent that it is not easy to sustain the onward movement when two, three, or four harmonies have to be provided for each note of the chant and the chant itself moves within a narrow range. The music comes to life chiefly at those points where the cantus firmus itself is decorated—as in the final measures, with their gently overlapping descending lines.

English liturgical organ music is seldom featured in recital programs or recordings and the scope for its use within present-day liturgies is limited. Yet much of it certainly deserves performance. The two most distinguished members of the school, Tallis and Blitheman, lived on well beyond the date when Catholic services ceased in England (Tallis died in 1585, Blitheman in 1591), and it is likely that some of their plainsong-based music is post-Reformation, written for other than liturgical purposes and possibly intended for virginal as much as for organ. In this category are Blitheman's six highly inventive settings of the antiphon *Gloria tibi Trinitas* (Mulliner, Nos. 91–96) and Tallis's two famous *Felix namque* settings, Nos. 109 and 110 in Fitzwilliam and dated respectively 1562 and 1564 in that source. Both of the Tallis works include the intonation and the Alleluia and both explore a great range of figurations; they summarize the techniques of the liturgical organ school and at the same time look forward to many typical features of the virginalist style. The second *Felix namque* was the more widely circulated and is another piece that Byrd certainly knew, since it has some close structural and motivic parallels with the younger composer's early Fantasia in A minor (MB 27/13).

Before we turn to a fuller account of Byrd, it remains briefly to consider the secular keyboard tradition of the midcentury, as represented by the Dublin Virginal Manuscript of c. 1570 and a few other fragmentary sources. The 30 pieces of Dublin are all untitled but there are several that are unmistakably pavans and galliards and others having the

EXAMPLE 2.6. Preston, *Beatus Laurentius*

character of almans and corantos. Continental influences are apparent in settings of Franco/Flemish dance tunes, such as No. 15, the [*Almande du Prince*] published by Susato in 1551, and in the use of the Italian grounds *passamezzo antico* (Nos. 1–2) and *romanesca* (No. 9). No. 10, however, is based on the English ground "Goodnight" and appears to be another example of a keyboard duet, requiring a bass compass down to low C.[6] The piece includes four "divisions" on the 8-measure ground, and except for the final measure it is in three strict parts. But there is an element of flexibility in the introduction of new figurations at unexpected points; triplets, for example, first appear in the final measure of statement 2, and there is a return to duple division of the beat at m. 6 of statement 4.

The Dublin Virginal Manuscript includes five pavan/galliard pairs in all of which the material of the galliard is fashioned in some way from that of the pavan (additionally, Nos. 1 and 2 are linked by their common use of the *passamezzo antico* ground). These dances are mostly cast in strains of four or eight measures and sometimes varied repeats are written out; the amount of extra decoration, however, is modest. The most sophisticated of the pavans are Nos. 3 and 21 in the manuscript, the former being the piece attributed to "mastyre tayler." Both have three equal strains closing respectively on tonic, dominant, and tonic, and both incorporate imitative elements into the basically regular design. However, strain III of Tayler's pavan is less concerned with imitation, adopting instead a more rhythmic, alman-like character. Example 2.7 shows the varied repeat of this strain. Only the final 1½ measures differ from the first statement, but the figurations will have a familiar appearance to players of a slightly later repertory.

Tayler's pavan could conceivably be a keyboard arrangement of a consort original in four parts, and this does appear to be the case with

EXAMPLE 2.7. Tayler, Pavan, last four measures

No. 21 in Dublin, which occurs elsewhere as a consort work. The pavan in C minor by Newman in the Mulliner Book (No. 116) is another keyboard dance that, as John Ward claims, "has all the earmarks of an arrangement of ensemble music" (Ward 1983, xi). But this same source does contain one extended dance movement that, equally, has the hallmarks of an original keyboard work. It is the [Galliard in F] (No. 2), one of a small group of late additions (c. 1575) to the manuscript. It consists of two 8-measure strains, each with thoroughgoing varied repeats; this 32-measure scheme is then subject to two further variations making a piece of 96 measures in all (plus a concluding measure). There are occasional hints of an independent alto or tenor part but the texture is largely right- hand figuration against left-hand chords; it is the variety of this figuration, ranging freely over nearly two octaves (c' to a'') that is the main focus of interest. A slight holding back of the onward flow at the beginning of the second main section (mm. 33–34) recurs, and indeed the idea is carried further, at the beginning of the third section (mm. 65–69). After Aston's Hornpipe this piece is the most substantial English "secular" keyboard work in pre-Byrd sources, and its method of creating a larger structure is mirrored in certain later works, such as Byrd's tripartite setting of the Italian song "Chi passa" (MB 27/19).

William Byrd (1539 or 1540–1623)

Byrd held a commanding position in English music of his time, comparable to that of Britten in the twentieth century. He cannot be regarded as primarily a composer of keyboard music; indeed, his own view was that "There is not any Musicke of Instruments whatsoever, comparable to that which is made of the voyces of Men."[7] Nevertheless, his best keyboard music displays the inventiveness and assured technique so consistently shown by his vocal music; much of it also has the manner "naturally disposed to Gravitie and Pietie" that Peacham saw reflected in Byrd's motets. And in one respect Byrd's achievement in keyboard music was more remarkable than in his other compositions: the music of the Nevell book of 1591 demonstrates a confident handling of largescale forms in purely instrumental terms that appears to be entirely without precedent.

Born in late 1539 or 1540 (Harley 1997, 14), Byrd served as organist of Lincoln Cathedral from 1563 to 1572. His appointment as a Gentleman of the Chapel Royal probably dates from February 1571/2,* not two years earlier as has generally been stated in biographies of the composer (Shaw 1991, 3). In

---

*Until 1752 in England the number of the year changed on 25 March. Hence February 1571/2 refers to February 1571 (old-style dating), February 1572 (new-style dating).

1575 he published jointly with Tallis a volume *of Cantiones Sacrae* (literally, sacred songs; these pieces are usually referred to as motets). As he approached his fiftieth year Byrd ventured into print again with two collections of English songs (1588 and 1589) and two of *Cantiones Sacrae* (1589 and 1591). Also from this period is the Nevell book, which was evidently commissioned as a presentation volume for "Ladye Nevell": the pieces are ordered with some care and the volume was copied in a most elegant hand by John Baldwin. Like the contemporary printed anthologies, Nevell appears to contain the composer's own selection of his best work to date.

Byrd's next project was the publication of the three Masses, which, although issued without title pages and dates, have now been shown to have been printed during the years 1592–95. Further collections of Latin and English vocal music followed in 1605, 1607, and 1611, and it was not until 1612 or 1613 that Byrd's first and only publication of keyboard music appeared. *Parthenia or the Maydenhead of the first musicke that ever was printed for the Virginalls is* a relatively small volume printed from engraved plates, containing eight pieces by Byrd, seven by John Bull, and six by Orlando Gibbons. Byrd's contribution includes both revised older material and some very recent pieces. He lived until 1623, but apart from four short contributions to Leighton's *Teares or Lamentacions of a Sorrowful Soule* of 1614, nothing more was printed and there is no evidence that he composed any more music.

Oliver Neighbour's *The Consort and Keyboard Music of William Byrd* (1978) is a classic of its kind, giving a fully rounded picture of Byrd's outstanding contribution to the instrumental genres of his day. Even the titles of the relevant chapters serve to indicate the range of the keyboard music, which totals about 120 pieces if all the dance movements are counted separately: Organ Antiphons and Hymns; Grounds and Related Pieces; Variations; Almans, Smaller Dances, Arrangements, Descriptive Music; Pavans and Galliards; Fantasias and Preludes. Although nearly every one of Byrd's works has some distinct feature that gives it a character of its own, in our own discussion we can do no more than select a handful of pieces. Byrd was one of those composers who would tackle a new idea or problem each time he put pen to paper.

It seems likely that he was composing keyboard music as early as the 1560s and continued until 1612; there are various kinds of evidence toward establishing a chronology. Nevell is helpful here, both for what it contains and what it excludes. The latter falls into two groups: pieces that on stylistic or other grounds can be assigned to a "pre- Nevell" period, and those that for similar reasons can be regarded as late works. The "other grounds" include clues that are occasionally to be found in the names of dedicatees, in the tunes Byrd chose for writing variations, or in settings he made of other people's compositions.

Among Byrd's earliest works (not in Nevell) are undoubtedly his

EXAMPLE 2.8. Byrd, *Clarifica me Pater I*

Plainsong: D   D   D

few surviving plainsong settings, which resemble in their basic procedures the organ music of the previous generation. They cannot have
been intended for liturgical use; rather, their purpose seems to have
been technical, an exploration of musical possibilities against the restric-
tions of a cantus firmus.

His three settings of *Clarifica me Pater* (MB 28/47–49) make an interesting contrast to Tallis's; they are much more varied but equally suitable for performance as a group. The first, mainly a 2, "breaks" the
plainsong in the bass. The opening notes of the chant are paraphrased
as a rhythmically flexible motive spanning a fifth (Ex. 2.8). This motive is
treated in imitation at the start and recurs in the upper voice a 4th
higher in m. 6, and a 4th higher again in m. 13. This last entry is preceded by a decorated Phrygian cadence on A, which is balanced by a
slightly more emphatic perfect one on F in m. 31. At this point triple
meter (tripla) is introduced; the chant now appears more plainly in the
bass but the upper part increases both in rhythmic interest and in melodic
range. It is instructive to look at those points in the piece where clear
points of articulation occur in the treble line (these do not necessarily coin-
cide with changes of figuration). Table 2.1 indicates the resulting phrase
and tonal structure. The $3\frac{1}{2}$-measure phrase, the only interruption to the
pattern of increasing phrase lengths, comes at the start of the tripla section, where the listener is adjusting to a new rhythmic character. One no-
tices also the careful placing of ornaments to pinpoint cross-rhythms or to
draw attention to the opening or closing notes of the treble phrases.

TABLE 2.1
Byrd, *Clarifica me Pater I*

Measures	Phrase length	Cadence degree
1–6	$5\frac{1}{2}$	C
6–13	7	A
13–20	$7\frac{1}{2}$	G
21–31	$10\frac{1}{2}$	F
31–34	$3\frac{1}{2}$	E
35–47	13	D

The second *Clarifica* has some similarities to the first in its placing of intermediate cadences and of new rhythmic patterns. Its texture, however, is entirely different. The chant in the uppermost of three voices is virtually undecorated and transposed up a 5th from D to A. The two lower voices add counterpoints that begin in fairly sober canonic fashion but become increasingly playful as the piece proceeds. The third setting is different again: in four parts, with the chant in the alto. The sectional structure is almost too clearly defined here, with cadences on tonic (D) in m. 11, subdominant in m. 28, and tonic in m. 56—three sections of increasing length, each developing its own imitative point against the theme (and, incidentally, with melodic peaks on f″, g″, and a″, respectively). With its evenly flowing polyphony this piece has little of the element of fantasy apparent in the other two settings; rather, it approaches the world of Tallis's *Clarifica* pieces and the third verse of Blitheman's *Eterne rerum conditor*.

A further group of evidently early works are the Hornpipe and the three grounds, Nos. 9, 43, and 86 in the MB edition. All are lengthy compositions constructed on short ground basses. The Ground in G (MB 28/86), for example, has 38 statements of its 4-measure ground. The opening of the piece is shown in Example 2.9. Throughout, the music cannot stray far from the I, V, and IV chords implied by the ground, yet by various means other than harmonic Byrd achieves a convincing overall design. The initial variations build up slowly—beginning in the middle register of the keyboard, introducing hints of imitation (mm. 17–20) and then longer imitative themes (mm. 25ff), syncopations (mm. 37ff), written-out trills (mm. 45ff), and eighth-note running figures of irregular length, shared between the hands (mm. 61ff). By mm. 95–100 the ground as such is present only in the listener's mind, for both hands are now involved in eighth-note runs. The tension built up thus far is released at m. 101 by a change to tripla ($^9_4$ in transcription) and a dance-like character. The first 12 measures of this dance are followed (mm. 113–124) by a reworking of the same melodic material (the

EXAMPLE 2.9. Byrd, Ground in G

4-measure ground continuing all the while). Thereafter, running passages become prominent again, now with 18 notes to the measure rather than 12 as previously. Perhaps out of consideration for the player Byrd does not reintroduce the idea of eighths in both hands! Once more the tension is released at m. 145 by a return to 3/2 meter and slower note values, and a majestic final pair of variations with closely packed imitations. The somewhat conventional cadential melody in the penultimate bar requires a considerable slackening of tempo in performance. Byrd's overall plan for this piece—two carefully controlled "crescendos," the second reaching its goal in less than half the time of the first—is simple but undeniably effective, and there is much refined detail on the way.

The copying of Nevell was completed in 1591 and the music therein may be taken as representative of Byrd's mature keyboard style, although a few of its 42 pieces undoubtedly date back to his earlier years. *The Hunt's Up* (MB 27/40) is one of them; based on a ground, it has something of the same character as the piece just discussed. Here, however, the ground is 16 measures long, and each of the 11 variations is of a more distinct character. An apparently earlier version of the piece, with 12 variations, is found in Fitzwilliam (No. 59). The discarded variation uses eighth- note movement in both hands, similar to that of the Ground in G. (In the third edition of MB 27, the earlier version is given as No. 40 and the later one as No. 41.)

The contents of Nevell are arranged in two main groups, each beginning with a piece dedicated to Lady Nevell herself: no. 1, "my ladye nevels grownde," and No. 26, "A voluntarie for my ladye nevell." Within the first group is a sequence of nine pavans, seven of them with associated galliards (Nos. 10–25); the second group includes seven sets of variations on song-tunes, as well as further grounds. Near the end (Nos. 39–40) is a tenth pavan and galliard, "mr. w. peter," which must have been written while the book was being compiled in about 1590. The dedicatee was only about 15 years old at this time.

"The firste pavian" and its galliard (MB 27/29a & b) must be among the earlier pieces in Nevell. The pavan is described in another source (Fitzwilliam) as "the first that ever hee made."[8] It exists also in a version for five-part consort.[9] The consort version almost certainly came first, and it seems therefore that this is another example—the most significant to date—of a consort dance transferred to the keyboard. The keyboard version, unlike its model, has varied repeats, and in these, as Davitt Moroney has eloquently put it, "the fingers start to assert themselves, in defiance of the strict polyphony [of the consort pavan], and a new style is born...."It is the exact moment when a great composer set out tentatively on a new path."[10]

In all essential respects the great majority of Byrd's pavans and galliards agree with Morley's descriptions of the two dances in his *Introduction* of 1597. The pavan, Morley writes, is a kind of staid music, ordained for grave dancing, and most commonly made of three strains, whereof every strain is played or sung twice; a strain they make to contain 8, 12 or 16 semibreves as they list, yet fewer than eight I have not seen in any pavan . . . in this you must cast your music by four. . . . After every pavan we usually set a galliard (that is, a kind of music made out of the other) . . . a lighter and more stirring kind of dancing than the pavan, consisting of the same number of strains; and look how many fours of semibreves you put in the strain of your pavan, so many times six minims must you put in the strain of your galliard. (Morley 1597/1971, 181; 1597/1952, 296)

Byrd's pavan strains are usually 16 semibreves long, and those of his galliards almost invariably run to 24 minims (8 measures of $\frac{3}{2}$), which is in line with what Morley recommends. In two of the Nevell pavans (Nos. 2 and 4) and in some others outside that source the strains are of 8 semibreves. In only one Nevell pair (the sixth) is there any noticeable thematic resemblance between the two dances. Morley does not refer to the decoration of repeated strains, but this is an important feature of Byrd's keyboard dances. Typically, the polyphonic interplay of a first statement will be only partially retained in the repeat. The texture will be lightened somewhat and a certain amount of figurative writing—unpredictable in its placing and its extent—introduced in both hands.

The "Petre" pavan and galliard (MB 27/3a & b) must have been highly regarded by Byrd himself because they reappear in *Parthenia*.[11] The pieces are in G minor with a two-flat signature. Though not linked thematically, they complement one another in a number of less obvious ways. A simple table (Table 2.2) showing no more than the opening and closing chords of each strain demonstrates Byrd's usual procedure of closing I in the tonic and II on a related chord. (Neighbour's useful convention for referring to the strains as I, II, III is followed here.)

TABLE 2.2
Byrd, Pavan and Galliard, *Sir William Petre*

	Pavan	Galliard
I	G minor–G major[12]	G minor–G major
II	G minor–D major	B-flat major–F major
III	G major–G major	F major–G major

The table also appears to indicate that the pavan stays "closer to home" than the galliard; however, intermediate modulations to B flat and F (in

EXAMPLE 2.10. Byrd, Pavan *Sir William Petre*, mm. 69–72

that order) occur during the course of both I and II in the pavan, and in III the key of B flat is again introduced, in a rather unexpected way following a half-close (imperfect cadence) in G minor (Ex. 2.10). This half-close comes one bar sooner than expected, so the division of the strain is into 7 + 9. The shorter (8-measure) strains of the galliard allow less time for internal modulations. II has two balancing phrases closing respectively on B flat and F (the latter sounding like the dominant of B flat). III, beginning in this F/B-flat area, reestablishes G minor in its fourth measure and so, as in the pavan, the final strain divides irregularly (3 + 3 + 2).

These are exceptionally inventive pieces. Each displays an onward progression of ideas in which the varied repeats play an essential part. As each motive is introduced its possibilities are thoroughly explored, but there is little recall of earlier material of the kind that lends coherence to instrumental structures in later centuries. One exception is the use of a rather unusual "broken" texture in mm. 41–44 of the pavan and mm. 29–31 of the galliard. Byrd employed a similar figuration for the coda of the pavan, but when he revised the piece for *Parthenia* he substituted a shorter and simpler ending (Neighbour 1978, 194–95).

No extract of a few measures can represent these pieces adequately, but strain I of the galliard (Ex. 2.11) does illustrate in relatively few notes Byrd's characteristic way of matching a closely imitative texture to the metrical demands of the dance. The imitative point, in its two forms (x and y), plays an important part in the construction of the melody, with its two phrases. This melody cadences in m. 4 on the dominant, and in m. 8 in the tonic, but its second phrase is slightly longer, beginning as it does on beat 3 of m. 4 (the same small imbalance is observed also in strain I of the pavan). The "early start" to phrase two gives a little more space for the approach to the cadence in m. 8. A further disturbance of the 4 + 4 phrasing is created by the unharmonized opening, which gives m. 1 the character of an upbeat and creates the expectation of a fugal texture. Beneath the melody, there is a constant undercurrent of references to the motive, form "y" appearing in the alto before it is taken up by the melody. Ornamentation is applied to the motive in a consistent fashion. It has a rhythmic and not merely decorative role to play, clearly

EXAMPLE 2.11. Byrd, Galliard *Sir William Petre*

suggesting a $\frac{6}{4}$ cross-rhythm in m. 1 and, in mm. 3–6, occurring on every fourth quarter-note beat with rather more ambiguous effect.

The use of a single imitative point throughout the first strain also occurs in the pavan, but it is not applied to subsequent strains in either dance. In mm. 7–8 of Example 2.11, the eighth-note decoration of the melodic cadence is imitated by the alto; this exchange prepares us for the predominantly eighth-note movement of the varied repeat. In this *reprise*, every one of the imitative entries is identifiable, either in decorated form or not. This is in keeping with the generally dense writing of the pair, but as mentioned above, it is not quite Byrd's usual practice.

The following piece in Nevell, the Fantasia in D minor (MB 28/46), may well be another recently composed addition to the manuscript. It is one of three of similar design, the others being the Fantasia in C (MB 27/25) and the Voluntary for My Lady Nevell (MB 28/61). These three no longer have the sectional structure of the early A-minor Fantasia with its links to Tallis's second *Felix namque*, but they do retain one feature from those works, namely a self-contained introductory passage closing in the tonic. Thereafter, the music runs on more or less continuously, in a colorful succession of sections referring to different styles; for example, in the D-minor piece, the madrigalian homophonic phrase with its low echo (mm. 30–34), and the reference (mm. 51–53) to the old style of "My lady careys dompe." As in the Petre pieces, one idea follows another in a seemingly inevitable flow, and here of course the music does not have to be encompassed within regular dance strains. Yet toward the end of all three pieces Byrd does apply a feature reminiscent of his dance forms. A portion of music occurs that could almost be a pavan strain, immediately followed by its varied repeat and a brief coda. The device helps greatly in bringing these extended pieces to a convincing close.

ILLUSTRATION 2.3. The opening of Byrd's variations on *Walsingham*, from a manuscript of c.1600 (London 30486, f. 2). The six-line staves are a regular feature of English keyboard sources from 1591 to c.1700. Reproduced by kind permission of the British Library.

Byrd's only dated keyboard piece is *The Woods So Wild* of 1590 (MB 28/85). Again, it must have been copied into Nevell almost as soon as it was composed. Like *Walsingham, The Carman's Whistle, Sellenger's Round,* and several other works with well-known titles, it is a set of variations on a popular tune. Nevell gives the title as "Will yow walke the woodes soe wylde," a text that fits the opening phrase of the melody.

As a group, Byrd's song variations are arguably the most character-ful of all his keyboard works. They vary greatly in length and complex-ity, each piece seeming to be perfectly matched to the qualities of the chosen melody. The starting point may well have been his own varia-tions on ground basses, for which he did have models of a kind. *The Woods So Wild* is an apposite example, since it contains elements of both the song variation and the ground.

The opening eight measures are shown in Example 2.12a. (In vir-ginalist variation sets, the initial statement is regarded as the first varia-tion, with the next treatment of the theme being numbered "2" in the sources, and so on.) The bass alternates between F and G—obviously reminiscent of Aston's Hornpipe, and suggestive of a ground bass. This led Byrd to devise a set of 12 variations, the theme as such appearing in only half of them (vars. 1–3, 6–7 and 12). In the others, the music is con-structed over or around the bass.

Of the "theme" variations, Nos. 3 and 6 have the melody in a mid-dle voice; the equally spaced 2, 7, and 12 have it more prominently be-ginning on f ″. In the last variation the theme is more richly harmonized (i.e., with more chord changes), calling perhaps for a slight broadening of tempo in performance. The "bass" variations all feature imitative (al-most canonic) dialogues in the accompanying voices; in vars. 4, 5, 8, and 11 the motives employed relate to the theme (Ex. 2.12b), but in 9 and 10 they are more independent. Eighth-note movement in vars. 6 and 7 leads to the most emphatic cadence so far at the end of 7; var. 8 falls back to quarter-note movement, but 9, 10, and 11 gradually reintroduce eighths before the final broadening of var. 12. The overall pacing is re-markably similar to that of the much earlier Ground in G.

"At some time after 1590 [Byrd] evidently became dissatisfied with the rather hasty preparation at the end of var. 11 for the return of the melody in the final variation. . . . He accordingly inserted two new varia-tions to effect the transition more gradually" (Neighbour 1978, 157). These extra variations, and a consequent adjustment to the beginning of the final variation, are found in Fitzwilliam and Forster's Virginal Book (dated 31 January 1624/5). They are not altogether satisfactory. The beginning of the new var. 12 holds up the onward flow and seems somewhat out of place; on the other hand, its second half is very similar to var. 6. Likewise, var. 13 recalls 7 (and 3). The original opening of the final variation (Ex. 2.12c) has a hint of the "ground" in the middle

EXAMPLE 2.12. Byrd, *The Woods So Wild*

register that is partly lost in the revision. So, all in all, this is perhaps a case in which the composer's first thoughts were better.

For a brief consideration of Byrd's later keyboard style the obvious starting point is *Parthenia*. Two named dances here were probably very recently composed: the galliard *Mistress Mary Brownlow* (MB 27/34) and the pavan *The Earl of Salisbury* together with the two galliards that follow it (MB 27/15a–c). Born in about 1591, Mary Brownlow was married in November 1613; perhaps her galliard was commissioned as an engagement present. (*Parthenia* itself was dedicated to a betrothed couple, Prince Frederick, Elector Palatine of the Rhine, and Princess Elizabeth, daughter of James I.) Robert Cecil, Earl of Salisbury, died in May 1612 and Byrd's famous pavan was almost certainly written in memory of him. It is quite unlike Byrd's other pavans in its simple melodic style and its two strains without varied repeats. It foreshadows in an extraordinary way a type of binary structure that was still being widely applied a century later—strain I closing on the dominant, and II featuring repeated or sequential material in a related key before the return to the tonic.

Mistress Mary Brownlow shows another direction in which Byrd's later keyboard style developed: toward more ornate writing and the exploration of diverse and rapidly changing figuration. In part he was responding to the innovations of his younger contemporaries, particularly John Bull. Some of the rather "unByrdlike" ideas in this galliard turn out to be subtly adjusted quotations from a galliard in D by Bull (MB 19/113; see Cunningham 1984, 135–39).

Outside *Parthenia*, two late pavan/galliard pairs seem again to be "commentaries" on the music of younger contemporaries. The pair in C (MB 27/33) has a quotation from Bull's *Lord Lumley* pavan (MB 19/129a) and, according to Neighbour, Byrd's "object was to put to the test the principles underlying Bull's keyboard style in general" (1978, 210). Similarly, the pair in F (MB 28/60) uses, and improves upon, several motives from a pair in the same key by Morley (Neighbour 1978, 206–9).

Involvement with other composers' music manifests itself in another way in Byrd's highly decorative arrangements of Dowland's *Lachrymae* pavan (MB 28/54) and a galliard by James Harding (MB 28/55). And finally, two evidently late examples of the variation form are the superb sets on *John come kiss me now* (MB 28/81) and *O Mistress mine* (MB 28/83). The latter has just six variations on a rather long theme. The melody is in the top voice throughout, and although it sometimes takes up the decorative motives going on below, its outlines remain clear. *John come kiss me now* is a shorter (8-measure) theme with 16 variations, the melody appearing in tenor, bass, and alto positions as well as soprano. With its great variety of accompanying counterpoints, its technical demands on the player (especially in the "cumulative" vars. 9–14), and its noble final pair of variations, this work summarizes (if any one work can) Byrd's achievements as a keyboard composer.

Performance Practice

The performance practice of virginalist music is relatively uninvestigated, and it may well be that much potentially valuable evidence simply has not survived. Even the choice of instrument is not a straightforward matter. It will be remembered that in the years of Byrd's maturity, English organ building was at a low ebb; perhaps on account of this, almost all of his keyboard music seems to have been conceived primarily in terms of the harpsichord. Yet he was an organist by profession; as late as 1607 he was still describing himself as "Organista Regio" on the title page of his *Gradualia*, book II. Flexibility of medium was a strong feature of Elizabethan music. Players today may well find that many of Byrd's keyboard pieces (not just the plainsong settings) can be performed successfully on an organ with light, clear registration, as well as on harpsichords of different kinds.

None of Byrd's keyboard music rises above a″ or descends below C. The lowest C sharp and E flat are never used, and high g″ sharp hardly ever—although one piece, *Hugh Ashton's Ground* (MB 27/20), seems to make a special feature of this note (Moroney 1993, 81–82). A few pieces from all stages of Byrd's career make use of F sharp and G sharp in the lowest octave, but in the great majority (including all those in *Parthenia*) these notes are not used.[13] It may be, therefore, that Byrd was often content to write for instruments with the C/E short octave. Measure 71 of the Petre pavan (Ex. 2.10) is actually easier to play on such an instrument, and there is a similar instance at m. 80 of *O Mistress mine*. Davitt Moroney has recently shown that fully half of Byrd's keyboard works can be accommodated on a 38-note keyboard (F,G,A—g″,a″), an unexpectedly limited compass that is also adequate for the idiomatic keyboard pieces of Royal App. 58 and Tallis's two *Felix namque* settings.

Apart from the instrument itself, there are many aspects of performance to be considered in relation to any early keyboard repertory: pitch level, tuning, tempo, articulation, the amount of *rubato* and other modifications to notated rhythms, the use or otherwise of original fingering systems, and ornamentation (or gracing, to use the earlier English term). The last of these has been the subject of widest debate in the case of the virginalists, for the obvious reason that there is no trustworthy contemporary explanation of the two familiar signs, the single stroke and the double stroke through the stem. The latter is much the more common, occurring in such a wide variety of contexts that it must be regarded as a general-purpose sign: "play an ornament of some kind." Occasionally, copyists of Byrd's music used the double stroke as an abbreviation for an upper-note trill with termination (afterbeat). For example, in m. 19 of the Fantasia MB 28/46, one source (London 30485) has a written-out trill of eight sixteenths (Ex. 2.13a); in Nevell, Baldwin, who was running out of space at the end of a line, substituted a minim e′ with two-stroke ornament. It follows that one possible interpretation of the double stroke is such a trill, especially in cadential or quasi-cadential contexts like this one. Sometimes the afterbeat is written out, as in Example 2.12a, m. 7; a similar example, from a print of 1663, is in Example 2.25, m. 4. (The exact number of repercussions is variable, since in

EXAMPLE 2.13. The double-stroke ornament

EXAMPLE 2.14. The single-stroke ornament

written-out graces of this kind the number of notes often varies between sources.) But this realization will not be appropriate in most instances and a number of alternatives are shown in Example 2.13b–e. The short upper-note trill (b) may be regarded as the standard interpretation. In the last decades of the seventeenth century, the two-stroke sign was adopted for the "shake" (upper-note trill without termination). Alan Curtis has observed "it is inconceivable that this most basic of ornaments, present throughout the history of the literature for harpsichord and related instruments, should not have been used by the Virginalists" (Curtis 1969, 209–10). The lower mordent (c), the obverse of (b) and almost as widespread in harpsichord literature, will be found effective in certain contexts, such as on opening notes or on notes that are part of an ascending group (see Ex. 2.8, m. 1). Interpretation (d) is appropriate for notes within fairly rapid stepwise descending groups (Ex. 2.11, m. 7, soprano fourth note; m. 8, alto second note). The final suggestion (e) was included by Thurston Dart in many of his editions; where the ornament is on a very short note there is hardly time for anything more elaborate.

The single stroke, occurring much less frequently, may have had a more precise meaning, although whether this remained constant between, for example, 1570 and 1620 is doubtful. It may occasionally have been used to define one of the possible meanings of the double stroke (the lower mordent?). Dart suggested that it "seems to mean" a slide from a third below (Ex. 2.14a), and there is some support for this in Edward Bevin's tiny piece "Graces in play" dating from c. 1630 (Ex. 2.14c; from London 31403, f. 5). It is noticeable that in Byrd's music the single stroke is often applied to the highest note of a small group. There are over 20 examples in the first 50 measures of his Hornpipe, and in every case an ornament involving lower auxiliary notes is suitable (either a or b of Ex. 2.14). The passage also includes several double strokes, and one thing at least is clear: in this early piece Byrd was making a definite distinction between the two signs. As time went on he seems to have used

EXAMPLE 2.15. Byrd, *O Mistress mine*, m. 7

the single stroke less. There are none at all in his pieces in *Parthenia*. In *O Mistress mine* there are just four examples, the first of which is shown in Example 2.15. The slide, whether on or before the beat, produces consecutives and, in view of the held alto g', it seems that here the mordent (g"–f'♯–g") is the only possible interpretation.

The Later Virginalists

"It is interesting to see combined in Byrd qualities which become more marked in his younger English contemporaries: the boldness and brilliance of Bull, the grave serenity of Gibbons and the romantic charm of Farnaby." Writing over 70 years ago, Frank Howes (1928, 142) pinpointed Byrd's role as the inspiration for a whole new generation of keyboard composers. We do not know for certain whether any of the three he names was actually a pupil of Byrd's, but like a good teacher, he seems to have drawn from them the qualities in which each excelled. Two who did describe Byrd as their "master" were Thomas Morley and Thomas Tomkins.

The Fitzwilliam Virginal Book has 297 pieces, with about 30 composers named; the most strongly represented, after Byrd, are John Bull, Giles Farnaby, and Peter Philips. Until recently it was generally accepted that the manuscript was copied c. 1613–19 by Francis Tregian while imprisoned in the Fleet as a Catholic recusant (Thompson 2001 offers "an alternative view," and reveals that Tregian died in 1617). A marked Catholic bias has been observed in the book, not only in the composers included but also in the names of dedicatees (e.g., the Lord Lumley of Bull's pavan); this may account for the relatively few pieces by Gibbons. The most important source for the latter is Cosyn's Virginal Book of 1620, which also contains music by Bull and by Cosyn himself. (Cosyn's keyboard music is now accessible in transcription in Memed 1993.) In all, about 40 manuscripts containing English keyboard music survive from the first half of the seventeenth century, in addition to the printed source *Parthenia* with its music by the "three famous Masters" Byrd, Bull, and Gibbons.

In such a repertory it is only to be expected that a number of works are of uncertain authorship. Occasionally, anonymous works can be attributed to particular composers with some degree of confidence: examples are a short untitled fantasia in Oxford 1142A, probably by Gibbons (MB 20/49), and the untitled and possibly incomplete ground in London 30485 that may be by Weelkes (MB 55/38). More frequently, attributions in the sources must be treated with caution. In this category is a group of plainsong hymns and Alleluia settings ascribed to Bull in London 23623 (MB 14/39 and 45-49); the copyist of this source was inclined to attribute everything to Bull without much discrimination. An intriguing example of conflicting attributions is *Go from my window,* an imaginative work of which there are two copies in Fitzwilliam. No. 9 in the manuscript consists of seven variations on the theme, attributed to Thomas Morley; No. 42 has the same music (with minor variants) plus an eighth variation, attributed to John Munday.

In the forms they used, the later virginalists were largely content to follow Byrd's lead. Sometimes, indeed, they dealt with the same material. *Go from my window* is a case in point, although here there is a small possibility that Byrd's variations postdate those of Morley/Munday. *Walsingham* was set by Bull in a way that seems designed deliberately to contrast with Byrd's setting. Gibbons wrote variations on *The Woods So Wild;* Tomkins set *Fortune.* Bull and Tomkins followed Byrd in writing fantasias on the hexachord theme "Ut re mi fa sol la." Byrd's Passamezzo [antico] pavan and galliard seem to have been models for a pair on the same bass by Philips (dated 1592) and for a Passamezzo pavan by Morley.

In adopting a similar range of forms to those employed by Byrd, his successors inevitably followed their own proclivities to a certain extent. Bull and Tomkins wrote an unexpectedly large amount of highly figurative plainsong-based music; Gibbons developed a type of free fantasia more unified in rhythmic character than is usual with Byrd. Almost all the virginalists explored the pavan and galliard form, often departing from the structure "by fours" advocated by Morley, and aiming to achieve (to judge from many of the titles) a wider range of expression. Many of these works are on a substantial scale, as long as or longer than comparable examples by Byrd, but they rarely display the same structural control. Length often seems to be achieved by "more of the same" rather than by a process of evolution from simple beginnings. Gibbons's *The Woods So Wild* compares unfavorably with Byrd's set on this theme; the most striking harmony and ingenious polyphony occur in the first variation, and the subsequent variations, for all their technical brilliance, do not sound like a logical consequence of the opening. Gibbons is certainly more successful in his extended fantasias, but much of the best work of the later virginalists is in smaller forms, or standard ones treated more concisely. Particularly attractive to modern players are the "character pieces" such as Bull's *My Self* or Martin Peerson's exquisite *The Fall of the Leaf.* In structure and effect these descriptive pieces are often quite similar to the shorter dances such as the alman and coranto.

To judge from the music that survives, the most prolific of the virginalists was John Bull. He wrote comparatively little for other media, and his keyboard music is very much "player's music." Thurston Dart painted a memorable picture of Bull playing a fine chamber organ at a city feast in 1607, and making "a cheerful noise with dances, variations, preludes and brilliant improvisations of every kind" (MB 19, 2nd ed., xvii). Tomkins described pieces of his as "Excellent for the hand," whereas comparable works by Byrd were "Excellent for matter" or "For substance." Born in about 1563, Bull was appointed organist of

Hereford Cathedral in 1582, and Gentleman of the Chapel Royal in January 1585/6. Apparently he succeeded his master, Blitheman, as one of the organists of the Chapel in 1591. In 1601–02 he traveled abroad for about 18 months, during which time he may have met Sweelinck. In 1613 he left England for good, going first to Brussels and thence to Antwerp, where he was Cathedral organist from 1617 until his death in 1628.

For Bull's music up to 1613 the principal sources are Fitzwilliam and a manuscript now in the Paris Bibliothèque Nationale, Paris 1185. The earlier layer of Paris 1185 contains about 75 pieces carefully ordered by final (key) and all anonymous. Many of them are, however, identified elsewhere as Bull's, and the good quality of the texts has led some scholars to propose that this layer is in Bull's hand, and that many of the unique texts are works by Bull. Whoever the copyist was, the "Bull" section was probably completed by about 1611. The MS later came into the possession of Cosyn, who added about 50 more pieces and an index dated 1652. As for the Fitzwilliam book, there is no evidence that anything Bull composed after 1613 found its way into that source.

Among Bull's plainsong settings are no fewer than 12 In Nomines (MB 14/20–31). The In Nomine was a specifically English instrumental form, a piece for consort or keyboard using the antiphon *Gloria tibi Trinitas* as a cantus firmus. (The four-part In Nomine section of John Taverner's six-part mass *Gloria tibi Trinitas* was justly admired, and instrumental arrangements were made of it in the mid-sixteenth century. This encouraged composers to write new instrumental pieces on the same cantus firmus. Blitheman's six settings in the Mulliner Book have their correct title, *Gloria tibi Trinitas*, but many others were illogically called In Nomine after the Taverner model.)

Table 2.3 gives certain details of Bull's In Nomines. The number of voices is not adhered to strictly: except in No. I, extra notes are added at the final cadence and occasionally elsewhere. Column 2 shows the voice carrying the cantus firmus (Soprano, Middle, Bass) and column 3 the pitch of its first (and last) note. It will be seen that only No. XII has the Dorian-mode chant at its "original pitch." The rhythm given to each cantus firmus note is also subject to variation; in all the settings some "breaking" of the chant occurs. But the normal repetition of the cantus firmus notes does suggest that the composer had in mind performance on the harpsichord rather than (or as well as) on the organ.

The first six settings occur in the same order in both Paris 1185 and Paris 1122 (as two groups of three), an arrangement that may well derive from the composer. Perhaps he was emulating Blitheman's set of six. The remaining six are separate compositions.

The accompanying counterpoints are generally of increasing complexity throughout a piece, and seldom make any thorough use of imitative motives. Nos. I–III, VI, and IX–XI have closing sections in tripla,

TABLE 2.3
In Nomines by John Bull

	No. of Voices	C.f. voice	C.f. pitch	C.f. rhythm
I	3	B	A	o o
II	3	M	a	o o
III	3	S	a′	o ♩
IV	3	B	A	o o
V	3	M	a	o o
VI	3	S	a′	o. *
VII	3	M	a	o o
VIII	free	S	a′	o o
IX	4	B	A	o o ♩ ♩
X	3	S	a′	o ♩
XI	3	S	a′	o ♩
XII	3	S	d′	o ♩

*o ♩ in Paris. 1122

which in No. II (for example) involves a maximum of 24 notes to each breve value of the cantus firmus, as opposed to 16 previously. The most adventurous setting is No. IX, in which each cantus firmus note is extended to the value of 11 quarter notes. Example 2.16 shows the music for note 19 of the chant. By breaking the plainsong at one point Bull engineers a change of harmony and a hint of a cadence. This is typical of the careful working out from measure to measure, but the piece as a whole becomes rather diffuse because of the great diversity of accompanying motives, which have little in common beyond their mainly stepwise movement. Perhaps the most successful of these settings is the simplest and probably the earliest, No. XII. The soprano cantus firmus beginning on d′ keeps the music in a sonorous low register. The piece falls into three distinct sections (mm. 1–18, 19–31, 32–58). The transitions between them are well managed, m. 18 and m. 31 both featuring a slight disturbance in the previously established pattern that prepares the attentive listener for a change in figuration.

EXAMPLE 2.16. Bull, *In Nomine IX*, mm. 55–57

About a dozen pavan/galliard pairs by Bull survive, and as many separate galliards. Again, the simpler works may well appeal most to players today, such as the pair *St. Thomas Wake!* (MB 19/126a & b) and the galliard in D minor (MB 19/70): these pieces were published in *Parthenia*. Among the more extended dances are the pavan and galliard variously described as "Chromatic" and "Queen Elizabeth's" (MB 19/87a & b). They may have been written in 1603 as a memorial to the Queen. The strain lengths are not quite as regular as one would expect from Byrd (pavan: 16, 18, 16 semibreves, with varied repeats; galliard: 12, 8, 12 dotted semibreves). The outline tonal plan, however (see Table 2.4, showing first and last chords of strains), is similar to what Byrd might have devised in a minor-key pair.

This pair is only intermittently chromatic. Strain II of the pavan features half-note themes ascending and descending in semitone steps, but the music stays close to the tonic and subdominant areas, eventually closing on the dominant. Strain III is effectively in A major throughout. The only extensive modulation is in strain III of the galliard, where there are cadences at 2-measure intervals on A major, E major, B major, and F-sharp major—a progression that implies a tuning system approaching equal temperament. But this event occurs too late in the day to be fully effective. One other notable feature is the use in strain III of the pavan of a cantus firmus–like theme in the soprano. A number of other pavans by different composers use a similar device at this point, and it has never been satisfactorily explained whether these are "borrowed" themes of some kind, or made-up ones based on the hexachord.

Comparatively little of Bull's music dates from after his departure from England in 1613. One piece, a fantasia on a theme of Sweelinck (MB 14/4), is dated 1621. Some other works found only in continental sources can be regarded as late. Among them are two *Salve Regina* settings (MB 14/40, 41), two arrangements of Palestrina's madrigal *Vestiva i colli* (MB 14/8, 9), and some variations on Dutch carol tunes. One of the latter, the Prelude and Carol *Laet ons met herten reijne* (MB 14/56), has some original organ registrations: "Cornet," "Crumhorne," and "Voll Register." Also effective on the organ are the variations on *Revenant* (MB 19/100), a tune more widely known as *More Palatino* and set by many

TABLE 2.4
Bull, Chromatic Pavan and Galliard

	Pavan	*Galliard*
I	A minor–A major	A minor–A major
II	A minor–E major	G major–D major
III	E major–A major	D minor–A major

continental composers, including Frescobaldi and Sweelinck. Each of the six variations is in a strict number of parts (respectively 3, 3, 2, 3, 2, 4). The tune itself, virtually unchanged, remains in the treble except in var. 4, where it is placed in the tenor. The accompanying lines can be tenuously related to the theme (Ex. 2.17), but they are also interesting melodies in their own right. Rhythmically, the variations are paired: vars. 1–2 add eighth-note counterpoints to the theme and vars. 3–4 add sixteenth-note ones, while vars. 5–6 feature continuous triplet eighth notes against the occasional duplets of the theme itself. Cunningham has observed that the metrical conflict is preserved "right up to the final cadence, producing an effect that could be used to advantage by a good player" (1984, 204–5). In this attractive piece the elements of Bull's style are pared down to essentials.

Two close contemporaries of Bull are Peter Philips (c. 1560–1628) and Giles Farnaby (c. 1565–1640). Philips, a Catholic, spent almost all of his career abroad. He traveled to Rome in 1582 and from 1585 to 1590 was in the service of Lord Thomas Paget in Italy, Spain, France, and the Netherlands. He met Sweelinck in Amsterdam in 1593, and from 1597 onward was court organist at Brussels. Much of his music (Latin motets and Italian madrigals) was published in Antwerp. Relatively little of his keyboard music has been preserved—there are about 30 pieces in all. Of these, 19 are in Fitzwilliam, copied as a single group, Nos. 70–88 in the manuscript. Some pieces have dates, ranging from 1580 to 1605. Obviously, Philips's keyboard music, unlike that of Bull's exile, found its way back to England. Like Bull, Philips was an important figure in transmitting the features of English keyboard style to the Continent.

Sweelinck made an arrangement of Philips's Pavan in G (No. 85 in Fitzwilliam, dated 1580 and described as "The first one Philips made"; once again, it was originally for consort). The unusual proportions of this work betray a composer of some originality: strains respectively of 13, 11, and 14 semibreves, with an effective extra semibreve following the varied repeat of II. Strain II itself works a single point with considerable skill. Strain III is one of the earliest of those with a cantus firmus theme. The supporting chords, in a regular rhythmic pattern, repay study; they reveal a strong sense of harmonic direction.

Two fine pavan/galliard pairs are those entitled *Paget* (Fitzwilliam, Nos. 74 and 75), perhaps dating from 1590, and *Dolorosa* (Fitzwilliam,

EXAMPLE 2.17. Bull, *Revenant*, openings of vars. 3 and 5

Nos. 80 and 81), dated 1593 and written during a brief spell of imprisonment. Here the underlying proportions are "by fours," but still handled with an element of the unexpected. The *Paget* pavan has strains of 16, 16 (divided 9 + 7), and 32 (divided 20 + 12) semibreves; in *Dolorosa* the tally is 16, 24, 32. In both pairs the galliard reworks quite closely material from the pavan; this often involves a simplification of the ideas. Example 2.18 illustrates this from strain III of *Dolorosa*, which also shows Philips exploiting the sonorities possible on the short-octave instrument.

No fewer than nine of the Philips works in Fitzwilliam are intabulations in the Italian vein of madrigals or chansons. The originals are by Marenzio, Caccini, Striggio, Lassus, and in one case *(Fece da voi)* Philips himself. The arrangements have an unpredictable quality, like the written-down improvisations of a player possessed of both proficient technique and fertile imagination. These pieces require very flexible performance; in a recital program they would make a good foil to works with more regular rhythmic patterns, such as Philips's Passamezzo [antico] Pavan and Galliard (Fitzwilliam, Nos. 76 and 77).

Most of the virginalists were professional organists, but Giles Farnaby was a joiner, possibly a maker of keyboard instruments. Technically, there are a few rough edges in his music, but few would disagree with Richard Marlow's opinion that he is "an instinctive composer with something original to say . . . his music is spontaneous, vital, almost innocent at times" (MB 24, xiii).

Farnaby published a book of canzonets in 1598 and in the same decade contributed to the printed psalters of East and Barley. His keyboard music, however, seems to have had very limited circulation. Of the 53 pieces in the MB edition, all but two are found only in Fitzwilliam. Many of them are arrangements, settings of popular tunes such as *Tell me Daphne* or *Paul's Wharf* or decorative versions of pavans by Dowland and others. One fantasia-like piece (MB 24/11) is in fact a transcription

EXAMPLE 2.18. Philips, *Dolorosa* Pavan (mm. 103–109) and Galliard (mm. 42–45)

of Farnaby's own canzonet "Ay me poor heart" (No. 15 of his 1598 collection). His "free" fantasias often start well, with distinctive and malleable ideas, but the composer was generally unable to maintain a consistent level of interest throughout these longer works, and there is an element of note spinning in the running figurations with which they invariably end.

Farnaby's originality is more apparent in smaller-scale compositions. His [Alman] for Two Virginals (MB 24/25) is thought to be the first piece ever written for two keyboards. The second player is given an elaborated version of the first player's music. Since both are self-sufficient, and the piece is very short, it might be effective in performance for the two versions to be played first separately, and then together. The jig (MB 24/27) consists of four variations on a theme with an engaging 9-measure structure.[14] The fourth variation makes considerable demands on the performer, with the theme in broken octaves (plus ornaments) in the left hand against right-hand sixteenth notes. The character pieces *His Dream, His Rest,* and *His Humour* (MB 24/50, 51, 53), occurring consecutively in Fitzwilliam, make an effective suite in spite of the fact that *His Dream* has final D, and the other two, final G. *His Humour* is a kind of musical joke in which various stock motives of Elizabethan music are gently parodied: sudden chromaticism, facile imitative tags, and the hexachord—uphill and down again.

Farnaby chose some attractive tunes to vary, none more so than *Loth to Depart* (MB 24/41), on which he composed six variations. The 8-measure theme falls into four equal phrases, and it has to be admitted that there is a tendency in Farnaby's piece for the music to fall into 2-measure segments. But the whole is shaped by the gradual introduction of shorter note values through vars. 1–5, culminating in a richly harmonized final statement. It is clear to the listener that var. 6 is the moment of final leave-taking, delayed only by the backward glance of the beautifully judged extra bar at the end.

The youngest contributor to *Parthenia*, Orlando Gibbons (1583–1625), can be compared to Byrd in that he contributed with distinction to many of the musical genres current in his day. The skillful polyphony and the general mood of restraint observed in his anthems, madrigals, and consort music also inform his keyboard music. He had a considerable reputation as a player, being appointed organist at the Chapel Royal sometime before 1615, virginalist to King James I in 1619, and organist of Westminster Abbey in 1623. The virtuoso performer can be observed in the rapid passage work of *The Queen's Command* (No. 20 in *Parthenia;* MB 20/28) and a few other pieces, but on the whole Gibbons's keyboard music is more "for substance" than "for the hand."

The fantasias in MB 20, Nos. 7–15, are certainly substantial works. They are all effective on the organ, even though one of them, the "Fantazia of foure parts" (MB 20/12), was included in the "virginalls" publication *Parthenia*. The editor of MB 20, Gerald Hendrie, suggested that Gibbons may have revised the piece for print, enlivening the rhythm in places and so making it more suitable for the virginals. The fantasia MB 20/7 is described in its only source, Cosyn's Virginal Book, as "A Fancy for a double Orgaine," and appears to be the first known piece to exploit the two manuals found on early seventeenth-century organs. The manuals are described as "ten[or]" and "base," the compass of the former (Choir organ) evidently descending to c and of the latter (Great organ) to C. Most of the way through, the piece is presented as a dialogue played by the left hand alternately on Choir and Great, accompanied by two right-hand voices on the Choir. Toward the end (m. 66 onward) the texture expands to four voices, and Cosyn's manual indications seem to fit the music less comfortably; this perhaps calls into question whether Gibbons himself designed the work for two manuals (Wulstan 1985, 123).

Nevertheless, the Fantasia for Double Organ does proceed differently from a "normal" fantasia treating a succession of polyphonic points in turn. Only the opening and closing paragraphs (mm. 1–14, 66–80) make thorough use of imitation; the motives employed are shown in Examples 2.19a and f. In between, the music is freely polyphonic, the main events being not new points of imitation but the entries of the "base" element of the left-hand dialogue. All these entries are different (varying in length from two to seven measures), but they all incorporate, in diminished note values, elements from Example 2.19a, as illustrated in Examples 19b–e. Thematically, then, the fantasia evolves by gradual stages from the opening point to the concluding one. The cadences of the "base" phrases form the main points of articulation—for example, m. 24 (on F), mm. 30, 37, and 54 (all on D, with tierce de Picardie), and m. 60 (on A). If the piece is played on two manuals, the best solution for the problematic closing passage is probably for the right hand to transfer to the Great manual on the second note of m. 66, both hands remaining on that manual until the end.

Three more pieces from *Parthenia* call for brief comment. The pavan and galliard *Lord Salisbury* (MB 20/18–19) are Gibbons's only linked pair; there are motivic and harmonic connections among all three strains, but they do not extend beyond the first few notes (in II the galliard diminishes the pavan's rhythm, retaining the melodic shape and

EXAMPLE 2.19. Gibbons, Fantasia for Double Organ, selected motives

(a) mm. 1-2

(b) mm. 17-18

(c) mm. 22-23

(d) mm. 27-28

(e) mm. 63-64

(f) mm. 66-67

EXAMPLE 2.20. Gibbons, Pavan *Lord Salisbury*, and Dowland, *Lachrymae* Pavan, opening motives of strains

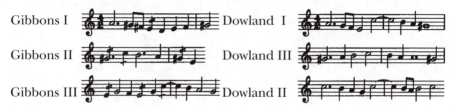

the accompanying part a tenth lower). These pieces are no less intense than the pavans that Dowland described as "passionate," and it is interesting to note that Gibbons's pavan is one of many[15] that echo the material of Dowland's most famous work, the *Lachrymae* pavan (Ex. 2.20). Gibbons's sharpening of the 7th and 6th degrees in the descending minor scale adds a special pathos at the outset.

The final piece in *Parthenia,* strangely enough, is a prelude (MB 20/2). Most virginalist preludes seem to have been independent pieces; perhaps it was normally left to players to select a prelude in the appropriate key to precede a fantasia or pavan/galliard pair. This particular example survives in a dozen manuscript copies and evidently retained its popularity well into the eighteenth century. It is not hard to see why, for it is one of those pieces that seems ahead of its time, with hints of threepart invertible counterpoint, sequential writing (including 7-6 suspensions), and tonally directed harmony.

The last of the virginalists was Thomas Tomkins, a composer who in his later works pursued his own lines of musical thought irrespective of new trends in the world around him. Born in 1572, he was older than Gibbons but outlived him by more than 30 years. He wrote most of his keyboard music in his last decade, 1646–56, after the Civil War had forced him to resign his organist's post at Worcester Cathedral.

Five pieces by Tomkins are in Fitzwilliam, probably written by 1615. The first (MB 5/56) is a Pavan in A minor (strain lengths: 16, 20, 26), originally for five-part consort. Varied repeats are added in the keyboard version, with unusually florid motivic transitions between the strains. The second Tomkins work in Fitzwilliam is a Ground in G (MB 5/39). Its theme has the same rhythm (in halved note values) as that of Byrd's Ground in G (Ex. 2.21). It also has a curious resemblance to "Up Tails

EXAMPLE 2.21. Tomkins, Ground in G

All," a tune set by Farnaby (MB 24/48). With its constant return to D-B-D, it must have posed quite a compositional challenge. One imagines that Byrd could have given this theme to his pupil Tomkins and suggested a strategy for the plan of the whole, which Tomkins followed assiduously, though at times rather mechanically. Variations 1–26 build up slowly to continuous sixteenth movement in both hands; 27–35 employ tripla; 36 is the climax of rhythmic elaboration; and 37–45 form an expansive final group. During the course of the work the theme is placed in treble, bass, tenor, and alto positions—the last only in var. 41, with a treble descant that functions as a central apex to the final group of variations. The piece is rounded off by a coda appropriately marked "[Quasi senza tempo]" in the Fuller Maitland and Barclay Squire edition of Fitzwilliam. An extended plagal cadence decorated by scales, it is a distant successor to the coda of Tallis's second *Felix namque* setting.

One composition by Tomkins is dated 1637: the *Offertory* (MB 5/21), which in spite of its title is similar to the piece just discussed. It is based on a short theme, apparently derived from the plainsong intonation of *Felix namque,* varied as many as 64 times. Possibly also from the 1630s, but a good deal less elaborate, is the *Fancy for two to play* (MB 5/32). This is one of two keyboard duets that Tomkins copied into London 29996, the other being an In Nomine by Nicholas Carleton (d. 1630): "A verse for two to play on one virginall or organs." Tomkins described his own piece as "Another of the like," but it is a much more appealing work than Carleton's. "The Treble partes" begin with what Kerman would describe as a three-part "cell," answered five semibreves later and an octave lower by "The Base parte." The rest of the first section, up to the tonic cadence in m. 20, is constructed on a series of imitative points. Tomkins here uses the four hands to produce a richer polyphony than can be conveniently encompassed by two. The livelier and shorter second section takes up the opening idea of antiphonal exchange between the two players. Considering that this is one of the very first keyboard duets, the piece shows a remarkable appreciation of the potentialities of the medium. Beyond that, a feature that contributes to its success in performance is the kinship that exists among the various motives employed.

The sole source for almost all the keyboard music of Tomkins's last decade is a manuscript in his own hand, Paris 1122. In MB 5 Stephen D. Tuttle published a detailed account of this important source, summarizing the position regarding its compilation as follows:

> The manuscript was apparently started by [Tomkins] as a collection of pieces by various composers, for the first seventy-one pages contain works of Byrd and Bull, as well as some of his own, all copied in a fair hand. After page 71 he abandoned his original idea of a collection and used the remaining pages for composing new works or perhaps, in some cases, for revising earlier ones. (p. xiii)

There are about 50 pieces by Tomkins in Paris 1122, of which over 30 bear dates, ranging from 9 November 1646 to 8 September 1654. On stylistic grounds it is likely that most of the undated pieces also belong to these years.

Among the dated works are examples of plainsong settings, fantasias, pavans and galliards, and one variation set *(Fortune)*. It is almost as if Tomkins set out, in retirement, to sum up more than a century of English keyboard styles. The notion is not altogether fanciful; one of the items in Tomkins's large library was the manuscript London 29996, with its collections of liturgical organ music, to which he made a number of annotations.

The immediate models for his own plainsong pieces, however, were Byrd and Bull. *Clarifica me Pater,* September 1650 (MB 5/4), follows Byrd's second setting in placing the chant, transposed up a fifth, in the soprano, with two imitative voices below. The six In Nomines, two of which appear in two versions, may be compared to those of Bull in their general layout (Table 2.5). Tomkins follows Bull's transpositions and his rhythmic treatment of the chant in $\frac{3}{2}$ meter. But he does not place the cantus firmus in the middle voice, and in duple meter examples the chant values are only half the length of Bull's, which is probably an advantage. In composing the accompanying counterpoints Tomkins followed the usual procedure of gradually diminishing note values, but the process is tautly controlled and each motive is made to earn its keep. Some of the more rapid figurations do resemble those of Bull quite closely (compare, for example, MB 5/11, mm. 31–33, with MB 14/30, mm. 35–39).

Two pavans will serve as final examples. *A Sad Pavan for these Distracted Times* (MB 5/53) is dated 14 February 1649. This is presumably an "old style" date, and thus Tomkins wrote this piece just over a year after the execution of Charles I. The piece is not particularly chromatic, but it is wayward in its tonal structure. As Table 2.6 indicates, the strains begin rather far on the flat side before closing more conventionally on tonic, dominant, and tonic (the piece has a one-flat key signature). The strain lengths are highly irregular (28, 27, 36) and there are no varied repeats.

TABLE 2.5
In Nomines by Tomkins

MB no.	No. of voices	C.f. voice	C.f. pitch	C.f. rhythm
5/6	3	S	a′	○ ♩
7	3	B	A	○ ♩
8	3	B	A	○ ♩
9	3	S	a′	○
10/11	3	S	a′	○ ♩
12	3	B	A	○

TABLE 2.6
Tomkins, *A Sad Pavan*

I	C minor–G major
II	E-flat major–D major
III	E-flat major–G major

Notwithstanding the dotted rhythms that appear briefly toward the end of strain II and more extensively in III, the dance element is wholly absent from this piece. The music displays Tomkins's characteristic economy, each strain being built on a single motive. These motives move almost entirely by step and hence are undemonstrative, even withdrawn in character; they are subject to constant rhythmic and textural variation, which adds to the unsettled feeling of the work.

By contrast, the *Short Pavan*, 19 July 1654 (MB 5/55), returns to a straightforward tonal scheme and regular 8-semibreve strains, into which Tomkins skillfully weaves imitative figures in the time-honored fashion. These three strains could easily be arranged for four-part consort. The varied repeats have something to add, each one reaching a higher melodic peak than the undecorated statement. In this serene work Tomkins, now over 80 years old, recaptured the youth of English instrumental dance forms.

The Mid-Seventeenth Century

Tomkins was writing in the middle years of the seventeenth century, but in what was by then a very old-fashioned style. When we turn to other keyboard music written in England between the 1620s and the Restoration, we find a very different repertory, consisting mainly of simple settings of popular tunes and short dance movements. Much of this music remains unpublished. There have, however, been some valuable editions and studies of representative sources, such as *Parthenia In-Violata* (1624 or 1625); three manuscripts now in Paris and one in New York;[16] Elizabeth Rogers's Virginal Book (27 February 1656/7); and a print that was first issued just three years after the Restoration, *Musicks Hand-maide*, 1663.

The sequel to *Parthenia*, *Parthenia In-Violata or Mayden-Musicke for the Virginalls and Bass-Viol*, is the second printed source of English keyboard music. Strictly speaking, it is a consort source, because its 20 pieces are scored for keyboard and bass viol, but the keyboard part is self-sufficient and none of the several manuscript concordances includes a bass viol part; furthermore, the viol's role is limited to reinforcing the keyboard's bass line. All the pieces are given anonymously; two are ascribed elsewhere to Bull and one to Edmund Hooper (c. 1553–1621; organist of Westminster Abbey from 1606). The book is undated, but it may well have been issued between December 1624 and May 1625 as a wedding present for Prince Charles of England (who played the viol) and Princess Henrietta Maria of France (who played the virginal) (Dart, *Historical Introduction* to 1961 facsimile edition).

Unlike its predecessor, *Parthenia In-Violata* has no pavans, galliards, or fantasias. From their titles the first eight pieces could all be settings of masque tunes; No. 2, *The Lordes Mask*, is certainly in that category.[17] No. 9 of *Parthenia In-Violata* is entitled "Miserere," but the plainsong, concealed in an inner part, is hardly compatible with the coranto-like character of the piece. Three items (Nos. 10, 15, 16) are headed "Almaine." These are short binary-form pieces, without varied repeats. Nos. 12, 19, and 20, all untitled, are alman-like but with varied repeats; Nos. 11, 13, 14, 17, and 18, also untitled, are in effect corantos, again with varied repeats. Almans, corantos, and settings of masque tunes all occur among the shorter pieces in Fitzwilliam, and also feature quite prominently in the music of Orlando Gibbons. So in the forms represented, *Parthenia In-Violata* can be seen as a link between the music of the virginal school and the fashions that would dominate keyboard music during the middle years of the century.

From about 1620 onward the alman (almaine, almaygne, almand) replaced the pavan as the main duple-meter keyboard dance in England. It was destined gradually to become more elaborate, as the pavan had done previously. The dozen or so examples in Fitzwilliam are usually of two strains only, without varied repeats. Of the three pieces called "Almaine" in *Parthenia In-Violata*, the most interesting is No. 16. Its two sections, of 8 and 11 measures, both close on the tonic, A. The melody is echoed in canonic fashion in a middle voice (mm. 3 and 5) or in the bass (mm. 10, 12–13), and toward the end there is a passage of freely imitative polyphony that recalls the last strain of Gibbons's *Lord Salisbury* pavan (Ex. 2.22).

The triple-meter coranto is also represented by about a dozen

EXAMPLE 2.22. Almaine, *Parthenia In-Violata*, No. 16, mm. 14–17, for keyboard and bass viol

examples in Fitzwilliam. They are straightforward pieces, usually with the time signature 3 and seldom employing any cross-rhythm effects. They are not yet linked to almans in this source; Nos. 200 and 201 are "An Almain" and "Corranto" both in G, but their placing together is no doubt an accident. Similarly independent are the pieces in coranto style in *Parthenia In-Violata*. No. 11 makes an even denser use of imitation than No. 16. It, too, has strains of 8 and 11 measures, both closing on the tonic, which in this case is G. The decoration applied in the varied repeats is modest, so the polyphonic aspect of the first statements is retained.

The kind of repertory covered by an English keyboard player in the 1630s is preserved in Paris 1186, a manuscript of nearly 200 pieces compiled by "R.Cr." (who has not been identified). A handful of pieces by the compiler have dates—1635, 1636, and 1638. Some virginalist music is included, but not in very good texts; Byrd's *The Woods So Wild*, for example, is reduced to its first two variations. There are simple versions of masque tunes and popular songs, pieces in alman style (often untitled), corantos and jigs, and arrangements of vocal music both sacred and secular. Almost everything is anonymous. The editor, Martha Maas, has suggested that "the writer may have been a professional musician attached to a private household where music of these several kinds would have been demanded of him" (*English Pastime Music*, viii). Many of the pieces, however, are well within the capabilities of an amateur player.

A similar miscellany, but in at least five hands and compiled over a longer period (1620 or before–c. 1660) is Drexel 5612. The first copyist entered a good deal of virginalist music by Byrd and others. Pieces added by the later scribes were on the whole much shorter and simpler. A few composers' names appear, among them [Edmund] Hooper, Thomas Holmes (1606–38, organist of Winchester Cathedral), and Leonard Mells (court violinist in the 1620s and 1630s).

The repertory of the 1650s, not so very different from that of the 1630s, is represented by "Elizabeth Rogers hir Virginall Booke" (hereafter Rogers), which has the date 27 February 1656 on its first leaf. At least two hands have been identified, and again there is a cross-section of music for domestic use, including original keyboard works, settings of well-known tunes, and some anthems and songs arranged on two staves with text. Byrd's "Battle" suite appears in the book, and a number of pieces refer to more recent political events—*Sir Thomas Fairfax's March*, *Prince Rupert's March*, *Rupert's Retreat*, and *When the King enjoys his own again*.[18]

The dance music in Rogers includes courants and sarabands by "Beare," undoubtedly a member of the French de la Barre dynasty. He is one of several French musicians whose work appears in midcentury English sources.[19] It is not always easy to distinguish French elements from native English ones in music of this period; many aspects of style

EXAMPLE 2.23. "Corrant Beare," Elizabeth Rogers's Virginal Book, No. 23

had an international currency. In the extract from "Corrant Beare" (Rogers No. 23; Ex. 2.23) we may regard as typically French the graceful melodic line of which the ornaments seem an integral part, and the "broken" style of the left-hand accompaniment *(stile brisé)*, which is often said to derive from the texture of lute music. The ornament sign itself, however, is still the virginalist double stroke (English ornament signs were added as a matter of course to continental pieces, which appear without them in continental sources), and broken-chord patterns such as that in the last measure of the example are found in English music at least a century earlier. The extract does illustrate the play of $\frac{3}{2}$ against $\frac{6}{4}$ typical of the French courante, which is not very common in earlier English corantos.

Paris 1186, Drexel 5612, and Rogers all include arrangements of tunes that also occur in John Playford's publication *The English Dancing Master* (London, 1651, and subsequent editions). "Blewcapp" is one such. Example 2.24 shows the first of its two strains; further comment is unnecessary. The tune of *The Nightingale* is set for lute in Thomas Mace's *Musicke's Monument* of 1676 (201), and keyboard versions, largely independent of each other, are found in Paris 1186 (two settings, one attributed to Henry Loosemore), Drexel 5612 (two), and Rogers. Because the tune itself is attractive—incorporating a modest amount of birdsong imitation—the keyboard arrangements have a certain charm. The meter is that of an almain. The two 12-measure strains both close on the tonic (C) but the stressing of the subdominant chord at the beginning of the second one provides some harmonic variety (see Ill. 2.4).

As for named dances, the majority are still separate movements. But some pairings do occur, marking the early stages in the development of the suite. In Drexel 5612, an "Almaine" and "The Saraband," the latter attributed to "Mr. Mels," are clearly linked thematically in both strains,

EXAMPLE 2.24. "Blewcapp," Drexel 5612, p. 181

ILLUSTRATION 2.4. Elizabeth Rogers's Virginal Book (London 10337), f. 9. An anonymous setting of *The Nightingale*. Reproduced by kind permission of the British Library.

although the underlying harmonies are clumsy in the extreme. Rogers has two pairs of dances by Thomas Strengthfield, a composer unknown outside this source: Nos. 14–15, "Almaygne"—"The Corrant to the last Alm.," and Nos. 17–18, "Almaygne"—"Corrant to the former Alma." These two pairs exhibit some slight motivic similarities of a kind that might or might not be deliberate. Other groups of two or three dances in the same key occur in Rogers, and it is possible that they were in-tended—at least by the copyist—to be played consecutively.

The grouping of dances into suites is somewhat clearer in *Musicks Hand-maide Presenting New and Pleasant Lessons for the Virginals or Harpsy-con,* published by John Playford in 1663. Nos. 3–6 consist of an Ayre, Corant, Saraband, and Jig, all in G, the last attributed to Benjamin San-dley. Nos. 7–9 are Ayre, Corant, and Saraband, with the name of William Lawes attached to the last; Nos. 13–15 are Allmaine—Coranto—Saraband, without ascription. Nearly all the pieces in *Musicks Hand-maide*—dances and named tunes—are in binary form, with a single melodic line in the right hand and supporting left-hand harmonies in no more than two parts. There are no varied repeats. The publication rep-resents the extreme point in the simplification of English keyboard music. Even the works added when the book was reprinted in 1678 show a little more contrapuntal interest.

A typical example from the 1663 issue is No. 42, an Ayre by Ben-jamin Rogers. It is so short that it can be quoted in its entirety (Ex. 2.25). Its first two measures are an almost direct quotation from *The Kinges Morisck* (No. 1 of *Parthenia In-Violata*). The supertonic close to the first strain is unusual, as is the absence of a first repeat (which is made quite clear in the original print; the reason is doubtless the avoidance of con-secutives). The second strain, beginning with an upside-down version of the opening motive, should presumably have the same rhythm applied to it, but how far this should affect the rest of this miniature piece is a matter for the good taste of the player. The next item, a Coranto also in

EXAMPLE 2.25. Rogers, Ayre

C, has generally been assumed to be by Rogers as well, but it is a variant of the piece attributed to "Beare" in Rogers and shown in Example 2.23.

Playford's Preface "To all Lovers of Musick" is of interest for its comments on the instruments, the potential users, the music itself, and one possible reason for its very simple textures:

> . . . the *Virginals;* an instrument of much delight and variety of harmony, as being the same with the *Harpsycon* and *Organ;* which excellency hath made it the delight of many young ladies and gentlewomen, whose accommodation induced me to select these new and pleasant lessons, which are not only easy but delightful for young practitioners, being most of them late tunes and dances set to the virginals after the newest mode, and are so composed that the treble violin may play the tunes along with the virginals, which will be a pleasant consort.

The Age of Purcell

English keyboard music of the Restoration had its own "three famous Masters" in Matthew Locke (c. 1622–77), John Blow (1649–1708), and Henry Purcell (1659–95). All three were professional organists, and although keyboard music formed only a small part of their output, a good proportion of it was published. In the music of these three and their contemporaries, a clear distinction now existed between music for harpsichord or spinet and that intended for organ. The former consisted principally of suites (seldom identified as such). The makeup of suites varied, but they often included the sequence almain–corant–saraband, preceded and/or followed by other items. For the organ, the standard form was the single-movement voluntary. Voluntaries normally incorporated some quasi-fugal writing, thus reestablishing a tradition that had been broken during the period of the Civil War and Commonwealth.

Organ music was not the only aspect of English music that took a new lease on life at the time of the Restoration. Composers were once again able to enjoy royal patronage: Locke, Blow, and Purcell were all "Composers in Ordinary" to the King, as well as holding appointments as organists of royal chapels. They also had the opportunity to provide songs and incidental music for the newly opened theatres. Several of Purcell's published harpsichord pieces are arrangements from his theatre music.

To some degree it is possible to trace the development of Restoration keyboard music through the printed sources, which increase in number toward the year 1700. All of them, incidentally, like *Parthenia* and *Parthenia In-Violata*, were printed from engraved copper plates. A small oblong format was preferred, convenient for placing on the music desks of harpsichords and spinets.

Most of Locke's keyboard music is found in *Melothesia*, published in 1673. This book, according to the title page, was "All carefully reviewed by M. Locke, Composer in Ordinary to His Majesty, and Organist of Her Majesties Chappel." This last refers to the Catholic Chapel of Queen Catherine, at Somerset House. *Melothesia* ("setting of melody") contains not only harpsichord and organ music but also "Certain General Rules for Playing upon a Continued-Bass." This, the first surviving explanation of figured bass to be printed in England, is reproduced in facsimile in Christopher Hogwood's excellent edition of the complete *Melothesia*. The prefatory material also gives the symbols and names for five different ornaments: forefall, backfall, shake, forefall and shake, and beat. In the music itself the signs are placed above or below the notes, rather than through the stem as still applied in the first issue of *Musicks Hand-maide*. Explanations of the signs in musical notation were apparently not printed until *The Harpsicord Master* of 1697 (see below). This more precise usage of ornament symbols is evidence of French influence, though the meaning of the symbols differs in some cases from that which applies in French sources.

Melothesia begins with 21 harpsichord pieces by Locke and ends with 7 organ pieces by him (see Ill. 2.5). In between is music by several little-known contemporaries, including Christopher Preston, John Roberts, and William Gregory. The concept of the suite is taken a stage further in *Melothesia:* most of its 61 harpsichord pieces are in groups of 4 or 5 united by key, although sometimes a "suite" contains items by more than one composer. For example, Locke added a "Horne Pipe" of his own to complete a Suite in D minor (almain–corant–saraband) by William

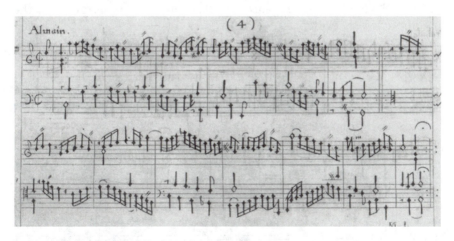

ILLUSTRATION 2.5. *Melothesia*, 1673, p. 4. The Almain from Locke's first suite. Reproduced by kind permission of the British Library.

EXAMPLE 2.26. Roberts, Corant and "La Double" (*Melothesia*, No. 28)

Gregory. The first 7 pieces in the book, all in C major, are entitled Prelude, Saraband, Prelude, Almain, Corant, Gavott, and Country Dance.
In his edition Dart took this to be a six-movement suite with alternative
preludes and the saraband misplaced. It is more likely that Locke intended the first two pieces to be independent, No. 1 being an introductory prelude to the whole collection along the lines of the first piece in
Musicks Hand-maide, and No. 2 "a demonstration of the more modern
variation method, verging on the French *double*" (Hogwood 1987, v).
Like many early keyboard sources, *Melothesia* betrays a clear pedagogical
intent, evident in the relative simplicity of the first few pieces by Locke
and the gradual introduction of technical problems and new keyboard
textures. Later in the volume (No. 28) is a corant by John Roberts in
which the two 8-measure strains have varied repeats labeled "La Double" (Ex. 2.26). In these repeats, the "broken" style reminiscent of the
lute idiom is very evident.

There are four suites by Locke in *Melothesia.* The third one, again in
C, has five movements, prelude–almain–corant–saraband–jig. The prelude (Ex. 2.27) must obviously by played very freely; although notated in
exact values it approaches the style of the "unmeasured" French preludes. The slur in m. 1 indicates sustaining of the notes concerned. The

EXAMPLE 2.27. Locke, Prelude (*Melothesia*, No. 12)

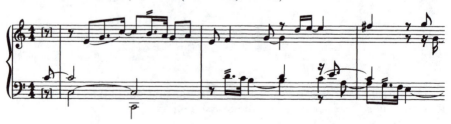

EXAMPLE 2.28. Locke, Almain (*Melothesta*, No. 13)

almain (Ex. 2.28) illustrates the extent to which this dance had slowed down and become texturally more complex by the 1670s. The upbeat should probably be given its full value in performance (Caldwell 1973, 176). This example has a short opening phrase closing on the tonic, a first strain closing on the dominant, and strain II taking that chord as its starting point. These are regular features of countless binary movements of the late seventeenth and eighteenth centuries. More idiosyncratic, even personal to Locke, is the way modulation is used within each strain. Measures 4–6 hint at D minor, C major, F major, D minor, A minor; in strain II, mm. 11–15 move through D minor, A minor, F major, G major, F major, D minor, G minor, G major. This constant touching upon different keys produces a rather unsettled feeling in the listener. The wayward effect is reinforced by the fact that there is hardly any reuse of melodic or rhythmic motives in the piece. Nonetheless, Locke has the skill to redress the balance in the last three measures, which over a slower harmonic foundation (chords IV–V–I) do make more consistent use of descending sixteenth-note figures. The two strains, incidentally, are both of nine measures, and the two strains of the following corant are both of six measures; this symmetrical planning is typical of Locke, even though within each strain there is little feeling of regular phraseology. The corant (Ex. 2.29) does not feature any audible element of $\frac{3}{2}:\frac{6}{4}$ cross-rhythm, though other examples do, for example, *Melothesia*, Nos. 19 (Locke), 24 (Preston), and 28 (Roberts).

In performance, the rhythmic character of this and many similar examples is, once again, a matter of taste. The dotted rhythms in m. I may well have been "tempered" to something like ♩♩♪ ♩♪ ♩, and the same interpretation would then be applied to the left hand in m. 2. The upbeat in this case would require shortening. The saraband, of which the melody only is shown in Example 2.30, is in simple 3 time without

EXAMPLE 2.29. Locke, Corant (*Melothesia*, No. 14)

EXAMPLE 2.30. Locke, Saraband (*Melothesia*, No. 15), melody only

upbeat, and with some stressing of the second beat chiefly by means of ornamentation. In many earlier (midcentury) sarabands the melody begins with three eighth notes at the same pitch, a convention of which a trace remains in this example. Finally, the jig of Locke's third suite (melody in Ex. 2.31a) has the characteristic hornpipe rhythm familiar to modern listeners from Handel's Water Music. Once again the overall dimensions are evenly balanced: a repeated A section of 7 measures is followed by a B section of 14. A is a regular 4-measure phrase extended by a tag that echoes its closing rhythm (♩♩ ♩♩) three times; like a rhyme, the tag appears again at the end of the B section. In the final notated bar (Ex. 2.31b), leading neatly back to the sign, the slurred eighths almost certainly indicate performance in the manner of the French "couler": ♪♩ or ♫. .

Locke's organ pieces in *Melothesia* are almost the only ones of his that survive. They are not called voluntaries; the first six are headed "For the Organ" and the last one "For a Double Organ." Nos. 1 and 4–6 are short, less than 20 measures of common time ($\frac{4}{4}$ in transcription). Each treats a single theme in fugal style, echoing the rich textures of the English viol fantasies. No. 2 (in F) is similar, but the fugal writing is preceded by a 10-measure introduction that begins chordally. No. 3 (in A minor) is also bipartite, but the first section is itself fugal, on a rather chromatic subject.

Locke's double-organ piece has a number of novel features. It was not the first such work since that by Gibbons mentioned earlier; there are, for example, three by John Lugge, organist of Exeter Cathedral from 1603 to 1647 (Locke was a choirboy there). Locke begins appropriately with two subjects, one an old-fashioned ricercar soggetto, the other a very up-to-date French march, which are worked together in invertible counterpoint. The right hand, as well as the left, has solos on the Great organ. From about m. 20 Locke abandons his double fugue: the third and fourth entries on the Great (mm. 24, 29) are of a new theme in sixteenths. This leads to a brief passage of antiphonal exchange between

EXAMPLE 2.31. Locke, Jig, (*Melothesia*, No. 16), melody only, mm. 1–4 and 17

the two manuals before the piece is brought to an end with both hands on the Great. Locke's tendency to move on to a new idea rather than explore an old one is still apparent, especially in the latter part of this piece. It is interesting to note, however, that the beginning of the "coda" on the Great (mm. 33–34) recalls the material of an earlier episode on the Choir (mm. 22–23).

Half a dozen more pieces by Locke were printed in 1678, the year after his death, in a revised edition of *Musicks Hand-maide*. This revision added 22 "lessons" to the 53 in the earlier issue. Of the Locke pieces, most (if not all) are arrangements—not necessarily by the composer himself. The Ayre–Saraband pair Nos. 66–67 and the Ayre No. 68 derive from Locke's music for the masque *Cupid & Death* (1659; original versions in MB 2, pp. 24, 25, 47); the Alman No. 64 is an arrangement of the Ayre from the seventh suite of his *The Little Consort* (MB 31, p. 83), in which not a great deal remains of the original middle part.

Next in the line of extant English keyboard prints is *The Second Part of Musick's Hand-maid*, published in 1689 by Henry Playford (John's son) (Ill. 2.6). Playford's address "To the Reader" announces that the music

ILLUSTRATION 2.6. The title page from *The Second Part of Musick's Hand-Maid*, 1689. The illustration was also used on the title page of *Musicks Hand-Maide*, 1663. Reproduced by kind permission of the British Library.

has been "Composed by our ablest Masters, Dr. John Blow, Mr. Henry Purcell &c. the Impression being carefully Revised and Corrected by the said Mr. Henry Purcell." Several of the 18 pieces by Purcell are arrangements; where the models are his own songs, one cannot be sure that Purcell himself made the keyboard settings, but it seems that at least he must have approved them. The best known is *A New Ground* in E minor, a setting of the song "Here the deities approve" from the ode *Welcome to all the pleasures* (1683). The opening bars give some indication of the style Purcell considered appropriate for continuo realization. The vocal part (originally alto) is placed an octave higher in the arrangement, with some additional decoration both written out and indicated by ornament symbols.

No. 20 in *The Second Part of Musick's Hand-maid* is a similar kind of setting of a song written over a five-measure ground (Ex. 2.32). It is without title or ascription. Thurston Dart identified a three-part version of this piece in London 22100: "A Song upon A Ground 'Scocca pur, tutti tuoi strali' by Mr. Baptist." Dart took this to refer to Giovanni Battista Draghi, an Italian who had settled in London by 1667 (he succeeded Locke as organist to Queen Catherine and later [1707] published a collection of six harpsichord suites). But the editor of Draghi's harpsichord works, Robert Klakowich, has argued that "Baptist" here refers to Lully, since "Scocca pur" exists in various French sources close to that composer. This leaves a question mark over the piece in *The Second Part of Musick's Hand-maid*—could the setting be by Purcell? The 5-measure ground might have attracted him, and he was closely involved in the production of the book. Yet there is little inspiration in the arrangement as such and the piece is perhaps best left anonymous.

Also given anonymously, but certainly by Purcell, is the "Suit of Lessons" in C (prelude–almand–corant–saraband–jig) with which the

EXAMPLE 2.32. Ground: "Scocca pur"

1689 print ends. The third and fourth movements reappear in the fifth suite of the *Choice Collection* of 1696, to which we now turn.

Eight suites by Purcell were printed in 1696, the year after the composer's death, in *A Choice Collection of Lessons for the Harpsichord or Spinnet Composed by the late Mr. Henry Purcell Organist of his Majesties Chappel Royal, & of St. Peters Westminster* [Westminster Abbey]. This collection was issued by Purcell's widow, Frances, and the exact constitution of the suites may not in every case have been Purcell's own; Suite No. 3 contains only prelude–almand–courante, and the final movements of the last two suites are arrangements.[20] Nevertheless, for the music it contains this is probably the most important of all seventeenth-century English keyboard prints, its only rival being *Parthenia*.

Except for Nos. 1 and 3 (both in G), each suite is in a different key and each has a character of its own—from the unpretentious No. 1 to the sombre No. 7 in D Minor, with its opening almand "Bell-barr," marked "very slow." All except No. 7 have opening preludes, more Italianate in style than the dance movements, whose ornamented melodic lines still betray French influence. The prelude of Suite No. 5 in C is another of those pieces that seems to step into the future—it is hard to avoid thinking of Bach in connection with it. Not only does it have a refreshing rhythmic drive and motivic economy, but the tonal plan is forward looking: dominant halfway (mm. 10–17), balanced by hints of the subdominant key toward the end (mm. 31–32), approached by means of a confident cycle of fifths progression (Ex. 2.33). While the rest of the fifth suite may not quite measure up to the prelude, an effective recital item can be produced by adding to the four movements of 1696 (prelude–almand–corant–saraband) the jig printed in 1689 (Caldwell 1973, 185).

The second suite, in G minor, is a consistently fine work with four well-matched movements (though, as usual, they are not linked thematically). The prelude, with its almost continuous sixteenth-note movement, is a more ruminative piece than that of Suite 5, but its tonal scheme is equally secure—the structure being articulated by intermediate cadences first on the dominant and then in related major keys (F and B flat). In the almand, the bass part is worth noting; in the first strain it

EXAMPLE 2.33. Purcell, Suite No. 5, Prelude, mm. 28–31

Example 2.34. Purcell, Suite No. 2, Corant, mm. 4-7

rises by step through a tenth from G to b, thence similarly down to d for the "half-close" cadence. A similar sense of purpose informs the melodic line of the ensuing corant, with a beautiful rising sequence occupying the center of the first strain (Ex. 2.34) and a no less striking descending sequence leading to the cadence of strain II. In contrast to the first three movements, the final saraband is symmetrical in its phrase structure. In fact, it proceeds "by fours," with two strains of 8 measures each and a 4-measure *petite reprise* (i.e., a further repetition of the second half of the second strain) to round off the dance and the whole suite.

In 1697 the London publisher and instrument maker John Walsh made his first incursion into keyboard music with *The Harpsicord Master,* of which the only known copy was discovered by Robert Petre in 1977 in Auckland Public Library, New Zealand. The music, by Jeremiah Clarke, John Barrett, and others, consists largely of arrangements. The first Piece, however, is a "Prelude for the fingering" by Purcell.[21] Preceding that are some "Instructions for Learners" that, according to the title page, had been written by Purcell at the request of a friend. These instructions, reprinted in many subsequent collections, deal with the rudiments of pitch and note values, and also cover "Rules for Graces" and the fingering of scales (in C major). Almost all modern editions of keyboard music by Purcell and his contemporaries include a transcription and/or discussion of the "Rules for Graces" (Ill. 2.7).

The claim that the "Instructions" derive from Purcell's own manuscript seems genuine enough, yet the interpretations of the graces are in need of some amendment. The explanation of the battery (a spread chord) is plainly confused. The shake (//) is shown as plain eight-note trill beginning on the upper note, but the number of repercussions must obviously vary according to context. Similarly, the upper and lower appoggiaturas (backfall, forefall) are shown in a "Scotch snap" rhythm (♪♩.), which will be variable in performance. It is normally assumed that a tie should be added to the explanation of "plain note and shake" (Ex. 2.35a). Most problematic is the interpretation of the beat. As was first suggested by Howard Ferguson, it is possible that the realization given is actually that of the "forefall & beat," and that the beat should be the equivalent of the continental lower mordent—a simpler, less

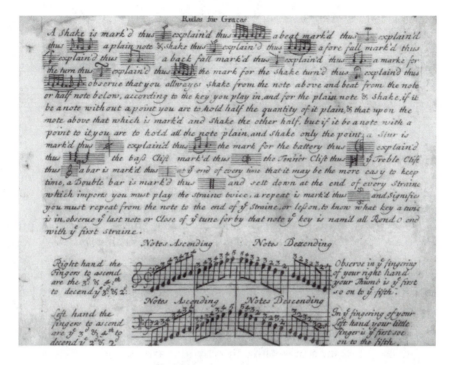

ILLUSTRATION 2.7. "Rules for Graces" and fingering for scales, as reprinted in *The Second Book of the Harpsicord Master* (1700). The left-hand fingering here, and in virginalist sources, is the reverse of the modern convention. Reproduction by kind permission of the Royal College of Music, London.

mannered interpretation that is never inappropriate in performance (Ex. 2.35b). It is true that the writer of the "Rules" went on to say "observe that you allwayes shake from the note above and beat from the note or half note below," but this may merely have been intended to stress that the shake is an alternation with the note above and the beat with the note below (Ferguson 1975, 152). In the first two measures of Purcell's Almand "Bell-barr" (Ex. 2.36) both graces (beat and forefall &

EXAMPLE 2.35.
(a) Plain note and shake

(b) beat

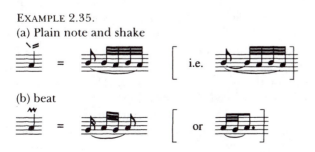

EXAMPLE 2.36. Purcell, Suite No. 7, Almand

beat) appear. The three "beats" in m. 1 are, for melodic and harmonic reasons, all best played as simple three-note mordents. This will also make a greater distinction between the two ornaments on high a″.

The third "master" of Restoration keyboard music, John Blow, published six harpsichord suites. *A Choice Collection of Lessons for the Harpsicord, Spinnet &c . . . By Dr. John Blow* (1698) contains four "Sett's," and two further publications of 1700 include one more suite each: *A Choice Collection of Ayres* by various composers, issued by John Young, and *The Second Book of the Harpsicord Master,* issued by John Walsh. Three individual movements published in 1698 had previously appeared in *The Second Part of Musick's Hand-maid* of 1689, and in one case, the saraband of Suite No. 4, it is interesting to see how the rhythms are notated more precisely in the later source (both are shown in Howard Ferguson's edition of Blow's suites [1965]).

Blow was a more prolific writer of keyboard music than either Locke or Purcell. The six published suites represent only a small proportion of his harpsichord music. Nevertheless, they show a wide-ranging musical invention. In particular, each piece has a distinct rhythmic character. Blow is somewhat the opposite of Locke in that he handles his musical material very economically (sometimes, one feels, almost too much so). His writing for the harpsichord is resourceful, with a well-judged use of its highest and lowest registers.

Only one of Blow's printed suites is in a major key—No. 4 in C ([almand]–corant–saraband–gavott). It is an appealing work whose "open" key is matched by a directness of melody and clarity of design. The tonal planning seems to extend over the four movements, in that the first and last limit themselves to the tonic and dominant keys, whereas strain II of the corant moves through D minor and G minor, and strain II of the saraband through A minor. Strain II of the corant is also remarkable for its melodic bass part—in quasi-canon with the right-hand tune much of the way, and even taking the leading role in mm. 23–26.

Quite different in character is Suite No. 2 in D Minor, with its rather untypical three-movement layout, ground–[rondo]–minuet. A number of contemporary suites begin with almand/grounds. This one could have started life as a two-strain almand (mm. 1–4, 9–12). Blow perhaps saw possibilities for variation in the stepwise descending bass of strain I; he first added decorated repeats to the two strains (mm. 5–8, 13–16), and then (perhaps later) appended a further variation on the whole 16-measure structure. The form of the second movement can be shown as A A B A C A D A; the episodes again explore related keys in a fairly methodical way. The final minuet recalls the medieval technique of isorhythm. Its 12-measure strains proceed entirely in 3-measure phrases, all of which have similar rhythms in both hands. Blow skillfully makes the melody slightly more active in the penultimate "unit," giving the impression of a longer (6-measure) phrase to complete the piece.

Unlike their harpsichord suites, the organ voluntaries of Blow and Purcell remained unpublished in the seventeenth century. As usual, no autograph manuscripts survive; the voluntaries were transmitted by the traditional process of hand copying, and the attendant problems of determining authorship and establishing a reliable text are even greater than usual with these pieces. About 30 voluntaries can be attributed to Blow, and hardly more than 2 or 3 to Purcell. A Voluntary on the Old 100th, the only English work of its kind from the seventeenth century, is ascribed to Purcell in a manuscript of c. 1700; an apparently earlier version, attributed to Blow, survives in an early nineteenth-century printed source derived from a manuscript now lost.

Alongside their Chapel Royal appointments, both Blow and Purcell were organists of Westminster Abbey (Blow from 1668 to 1679 and again from 1695 to 1708; Purcell in the intervening period). They would have played voluntaries, either improvised or written down, before or after services, or as an introduction to the anthem. The most frequent title for Blow's organ pieces in the manuscripts is "verse," a term that draws attention to their liturgical context. Nearly all of them begin fugally. In many examples the fugue subject sooner or later gives place to, or is combined with, figurations in faster note values. The subjects, and hence the pieces based on them, are very diverse in character. No tempo indications appear against them, but some, clearly fairly fast, are of the Italianate canzona type; others, rhythmically more variable and more highly ornamented, seem to require a more measured performance. Voluntaries Nos. 3 and 12 in Shaw's edition (1958) illustrate the two types (Ex. 2.37a and b). No 16 is in two movements (Ex. 2.38a and b), the second being the only example of triple meter in the 30 voluntaries.

EXAMPLE 2.37. Blow, Voluntaries Nos. 3 and 12, opening themes

EXAMPLE 2.38. Blow, Voluntary No. 16
(a) mm. 1–2   (b) mm. 38–39

(c) mm. 36–37 (78–79 almost identical)

Caldwell has questioned whether the movements belong together (1973, 168), but there is a certain thematic resemblance between their subjects, and, unusually, both movements proceed mainly in even eighth notes. The same cadence—admittedly a common formula—is used for both (Ex. 2.38c).

Nos. 25 to 29 in Shaw's edition are for double organ. No. 25, like the Locke example discussed above, has a two-part structure. The opening theme forms the subject for a three-part fugal exposition on the "Little Organ" before being introduced as a left-hand solo on the Great (m. 8); there is a further left-hand entry of the theme in m. 22. The second, more canzona-like theme is introduced in m. 28, with Great "solos" at m. 30 (left hand), 32 (right hand), 37 (left hand), and 40 (right hand—with both hands now on Great, until the end). The cadence formula of no. 16 appears again in the final measures.

Purcell's most famous organ piece is *his* Voluntary for Double Organ, in D minor. This undoubted masterpiece will fittingly conclude our survey. In its outlines and even its final cadence it is quite similar to the Blow piece just discussed, but Purcell makes his materials go much further and his scheme of entries is more methodically worked out.

Once again there are two themes utilized consecutively. The fugal opening section (mm. 1–13), with both hands on the quieter manual, has no fewer than eight entries of the first theme, some in stretto (i.e., overlapping). The balancing final section (mm. 66–81), with both hands on the Great, is a fugato based on the more canzona-like theme II. In between are eight solo entries on the Great. A final table (Table 2.7) will perhaps best illustrate how Purcell achieves a balance between symmetry and variety in this scheme. It will be seen that the solos based on theme I are separated by short interludes on the Choir organ; these are abandoned once the theme II entries begin. As the final column shows, the music is not limited to tonic and dominant keys during the course of the

TABLE 2.7
Purcell, Voluntary for Double Organ

Measures	Theme	Hand	Key of solo entry	Key (chord) at end of solo
14–19	I	Left	D minor	D minor (dominant)
23–28	I	Right	D minor	F major (dominant)
30–36	I	Left	A minor	C major (dominant)
38–45	I	Right	A minor	D major (tonic 1st inversion)
*48–51	II	Left	D minor	A minor (submediant)
52–57	II	Right	D minor	A minor (dominant)
57–61	II	Left	A minor	F major (tonic 2d inversion)
62–65	II	Right	F major	F major (dominant)

*Actually last eighth of 47 (upbeat to theme II).

first seven entries, but Purcell does mark the end of the theme I entries (m. 45) with a fairly deliberate tonic cadence. And the "$^6_4$" chord in m. 61, curiously left hanging in the air, finds its eventual resolution in m. 65.

Such details, and the purposeful underlying structure, do not of course entirely account for the success of Purcell's piece. It also has a strong element of fantasy in the many bold harmonic touches and in the rhapsodic passagework, ranging widely over the keyboard, that tends to occur toward the end of each solo entry.

Even these features do not explain why we should feel that a work of this caliber somehow reflects the composer's own personality. We can go so far in identifying the elements that go into the making of a piece of music, and in relating the resulting score to contemporary instruments and methods of performance; yet in the music of composers like Purcell, Tallis, Byrd, or Gibbons (not to mention a host of others outside the scope of this chapter), there is something more. It cannot be defined in words, but happily it can be conveyed by the sensitive player and recognized by the perceptive listener.

Guide to Literature and Editions

Most of the liturgical organ repertory is in vols. 6 and 10 of *Early English Church Music* (EECM), and almost all of the remainder can be found in vol. 1 of *Musica Britannica* (MB). The latter is an edition of the

Mulliner Book, which, with its cross-section of sacred and secular music, constitutes in itself a fascinating anthology from the mid-sixteenth century. The MB series has subsequently included the collected keyboard works of Tomkins, Bull, Gibbons, Giles and Richard Farnaby, Byrd, and Philips. Volume 55 in the series, *Elizabethan Keyboard Music,* is devoted principally to material from two important Byrd sources, London 30485 and Forster's Virginal Book, while volume 66, *Tudor Keyboard Music c. 1520–1580,* edited by John Caldwell, contains pieces from Royal App. 56 and 58, Tallis's two *Felix namque* settings, and a variety of other music.

The Fuller Maitland/Barclay Squire edition of the Fitzwilliam Virginal Book, familiar in a reprint by Dover Publications, remains indispensable for all who study the virginalists, and includes some music not at present available elsewhere. Some volumes in the *Early Keyboard Music* series (EKM) published by Stainer & Bell, London, derive mainly from the Fitzwilliam manuscript–for example, the *Complete Keyboard Works* by Morley (EKM, 12 and 13) and Tisdall (EKM, 14). Other volumes in this useful series offer selections of music from the MB editions: EKM, 1 and 2 (Tomkins), EKM, 3 (the Mulliner Book), EKM, 8 (Bull), EKM, 25 and 26 (Gibbons), and EKM, 33 and 34 (Byrd). These selections are not listed separately in the Bibliography.

For music of the "transition" period there are editions both of complete sources (*Parthenia In-Violata, Elizabeth Rogers Hir Virginall Booke*) and of selections from sources (*English Pastime Music,* containing pieces from Paris 1186, 1186bis, and 1185; *English Court and Country Dances of the Early Baroque,* containing pieces from Drexel 5612). As for the Restoration "masters," the complete keyboard works of Locke, Purcell, and Blow, are available in reliable editions–among them volumes 69 and 73 of MB, devoted respectively to the organ music and harpsichord music of Blow.

A particularly valuable anthology–not least for its prefatory material–is Howard Ferguson's *Early English Keyboard Music.* The two volumes include several works mentioned in the above chapter, including the [Galliard in F] from Mulliner, the variations on *Go from my window* by Morley/Munday, Gibbons's *Lord Salisbury* pavan and galliard, Tomkins's *A Sad Pavan,* the anonymous ground "Scocca pur," and the complete Suite No. 2 by Purcell. The three English volumes of Faber's Early Organ Series are of course limited to pieces considered appropriate for the organ. Volume 1 includes Byrd's three *Clarifica* settings and a piece by Blitheman not in Mulliner, and vol. 3 has a voluntary by Locke not in *Melothesia.* The texts presented in these volumes preserve more features of the original notation than is usual in editions of this music.

For further reading the best starting point is John Caldwell's *English Keyboard Music Before the Nineteenth Century,* to which his more recent contribution to vol. 6 of the *New Oxford History of Music* (covering the period 1630-1700) will form a useful supplement. Oliver Neighbour's exceptionally perceptive study *The Consort and Keyboard Music of William Byrd* has already been mentioned; to it may be added the extensive notes by Davitt Moroney accompanying his widely acclaimed recording of Byrd's complete keyboard music (Hyperion, CDA 66551/7, 1999). Finally, two fine pieces of writing by the late Thurston Dart can be recommended, almost as much for style as for content (indeed, the keyboard repertoire as such is not their main concern). They are his Foreword to Harman's edition of Morley's *Introduction* and his Historical Introduction to the facsimile edition of *Parthenia In-Violata*.

Notes

1. The term "virginalists" is a convenient one and will be used in this chapter, but it should be borne in mind that their music would have been played not only on the rectangular virginals, but also on other types of harpsichords and on the organ.

2. Pieces in the *Musica Britannica* and *Early English Church Music* editions will be referred to in this form. MB 27/39 means piece no. 39 in volume 27 of *Musica Britannica*.

3. *Seven Dances from the Court of Henry VIII,* ed. Peter Holman (Earlham Press, Corby, 1983). Holman regards *The Crocke* as two separate pieces.

4. See also Denis Stevens in EECM, 10, xi. Stevens mentions the possibility of a second player supplying the plainsong notes (at the written pitch) on another organ, but considers it unlikely, since *"Felix namque,* being part of the Lady-Mass, would have been played in the Lady-chapel; and there it seems doubtful whether one would ever find two organs."

5. Faburden is a fifteenth-century technique for improvising three-part polyphony on a plainsong. The chant itself was sung in parallel fourths, below which a third voice sang a slightly different melody, generally a third below the middle voice, but a fifth below at the beginning and end and at certain other points; this produced a series of 6/3 chords with occasional 8/5 ones.

6. In John Ward's edition of 1983 the ground covers the range c to g, but if the D clef in the MS refers to the D below middle C (as Ward suggests on p. xii), the ground should be an octave lower.

7. This is the seventh of Byrd's "Reasons briefely set downe ... to perswade every one to learne to sing," which appear in his *Psalmes, Sonets, & Songs* of 1588.

8. The source for this information is unknown, but it is unlikely that it derives from the work's placing in Nevell.

9. Printed in *The Byrd Edition* 17/14 (ed. Kenneth Elliott, London, 1971).

10. Sleeve notes to Moroney's recording (1986) of *William Byrd: Pavans and Galliards* (Harmonia Mundi HMC 1241.42).

11. William Petre had been knighted in 1603 and so the title in *Parthenia* is "Pavana. Sr: Wm: Petre."

12. In minor-key pieces throughout the sixteenth century, sectional and final cadences nearly always feature a "tierce de Picardie" (sharpened third).

13. In the Earl of Salisbury's second galliard *(Parthenia,* No. 8; MB 27/15c), m. 7,

the second bass note, G, is without the expected sharp.

14. Two simple variations on an 8-measure version of the tune are in Paris 1186 (c. 1635), with the title "A Scottish Jigge"; see Maas, *English Pastime Music,* No. [24].

15. Including the three pavans immediately preceding this one in the MB edition (MB 20/15–17).

16. *English Pastime Music* (ed. Maas) and *English Court and Country Dances of the Early Baroque* (ed. Gervers); see Bibliography.

17. Masques were lavish dramatic entertainments produced at court and at the Inns of Court. They were especially popular during the reign of James I, but continued as private entertainments right up to the Restoration. The simple keyboard arrangements of tunes from the masques are the equivalent of present-day sheet-music versions of songs from musicals.

18. Thomas, Lord Fairfax, was commander of the Parliamentary army in the Civil War and was one of those who took part in the trial of King Charles I. Prince Rupert, son of Frederick and Elizabeth (the dedicatees of *Parthenia),* led the Royalist cavalry; he suffered defeat at the battle of Naseby in 1645.

19. Other manuscripts including French music are Drexel 5611 and Oxford 1236, both dating from c. 1650. Music by the Italian Frescobaldi also occurs in a number of English manuscripts, such as Oxford 1003 and 1113 and London 36661.

20. Suite No. 4 in A Minor (prelude–almand–corante–saraband) exists in an apparently earlier version with an entirely different prelude in Oxford 1177 (see Ferguson's edition). Another form of this suite occurs in a Purcell keyboard autograph that has recently come to light, in which the almand and corante are associated with a previously unknown jig. For an account of this manuscript and its discovery by Lisa Cox, see Price 1995.

21. Not in Ferguson's edition of Purcell's keyboard works; first modern printing (ed. Robert Petre) in *Early Music* 6 (1978): 375.

Selected Bibliography

EDITIONS

Anne Cromwell's Virginal Book, 1638. Ed. Howard Ferguson. London, 1974.

Blow, John. *Complete Organ Music.* Ed. Barry Cooper. MB, 69. London, 1996.

——. *Complete Harpsichord Music.* Ed. Robert Klakowich. MB, 73. London, 1998

——. *Thirty Voluntaries and Verses for the Organ.* Ed. Watkins Shaw. 2d ed. London, 1972.

British Library MS Add. 23623. Facsimile edition, with Introduction by Alexander Silbiger. SCKM, 18. New York, 1987.

Bull, John. *Keyboard Music I.* Ed. John Steele and Francis Cameron, with introductory material by Thurston Dart. MB, 14. 3d ed. rev. Alan Brown. London, 2001.

——. *Keyboard Music II* Ed. Thurston Dart. MB, 19. 2d ed. London, 1970.

Byrd, William. *Keyboard Music I and II.* Ed. Alan Brown. MB, 27 and 28. 3d ed. of I. London, 1999. 2d ed. of II. London, 1985.

——. *My Ladye Nevells Booke* (1591). Ed. Hilda Andrews. London, 1926. Reprint. New York, n.d.

——. *Three Anonymous Keyboard Pieces Attributed to William Byrd.* Ed. Oliver Neighbour. Borough Green, 1973.

Clement Matchett's Virginal Book (1612). Ed. Thurston Dart. EKM, 9. 2d ed. London, 1969.

Draghi, Giovanni Battista. *Harpsichord Music.* Ed. Robert Klakowich. Recent Researches in the Music of the Baroque Era, 56. Madison, WI, 1986.

The Dublin Virginal Manuscript. Ed. John Ward [new edition]. London, 1983.

Early English Church Music (EECM). London, 1963–.

Early English Keyboard Music: An Anthology. 2 vols. Ed. Howard Ferguson. London, 1971.

Early Tudor Organ Music I: Music for the Office. Ed. John Caldwell. EECM, 6. London, 1966.

Early Tudor Organ Music II: Music for the Mass. Ed. Denis Stevens. EECM, 10. London, 1969.

Elizabethan Keyboard Music. Ed. Alan Brown. MB, 55. London, 1989.

Elizabeth Rogers Hir Virginall Booke. Ed. Charles Cofone. 2d ed. New York, 1975.

English Court and Country Dances of the Early Baroque. Ed. Hilda Gervers. CEKM, 44. Neuhausen–Stuttgart, 1982.

English Pastime Music, 1630–1660. Ed. Martha Maas. Madison, WI, 1974.

European Organ Music of the Sixteenth and Seventeenth Centuries. Vol. 1: *England c. 1510–1590.* Vol. 2: *England 1590–1650.* Vol. 3: *England 1660–1710.* Ed. Geoffrey Cox. Faber Early Organ Series. London, 1986.

Farnaby, Giles and Richard. *Keyboard Music.* Ed. Richard Marlow. MB, 24. London, 1965.

The Fingering of Virginal Music. Ed. Peter le Huray. EKM, 38. London, 1981.

The First Part of Musick's Hand-maid (1663). Ed. Thurston Dart. EKM, 28. London, 1969.

The Fitzwilliam Virginal Book. Ed. J. A. Fuller Maitland and W. Barclay Squire. Leipzig, 1899. Reprint. New York, 1963.

Gibbons, Orlando. *Keyboard Music.* Ed. Gerald Hendrie. MB, 20. 2d ed. London, 1967.

The Harpsicord Master (1697). Facsimile edition. Ed. Robert Petre. Wellington, N.Z., 1980.

The Harpsicord Master (1697). Ed. Christopher Hogwood. Oxford, 1980.

The Harpsicord Master II and III (1700 and 1702). Facsimile edition, with Introduction by Richard Rastall. Clarabricken, 1980.

Locke, Matthew. *Keyboard Suites* [and miscellaneous pieces]. Ed. Thurston Dart. EKM, 6. 2d ed. London, 1964.

——. *Organ Voluntaries.* Ed. Thurston Dart. EKM, 7. 2d ed. London, 1968.

——. [and other composers]. *Melothesia* (1673). Ed. Christopher Hogwood. Oxford, 1987.

Lugge, John. *The Complete Keyboard Works.* Ed. Susi Jeans and John Steele. London, 1990.

Melothesia (1673). Facsimile edition. New York, 1975.

Morley, Thomas. *Keyboard Works I and II* Ed. Thurston Dart. 2d ed. London, 1964.

The Mulliner Book. Ed. Denis Stevens. MB, 1. 2d ed. London, 1964.

Musica Britannica. (MB). London, 1951–.

Nederlandse Klaviermuziek uit de 16e en 17e Eeuw. Ed. Alan Curtis. Monumenta Musica Neerlandica, 3. Amsterdam, 1961. [Includes some Elizabethan music.]

Parthenia, (1612–13). Facsimile edition. New York, 1985.

Parthenia. Ed. Thurston Dart. EKM, 19. 2d ed. London, 1962.

Parthenia In-Violata (1624–25). Facsimile edition, with Historical Introduction by Thurston Dart. New York, 1961.

Parthenia In- Violata. Ed. Thurston Dart. New York, 1961.

Priscilla Bunbury's Virginal Book. Ed. Virginia Brookes. Albany, CA, 1993.

Philips, Peter. *Complete Keyboard Music.* Ed. David Smith. MB, 75. London, 1999.

——. *Eight Keyboard Pieces.* Ed. John Harley. EKM, 41. London, 1995.

Purcell, Henry. *Complete Harpsichord Music.* 2 vols. Ed. Christopher Kite. London, 1983.

——. *Complete Harpsichord Works.* 2 vols. Ed. Howard Ferguson. EKM, 21, 22. 2d ed. London, 1968.

——. *The Organ Works.* Ed. Hugh McLean. 2d ed. London, 1967.

Rogers, Benjamin. *Complete Keyboard Works.* Ed. Richard Rastall. EKM, 29. London, [1973].

The Second Part of Musick's Hand-maid (1689). Ed. Thurston Dart. EKM, 10. 2d ed. London, 1968.

Tallis, Thomas. *Complete Keyboard Works.* Ed. Denis Stevens. New York, 1953.

Ten Pieces by Hugh Aston and Others. Ed. Frank Dawes. London, 1951.

The 'Lynar' Virginal book [12 pieces by Bull and others.] Ed. Pieter Dirksen. EKM, 42. London, 2002.

Tisdale's Virginal Book. Ed. Alan Brown. EKM, 24. London, 1966.

Tisdall, William. *Complete Keyboard Works.* Ed. Howard Ferguson. EKM, 14. 2d ed. London, 1971.

Tomkins, Thomas. *Keyboard Music.* Ed. Stephen D. Tuttle. MB, 5. 2d ed. London, 1964.

Tudor Keyboard Music c. 1520–1580. Ed. John Caldwell. MB, 66. London. 1995.

Two Elizabethan Keyboard Duets [by Carleton and Tomkins]. Ed. Frank Dawes. London, 1949.

Weelkes, Thomas. *Keyboard Music in Facsimile,* with introduction and transcriptions by Desmond Hunter. Clarabricken, 1985.

LITERATURE

Bailey, Candace. "English Keyboard Music, c. 1625–1680." Ph.D. dissertation, Duke University, 1992.

——. "New York Public Library Drexel MS 5611: English Keyboard Music of the Early Restoration." *Fontes Artis Musicae* 47 (2000): 51–67.

——. *Seventeenth-Century British Keyboard Sources.* Warren, MI, 2003.

——. "William Ellis and the Transmission of Continental Keyboard Music in Restoration England." *The Journal of Musicological Research,* 20 (2001): 211–242.

Borren, Charles van den. *Les Origines de la musique de clavier en Angleterre.* Brussels, 1912. Translated by James E. Matthew as *The Sources of Keyboard Music in England.* London, 1915.

Brookes, Virginia. *British Keyboard Music to c. 1660: Sources and Thematic Index.* Oxford, 1996.

Brown, Alan. "'The Woods So Wild': Notes on a Byrd text." In *Sundry Sorts of Music Books: Essays on the British Library Collections, Presented to O. W. Neighbour on his 70th birthday,* ed. Chris Banks, Arthur Searle, and Malcolm Turner, 54–66. London, 1993.

Caldwell, John. *English Keyboard Music Before the Nineteenth Century.* Oxford, 1973.

——. "Keyboard Music: 1630–1700." In *New Oxford History of Music,* vol. 6, ed. Gerald Abraham, 505–89 (section on England, 578–89). Oxford, 1986.

——. "Keyboard Plainsong Settings in England, 1500–1660." *Musica Disciplina* 19 (1965): 129–53.

——. *The Oxford History of English Music.* Vol. I (main sections on keyboard music, 339–44, 486–96). Oxford, 1991.

——. "The Pitch of Early Tudor Organ Music." *Music & Letters* 51 (1970): 156–63.

Clutton, Cecil, and Austin Niland. *The British Organ.* London, 1963. 2d revised edition. 1982.

Cooper, Barry. "Keyboard Music." In *The Blackwell History of Music in Britain,* vol. 3, ed. Ian Spink, 341–66. Oxford, 1992.

——. "The Keyboard Suite in England before the Restoration." *Music & Letters* 53 (1972): 309–19.

Cox, Geoffrey. *Organ Music In Restoration England: A Study of Sources, Styles and Influences.* 2 vols. New York, 1989.

Cunningham, Walker. *The Keyboard Music of John Bull.* Ann Arbor, 1984.

Curtis, Alan. *Sweelinck's Keyboard Music: A Study of English Elements in Seventeenth-Century Dutch Composition.* Leiden and London, 1969.

Dart, Thurston. "New Sources of Virginal Music." *Music & Letters* 35 (1954): 93–106.

Dirksen, Pieter. "Perspectives on John Bull's Keyboard Music after 1613." In *XVIIe, XIXe, XXIe siècle: Bruxelles, carrefour européen de l'orgue,* ed. Jean Ferrard, 31–39, Brussels, 2002.

Ferguson, Howard. *Keyboard Interpretation from the 14th to the 19th Century: An Introduction.* London, 1975. 2d revised edition. 1987.

——. "Repeats and Final Bars in the Fitzwilliam Virginal Book." *Music & Letters* 43 (1962): 345–50.

Flynn, Jane. "A Reconsideration of the Mulliner Book (British Library Add. Ms 30513): Music Education in Sixteenth-Century England." Ph.D. dissertation, Duke University, 1993.

Gaskin, Hilary. "Baldwin and the Nevell Hand." In *Byrd Studies,* ed. Alan Brown and Richard Turbet, 159–73. Cambridge, 1992.

Glyn, Margaret. *Elizabethan Virginal Music and Its Composers.* London, 1934.

Harley, John. *British Harpsichord Music,* 2 vols. Aldershot, 1992–94.

——. "Ornaments in English Keyboard Music of the Seventeenth and Early Eighteenth Centuries." *Music Review* 31 (1970): 177–200.

——. *William Byrd: Gentleman of the Chapel Royal.* Aldershot, 1997.

Harrison, Frank L. *Music in Medieval Britain.* London, 1958. 2d edition. 1963.

Howes, Frank. *William Byrd.* London, 1928.

Hunter, Desmond. "The Application of (Ornamental) Strokes in English Virginal Music: A Brief Chronological Survey." *Performance Practice Review* 9 (1996): 66–77.

——. "My Ladye Nevells Booke and the Art of Gracing." In *Byrd Studies,* ed. Alan Brown and Richard Turbet. Cambridge, 1992, 174–92.

Irving, John. "Byrd and Tomkins: The Instrumental Music." In *Byrd Studies,* ed. Alan Brown and Richard Turbet, 141–58. Cambridge, 1992.

Johnstone, H. Diack. "Ornamentation in the Keybaord Music of Henry Purcell and His Contemporaries." In *Performing the Music of Henry Purcell,* ed. Michael Burden, 82–104. New York, 1996.

Klakowich, Robert. "*Scocca pur:* Genesis of an English Ground." *Journal of the Royal*

Musical Association 116 (1991): 63–77.

Le Huray, Peter. "English Keyboard Fingering in the 16th and Early 17th Centuries." In *Source Materials and the Interpretation of Music,* ed. Ian Bent, 227–57. London, 1981.

——. *Music and the Reformation in England, 1549–1660.* Cambridge, 1967. Reprint. 1978.

Lowinsky, Edward. "English Organ Music of the Renaissance." *Musical Quarterly* 39 (1953): 373–95, 528–53.

Maas, Martha. "Seventeenth-Century English Keyboard Music: A Study of Manuscripts Rés. 1185, 1186, and 1186bis of the Paris Conservatory Library." Ph.D. dissertation, Yale University, 1969.

Maxim, Christopher. "A Little-known Keyboard Plainsong Setting in the Fitzwilliam Virginal Book: a Key to Tallis's Compositional Process?" *Early Music* 29 (2001): 275–82.

Memed, Orhan. *Seventeenth-Century English Keyboard Music: Benjamin Cosyn.* 2 vols. New York, 1993. [Contains complete transcription of Cosyn's keyboard music.]

Morley, Thomas. A *Plaine and Easle Introduction to Practicall Musicke* (1597). Facsimile edition. Farnborough, 1971.

——. *A Plaine and Easie Introduction to Practicall Musicke* (1597). Ed. R. Alec Harman, with a foreword by Thurston Dart. London, 1952.

Moroney, Davitt. "'Bounds and Compasses': The Range of Byrd's Keyboards." In *Sundry Sorts of Music Books: Essays on the British Library Collections, Presented to O. W. Neighbour on his 70th birthday,* ed. Chris Banks, Arthur Searle, and Malcolm Turner, 67–88. London, 1993.

Neighbour, Oliver. *The Consort and Keyboard Music of William Byrd.* London, 1978.

——. "Some Anonymous Keyboard Pieces Considered in Relation to Byrd." In *Byrd Studies,* ed. Alan Brown and Richard Turbet, 193–201. Cambridge, 1992.

O'Brien, Grant. *Ruckers: A Harpsichord and Virginal Building Tradition.* Cambridge, 1990.

Pollack, Janet. "A Reevaluation of Parthenia and Its Context." Ph.D. dissertation, Duke University, 2001.

Petre, Robert. "A New Piece by Henry Purcell." *Early Music* 6 (1978): 374–79.

Price, Curtis. "Newly Discovered Autograph Keyboard Music of Purcell and Draghi." *Journal of the Royal Musical Association* 120 (1995): 77–111.

Rasch, Rudolf. "The Messaus-Bull Codex London, British Library, Additional Manuscript 23.623." *Belgisch Tijdschrift voor Muziekwetenschap* 50 (1996): 93–127.

Ripin, Edwin M., et al. *Early Keyboard Instruments.* The New Grove Musical Instrument Series. New York, 1989.

Russell, Raymond. *The Harpsichord and Clavichord: An Introductory Study.* London, 1959. 2d edition. 1973.

Shaw, Watkins. *The Succession of Organists of the Chapel Royal and the Cathedrals of England and Wales from c. 1538.* Oxford, 1991.

Smith, David. "The Instrumental Music of Peter Philips: Its Sources, Dissemination and Style." Ph.D. dissertation, University of Oxford, 1994.

Stevens, Denis. *The Mulliner Book: A Commentary.* London, 1952.

——. *Thomas Tomkins 1572–1656.* London, 1957. 2d revised edition. 1967.

Thompson, Ruby Reid. "Francis Tregian the Younger as Music Copyist: a Legend and an Alternative View." *Music & Letters* 82 (2001): 1–31. [Response by David Smith in *Musical Times* 143 (2002): 7–16.]

Willetts, Pamela. "Benjamin Cosyn: Sources and Circumstance." In *Sundry Sorts of Music Books: Essays on the British Library Collections, Presented to O. W. Neighbour on his 70th birthday,* ed. Chris Banks, Arthur Searle, and Malcolm Turner, 129–45. London, 1993.

Wulstan, David. *Tudor Music.* London, 1985.

MANUSCRIPT SHORT TITLES

Cosyn's Virginal Book	*GB-Lbl* R.M. 23.1.4
Drexel 5611	*US-NYp* Drexel 5611
Drexel 5612	*US-NYp* Drexel 5612
Dublin (Virginal Manuscript)	*EIRE-Dtc* D.3.30/i
Fitzwilliam (Virginal Book)	*GB-Cfm* Music MS 168
Forster's Virginal Book	*GB-Lbl* R.M. 24.d.3
London 22100	*GB-Lbl* Add. 22100
London 23623	*GB-Lbl* Add. 23623
London 29996	*GB-Lbl* Add. 29996
London 30485	*GB-Lbl* Add. 30485
London 30486	*GB-Lbl* Add. 30486
London 31403	*GB-Lbl* Add. 31403
London 36661	*GB-Lbl* Add. 36661
Mulliner (Book)	*GB-Lbl* Add. 30513
Nevell (My Ladye Nevells Booke)	*GB* private collection
Oxford 1003	*GB-Och* 1003
Oxford 1113	*GB-Och* 1113
Oxford 1142A	*GB-Och* 1142A
Oxford 1177	*GB-Och* 1177
Oxford 1236	*GB-Och* 1236
Paris 1122	*F-Pc* Rés. 1122
Paris 1185	*F-Pc* Rés. 1185
Paris 1186	*F-Pc* Rés. 1186
Paris 1186bis	*F-Pc* Rés. 1186bis
Robertsbridge (fragment)	*GB-Lbl* Add. 28550
Rogers (Elizabeth Rogers's Virginal Book)	*GB-Lbl* Add. 10337
Royal App. 56	*GB-Lbl* Royal App. 56
Royal App. 58	*GB-Lbl* Royal App. 58

CHAPTER THREE

France

Bruce Gustafson

Scholars of French music of the seventeenth and eighteenth centuries have tended to avoid the word "baroque," recoiling from its etymology of misshapen pearls, and have preferred the term "classic" to accord with the great emphasis on Greek and Roman antiquity that pervaded French taste in the visual arts, theatre, and the newly created French opera (*tragédie lyrique*), whose name as well as form referred to classical tragedy. The earliest French keyboard music of consequence comes from the Renaissance, when the publisher Attaingnant brought out seven volumes of organ and harpsichord music in 1531. Nothing more is known until nearly a century later, when in the 1620s Titelouze published a large number of his organ works, which he thought to be the first ever published in France. They stand apart stylistically from their sixteenth-century predecessors, but give little hint of the "classic" style that was to appear after another hiatus of two generations. There is no significant harpsichord music from this "preclassic" period.

The classic repertory comes from the last two-thirds of the seventeenth century and the first third of the eighteenth, and, particularly in the case of harpsichord music, seems to have been born a mature style. As France herself entered a new era when Louis XIV became king in 1643, keyboard music came into a golden age, that of the Couperins (Louis and his famous nephew François), Chambonnières, d'Anglebert, Jacquet de La Guerre, Grigny, Nivers, Lebègue, Marchand, and others. Most of these composers were both organists and harpsichordists, but they created musical styles for the two instruments that were—with some exceptions—quite distinct.

Organ Music

The organ repertory comes down to us primarily through published collections of the works of individual composers: the earliest (Attaingnant and Titelouze) were printed, as was a set of fugues by Roberday in 1660; after 1665 came books by Nivers, Lebègue (three each), Gigault, Boyvin, d'Anglebert (five fugues and a *quatuor* appended to his harpsichord pieces), Jullien, François Couperin, Chaumont, Grigny, and Louis Marchand. Significant organ music was published in the early eighteenth century as well, but this is beyond the scope of the present study. Considering the number of churches that had large organs, it is perhaps surprising that very few manuscripts from the inhabitants of those lofts have survived. However, two of the most important discoveries made in the world of French music in the last half century are of manuscripts. The first contains the organ works of Louis Couperin; unfortunately, it remains frustratingly unavailable (Oldham 1960). The second is an enormous collection of mostly anonymous Parisian organ music from the latter part of the seventeenth century that was brought to Montreal by an organist in 1724 (Gallat-Morin 1988). Like the smaller manuscripts that we know, it tells us much about what a French organist actually played.

Organ music in France before 1700—and for a century and a half beyond—was more wedded to its function in the liturgy and to the peculiarities of its instrument than was that of any other culture. Abstract works—fugues, fantasies, preludes, toccatas, and the like—exist only exceptionally, and were more often than not, composed as didactic examples of composition. While two types of pieces—the offertory and the completely extraliturgical sets of variations on noëls—did develop considerable scope, the principal genre was the "verset," a short composition that, was played in place of one pharse (one verse) of plainchant, the ensuing verse being sung by the choir. The organ itself developed in France in ways that were not only unlike those of other countries, but that dictated the musical textures of the repertory to an extreme.

Plainchant in France

Before the organ repertory can be addressed, a word must be said about the singing with which it so closely interacted. During the seventeenth century there was a major movement to reform the practice of Gregorian chant in France. The intent was to purify the chants, but unlike later reforms this one was not based on a scholarly reevaluation of medieval manuscripts. Rather, the church musicians reconciled the melodies as they knew them to rules of Latin grammar and diction, often not recognizing the extent to which the contempoary mucial style was influencing their judgment. Guillaume-Gabriel Nivers, one of the most important composers of organ music, published a *Dissertation sur le chant gregorien* (1683) that summarizes the precepts of the reform, and he also edited chant books that were widely used.

The new style reduced the notation almost exclusively to two note shapes, the *longue* (◳ or ◳) and the *breve* (◆), which had essentially a 2:1 ratio, almost as specific as the modern whole note to the half note. Dots were also interpreted more or less as in secular notation: between two *breves* the dot extended the value of the first at the expense of the second; between a *longue* and a *breve,* one dot added half the value of the *longue* (so that the *longue* now equaled three *breves*), leaving the value of the second note unchanged. The placement of *breves,* which Nivers and others fixed in their editions of the chant repertory, was calculated according to the text. Strophic chants, such as hymns, were sung metrically, with the rules of text declamation being broken as needed, the problem attributed to a poetic fault. The tempo for all chants was determined both by the nature of the text and the importance of the liturgical occasion—the more important the feast, the slower one sang the chants. "Excessive" melismas were excised from the historical melodies, and accidentals introduced as obviously necessary *musica ficta.* While Nivers scorned tasteless embellishment of the chants, he thought it entirely natural to add *ports de voix;* other sources went further in stipulating the addition of trills. The *Missa cunctipotens genitor Deus* was the ordinary most used for important occasions, and it was for this set of chants that most of the extant organ masses were composed.[1] A comparison of Nivers's version (Ill. 3.1) with that in the current edition of the *Liber usualis* (Mass IV) will reveal eliminations of "superfluous" notes and a regularization of the placement of *breves* to conform with Nivers's rules for reflecting the structure of the text.

The movement toward correction—and therefore modernization, although this was not a stated goal—reached its most extreme in *plainchant musical,* which is the name of both the style and a corpus of newly composed melodies. Henri Dumont published five mass ordinaries in 1669 that became the most famous examples of *plainchant musical.* The music is entirely monophonic and is notated in *longues* and *breves.* Each cycle remains in a single tone, unlike the Gregorian models, and the melodies adhere strictly to the rules codified by Nivers, the father of the genre.

Chant was not usually sung unaccompanied in seventeenth-century France. The norm was to have a serpent double the melody, keeping the choir on pitch and providing musical leadership. Monophony was not the only style of performance, however, and strophic chants such as the Magnificat, hymns, and psalms (the same ones that were realized metrically) were very frequently performed in *fauxbourdon;* continuo-like

ILLUSTRATION 3.1. The Kyrie "Cunctipotens genitor Deus," Gloria, Sanctus, Agnus Dei, and Ite missa est, as edited by Nivers (*Graduale Romanum,* Paris, 1697). *(continued)*

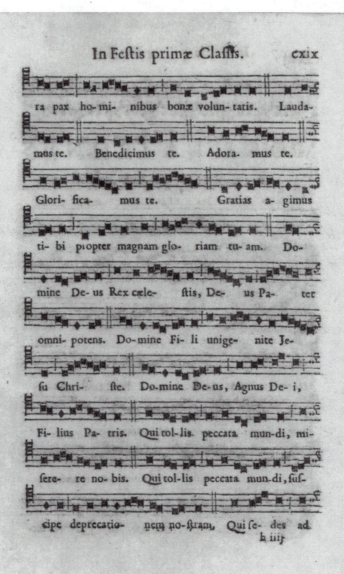

ILLUSTRATION 3.1. *(continued)*

(continued)

ILLUSTRATION 3.1. *(continued)*

organ accompaniment was also known, although it is difficult to determine how widespread the practice was.

Liturgy and the Organ

Liturgy comprises not only actions but also words, albeit ones that are highly symbolic and evocative. The French organist's primary task was to play when texts would otherwise have been sung, ending in such a way that the next phrase of the text could be sung. This *alternatim* practice, of course, fractured the texts because the organ caused half of the words to remain unstated. Church authorities resisted and regulated it for centuries, and it caused considerable friction. The faithful were supposed to contemplate the missing words, or even to murmur them; by the middle of the seventeenth century Nivers declared that the main source of misunderstanding between organist and choir was the latter's virtual shouting of the words while the organist played, creating such cacophony that, among other things, they couldn't find their pitch for the next verse. Alternatim practice was officially banned by a *Motu proprio* in 1903, but even then it was still not completely suppressed in France. In our period, improvising versets was cultivated as the highest art of the French organist, and *alternatim* practice was the norm for most important services, even if it was considered second best to vocal polyphony for at least the Kyrie and Gloria.

If the choir were to sing polyphonic settings of the texts rather than chants, the organ would generally play before, and perhaps after, each choral work. The organist also might provide a frame for extraliturgical choral pieces such as motets sung at the time of the offertory or communion. There is, however, some evidence of the organ supplying versets in alternation with polyphony, as in a Mass by Charpentier. An organ also might accompany the choir's polyphony, continuo fashion.

There are numerous regulatory "ceremonials" from specific French dioceses that stipulate when the organist might or might not play, and in which versets the chant that is not being sung should be audible. Some general statements are possible because the individual ceremonials that we know are consistent in outline, though certainly not in detail. The most important one applied to the diocese of Paris and was written in 1662.[2] The organist was expected to play not only at mass, but for the important offices and ceremonies: first vespers, matins, lauds, second vespers, benediction, and sometimes terce, compline, and various processions. Contracts between churches and organists sometimes specified as many as 400 services for which the organist was to play. Each of these services had its own liturgy, of course, and together they could demand well over 100 versets to be played on a single day. When one adds to this matrix a myriad of local practices, it becomes obvious why the art of playing the organ was synonymous with the art of improvisation; to write out all those little pieces and then locate them when needed would have been more trouble than it was worth.

The organ music that does come down to us represents models of an improvisational art by famous masters. It had the potential of being a mere stock of functional, easy versets with which the untrained could make do, and this became the lamentable norm late in the next century. But for the period under consideration, commercial exploitation of the ignorant was not an important factor. By virtue of its liturgical importance, the mass was the ceremony for which most composers published versets. Second in importance are versets that substituted for verses of office hymns, most notably at vespers; the Te Deum stands apart because of its length and regularity of use. Vespers occasioned music of great importance in general, and it was there that the canticle Magnificat was sung; therefore, we have many surviving versets for it, most of which could also be used for the Benedictus, the other great canticle, sung at the musically less imposing office of lauds. A ceremony that was often appended to vespers or incorporated into the mass, benediction, became a virtual concert in seventeenth-century France, but we have no organ music composed specifically for it.

In spite of the emotional range of this music, reflecting the mood of the text for which the verset substituted was not a consistent aim. That is, the texts and the associated chants were treated essentially as abstract entities with infrequent need of literal musical interpretation. Although composers did not always comply with the ecclesiastical mandates, the mood for all organ music was supposed to be serious and distinct from the secular world. Certain words and liturgical actions merited special consideration because of their holiness. The organist accomplished this in two ways: (1) by reference to the appropriate chant, quoting it literally as a cantus firmus or creating themes that were inspired by the rhythm of the words; or (2) by the choice of registration, some of which carried implications of greater or lesser seriousness. On the whole, however, French organ music is grounded in musical rather than theological values. Versets might or might not make reference to the Gregorian chant for which they were substituting, but as long as they ended properly to give the pitch for the ensuing chant they could be used. This is what led to grouping versets by tone, creating a dictionary of versets from which one could extract what was needed for any liturgy. Nivers published such groupings in his first book in 1665, which were much later–and very inappropriately–called "suites."

THE MASS

The typical organ mass provided versets for the ordinary of the mass except for the Credo, the fundamental statement of Christian belief, all of whose words were to be sung:[3] Kyrie, Gloria, Sanctus (including the Benedictus[4]), Agnus Dei, and Ite missa est. Additionally, there was music for three places in which organ solos were used to cover liturgical action: the Offertory, Elevation, and Communion. This gives a total of just over 20 movements in an "organ mass" (see Table 3.1 for a schematic design; specific cases varied in detail).

According to the Parisian ceremonial of 1662, the organ began the Kyrie, alternating with the choir through the ninefold repetitions, so that it also ended the cycle. (Again, other practices coexisted; for example, there is evidence of the number of alternations being reduced when the choir was singing polyphony.) After the priest intoned the first line of the Gloria, the organ began the alternation, following the same line divisions as are found in more modern practice until the final verse, which was usually begun at "in gloria Dei Patri," rather than at "Amen." The Offertory was the first of the three movements that did not replace chant. It provided music during a liturgical action that did have associated texts for the celebrant, but not for the choir. Later in the service came the Sanctus, again begun by the organ. The end of the Sanctus varied, however, with at least three possibilities related to music for the elevation of the host, which was an important and extroverted musical moment in the French liturgy of the period:

1. An organ verset substituted for the Benedictus and then a second independent organ solo was played for the Elevation.

2. A single organ piece substituted for the Benedictus and covered the Elevation.

3. The Benedictus was sung as the last section of the Sanctus, with an organ Elevation following.

The Agnus Dei has a clear tripartite form, and the organ began, as it did in all of the ordinary except when the priest gave the opening phrase. Music associated with communion came either during the distribution of the elements or at the antiphon that preceded the liturgical action. At the end of the mass the important words "ite missa est" were sung by the priest, but the organ substituted for the response, "Deo gratias." In France, there followed a psalm verse ("God save the King," from Psalm 19) and there might then be a procession, a "sortie."

Musically, there are two categories of organ mass: those that are designed to accommodate the "normal" chants (the *Missa cunctipotens*, Ill. 3. 1), and those that used chants particular to a congregation. The *Missa cunctipotens* demanded a specific tonal organization, as is noted in Table 3.1;[5] the new masses in *plainchant musical* presented all of the melodies in the same tonality; and those constructed from miscellaneous chants could have any sort of tonal organization. Thus, an organ mass other than one for the *Missa cunctipotens* not only refrained from quoting chant melodies but presented all of the versets in a single tonality; with such works at hand in several tonalities, the organist could select the versets according to the necessities of the individual situation.

TABLE 3.1
A Hypothetical Organ Mass in Accordance with the 1662
Parisian Ceremonial

The movements in a typical published organ mass are numbered,
followed by the closing pitch necessary to accommodate the ensuing
sung verse of the *Missa cunctipotens genitor*. Variant divisions of the texts
are given in the columns on the right. Full texts, given for Ordinary items,
are in quotation marks.

Roman type:	the organ substituted for some or all of the text.
Italics:	normally sung.
Bold:	cantus firmus was supposed to be audible.
<u>Underlining:</u>	the organist was to play "gravely, softly, sweetly, etc."

	Introit	
1. d	**"Kyrie eleison.**	
	Kyrie eleison,	
2. d	Kyrie eleison.	
	Christe eleison.	
3. d	Christe eleison.	
	Christe eleison.	
4. d	Kyrie eleison,	
	Kyrie eleison.	
5.	**Kyrie eleison."**	
	"Gloria in excelsis Deo, [Priest]	
6. e	**Et in terra pax hominibus bonæ voluntatis.**	
	Laudamus te.	
7. e	Benedicimus te.	
	Adoramus te.	
8. e	Glorificamus te.	
	Gratias agimus tibi propter magnam gloriam tuam.	
9. e	Domine Deus, Rex cælestis, Deus Pater omnipotens.	
	Domine Fili unigenite Jesu Christe.	
10. e	Domine Deus, Agnus Dei, Filius Patris.	
	Qui tollis peccata mundi, miserere nobis.	
11. e	Qui tollis peccata mundi **suscipe deprecationem <u>nostram</u>**.	
	Qui sedes ad dexteram Patris, misere nobis	
12. e	Quoniam tu solus sanctus.	
	Tu solus Dominus.	
13. e	<u>Tu solus altissimus, Jesu Christe.</u>	
	Cum Sancto Spiritu.	*Cum Sancto Spiritu,*
		in gloria Dei Patris
14.	**In gloria Dei Patris, Amen."**	Amen."

	Collect		
	Epistle		
	Gradual		
	"Alleluia" [or] *tract*		
	Prose (sequence)		
	Gospel		
	"Credo. . ." [organ specifically prohibited]		
15.	Offertory		
	Preface		
16. f	**"Sanctus.**		
	Sanctus,		
17. f	Sanctus, Dominus Deus Sabaoth.		
	Pleni sunt cæli et terra gloria tua. Hosanna in excelsis."		
18.	"Benedictus qui venit in nomine Domini. Hosanna in excelsis."	"Benedictus qui venit in nomine Domini. Hosanna in excelsis." & <u>Elevation</u>	*"Benedictus qui venit in nomine Domini, Hosanna in excelsis."*
	Canon [Priest, silently]	*Canon* [Priest, silently]	*Canon* [Priest, silently]
18a.	<u>Elevation</u>		<u>Elevation</u>
	"Pater noster. . ."		
19. f	**"Agnus Dei,** qui tollis peccata mundi: miserere nobis.		
	Agnus Dei, qui tollis peccata mundi: miserere nobis.		
20.	Agnus Dei, qui tollis peccata mundi: dona nobis pacem."		
21.	<u>Communion</u>		
	Post-communion prayer		
	"Ite missa est. [Priest]		
22.	Deo gratias."		
	"Domine, salvum fac Regem, et exaudi nos in die quam invocaverimus te."		
	Procession		

According to the 1662 ceremonial, one ought to hear the appropriate chants in certain phrases of the mass if the organ substituted for them, as is indicated in Table 3.1. Composers by no means followed these rules, but they were at least aware of them. In the versets written for the *Missa cunctipotens,* they did in general comply; for other groupings of chants, the possibilities were simply too numerous and composers wrote all-purpose versets. However, Raison did provide blank space in his *Livre d'orgue* (1687) for the individual organist to write in the opening chant of each item; he also offered in the preface to compose a verset on those chants if the organist contacted him individually, so that a correct mass for the specific congregation would exist.

HYMNS

Because of their strophic design, hymns naturally lend themselves to *alternatim* performance. They are made up of individual verses that are syntactically—and often logically—distinct entities, and the omission of alternate verses is therefore not as disruptive as it is in the mass. Hymns were sung at the offices, most notably vespers. The 1662 ceremonial stipulated that the cantus firmus (the plainchant for the hymn) should be audible at least in the first verset, and here composers complied.

THE TE DEUM

The Te Deum was a very special hymn, sung not only at matins and after vespers, but separately as a sort of liturgy unto itself at moments of national or ecclesiastical celebration. It has one of the longest and most notable traditions of *alternatim* performance, and in the eighteenth century it elicited extraordinarily flamboyant organ playing for certain of its 16 versets. Before 1700, however, the versets did not suggest the tone poems of the future.

THE MAGNIFICAT AND BENEDICTUS DOMINUS DEUS

The two most important canticles were closely related. Because they were sung to reciting tones rather than having through-composed melodies, there was little impetus for organists to make melodic reference to the chants, although sometimes the first verset of a Magnificat does present the cantus firmus. With the simplest pattern of alternation (see Table 3.2), 6 organ versets were needed for the Magnificat; the Benedictus Dominus Deus required at least 7. Composers sometimes provided extra versets for the Magnificat (without quoting the chant in the first) so that they could be used for the Benedictus as well; there is no surviving cycle of organ versets written specifically for the Benedictus. To the Magnificat was attached an antiphon and the doxology ("gloria patri . . . Amen"). Depending on the importance of the day in the church year, the antiphon might be sung in one of three patterns: (1) once before the Magnificat; (2) before and after the Magnificat and its appended doxology; or (3) before and after the Magnificat itself, and again after the doxology. This provides several schemes for using organ versets to substitute for the repetitions of the antiphon, four of which are indicated in Table 3.2.

TABLE 3.2
Alternatim Practices for the Magnificat

Sung verses are in *italics.* Organ versets are numbered, showing four schemes that organists used. The first shows the minimum required (six), including one for the doxology. The second provides an extra verset to make enough versets to use for the Benedictus. The third and fourth schemes provide organ substitution for either the "amen" or the final repetition of the antiphon.

				Antiphon
1	1	1	1	"Magnificat anima mea Dominum;
				Et exultavit spiritus meus: in Deo salutary meo;
2	2	2	2	Quia respexit humilitatem ancillæ suæ, ecce enim ex hoc beatam me dicent omnes generationes;
				Quia fecit mihi magna qui potens est: et sanctum nomen ejus;
3	3	3	3	Et misericordia ejus a progenie in progenies: timentibus eum.
				Fecit potentiam in brachio suo: dispersit superbos mente cordis sui.
4	4	4	4	Deposuit potentes de sede: et exaltavit humiles.
				Esurientes implevit bonis: et divites dimisit inanes.
5	5, 6	5	5	Suscepit Israël puerum suum: recordatus misericordiæ suæ,
				Sicut locutus est ad patres nostros: Abraham et semini ejus in sæcula.
				Antiphon [repeated on triple feasts]
6	7	6	6	Gloria Patri et Fillo et Spiritui Sancto
				Sicut erat in principio et nunc, et semper: et in sæcula sæculorum. (Amen")
		7		Amen"
			7	Antiphon [repeated on double and triple feasts]

NOËLS

The last category of French organ music is the noël variation, the only nonliturgical genre of significance. It is peculiar to France more for its tunes and sociological role than its keyboard style. Noëls are Christmas songs that are used—then as now—as much outside church as within it, existing as a quasi-folk literature. The tradition of writing key-board variations for these tunes began in the seventeenth century and blossomed into a repertory that is the meeting point of popular culture and the sophisticated world of the organ. From the eighteenth century to the present day, Parisian churches have attracted Christmas crowds by advertising the performance of the traditional noëls for organ.

By the nature of their themes, such variations are quite different from liturgical organ music. The tunes were known in strongly rhythmic versions that had clear and mostly symmetrical phrase structures. From the beginning, keyboard composers emphasized figural patterns to make their variations, rather then using contrapuntal techniques and the sonority-based styles that developed in the liturgical repertory. Thus noëls are the only category of French keyboard music in this period in which there is little distinction between organ and harpsichord idiom—and this continues to be the case into the era of the piano. Nonetheless, noël variations were primarily intended for organ performance, and some do make use of idiomatic organ sonorities.

The Renaissance and Pre–Classic Periods

THE EARLY FRENCH ORGAN

The organs that gave life to the pieces published by Attaingnant in the sixteenth century and those composed by Titelouze at the beginning of the seventeenth had not developed the traits that would separate this national school of organ building from all others—or at least our limited knowledge of these older instruments does not permit us to recognize those qualities. Organs in northern France seem to have developed in the tradition of the Low Countries, slowly evolving from a blockwerk to an instrument with two manuals and independent 8′ pedal. Those in the south were heavily influenced by Italian building principles. Instru-ments varied greatly not only in size but in basic style, and no single tra-dition of registration had yet developed. Thus the theorist Mersenne (1636) was able to give a long list of possible registrations, but the com-poser Titelouze (1623, 1626) merely pointed out the contrapuntal clarity achieved by playing individual voices on separate manuals.

PIERRE ATTAINGNANT (C. 1494–1551/2)

The printer Attaingnant brought out three volumes of anonymous organ music in 1531 that stand as a cornerstone of French composition for organ. One volume contains intabulations of 13 motets, but the other two consist of music that appears for the most part to have been con-ceived for the organ: over 80 versets for two masses, magnificats on the eight tones, and a Te Deum; in addition, there are two preludes without liturgical attachment. In the very year of these publications, Parisian organists were said to be playing unseemly (presumably frivolously secular) music,[6] but this is nowhere in evidence in the surviving music. Rather, the versets are lean, contrapuntal, and continuous, often consisting of three more or less strictly maintained voices. They are straightforward in presenting the chant that is being adorned, which more often than not is in long notes accompanied by scalar, nonimitative counterpoint. They demand the homogeneous sound of a blockwerk style organ. Even long-note chant melodies have occasional ornamental figures that unite them with their accompanying lines and preclude their being intoned on a separate register, unlike the classic *plein jeu* with cantus firmus. There is also no suggestion of using antiphonal effects to contrast the two divisions possessed by many organs.

The first mass serves as proof that the liturgical practices outlined above were already essentially in place. The versets are basically for the scheme outlined in Table 3.1; the primary difference is that here there are seven versets for the Credo, in spite of the fact that organ substitution for these texts was already strictly forbidden. There is also no music to cover liturgical action (items 15, 18a, and 21 in Table 3.1), as all of the movements are based on the chants for which they substitute. The Kyrie is for the "Fons bonitatis" chant (Mass II in the modern *Liber usualis*), but the remainder of the mass uses the "Cunctipotens genitor" chants already discussed, with the addition of Credo I. The second mass in the volume uses the "Cunctipotens genitor" chants throughout.

The versets of our specimen mass vary greatly in length, from 8 to 45 measures, and there is similar variety in the treatment of the cantus firmus. It may migrate from one voice to another, and may disappear into figuration or remain in long notes. The melodic writing is dominated by scalar figurations, and the textures are generally sparce and nonimitative, giving no hint of the rich polyphony that was already typical of sacred vocal music in the second quarter of the sixteenth century.

JEHAN TITELOUZE (1562/3–1633)

Titelouze was born in what was then the Spanish Netherlands, where Italian, French, Dutch, and Spanish musical influences vied with each other. He spent his career as organist and priest at the cathedral in Rouen, entering into learned intercourse on musical theory with Mersenne in Paris. Although he did not become a French citizen until 1604, when he was in his 40s, his heritage was probably French, as there is evidence that "Titelouze" is a sixteenth-century corruption of "de Toulouse." He was about 60 when he published his two books of organ music in 1623 and 1626, and they serve therefore more as crown jewels of the sixteenth century than as harbingers of the style that was soon to emerge. He is the opposite of Frescobaldi—20 years his junior—who began publishing music more than a decade earlier and who developed a highly idiomatic keyboard idiom. Titelouze was grounded in the vocal motet, adapting it to the keyboard.

The two volumes contain nearly 100 versets, 39 in the first for 12 hymns, and 56 in the second for Magnificats on the eight tones. As in the versets published by Attaingnant (which Titelouze did not know), the chants are pervasive. For at least the first verset of each hymn he presents the cantus firmus in long notes, usually in the bass, although in later versets it may migrate. Virtually all of the other versets are fugues, with subjects based on the opening of the chant, and in the Magnificat versets—according to his preface—the rhythm of the subjects is calculated to reflect the words that the organ music is replacing. Unlike Attaingnant's collection, this music is almost entirely four-voiced and has creative counterpoint throughout, including much use of inversion. His style adheres to strict rubrics, but the very lack of freedom inspired invention.

The music does not exploit the possibility of colorful solo stops that his organs possessed. In the preface to the first book, Titelouze enthuses about modern French organs with two independent manual keyboards and pedal keyboard at 8' "to play the bass independently, without playing it in the manuals, the tenor on the second keyboard, the alto and soprano on the third." He says that this allows the voices to be clear even when they cross, but the voices do not cross in his music, and in any case he clearly intends his pieces to be playable by the hands only; in the second book's preface he notes that he has made an effort to make the pieces easier by constraining the distance between the voices, and already in the more demanding first book he suggests altering the voicing if the player's hands are too small to play the occasional tenths that are demanded.

The Magnificat on the second tone demonstrates both typical traits and some unusual gestures. Titelouze offers seven versets: the first scheme outlined in Table 3.2, with two choices for the fourth verset. He explains that this enables the organist to use them for the Benedictus Dominus Deus, although the motivic connection to the Magnificat phrases then becomes irrelevant. There is, typically, no presentation of the reciting formula in this set, though its intonation (four notes, omitting repeated tones) is presented in double breves in the soprano of the opening verset (see Ill. 3.2), and most of the fugue subjects can be seen to be very loosely related to the tone. All of the versets conclude on G, which is to say that Titelouze has transposed the tone up a fourth to create a comfortable singing range; this reflects the confusing conception of tone, mode, absolute pitch, and eventually tonality that was shared by the coming generations of French organists. Most of these versets have a cadence in the middle with a new subject for the second half, and the organist is given leave in the preface to stop at that cadence if church authorities will not allow the time for the full versets. Indeed, Titelouze had already truncated his form from the three sections used in his book of hymn versets, which were thought by unspecified critics to be too long. All of the Magnificat versets are close to 30 measures long, and

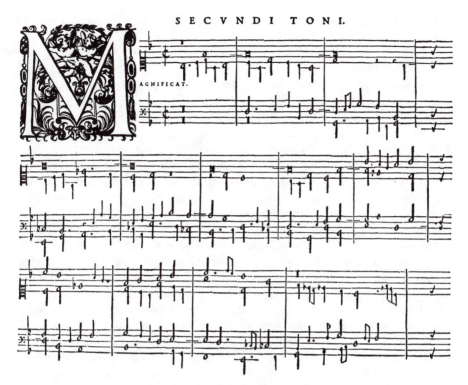

ILLUSTRATION 3.2. Jehan Titelouze, Magnificat on the Second Tone (*Le Magnificat, ou cantique de la Vierge pour toucher sur l'orgue, suivant les huit tons de l'Eglise,* 1626. Facsimile edition, Geneva: Minkoff, 1967). Reproduced with permission.

many have a concluding section that abandons the subject. In the fourth verset of the set at hand there is a burst of figuration in sixteenth notes at the end. The next verset provides an example of a chromatic subject (five ascending half steps: see Ex. 3.1) that suggests that he was not unaware of Italian stylistic developments. On the whole, however, Titelouze's style is an argument for the French virtues of austerity and

EXAMPLE 3.1. Titelouze, "Deposuit potentes" 2 from the Magnificat on the Second Tone, 1636, m. 16–20

sobriety. Bravura and pathos have little place in this magisterial counter-point.

THE INTERIM

Whether or not based on plainchant, fugal counterpoint remained the fundamental written vocabulary of French organists in the middle third of the century. One such work, a fantasy by the organist of Notre Dame, Charles Racquet, survives as a manuscript addition to Mersenne's 1636 treatise. Henri Dumont (1652, 1657, 1668), cited above as a modernizer of chant, sanctioned organ performance for a handful of surviving works that have more in common with music for instrumental ensemble or harpsichord than that for organ, using binary forms and cheerful duo textures. François Roberday (1660), on the other hand, sought the Italian muse in publishing a set of fugues in open score using themes—and in some cases whole pieces—by Frescobaldi, Froberger, and others. The development of mainstream organ music in the 1650s, however, can be seen in the music of the great Louis Couperin. What we know of the roughly 75 pieces shows a continuation of the essential vo-cabulary of Titelouze in a contrapuntally less rigorous fashion and with the injection of the division bass texture. That is, whether or not based on plainchant, the pieces are an appropriate length to be used as versets and are more often than not fugues (sometimes called fantasies) on a sin-gle subject. Either for an entire movement or beginning with the bass entry in a fugue, the upper voices often abandon their contrapuntal ac-tivity to accompany an athletic bass line that bounces back and forth be-tween tenor and bass ranges (as if alternating between high and low strings on a viol). Although the registrations are not specified, the char-acteristic melodic and textural qualities of the *basse de trompette* and *basse de cromorne* are obvious, and in some pieces in other styles registrations that were about to become a common language are already indicated.

The Classic Period

THE CLASSIC FRENCH ORGAN

By the 1660s organ design in France had evolved to its definitive shape. It cultivated a set of standardized sonorities, even though organs varied in size and coloristic possibilities. As in all organ traditions, there was a basic chorus of principal stops, going up through mixtures, but it is the emphasis on colorful tierce combinations, pungent reeds, and very broad foundation stops that identify the French classic sound. The reeds were not intended to reinforce the principal chorus, but were the founda-tion of a blazing chorus to be further spiced by cornets. The pedals were not essentially for playing bass lines at 16′, but for projecting a cantus fir-mus through the principal chorus in the tenor range or for supplying a quiet bass at 8′. Many instruments had separate incomplete keyboards for important solo stops, and some had a separate "echo" division that was muffled by being enclosed at the bottom of the organ case. The specifications for the organ of Saint-Sulpice in Paris, where Nivers was the organist, may be taken as typical. Of modest size, it nonetheless has the necessary stops for all of the classic registrations (see Table 3.3).

TABLE 3.3
The Organ of Saint-Sulpice (Paris)
Built by Vincent Coppeau, 1636
Renovated and Enlarged by François Ducastel, 1675

Grand-Orgue

1. Montre	16′	8. Tierce*	$1^3/_5'$	12. Trompette	8′
2. Montre	8′	9. Nazard*	$2^2/_3'$	13. Clairon	4′
3. Bourdon	8′	10. Flageolet	2′	14. Voix	
4. Prestant	4′	11. Cornet		humaine	8′
5. Doublette*	2′				
6. Fourniture					
7. Cymbale					

Positif

15. Montre	8′	21. Flûte	4′	24. Cromorne	8′
16. Bourdon	8′	22. Nazard	$2^2/_3'$		
17. Prestant	4′	23. Tierce	$1^3/_5'$		
18. Doublette*	2′				
19. Fourniture					
20. Cymbale					

Écho

25. Cornet

Pédale

26. Flûte	8′	27. Trompette	8′

Couplers:
  grand orgue-to-*pédale*
  positif-to-*grand orgue*
Tremblant fort
Tremblant doux

*Indicates stops that were divided at e′/f′.

REGISTRATIONS AND GENRES

Composers specified registrations both in extensive prefaces to their published organ books and within the scores. The instructions display an infinite variety in detail, but were schematically universal. Beginning with Nivers, composers understood these registrations to imply compositional genres as well. The following will serve as a glossary of the most important registrations and genres, with a sample realization on the organ at Saint-Sulpice given in parentheses.

Plein jeu, prélude. The chorus of flues from 8′ (16′ in larger organs) through mixture, a brilliant but not strident sound. Often the *pleins jeux* of the primary and secondary manuals *(grand plein jeu, petit plein jeu)* were used in contrast with each other (1–7; 15–20), with both the compositional and performance style understood to be light and animated on the *petit plein jeu* but majestic on the *grand plein jeu.* The *plein jeu* was generally used for relatively homophonic textures of three or four voices, enlivened by dissonances such as suspensions, ornamental figures, and some motivic imitation, particularly of rapid scalar motives. The genre may well have been influenced by the practice of fauxbourdon accompaniments of chants. The pieces were almost always in duple or quadruple meter, but even those that have sections in triple meter are not dancelike. Such movements were used virtually universally for the opening of a set of versets, and thus "prélude" and "plein jeu" were often synonymous. The texture might be pierced by a cantus firmus in long notes played on the pedal *trompette* in the bass or tenor (see Ex. 3.2), but neither reeds nor tierces were mixed with the *plein jeu.* Atypically, the petit *plein jeu* was used to accompany a *basse de trompette* (see below).

Jeux doux, fond d'orgue, concert de flûtes. Three related combinations. The first is a soft combination of closed and open flutes *(bourdon* and *flûte)* with or without the principals *(montre, prestant)* (e.g., 2, 3; or 16, 21). It was usually used as an accompaniment for solo stops. The combination was augmented as needed depending on the strength of the solo stop(s) (e.g., 3, 4; 2–5; or even with the 16′) and when it included all the flues at 16′, 8′, and 4′ it was called the "fond d'orgue." This was understood to imply great gravity, as in accompanying a *cromorne* or tierce solo in the tenor, and the slow-moving bass line might be played by the pedal *flûte* (perhaps with the manual stops coupled to the pedal). The softer flue

EXAMPLE 3.2. François Couperin, "Pleinchant du premier Kyrie, en taille," the opening *plein jeu of* the Parish mass, 1690, mm. 1–6.

combinations, emphasizing but not necessarily limited to the open and closed flutes, were called "concert de flûtes" or simply "flûtes" when they were used not to accompany a solo stop but alone or antiphonally between two or three divisions of the organ. The *tremblant doux* was used with this combination. Such pieces were often in trio texture with much use of parallel thirds for the upper voices.

Grand jeu. The loud reed stops, perhaps supported by the various cornet stops (e.g., 3, 4, 8–13; 16, 21–24), the whole often shaken by the *tremblant fort.* This blazing sound was the crown of the French classic organ. It was used for pieces that were usually sectional and largely homophonic, often with chords supporting passage work in either the soprano or bass. Very frequently these grand compositions featured dialogues among the divisions, often with rapid echo effects, and sometimes in large-scale, sectional forms. They often were used for the closing verset of a series and for offertories in masses.

Cornet, jeu de tierce, jeu de nazard. French organs had, relative to other national styles, a large number of third-sounding stops that were used in combination with octave and fifth-sounding stops (3, 4, 8, 9, 10: one possibility for a *jeu de tierce;* the modern term is *cornet décomposé*) or were part of a similar group of ranks that were on a single chest and drawn by a single knob (11), sometimes physically separated and playable from a separate keyboard (25; usually on a *récit,* but in an *écho* placement in Table 3.3; a *cornet séparé*). They were used for solos in all ranges, for fugues (as an alternative to a reed stop), and to augment or contrast with the *grand jeu.* The combinations could be amplified by the addition of other flues, including even the 16'. Large organs had tierce combinations that supported the 16' harmonic series (16', 8', $5\frac{1}{3}'$, 4', $3\frac{1}{5}'$) but composers did not develop distinctive genres for such variants. A similar combination without the tierce (3, 4, 9) used for solos in the treble was called *jeu de nazard.*

Récit: dessus, taille, basse. The choice of stops for *solos (récits)* allowed for considerable freedom, but composers did understand both the various stops and the three potential ranges as being suitable for specific musical styles. They were accompanied by the *jeu doux* or *fond d'orgue.* Most soprano *(dessus) solos* were lyrical, consciously imitating the supple vocal style of the *air de cour* or of the *tragédie lyrique.* The composition and performance of these versets ranged from the bold to the tender with the choice of solo: the *trompette* (rarely), *cornet, jeu de tierce, cromorne,* or *voix humaine.* Solos in the tenor *(taille)* are the most emotionally charged pieces in the repertory, contrasting serenity with effusive arabesques. They are almost exlusively played on the *cromorne* or *jeu de tierce,* with the pedal *flûte* supplying the bass. The translation "tenor" is misleading, however, as they typically emphasize the alto range, sweeping both up and down from it for emotional high points. Solos in the bass emphasized athletic virtuosity and were largely played on the *trompette* or *cromorne*; a significant number use the *jeu de tierce* for such movements, however, and the *voix humaine* is not unknown.

Duo. The same combinations that were used for solos were used in pairs for versets in two-voiced imitative counterpoint, except for the *voix humaine*. Duos provide the most varied possibilities for registration of all of the genres. The compositional style was closely related to the dances that were the foundation of harpsichord music, and indeed this was pointed out by Raison in 1687, but he did suggest that one should play a bit more slowly because of the "sanctity of the place."

Trio. There are two essential types of trio: the *trio à trois claviers* and the *trio à deux dessus*. In the first, the three voices participate equally in imitative counterpart and are played on three different colors; the upper two voices are on two of the combinations that would serve for a *récit* or duo, and the bass is the pedal *flûte*. This constitutes virtually the only figural writing for the pedals in the repertory. Related to the *trio à trois claviers* are dialogues between two *récit* registrations in which the two solo voices are brought together and accompanied by a nonimitative bass on the pedal *flûte,* creating trio texture. In the *trio à deux dessus,* two intertwining sopranos on one registration participate in imitative counterpoint with the bass; a duo registration is used, with the right hand playing the two soprano parts, which frequently move in parallel thirds or sixths, while the left hand takes the bass.

Fugue. Fugues, usually of four voices and displaying a wide variety of compositional approach, were played primarily on the *trompette* and/or *cromorne* supported by one or more foundation stops (*bourdon* and *prestant*). They were sometimes played on the *jeu de tierce* (e.g., Nivers). Grigny, as we shall see, cultivated a particular type of five-voiced fugue. French fugues are more closely related to the pre-classic repertory (and to the Italian ricercar) than any of the other classic genres. They were used with great regularity as the second verset of a series, following the *plein jeu* and providing learned seriousness between the opening majesty and the lightness or tenderness to follow.

The French classic repertory has often been criticized for an empty-headed preoccupation with registrations, containing pieces with little "content" and polluting the sacred environment with dance rhythms and operatic tunefulness. This view turns a blind eye to the increasing closeness of sacred and secular musical vocabularies throughout Europe in this period and misses the special genius of French music: the use of timbre as a structural element, as a major component of the "content." Let us now see how three composers used their coloristic vocabulary to create works of genius, individuality, and beauty.

GUILLAUME-GABRIEL NIVERS (C. 1632–1714)

When Nivers published his *Livre d'orgue contenant cent pièces de tous les tons de l'eglise* in 1665, he did not claim novelty, but we know of no earlier example of the classic language. We have seen that there were precedents for some elements of the style, but the sudden codification of this vocabulary seems to have no explanation. As his title suggests, Nivers grouped his pieces according to tone, and in fact he makes no reference to the intended liturgical function of the versets either by prefatory remarks or by references to chants. Rather, he presents 12 series of versets, each in a single tone. The opening 2 series have 10 versets, all the rest 8. Although no sequence of movements is strictly maintained, a general pattern is clear and would be appropriate for a Magnificat or hymn or a portion of a mass: prelude, fugue, five to seven movements exploiting various registrations and their associated textures, tempos, and moods, and a concluding *plein jeu*. In his preface Nivers explains both the registrations and the tempos for the various genres detailed above. All of them save the trio and tenor solo are present.

The second set of versets elucidates the new idiom. They are in the second mode on G, as we have seen with Titelouze, but Nivers explains that they can serve for the third mode transposed to "G re sol ut par ♭" (both of these suitable for alternation with high voices) or for the first mode, also transposed, for low voices. The harmonic vocabulary of the organ pieces themselves is on the verge of being G minor, with authentic cadences concluding each verset, but Nivers—a published expert on *ton* and chant—was still far from a truly tonal vocabulary. The ten versets are as follows: *Prélude, Basse [de] trompette, Fugue, [Récit de] cornet, Duo, Récit de cromorne, Fugue grave, Echo, A 2 C[h]œurs,* and *Plein Jeu.*

The framing *Prélude* and *Plein Jeu* are similar in style, and (his preface tells us) they are to be played very slowly. The use of the term "prélude" in this context is new in itself, though not completely unprecedented. Both are in a rich nonimitative and four-voiced texture and are 14 to 15 measures in length. In the first the voices enter singly, in the last as a chord. They differ in that the *Prélude* increases in motion from half notes to moving eighths, whereas the *Plein Jeu* has less individuality of lines, with half-note motion dominating.

The *Basse de trompette* is remarkably similar to those by Louis Couperin. After an imitative opening on the two-voiced *jeu doux*, the solo presents the motive that has been exposed. Scale passages in sixteenth notes and octave leaps to contrast with the tenor and powerful bass ranges abound. As in all of the succeeding movements except for the *Fugue grave*, Nivers calls for a relatively quick tempo *(plus gay* compared to *fort lent);* this is still one level below his quickest category, *fort léger.* The *Fugue* that follows is notated in even eighth notes, but Nivers cites it in the preface as an example of where one should play it as if noted in dotted values that one further exaggerated—the application of strong inequality—and that this goes along with a quick tempo. The contrapuntal techniques of the two fugues are similar: they are three voiced, have five or six entries of the subject commencing on the final or dominant of the mode (g or d), and use no inversion (although others of his fugues do). They differ in registration and melodic structure: the quick fugue (according to the preface) is to be played on a small *jeu de tierce* or *mediocre jeu* (probably a *cromorne*), the slow one on a large *jeu de tierce* with *tremblant* or the *trompette* without *tremblant*. The quick subject has even eighth notes in conjunct motion, while the slow one has longer, more varied values and is characterized by skips.

The solos for *cornet* and *cromorne* are both accompanied by the *jeu doux*, primarily in two-voiced texture. Both melodies are elegantly beautiful, consisting of highly ornamented phases that, in spite of some sequential varied repetition, give the effect of improvisation. Although in Nivers's *plus gay* category, they are highly expressive, and the first of them closes with a repeated chromatic ascent. They contrast with the *Duo* that separates them. Its simplicity, clear harmonic drive, and insistent dotted patterns evoke the world of the gigue (the variety in quadruple meter), and the opening imitation is related to quick fugues, although the subject appears only three times in the verset.

The *Echo* and *A 2 Chœurs* movements both exploit contrast between divisions, but in quite different ways. In the first case (Ex. 3.3) a *cornet* plays a melody accompanied by the *jeu doux*, with the last part of it played on the *écho* (e.g., 25 in Table 3.3). As the title suggests, the order of events is always loud followed by soft, and the repetition is generally shorter than the original statement. The two choirs of the succeeding movement (Ex. 3.4) are the *grand jeu* and *positif* (the *petit grand jeu*). The writing is largely homophonic and the alternations are frequent, but unlike an echo, a soft passage engenders a loud response, not repeating the exact same melodic material. The thematic writing for the *grand jeu* differs from that for the *plein jeu* in using energetic motives characterized by skips, dotted values, and sometimes running eighth or sixteenth notes.

The composers who followed Nivers in the remaining third of the century—Lebègue, Gigault, Raison, Boyvin, François Couperin, Jullien, Chaumont, Marchand, and Grigny—added two genres (the trio and solo *en taille*). What is remarkable is the extent to which the genres were already crystallized in Nivers's hands, allowing him to make vivid emotional statements in a commonly understood language.

EXAMPLE 3.3. Nivers, *Echo* in the second tone (*Livre d'orgue*, 1665), mm. 7b–10

EXAMPLE 3.4. Nivers, *A 2 Chœurs* in the second tone (*Livre d'orgue*, 1665), mm. 12b–16

FRANÇOIS COUPERIN (1668–1733)

When Couperin made his pair of organ masses public, it was not yet apparent that he would eventually be called "Couperin le grand." He was more experienced than his 21 years might suggest, however. His father had died when this future organist to the king was only 10, and it was already established that he would inherit the title of organist at the church of St. Gervais. Michel De Lalande was interim organist until François reached 18, but as Lalande maintained two other organ posts, it is likely that Couperin played at St. Gervais at a very early age. Lalande lent the luster of his two court titles to the prefatory material of the young master's first effort, certifying that it was "very beautiful and worthy of being given to the public." Couperin continued to play the organ for another 40 years, but his primary focus as a composer shifted to harpsichord and chamber music, and these two masses are the only organ works we have from him.

Only the title page and prefatory page were engraved, the rest being individually copied by hand. At this point in his career, Couperin had neither the funds nor the reputation to justify even a modest run that would demand engraving. Indeed, only three early manuscripts are known (1689–90 and c. 1720), and they have the considerable number of differences that one can expect in works that circulate in manuscript. Couperin's title page announces that the first mass, which we shall examine below, was "for the ordinary use of parishes from solemn feasts ['double masses']," and the second was "appropriate for monasteries and convents." That is, the first is designed to be used with the *Missa cunctipotens genitor Deus* (Ill. 3.1), while the second has no references to chant, and can be used in conjunction with the chants peculiar to the practice of individual convent or monastery chapels.

The Parish mass has 21 versets, following the scheme shown in Table 3.1, except that there is no Communion movement. Verset 18 is for the Benedictus, with no separate Elevation (scheme 2 of Table 3.1). Couperin complies with the dictates of the 1662 ceremonial in most of the instances where chant was supposed to be evident: the first and last couplets of the Kyrie (versets 1 and 5), the first of the Gloria, Sanctus, and Agnus Dei (6, 16, 19); he did not use the chant in the other two stipulated versets of the Gloria (11 and 14). As for the call for playing "gravely, softly, and sweetly" in Nos. 11 and 13 to reflect the words "suscipe deprecationem" and "tu solus altissimus," Couperin certainly obliged in the first case, writing a moving *tierce en taille*, but the dialogue of *cornet* and tierce for the latter verset does not suggest special reverence.

Each of the major sections (Kyrie, Gloria, Sanctus, and Agnus) begins with a *plein jeu,* with the cantus firmus in the pedal *(trompette).* But within the standardization is variety, as each cantus is treated differently: in the tenor (Kyrie, Ex. 3.2), bass (Gloria), in canon in tenor and bass (Sanctus), and alternately in tenor or bass (Agnus). Just as Nivers followed the prelude with a fugue for the reeds, Couperin writes one for the *jeux d'anches* for the second verset of the Kyrie and one for the *cromorne* in the Gloria. The two genres to develop after Nivers are here represented in beautiful specimens. There are two solos *en taille,* one for the tierce (No. 11) and one for *cromorne* (No. 18). In both cases the accompaniment is *fond d'orgue* with pedal *flûte,* and the solo line spins out with rhapsodic intensity. The second new genre is the trio (No. 10), here *à deux dessus,* two sopranos on the *cromorne* and the bass on a tierce combination.

The other movements of this mass display the great variety available within the standardized genres: for example, a dialogue of the reeds and tierces of the *grand orgue* and the *bourdon* with *larigot* of the *positif* (No. 9), a *récit* for the *voix humaine* that presents a dialogue of soprano and tenor on the stop (No. 12). The *Offertoire,* a category of the *grand jeu* genre unfettered by alternatim practice, stands apart from the versets because of its scope. Here it consumes 183 measures and exploits contrasts among three divisions: the *grands jeux* of the *grand clavier* and *positif* and the *cornet séparé.* The first of the three sections begins the dialogue, beginning and ending with majestic homophony on the *grand jeu.* This gives way to a sombre fugal section in the minor mode with two expositions, the first *en trio á trois claviers* for the *positif, cornet séparé,* and pedal *flûte,* the second on the *grand clavier.* The return to major brings a burst of energy, using the rhythm and imitation of a gigue that dances to a blazing conclusion 50 measures later. It is a stunning masterpiece of the French classic repertory.

NICOLAS DE GRIGNY (1672–1703)

Just as Bach summarizes his era without being typical of it, Grigny stands apart for the monumentality of his conceptions. Indeed, Bach himself thought highly enough of Grigny's organ book to copy it out entirely not long after it appeared in 1699, and it had wide enough appeal to merit a second printing in 1711. Grigny was born and died in Reims, and was organist of the cathedral there, the site of coronations of French kings. He was in Paris as organist of St. Denis at the time of his marriage at the age of 23 and returned to Reims within a year, but little else is known of his formative years. His one publication appeared in 1699 without preface, but with a wealth of commanding counterpoint, technical demands, pathos, and brilliance that transcend all that went before. It consists of music for a mass and five hymns, for a total of 42 versets. The mass uses the scheme outlined in Table 3.1, with both a Benedictus and an Elevation (18, 18a), and the whole volume concludes with a non-liturgical contrapuntal study on the *grand jeu* over two pedal points together lasting 76 measures.

His five versets for the Pentecost hymn "Veni Creator" illustrate his achievement. The general scheme is now familiar: opening *plein jeu* with a cantus firmus played by the pedals in the tenor, a fugue in second place using reeds and tierce sonorities, and closing with a *grand jeu* after a duo and *récit*. Only the opening verset makes reference to the plainchant. No movement, however, could be mistaken for the work of one of his predecessors. The *plein jeu* is denser, consisting of five voices rather than four. The fugue (Ex. 3.5) is also five voiced and of a type that is not known from any other composer: two voices are played on the *cornet séparé* in the soprano range, two on the *cromorne* in the tenor, and the fifth by the pedals. In general, Grigny demands more of the pedals than any Frenchman in this era. The duo that ensues is long (52 measures) and energetic, with unmistakable gigue rhythms. It is shot through with imitation, but its short-breathed phraseology and sequential repetition preclude any hint of pedantry. The *récit* is for the *cromorne* accompanied by the *jeu doux*. It is lyrical and ornate, but is the most conventional of the versets. The closing *grand jeu* is called a *dialogue*, but it is a splendid overture in the style of Lully. The opening 15 measures are in four-voiced homophony on the *grand jeu* in duple meter and with many dotted values in the soprano. This gives way to 55 measures of imitative play in $\frac{6}{8}$ on the *petit jeu* (*grand jeu* of the *positif*) with alternating solos in the soprano and bass on the *grand jeu*. The whole is symmetrically rounded out by 16 measures with the style but not the thematic material of the opening. The French school continued to produce splendid organ music in the classic idiom in the first decades of the eighteenth century, but no composer matched Grigny's ability to write dense and highly ornamented polyphony without sacrificing appealing flamboyance.

Example 3.5. Grigny, Fugue from versets for "Veni Creator" (*Livre d'orgue*, 1699), mm. 1–9.

Harpsichord Music

The rich brocade that is classic French harpsichord music has even fewer antecedents than the compatriot organ repertory. From the Renaissance we have four books published by Attaingnant, secular counterparts to the organ books discussed above, and then there is silence until the second half of the seventeenth century when a fully developed idlomatic harpsichord style was in place. There is no secular counterpart to Titelouze, and though there are many "French" pieces in Germanic manuscripts from the middle of the century, none can be shown to be anything other than German transcriptions of French lute music, or settings of French melodies. Two French manuscripts from the first third of the century give us some hints of what must have been composed then, but their contents are meager, and they provide us with no repertory of musical interest (Gustafson and Fuller 1990, "38a-Aberdeen": 384–85, and "34-Gen-2350/57": 398–400). Chambonnières was born just after the turn of the century, and some of the nearly 150 surviving pieces written by him were surely composed well before 1650, but they come to us mostly in versions from no earlier than 1670, frustrating any attempt to sift early from late. From the second generation of harpsichordists we have a comparable number of wonderful pieces by Louis Couperin, whose life extended only from c. 1626 to 1661, but again almost exclusively in readings that are much later. During the last 30 years

of the century, however, the French harpsichord style is well documented through published collections by Chambonnières (1670). Lebègue
(1677, 1687), Jacquet de la Guerre (1687), d'Anglebert (1689), and Louis
Marchand (1699), as well as much music from manuscripts of the period.

French harpsichord music of the seventeenth century was to a significant extent an improvisatory art. To be sure, composers notated their
pieces, and harpsichordists without compositional pretensions read
them off the page, but there is considerable evidence that "the piece"
was not as fixed an entity as the notation might suggest to the modern
eye. It is natural for us to want simply to find "the original" and to repro-
duce it faithfully, but we shall see examples of quite different versions of
a piece that can claim almost equal proximity to the composer, suggesting that we must search beneath the surface details of the notation to
find "the piece." Further, for a central portion of the repertory (more
than 300 pieces) the "original" is the Bauyn MS, a source as problematic in its readings as it is rich in music. For these reasons, some understanding of the sources and what they do and do not tell us is crucial to
penetrating the music (see also p. 16–18).

The Renaissance and Pre-Classic Periods

PIERRE ATTAINGNANT (C. 1494–1551/2)

Three of the four books of secular keyboard music that Attaingnant
published comprised intabulations of chansons by Claudin de Sermisy
and others. The fourth contains arrangements of dance tunes. Although
the music of the latter is purely instrumental in conception, the title is
equivocal about the intended instrument: *Quatorze Gaillardes, neuf
Pavennes, sept branles, et deux basses dances; le tout reduict de musique en la
tabulature du jeu d'orgues, espinettes, manicordions, et telz semblables instru-
mentz musicaulx.* That is, 30 miscellaneous dance movements (there are
only seven pavanes, not nine) of four different types are presented in the
notation of the organ, spinet, and clavichord or similar instrument. The
list of instruments, akin to those in the titles used for the publisher's
other keyboard books, is of some interest. First, it should be observed
that it describes the notation, not the music. It is quite true, however,
that sacred and secular keyboard textures had not developed the characteristics that in the future would wed them so closely to either the organ
or stringed instruments; while these dances were surely not intended primarily for organ performance, there is nothing about them that would
preclude it. The title also suggests the relative importance of keyboard
instruments in general, with organ at the top. The spinet *(espinette,* a rectangular virginal) was the primary stringed keyboard instrument of the
century, and it existed in profusion straight through the next century.
The citation of clavichord *(manicordion)* points to a path not taken, as

EXAMPLE 3.6. Anonymous, Pavane [1] (Attaingnant, *Quatorze Gaillardes, neuf Pavennes . . .,* 1531), after Heartz

France did not develop a tradition of clavichord playing or composition. Harpsichord (*clavecin*) is not mentioned specifically, but is presumably subsumed under *espinette.*

The music for all four secular books shares an ornamental melodic vocabulary. It makes use of much rapid figuration, often in stereotypical scalar or turning patterns. In the arrangements of the chansons the original vocal lines are quite rigorously preserved, but ornamented by these techniques. In the dance pieces there are frequently block chords in one of the hands to accompany the ornamented melody in the other. There is much tossing of patterns back and forth between the hands in these dances, creating an idiomatic division style long before the Elizabethans. The chanson intabulations show less variety of texture than do the dances, but they are much more than straightforward scorings of vocal music.

The opening pair of dances has a number of the typical elements of the style. It consists of a pavane (Ex. 3.6) and galliard on the same tune, one that is found in a collection of music for instrumental ensemble published by Attaingnant, and it was intabulated for lute as well. The tune was known as "La sguizera" in an Italian keyboard setting, and it is also found in Italy as "Danza de Bologna" and "Balleto amor constante." It has three strains, although the pavane and galliard versions differ in terms of which repetitions are written out in varied form (|:AA':|BB'|:C:| and |:AA':|:B:|:C:|); they both adhere to the melodic skeleton of the melody. Both open with even eighth notes that turn around the original melody, accompanied by rhythmic block chords in the left hand. Already in the third measure, however, the left hand introduces a scalar figure that is the basis for the figuration to follow in the right hand. In more than a third of the music the left hand carries the figuration, producing welcome changes of texture. The accompanying chords are primarily of rhythmic interest, once to the extreme of a ninefold repetition of a single chord.

THE INTERIM

One pavane by Jacques Cellier from Reims is our only direct evidence of composition for spinet in the second two-thirds of the sixteenth century (Rouen 971, ff. 34[r-v]; Ledbetter 1987, frontispiece). It is dated

1594 and has many of the characteristics just observed from more than 60 years earlier: the style is rooted in the practice of divisions. Forty years later, Mersenne illustrated two keyboard styles: abstract counterpoint (a *Fantaisie* by Charles Raquet) and diminution variations "which can be done on the organ or spinet" by Pierre [iii] de La Barre in Mersenne's *Harmonie Universelle* (1636; the Raquet piece was added in manuscript somewhat later). The plan of the diminutions was so mechanical, consisting of increasingly small note values for each variation, that only the incipits were printed. The two slight manuscripts cited earlier also suggest that harmonizations of popular tunes and some division-style passagework were the norm. This evidence would seem to fly in the face of the frequently encountered view that the classic harpsichord idiom developed from lute music. We shall see in the context of harpsichord transcriptions that in some ways it did, but it was not a gradual and pervasive infection. Rather, the old division style was suddenly displaced (almost entirely, the primary exception being variations called *doubles)* by the completely new one perfected by Chambonnières. As for the lute, Mersenne commented that lutenists and spinet players were "almost as different in their touch as in their style."

Mersenne also summed up the situation at the moment of change: two generations earlier Thomas Champion had excelled as a contrapuntist, and organ was linked with spinet stylistically; his son was known only for his spinet playing, but again Mersenne praises his knowledge (i.e., counterpoint) as well as digital prowess (skill in playing divisions). With the current generation, the instrument of choice has shifted from spinet to harpsichord and the praise is for the sensuous qualities of the music: beauty of melody and rhythm, fineness of touch, and aural sensitivity. An idiom that exploits–and is heavily dependent upon–the particular qualities of stringed keyboard instruments has been born.

The Classic Period

SOURCES AND VERSIONS OF PIECES

The Bauyn MS has long been recognized as the cornerstone of the repertory. It is the largest single source of seventeenth-century French harpsichord music, containing 345 pieces that provide readings of more than a third of all the extant seventeenth-century French works written originally for the harpsichord. It is the only source for half of Louis Couperin's harpsichord music and a third of Chambonnières's output. Its music was largely composed no later than the 1650s (Chambonnières was already well known in the 1630s and Couperin died in 1661), but the date of the manuscript itself has been very difficult to determine. Until recently it was assumed to come from just after the period of its repertory, but recent research shows that the manufacturer of its paper did not begin his business until 1676.[7] A second important manuscript suggests that the date of Bauyn's compilation was probably a decade or more later. The Parville MS is closely related to Bauyn in its readings of the 79 pieces that the sources have in common. A collation of the readings demonstrates that neither served as exemplar for the other. Parville contains transcriptions of works from 16 of Lully's dramatic works, the latest being *Acis et Galathée* (1686). This provides a *terminus post quem* of 1686 for the manuscript. The similarities between Parville and Bauyn suggest that the two may have been written at approximately the same time, thus the dating of Parville can be tentatively extended to Bauyn. Parville contributes some unique pieces and refines our understanding of Bauyn, but the latter remains the principal source.

Thus the central repository of the music of Chambonnières and Louis Couperin comes from as much as half a century after the music was composed. The style of the manuscript, since it is so far removed from the composers, becomes a significant issue in understanding the music. The Bauyn manuscript is the work of a single anonymous scribe, clearly an experienced—perhaps a professional—French copyist. The manuscript seems not to have been intended for practical use; the large folio format is cumbersome on a harpsichord music rack and much larger than any other French harpsichord manuscript. The contents of the collection were organized before the copying of at least the first two sections began; there are no gaps to allow for the addition of pieces at a later time, as is the case in other manuscripts that attempt a strict organization. The organization itself betrays an archival sensibility, as 28 pieces in a key, including a succession of 11 examples of the same dance type, can hardly be considered a performance grouping. Finally, the style of the headings of the pieces is unyieldingly redundant, citing the title and the name of the composer even in a series of over 100 pieces by the same composer.

The notational habits of this scribe can be examined by comparing the readings of the ten pieces copied more than once. In one case, copies follow in direct succession and are virtual duplicates, with the variants instructive of scribal habits of the tradition in which the Bauyn scribe worked. First there are a number of relatively inconsequential changes: layout on the page, clef changes, vertical alignment of notes, stem directions, substitution of tied notes for their single-note equivalent, and interchange of sharp and natural signs to cancel a flat. There are also a number of variants that illustrate a somewhat more radical renotation of the pieces by the scribe. Tied notes are equated with rests, as is appropriate for a nonsustaining instrument, and the same passage can be notated as either one or two "voices." Three notational formations that suggest a trill are used interchangeably. The arpeggiation of cadential chords is treated so casually as to put the choice figure in the realm of ornamentation rather than essential text, and double bars may or may not contain dots.

When one broadens the investigation to compare the readings of the whole spectrum of sources for seventeenth-century French harpsichord music, one finds not only more and less "corrupt" sources but differing versions of the same pieces that lay equal claim to being "correct." Clearly, many of the musicians who wrote these pieces down did not copy exactly what they had before them. Further, aural transmission played a role; we know, for example, that Hardel wrote down pieces by Chambonnières as the master played them (Le Gallois 1680/1976). Versions of pieces differ greatly in ornamentation, cadential arpeggiation, texture, voice leading, and repetition schemes. The sources suggest that these elements were all variables of performance, and we should not expect to find a single version of a piece that can be defended as "definitive" from these standpoints. LeGallois tells us that Chambonnières never played his pieces the same way twice.[8]

Example 3.7 compares three versions of the first strain of a Courante by Chambonnières. The first reading (Ex. 3.7a) was published by the composer himself, and the second (Ex. 3.7b) is from a manuscript in the hand of d'Anglebert, a close associate and his successor at court; the reason for the copy is that the younger composer wrote a double on the master's piece. The third version (Ex. 3.7c) is that of Bauyn and Parville, which are virtually identical, even down to a rare double dot (the differences—all indicated in the example—consist of one note, one dot, two ties, and two ornaments). In his preface Chambonnières explained that he was finally publishing his pieces because of the faulty manuscript copies that had circulated all over Europe and misrepresented him, but his example is one of many indications that the offending faults were not a matter of surface details such as ornamentation or clichés of arpeggiation. The Bauyn-Parville reading may be in the lamented category of transmission, but clearly d'Anglebert was much too close to the composer and too fine a musician himself to be accused of mauling the piece, and his version differs with Chambonnières's published one in matters much more profound than a few ornaments. In the very first measure, d'Anglebert gives the left hand more activity, linking the bass and tenor. The left-hand differences in the second measure are in notation, not notes, as d'Anglebert has written out sustained values that might easily be realized from the composer's notation. D'Anglebert has changed a harmonic detail as well, creating a chromatic passing tone in the melody in m. 3, and he creates a bridge to repeat the strain (where Chambonnières's print does not even have dots in the double bar). In general, d'Anglebert's version has a texture that is more sonorous and falls more comfortably under the hands (see especially m. 6). The Bauyn-Parville version, compared to either of the others, is a rather clumsy text. In m. 2 the shift in

EXAMPLE 3.7. The first strain of a Courante by Chambonnières in three versions (key signatures, clefs, and stemming have been normalized to facilitate comparison)

(a) Chambonnières *Pièces de clavecin,* v. 2, 1670

(b) D'Anglebert MS, c. 1677–80

(c) Bauyn MS, f. 48ʳ, and Parville MS, c. 1686–7? (Symbols found only in Parville are in square brackets, those that are only in Bauyn are dotted)

(continued)

accent to the last half note is diminished by having all voices move on the preceding note; the reading of the last beat of m. 5 confuses the melody altogether; the two gratuitous ties in Bauyn (apparently introduced by the scribe of Bauyn, as neither is in Parville: m. 5–6 and into the last lefthand d of m. 7) are errors of musical consequence; and square treatment of the final measure is primitive at best (see also the varied treatment of cadential arpeggiation in Ex. 3.10).

The first conclusion to be drawn from this comparison is that one is handicapped when the only source for a piece is Bauyn-Parville, and that must be borne in mind when essaying the works of Louis Couperin and much of Chambonnières, not to mention Hardel, Richard, and the other composers from whom we have fewer pieces. Second, we can assume at a minimum that the considerable changes of texture and melodic detail in d'Anglebert's version were not violations of his revered colleague's music; they must have been considered an appropriate rendering. But the relationship of any text in this repertory to the composer's intentions also comes into question. Was d'Anglebert fixing or rewriting the older master's piece as we know it from the 1670 print, or was he perhaps working from another version coming just as surely from Chambonnières? There are too many differences between the d'Anglebert and Bauyn-Parville versions to imagine that the anonymous scribes had a text that was actually based on d'Anglebert's, yet there are enough congruities of detail[19] to suggest that both Bauyn-Parville and d'Anglebert may be derived from the same original, one that must have come from Chambonnières and must have had significant differences in texture as well as ornament from the version he published. This is not surprising in view of Le Gallois's comment that he varied his pieces each time he played them, not to mention the ones Hardel took down by dictation. D'Anglebert was the first in France to adopt a style of notation that was rich in detail, and eventually François Couperin would complain that some harpsichordists didn't play his pieces with the ornamentation exactly as he wrote it. In the mid-seventeenth century the written text seems to have been a much less proscriptive document.

THE SUITE AND ITS DANCES

The suite was the only genre of classic French harpsichord music, if one sets aside the independent contrapuntal works that represent a continuation of the pre-classic idiom. There is little evidence that composers conceived the suite as a compositional unit, and in fact most did not use the term (or any other) as a generic heading for the tonal groupings of their pieces. Thematic connections among pieces are rare, and some that exist may be mere coincidence. Suites were not copied as a unit from one manuscript to another, perhaps because they were essentially performance orderings. Musicians compiled their own suites from existing pieces, creating manuscripts that present groups of dances by more than one composer. Parville is one such manuscript, and even more diverse suites were compiled by Charles Babel just after the turn of the century (London 39659). There are also manuscripts that present, in effect, anthologies of dances; in some, there is no organization at all, and in others the movements are grouped by tonality and in the general order of a suite, but in quantities that all but preclude treating them as performance units. The Bauyn manuscript uses the latter approach, as has already been suggested. When composers published their pieces, however, they ordered them in performing units, and these are our surest guide to composers' understanding of the harpsichord suite in the seventeenth century. That the published groupings were intended as performing orders was made explicit by d'Anglebert in a note explaining that "one plays" the gigue added at the end of a group transcriptions (p. 34 of the 1689 print) after the first gigue of the suite (p. 31).

The suites in the *pièces de clavecin* published between 1670 and 1700 range from 4 to 21 movements in length; the majority comprise 7 or 8 pieces. Of these 26 suites, more than half (14) begin with unmeasured preludes (one of these is a called *tocade*), and all but 2 have an allemande as the first dance; the exceptions are in suites by Chambonnières in which a pavane provides a similarly weighty beginning. Twice, Lebègue presented a pair of allemandes, but in all other cases a single example of the dance begins the series. The opposite is true of the courantes that follow in all of these suites; in all but 8 of the suites there are 2 or 3 courantes in succession, and in 2 of the exceptions there are 2 courantes present, but not in direct succession after the allemande.[10] A single sarabande follows the courantes, again in all but 8 of the suites; in 2 of the exceptional suites there are 2 sarabandes, and in the others there is no sarabande. What follows is one or more lighter dance(s), including a gigue in most cases (coincidentally, the number of exceptions is again 8). Certain composers had more specific notions of suite design. D'Anglebert and Jacquet de la Guerre place the gigue directly after the sarabande in all of their suites, as did Marchand (though in a manuscript copy of Marchand's single suite, the anonymous copyist felt free to change this order; Gustafson and Fuller 1990, 172–73, 294). Lebègue tended to end with a minuet, as did Jacquet de la Guerre in all 4 of her suites and Marchand in his. The most exceptional suites are those by d'Anglebert in which a group of transcriptions or other "miscellaneous" pieces (a set of variations of *les folies d'espagne* or an honorific *tombeau*) conclude or are appended to the suite.

A suite, then, was understood to begin with the weighty movements in the order allemande, courantes, sarabande, with an optional preface of an unmeasured prelude. The lighter dances that followed usually included a gigue, and often a minuet provided a cheerful conclusion. This somewhat loose definition of the genre accords with orderings for other solo instruments, again allowing for more rigorously maintained patterns for specific composers. The classic sequence of allemande–courante–sarabande–gigue is the skeleton of the French harpsichord suite, but not its body.

The individual dances are overwhelmingly binary in form. The pavane was typically in three strains, and chaconnes (and occasionally other dances) usually used a refrain strain (*grand couplet*) between contrasting strains (*couplets,* the whole said to be *en rondeau*). Most strains of pieces in this repertory are marked by some sort of double bar with dots, and there is abundant documentation that most strains in this style were repeated. It does not follow, however, that a double bar with dots was treated by contemporary performers in the same manner that musicians today interpret a modern repetition sign—as a specific instruction to return (once) to the beginning of the strain. Within harpsichord music, the clearest evidence for more freedom in repetition schemes is d'Anglebert's clear indication of a return to the first strain after the repetition of the second, resulting in the form AABBAABB or perhaps AABBAB (see also p. 18).[11] Equally clear-cut are concordant readings of the same piece that do or do not have an indication of a *petite reprise.*[12] Outside the harpsichord repertory, the strongest evidence that repetitions were treated very freely is the comparison of extant choreographies with notated dance tunes, where strains were and were not repeated in a number of patterns. A *rondeau* theme may be played once the first time, and twice after the first *couplet,* for example, and *petites reprises* may be added even though not indicated in the original score, and they may be played more than once.[13]

The following will serve as a glossary of the essential characteristics of the principal movements of suites. Unless otherwise stated, the dance movements are binary in form, the two strains are not typically unified thematically, and the second strain is often longer than the first.

Prélude, Tocade. The unmeasured prelude has a special fascination for modern musicians largely because its notation is so different from any other keyboard muisc; it seems to stand apart as an odd sort of French Sphinx. The genre was first cultivated by the lutenists who, like the harpsichordists, used a short series of elaborated chordal and scalar passages—sometimes nothing more than three or four arpeggios—to accustom the fingers to the instrument and the ear to the tonality, as Lebègue explained in a letter to a perplexed British harpsichordist.[14] The most typical notation for the harpsichord prelude was a series of whole notes, with slur-like lines indicating the duration of individual pitches or specifying groupings, usually enclosing the notes of a single harmony. They were unpretentious pieces, and they were used as a beginner's first lesson, as François Couperin suggests in introducing his own preludes in 1716–17. Some composers (notably Lebègue, d'Anglebert, and Jacquet de la Guerre) developed hybrid notations that included varied note values to distinguish ornamental notes, parallel to the semimeasured notation used for many lute preludes. More important, however, unmeasured notation was used for pieces of much greater musical substance, some of which were written under the clear influence of Froberger's toccatas. One, by Jacquet de la Guerre, is in fact titled *Tocade*. The simple prelude and the French toccata can both be seen in the works of Louis Couperin by comparing his *Prélude à l'imitation de Mr. Froberger* with the *prélude* that follows it in the Bauyn MS (Moroney edition [1985], Nos. 6 and 7). The former presents two extensive and harmonically complicated unmeasured sections that are separated by a rhythmically and melodically infectious fugue; the latter (beautiful though it is) comprises only four lines, much of which is elaborated tonic and dominant harmony (see Ill. 3.3).

Allemande, Pavane. The harpsichord allemandes show great rhythmic variety. They all maintain quadruple meter and make use of upbeat figures (particularly at the beginnings of the two strains), but their defining characteristics have more to do with texture and mood than with phraseology or rhythmic features that derive from dance. Within the context of the individual composer's style, they are the most learned compositions, being permeated by poignant or surprising harmonic events, motivic imitation—but not fugal gestures—and nonpropulsive rhythm. As is the case for several of the dance movements, the range of tempo is difficult to specify. A grave or majestic mood seems to have been the norm for the French harpsichordists, but both d'Anglebert and Lebègue did specify certain ones as *gaye,* and Jacquet de la Guerre's essays, some with much parallel motion, are more genial than serious.

ILLUSTRATION 3.3. Louis Couperin, *Prélude*, Bauyn MS, vol. 2, f. 12v.

The pavane exists only at the beginning of the classic repertory, with examples by Chambonnières and Louis Couperin. They are also in slow quadruple meter but cast in three strains rather than two. For the harpsichordists they were heavy compositions, tending toward four-voiced texture rather than the usual three. Chambonnières opened two of his published suites with pavanes rather than allemandes, and Louis Couperin's single and quite extraordinary example is in the tortuous key of F-sharp minor.

Courante. The French harpsichordists wrote more courantes than any other genre, by far. The dance dictates an almost continuous shifting of accent from three groups of two to two groups of three. The meter is almost always "3," three half notes per measure. The breaking up of harmonies in accompanimental parts lends itself naturally to effecting changes and ambiguities of accent, and constitutes the most identifiable cliché of the repertory. Like the allemandes, courantes are typified by upbeat figures. The hemiola qualities of the textures tend to undermine the sense of closure of melodic phrases, creating a sense of a series of short-breathed ideas that join together to span an entire strain. Much more than in the allemandes, the intended tempo is difficult to specify; theorists agreed that courantes were solemn, but the word itself means "running," and the more homophonic textures (compared to the allemandes) combined with strong rhythmic gestures suggest considerable energy. Lebègue paired a *courante gaye* with a *courante grave* in his first suite, but none in the French repertory has the even running note values of the Italian *corrente*.

Sarabande, Gaillarde, Volte. The harpsichord sarabandes, unlike most of their counterparts for lute, have a much more straightforward melodic orientation and structure than do the courantes, being in four-measure phrases of simple triple meter (usually "3," meaning $\frac{3}{4}$), and in spite of the typical displacement of accent to the second beat and frequent cadences onto the third beat. The simplicity of the phraseology, however, allowed for harmonic, textural, or ornamental complications in this dance that—in the French harpsichord repertory—seems always to have been understood as grave. This is sometimes reflected in thicker and lower textures, exploiting the rich tenor and bass of the instrument as the lutenists did with their *sans chanterelle* ("without top string") pieces.

Like the pavane, the gaillarde appears infrequently and only in the earlier part of this repertory; it was not, however, paired with the pavane as in the Renaissance. It had been a fast dance, and at least one example in the repertory at hand (No. 77 by Louis Couperin) is simple in texture and motivically lively. In most examples, however, it is similar to the sarabande in its gravity, and Chambonnières published one in place of a sarabande in a suite. There is one by d'Anglebert that is called "Sarabande grave en forme de gaillarde" in the Bauyn MS, and another (simply "gaillarde" in the 1689 print) is labeled "Sarabande, façon de gaillarde" there. The harpsichordists retained the triple meter and upbeats of the old dance, but hemiola accents are not pervasive. Another fast Renaissance dance that became associated with the sarabande to the point of confusion was the *volte* (Italian, *volta*, "turn"). One of the most famous of the sarabandes by Chambonnières, "Sarabande O beau jardin," is called *volte* in the Bauyn MS (though placed with other sarabandes), and Louis Couperin wrote another that could easily be called a sarabande (Gustafson 1979, inventories 35-I No. 80 and 35-II No. 53).

Gigue, Brusque, Canarie. In the hands of the harpsichordists, the gigue was essentially a fugal piece in lively compound meter (although some exist notated in dotted duple values,[15] and some in simple triple meter). The two strains both open imitatively, but this is sometimes obscured by a full-textured accompaniment; the opening themes of the two strains often bear a motivic relationship, but it is not habitually one of inversion, as was the norm with the Germans. In some cases gigues are more melodically oriented, with imitation appearing only in the second strain. Chambonnières wrote two pieces that circulated with the label *brusque* that are, in style, gigues. Closely related to the gigue is the canarie, a faster dance named for the Canary Islands, where it originated. It almost always uses a pervasive rhythm ($\flat\!\!\downarrow\!\downarrow|\downarrow.\flat\!\!\downarrow\downarrow$), and here the harpsichordists more often inverted the opening theme in the second strain.

Chaconne, Passacaille. The chaconnes are not only much more expansive than the binary dances, but they include some of the most exquisite passages in this repertory. Formally, there is considerable variety, with transpositions of primary or secondary material or shifts to the parallel mode sometimes providing harmonic diversions. Most are *en rondeau*, with the refrain presenting an elaboration of a simple bass pattern, often richly harmonized, such as 3–4–5–1 (used in five of Louis Couperin's chaconnes), or a descending tetrachord (1–7–6–5). The pattern is generally varied or otherwise incorporated into the full texture, as the literal use of an ostinato bass melody was not part of the French (or Italian) harpsichord idiom. The phraseology is usually in balanced 4-measure units in triple meter. The secondary strains of these *rondeaux* do not often use the same bass pattern as the refrain, but there are examples of the variation chaconne in which each strain uses a single pattern without returning to a refrain (e.g., the F-major chaconne by Lebègue). One of the most striking features of these pieces is their frequent exploitation of the resonant low regions of the harpsichord, a counterpart to the *sans chanterelle* style of the lutenists. Often composers contrasted the upper registers in some or all of the episodic strains with the rich and often dissonance-spiced refrain. A small number of these pieces were labelled *passacaille*, and theorists then as well as now have sought a distinction (that, for example, the *passacaille* was slower or was not *en rondeau*), but the harpsichordists seem not to have had a common understanding of any difference between the two dance forms. One example by Louis Couperin is called simply *chaconne* in Parville, but *chaconne ou passacaille* in Bauyn. The dance was a serious one, although not necessarily slow in tempo, and Louis XIV himself is known to have danced it.[16]

Minuet (menuet). Minuets are in simple triple meter, usually beginning and cadencing on the downbeat. The choreography of minuets involves hemiolas, and this is not infrequently reflected in harpsichord versions of the dance. The second half of a typical 8-measure strain is often a varied repetition of the first phrase, and harpsichordists frequently emphasized tunefulness further by using simple harmonies, thin texture (sometimes only two voices), and high tessitura. The tempo seems to have been moderately quick, but there are virtually no specific clues to tempo within the harpsichord repertory.[17] The dance was associated with the town of Poitou, which name therefore appears in the titles of some examples in this repertory.

Gavotte, Bourrée. These dances, like the minuet, became more important in the repertory in the latter part of the period under discussion, undoubtedly influenced by the many such dances that were transcribed from Lully's stage works. The harpsichord composers tended to use the same techniques as in the minuet to emphasize tunefulness. Both of these dances are usually in C or 2. The gavotte's phrases begin in the middle of the measure, reflecting the choreography, although this nicety of notation is not always maintained. It had a background as a slow movement (e.g., as described by Mersenne), but the courtly dance of the late seventeenth century was moderately quick. D'Anglebert marked two of his *lentement,* but these are the only suggestions of slowness for harpsichord gavottes. The bourrée, less common as a harpsichord movement, begins with an upbeat and is normally faster than the gavotte.

Tombeau. The French lutenists were the first musicians to take over the literary practice of writing a *tombeau* (lament) to commemorate a death. There are only two such pieces by harpsichordists, one by Louis Couperin on the death of the lutenist Blancrocher, the other by d'Anglebert on the death of Chambonnières, but they are among the most arresting pieces in the repertory. They do not share formal characteristics, as the latter is in the style of a gaillarde and the former is closer to a pavane.

Transcriptions

The importance of transcription to the repertory of French harpsichordists is easily underestimated because so little of the music is published in modern editions. In the original manuscripts the quantity of transcribed music is stunning. There are, for example, more than twice the number of harpsichord transcriptions of selections from Lully's operas than original harpsichord pieces by any composer. Many of these arrangements are, to be sure, rather perfunctory settings of favorite tunes, but even they demonstrate what was understood to be harpsichord idiom. The melody is generally embellished, but otherwise taken over literally. The bass, however, may be broken up by octave displacements or otherwise join with harmonic filler in the left hand. Thus the texture becomes more like original French harpsichord music, in which the bass has more linear identity than in lute music, but much less than in ensemble textures. The harpsichord bass is the weight of the "broken" texture, called (in modern times) *style brisé*. Example 3.8 presents three transcribers' versions of the same passage (Ex. 3.8a). Both anonymous harpsichordists (Exx. 3.8b and c) have adapted the original texture to harpsichord idiom, but the result in London 39659 is considerably more

EXAMPLE 3.8. Jean-Baptiste Lully, "Entrée d'Apollon" from *Le Triomphe de l'Amour* (1681)
(a) Lully (orchestral score)

(b) Parville MS, c. 1686–87

(c) London 39659, 1702

(d) D'Anglebert, *Pièces de clavecin*, 1689

(continued)

EXAMPLE 3.8. *(continued)*

Example 3.8. (*continued*)

elegant; d'Anglebert's version (Ex. 3.8d) is yet richer and more elaborate, translating the music into his own very idiomatic harpsichord style.

The vast majority of the transcriptions are of extracts from stage works. If the French, like the Germans, played lute music on the harpsichord, there is little evidence of it. Some of the few such transcribed lute pieces that do exist are by d'Anglebert, and his adaptations stand apart from all the *anonyma*. Ledbetter (1987) has studied those from lute music to show how d'Anglebert created harpsichord parallels for specific effects idiomatic to the lute. For example, where a lute tablature might have an oblique line to indicate the breaking of a chord, d'Anglebert delays the melodic note with a rest. Example 3.9 shows the difference between a literal transcription (Ex. 3.9a) and d'Anglebert's approach (Ex. 3.9b). In Perrine's notation (which was intended to be played on the lute) one sees an example of the *tirer et rebattre* technique, a strumming in which the forefinger goes back and forth on repeated chords, here with successively fewer notes to create a decrescendo. D'Anglebert first transposes the piece to a range that will sound rich but clear on the harpsichord, and then uses two ornaments to help get the same effect of diminuendo without the unidiomatic repeated striking of the same notes. What he does not translate from the lute original is equally telling. In general, he adds to the melodic top line to create an integral voice of prominence, and similarly creates something closer to a contrapuntal voice from the bass notes of the tablature. He increases the texture by elaborating the tenor line, and harmonies are often filled out and enriched. For example, a typical arpeggiation of the final chord of a strain in lute music might consist of rhythmicized octaves that are replaced in the harpsichord transcription by a breaking up of the full triad, richly voiced (see Ex. 3.10). This suggests that while harpsichordists certainly

EXAMPLE 3.9. Ennemond Gaultier, Courante "La petite bergère," m. 23
(a) Perrine, *Pièces de luth en musique*, 1680

(b) D'Anglebert MS, c. 1677–80

EXAMPLE 3.10. Ennemond Gaultier, Courante "l'Imortelle," close of first strain to the end

(a) Perrine, *Pièces de luth en musique*, 1680

(b) D'Anglebert MS, c. 1677–80

(continued)

EXAMPLE 3.10. *(continued)*

drew upon effects that were born on the lute, it was not at the expense of idiomatic keyboard techniques. On the contrary, the lute effects were sonic ideals that guided the harpsichordists in exploiting the possibilities of their own instrument.

JACQUES CHAMPION DE CHAMBONNIÈRES (1601/2–1672)

Chambonnières enjoyed an international reputation as the finest harpsichord composer and player in France. He was harpsichordist to both Louis XIII and Louis XIV, and he was still a legendary figure in the eighteenth century, when certain of his pieces continued to be copied into performers' manuscripts. His surviving output comprises just under 150 pieces, of which 60 were published two years before his death. The third suite of the first book illustrates most of the characteristics of the style he invented. There are eight movements in D, the first six in the minor mode: allemande "La Loureuse," courante "La Toute Belle," courante "de Madame," courante, sarabande, "Les Baricades," gigue ["La Madelainette"], and gigue. Descriptive or honorific titles were a custom of the lutenists, and so it is not surprising to see them here; these are not, however, character pieces in the eighteenth-century sense, and each movement is clearly grounded in the character of its dance type. In four of the movements the second strain is slightly longer than the first, in two they are exactly equal, and in two the second strain is about twice as long as the first.

The allemande begins richly, with low and close voicing, first in four voices, later mostly in three. The soprano dominates melodically, and the tenor is second in thematic importance. There is almost continuous eighth-note motion created by having one or another voice move successively to a harmonic or passing note (the essence of *style brisé*). The bass sometimes enters off the beat or emerges subtly into or out of a tenor line so that it is perceived as part of the composite rhythmic activity rather than a melodic foundation. At first contrasting motives provide the contrapuntal interest in what is essentially an accompanied melody, but in the second strain the tenor initiates a motive that is twice imitated. The three courantes are also essentially three-voiced, and while more homophonic than the allemande they do place much melodic interest in the tenor. The beautiful sarabande, if not as low as the opening of the allemande, largely eschews the soprano range used extensively by all of the preceding movements, and is more often in four-voiced texture. It has the expected even phrasing, but the opening 8-measure strain avoids simple tunefulness by diverting the melodic activity to the left hand. The 16 measures of the second strain begin with clear 4-measure phrases, but the melodic arch spans the later joints. "Les Baricades" is in style a gigue (not a courante, as the Bauyn MS has it). It and the next gigue both have clear-cut fugal openings for each strain, with the first and second themes sharing rhythms but not contours. In the second gigue, a third motivically related theme is introduced and then contrasted with the second; all but the cadential measures of the strain have a version of one or the other themes. The last gigue begins with full chords, disguising the imitation that is nonetheless present. In this suite are to be found all of the qualities cited by Mersenne: beauty of melody and rhythm, supple integration of the voices, and the demand for lightness and quickness of hand. With the benefit of hindsight, we can add that compared to his successors, Chambonnières grounded his pieces in a skillful but concealed contrapuntal frame, and this aspect of his style certainly has nothing to do with lute music.

JACQUES HARDEL (D. 1678)

Le Gallois tells us that Hardel was the best student and musical heir of Chambonnières. He carried on the style and, in the judgment of Le Gallois, was fully the equal of the master. Unfortunately, only a handful of his pieces survive, but they are indeed very fine works. There is a six-movement suite, a courante for lute, and what became one of the hit tunes of the seventeenth century, a gavotte to which Louis Couperin wrote a double. What is striking about these pieces is the control of texture, whether sumptuously full as in the allemande, or delicately balanced as in the second of the three courantes. One of the qualities that the pieces share with those of Chambonnières is a capacity for long-breathed melodies.

LOUIS COUPERIN (C. 1626–61)

It was Chambonnières who "discovered" Louis Couperin in the little town of Chaumes and opened the doors of Paris and the court for him. Couperin, at about 25, was already musically formed and was to have only a decade left in his brief life. His frame and influence were such, however, that nearly 20 years after his death Le Gallois saw him as

EXAMPLE 3.11. Louis Couperin, Passacaille [No. 27] (Bauyn MS), mm. 1–4

the foil to Chambonnières, each harpsichordist having founded a style of playing and composing that was distinctive and to which all others—save the crass and empty "brilliant" style that Le Gallois deplored—could be related. The rather inscrutable distinction cited by Le Gallois was that Chambonnières touched the heart and Couperin the ear. Their compositional styles have enough in common that one sarabande (No. 28 the Couperin works) is attributed in different places to both composers in the Bauyn MS, and no one has to date claimed the ability to discern which attribution is correct. There are, however, significant differences in the œuvres of the two composers. The first is perhaps because of happenstance of what has survived. We have no preludes and four mostly short chaconnes by Chambonnières, but the 16 preludes and 10 chaconnes/passacailles by Couperin are among the grandest works in the repertory. There are differences of melodic, textural, and especially harmonic vocabulary as well. Couperin's music is filled with exquisite harmonic surprises and touching dissonances. The refrain of the great C-major Passacaille (Ex. 3.11) artfully piles up a-b-c-d at the end of the first measure; rather than resolving, it changes color to a-b♭-c-d on the downbeat before the tension is slowly dissipated, slipping into a consonance on the second beat of the third measure and balancing the extraordinary pungency with three more beats of cadential simplicity, all of this voiced for maximum richness. It is no wonder that the music of this young man, though never printed, was treasured in manuscript by musical connoisseurs in the eighteenth century.[18] Just over 130 of his harpsichord pieces survive today.

JEAN-HENRY D'ANGLEBERT (1629–1691)

After the premature death of Louis Couperin came the published books of *pièces de clavecin by* Chambonnières (1670), Lebègue (1677, 1687), Jacquet de la Guerre (1687), and then d'Anglebert (1689). Like Louis Couperin, d'Anglebert was an organist, but he abandoned that instrument in favor of the harpsichord, and in 1662 he took over Chambonnières's duties as royal harpsichordist. The relationship between the two musicians was cordial, although the frequently encountered statement that they were teacher and pupil is supposition. Just under 100 works survive, more than half of which d'Anglebert published with the promise of a second book that was not accomplished in the two years before his death. As we have already seen, his tonal groupings are composed of two large sections, the first a suite of the usual dances and the second a group of transcriptions. Although his style is essentially within the common practice we have been discussing, his notation is not. His pieces were written with much more detail and precision than were those of any of his contemporaries, including a thicket of signs for ornaments (his table lists 29, compared to 6 for Chambonnières) and written-out *filigré.* Interestingly, although his music circulated relatively little, his ornament table (see Ill. 3.4) was the model for later composers, notably Gaspard Le Roux and J. S. Bach (in the *Clavier-Büchlein vor Wilhelm Friedemann Bach*). He also specified tempos much more than the other composers, usually with *lentement,* which he attached to sarabandes and gaillardes, as well as to some transcribed gavottes and a chaconne (also a transcription). All this attention to detail reflects a sensitivity to the nuances of harpsichord sonority that was unerring, as we have seen above (Exx. 3.8, 3.9).

ILLUSTRATION 3.4. Jean-Henry D'Anglebert, Table of Ornaments (*Pièces de clavecin,* Paris, 1689).

LOUIS MARCHAND (1669–1732)

Composers headed into the eighteenth century speaking the language of their predecessors until François Couperin's first book (1713) broke new ground. Louis Marchand's first book appeared in 1699, with one suite and an ambitious plan to publish a suite every other quarter, alternating between organ and harpsichord music. One more harpsichord suite actually appeared, after the turn of the century. The first suite contains nine movements whose order, as we have already seen, is traditional, but there are stylistic elements that point toward the future. The Prélude has the chordal and scalar gestures of an unmeasured prelude but is fully rhythmicized in quadruple meter, and even suggests binary form with a cliché cadence to the dominant at the midpoint. Motivic unity is greater than in the music of previous generations, with the head motive of the sarabande permeating both strains. The chaconne *(en rondeau)* has increasing motion in each *couplet,* with the last ones being both Italianate and virtuosic, more so than in similar gestures in Jacquet de La Guerre's A-minor chaconne. The century ended with quite wonderful harpsichord music.

Sometime during the latter part of this classic period a shadowy figure named Geoffroy penned over 200 extremely odd pieces (Gustafson 1979, inventory 37). Some are in the textures and styles of the mainstream composers, but others are two-voiced ditties in the style of the most rudimentary transcriptions. They are notable for idiosyncratic–or perhaps uncontrolled–chromaticism, and are an enigmatic postscript to the sumptuous repertory of seventeenth-century French harpsichord music.[19]

Guide to Literature and Editions

The Renaissance repertory has been treated to a number of scholarly editions, of which Albert Seay's is particularly instructive for presenting the original chansons in score with the keyboard arrangements published by Attaingant. Much of the early French organ repertory was edited by Alexandre Guilmant at the turn of the twentieth century in editions that, despite anachronistic registrations, are very reliable *(Archives des maîtres de l'orgue des XVIe, XVIIe et XVIIIe siècles,* including the works of Titelouze, Raison, Marchand, Dumage, Clérambault, Gigault, Grigny, Fr. Couperin, Boyvin, Guilain, Dandrieu, and Lebègue). Since 1967 Heugel has published a series *(Le Pupitre)* of largely French early music, including some for organ and much for harpsichord, under the general direction of François Lesure. Of the repertory discussed in this chapter it includes the works of d'Anglebert, Grigny, and Jacquet de la Guerre (vols. 54, 68, and 66). A heavily edited selection of Louis

Couperin's harpsichord music—along with some that is wrongly attributed to him—is included in the series (vol. 18), but the edition by Moroney is far preferable, especially for its prefatory remarks on the unmeasured preludes. Both of these editions take both the Bauyn and Parville MSS into account, unlike earlier editions of Couperin's works. The composer's organ music remains inaccessible in a privately held manuscript. An edition, promised decades ago (Oldham 1960), is finally forthcoming. Current views of editorial practice are illustrated by the two very different editions of Hardel's works. The Broude Trust has begun a series of critical editions (*The Art of the Keyboard*) that includes the works of Hardel, La Barre, and Richard; in preparation are the Bauyn MS, and the harpsichord works of d'Anglebert, Chambonnières, and Geoffroy. An ongoing series of inexpensive facsimile editions under the direction of Jean Saint-Arroman *(Le Musique française classique de 1650 à 1800)* includes reproductions of keyboard sources by d'Anglebert, Attaingnant, Boyvin, Chambonnières, Clérambault, Gaspard Corrette, Dumage, Gigault, Grigny, Jacquet de La Guerre, Jullien, Lebègue, Marchand, Nivers, Raison, and Titelouze. Minkoff also has an extensive facsimile series, often with more informed prefaces, including the Bauyn, Brussels 27220, and La Pierre MSS and keyboard books by d'Anglebert, Couperin de Turin, Grigny, Jacquet de La Guerre, and Nivers.

For a survey and discussion of the whole French classic organ repertory, there is nothing in English comparable to Gallat-Morin's comprehensive study of the *Livre d'orgue de Montréal.* Dufourcq's five-volume *opus magnum is* the summation of a life's work, dealing with the sources, cases, builders, music, and documentation. In English, Pruitt's articles on Nivers are helpful in understanding the broader repertory, and Douglass's book remains the best overview of the instrument and its registrations. Higginbottom's 1981 article compares the extant organ repertory with instructions of contemporary ceremonials. Liberman is particularly helpful for his explanation of the changing understanding of *ton* in French organ music. Fuller provides a fine provisional analysis of Louis Couperin's organ style in NG 2001 (6: 581–83); until the Oldham manuscript is made available for study, a more thorough discussion is difficult to imagine.

The seventeenth-century harpsichord repertory is discussed and exhaustively indexed in my 1979 thematic catalogue, which also lists editions for specific works and secondary literature; the third appendix of its successor (1990) on later repertory presents extensive corrections to the first work. Ledbetter's book is a perceptive stylistic and historical discussion of the relationship between lute and harpsichord idioms. The "letter" from Le Gallois is the richest original source of information about the playing of Chambonnières and Louis Couperin. Fuller has provided the only stylistic discussion to date of harpsichord transcriptions. For specialized studies (some in English) and original documentation, *Recherches sur la musique française classique,* edited by the late Norbert Dufourcq and his colleague Marcelle Benoit, is a treasure trove.

On unmeasured preludes, the published thesis by Prévost is rich in comparative data, although it was written just before an important manuscript came to
light in Brussels (Gustafson and Fuller 1990, 374–82).

Notes

1. The name derives from the medieval trope on the Kyrie, "Cunctipotens genitor
Deus." It was authorized for use in parishes for important feasts ("double feasts"), but
was not typically used in institutions other than parishes (e.g., convents and monasteries), and so the distinction is now sometimes made between a "parish mass" and a
"convent mass." An organ mass for the "Cunctipotens genitor" chants was also sometimes called a "double mass" because of its use at "double feasts."

2. Paris, Bibliothèque nationale de France B4 682; see Dufourcq 1971–82, 5: 47–50.

3. Practice did not always follow theory-at least in the sixteenth century-as a mass
published by Attaingnant does have versets for the Credo.

4. This text (see Table 3.1) is not to be confused with the canticle of the same name.

5. The Sanctus chants demand versets ending on g, but composers of organ masses, including Nivers, consistently pitched it on f.

6. Henricus Comelius Agrippa, *De incertitudine el vanitate scientiarum et artium*
(Paris, 1531), fol. 34.

7. The dating, with an illustration of the paper's watermark, is explained in *Die
Musik in Geschichte und Gegenwart*, 2nd edition (Kassel, 1994), Sachteil vol. 1, 1306–07.
More recent research on the arms stamped on the binding, from which the name
"Bauyn" derives, will be presented in the forthcoming critical edition of the manuscript.

8. "...toutes les fois qu'il joüoit une piece il y méloit de nouvelles beautés par des
ports de voix, des passages, & des agrémens differens, avec des doubles cadences.
Enfin il les diversifoit tellement par toutes ces beautez differentes qu'il y fasoit tou-
jours trouver de nouvelles graces" "...every time he played a piece, he introduced new
beauties, with grace notes, passages, and various embellishments, including *double
cadences*. In a word, he so diversified them with all these different adornments that
he disclosed ever fresh graces in them") (Le Gallois 1680, 70).

9. See, for example, the tenor line of m. 3, perhaps the aborted (in Bauyn-Parville)
melodic figure at the end of m. 5, and perhaps the last full beat of m. 6 (voiced differently).

10. In the last suite of Chambonnières's first book a sarabande intervenes between
two courantes, and at the end of his second book a gigue comes between the allemande and the three courantes.

11. The indications occur in his 1689 *Pièces de clavecin* in the form of directs after
the final double bars.

12. "Reprise" ("repetition" or "return") often appears as a label for the second
strain. A "small repetition" is a return to the last phrase of the dance.

13. The dances are through-choreographed, not repeating with the music, so that
the repetition scheme demanded of the music is unequivocal. See Rebecca Harris-
Warrick, "Contexts for Choreographies: Notated Dances Set to the Music of Jean-
Baptiste Lully," in *Jean-Baptiste Lully: Actes du colloque* (Laaber, 1990), 433–55, esp. 440
and App. B.

14. *Recherches sur la musique française classique* 17 (1977): 7–14.

15. This spawned a hybrid genre that might be called "gigue-allemande." A small
number of pieces have aspects of both dances, or exist in variant versions with the

two dance titles (Gustafson 1979, vol. 1, 65, n. 115).

16. On the difference between the French chaconne and passacaille, see also Alexander Silbiger, "Chaconne 4: France," *NG 2001*, 5: 412–14 and "Passacaglia 4: France," *NG 2001*, 19: 193.

17. D'Anglebert marked two transcribed minuets *lentement,* but this may have been a personal propensity, as he did the same for gavottes.

18. As Titon du Tillet tells us in *Le Parnasse françois* (Paris, 1732), 402–03.

19. This volume of harpsichord works is not to be confused with a manuscript volume of organ music "attributed," with absolutely no justification, to Geoffroy in a modern edition (*Le Pupitre,* vol. 53).

Selected Bibliography

EDITIONS

d'Anglebert, Jean-Henry. *Pièces de clavecin.* Ed. Kenneth Gilbert. Le Pupitre 54. Paris, 1975.

Attaingnant, Pierre (publisher). *Deux Livres d'orgue.* Ed. Yvonne Rokseth. Paris, 1925.

———. *Keyboard Dances from the Earlier Sixteenth Century.* Ed. Daniel Heartz. CEKM, 8. 1967.

———. *Transcriptions of Chansons for Keyboard.* Ed. Albert Seay. Corpus Mensurabilis Musicae, 20. 1961.

London, British Library Add.39659: Babell Ms. Facsimile edition with Introduction by Bruce Gustafson. SCKM, 19. New York, 1987.

Manuscrit Bauyn. Facsimile edition, revised with Introduction by Davitt Moroney. Geneva, 1998.

Chambonnières, Jacques Champion de. *Œuvres complètes.* Ed. Paul Brunold and André Tessier. Paris, 1925. Reprint. New York, 1967.

Couperin, François. *Œuvres complètes.* Organ masses in vol. 3. Ed. Paul Brunold, rev. Kenneth Gilbert and Davitt Moroney. Monaco, 1982.

Couperin, Louis. *Pièces de clavecin.* Ed. Paul Brunold, rev. Davitt Moroney. Monaco, 1985.

Grigny, Nicolas de. *Livre d'orgue.* Ed. Charles-Léon Koehlhoeffer. Le Pupitre 68. Paris, 1986.

Hardel, Jacques. *The Collected Works.* Ed. Bruce Gustafson. The Art of the Keyboard, 1. New York, 1991.

———. *Pièces de clavecin.* Ed. Denis Herlin. Le Grand Clavier, 5. Monaco, 1991.

Livre d'orgue de Montréal. ed. Élisabeth Gallat-Morin and Kenneth Gilbert. 3 vols. Montréal, 1985–88.

Nivers, Guillaume-Gabriel. *Premier Livre d'orgue, 1665.* Ed. Norbert Dufourcq. Paris, 1963.

Tilney, Colin. *The Art of the Unmeasured Prelude for Harpsichord, 1660–1720.* London, 1991.

LITERATURE

Anthony, James R. *French Baroque Music from Beaujoyeulx to Rameau.* Revised edition. New York, 1978. Revised as *La Musique en France à l'époque baroque de Beaujoyeulx à Rameau.* Paris, 1981.

DeBoer, Barbara. "The Harpsichord Music of Jean Nicolas Geoffroy," Ph.D. dissertation, Northwestern University, 1983.

Douglass, Fenner. *The Language of the Classical French Organ.* New Haven, 1969.

Dufourcq, Norbert. *Le Livre de l'orgue français, 1589–1789.* 5 vols. Paris, 1971–82.

Fuller, David. "Les Arrangements pour clavier des œuvres de Lully." In *Jean-Baptiste Lully: Actes du colloque,* ed. Jérôme de la Gorce and Herbert Schneider, 471–82. Laaber, 1990.

Gallat-Morin, Elisabeth. *Un Manuscrit de musique française classique, Étude critique et historique: Le Livre d'orgue de Montréal.* Montreal, 1988.

Gustafson, Bruce. *French Harpsichord Music of the 17th Century: A Thematic Catalog of the Sources with Commentary.* 3 vols. Ann Arbor, 1979.

"Shapes and Meanings of Slurs in Unmeasured Harpsichord Preludes." *French Baroque Music 2* (1984): 20–22.

———. and David Fuller. A *Catalogue of French Harpsichord Music: 1699–1780.* London, 1990.

Higginbottom, Edward. "Ecclesiastical Prescription and French Classical Organ Music." *Organ Yearbook* 12 (1981): 31–54.

———. "French Classical Organ Music and the Liturgy." *Proceedings of the Royal Musical Association* 103 (1976–77): 19–40.

LeGallois, Jean. *Lettre de Mr Gallois à Mademoiselle Regnault de Dolier touchant la musique.* Paris, 1680. Translated and annotated by David Fuller in "French Harpsichord Playing in the 17th Century–After Le Gallois." *Early Music* 4 (1976): 22–26.

Ledbetter, David. *Harpsichord and Lute Music in 17th Century France.* London, 1987.

Liberman, Marc. "The Organ Works of Nicolas Lebègue in the Context of Contemporary Theory and Practice." Ph.D. dissertation, Northwestern University, 1984.

Moroney, Davitt. "The Performance of Unmeasured Harpsichord Preludes." *Early Music* 4 (1976): 143–51.

Oldham, Guy. "Louis Couperin: A New Source of French Keyboard Music of the Mid Seventeenth Century." *Recherches sur la musique française classique* 1 (1960): 51–60.

Prévost, Paul. *Le Prélude non mesuré pour clavecin (France, 1650–1700).* Baden-Baden and Bouxwiller, 1987.

Pruitt, William. "The Organ Works of Guillaume Nivers." *Recherches sur la musique française classique* 13 (1973): 133–56; 14 (1974): 7–81; 15 (1975): 47–49.

Rokseth, Yvonne. *La Musique d'orgue au XVe siècle et au début du XVIe.* Paris, 1930.

Saint-Arroman, Jean. *L'Interprétation de la musique pour orgue.* Vol. 2. *L'Interprétation de la musique française, 1661–1789.* Paris, 1988.

Scheibert, Beverley. *Jean-Henry D'Anglebert and the Seventeenth-Century Clavecin School.* Bloomington, IN, 1986.

Troeger, Richard. "The French Unmeasured Harpsichord Prelude: Notation and Performance." *Early Keyboard Journal* 10 (1992): 89–119.

Van Wye, Benjamin. "Ritual Use of the Organ in France." *Journal of the American Musicological Society* 33 (1980): 287–325.

MANUSCRIPT SHORT TITLES

Bauyn Manuscript	*F-Pn* Rés. Vm^7 674–675
D'Anglebert MS	*F-Pn* Rés. 89ter
London 39659	*GB-Lbl* Add. 39659
Oldham Manuscript	*GB-L* private collection
Parville Manuscript	*US-BE* MS 778
Rouen 971	*F-Rm* MS 971

CHAPTER FOUR

Germany and the Netherlands

John Butt

Conrad Paumann (c. 1410–73) and the Buxheim Organ Book

The first instance of a single dominating personality in the history of keyboard performance coincides with the elevation of instrumental—and particularly keyboard—music to a level that was almost comparable with vocal music. Organs were, of course, already indispensable in the church and court life of German lands, but their performers and repertory were essentially anonymous. The spectacular career of the blind organist Conrad Paumann, and the survival of several major sources of keyboard music from the fifteenth century, together suggest a fundamental shift in the status of the keyboard medium. Paumann enjoyed much fame in his first position as organist of the church of St. Sebald, and subsequently town organist, in Nuremberg. Soon he became organist to the Duke of Bavaria and was promoted in concert—presumably as a status symbol of the Munich court—before Philip the Good of Burgundy, Emperor Frederick III, and ultimately in Mantua, three years before his death.

That comparatively few works by Paumann survive is hardly surprising in view of his blindness and the consequent presumption that he improvised most of what he performed. However, the preservation of *any* keyboard music in manuscript from this time suggests that some of the repertory was considered exemplary and, to some degree, "fixed" into identifiable pieces. Undoubtably the most significant music from Paumann and his circle is the collection of *Fundamenta*, notated exercises designed specifically to cultivate improvisation and dexterity at the organ. Here, then, notation provides a window into the countless improvisations of the age—performances that, although lost, can be approached and understood by the modern performer. It is extremely difficult to ascertain how closely the various surviving *Fundamenta* relate to Paumann's original teaching methods; two examples attributed to him exist in sources predating the Buxheim organ book and two of the four examples in Buxheim bear his initials or name. Wolff (1968) deals with many of the complex stylistic and chronological issues, showing that the two earlier examples already evidence Paumann's development of three-part texture for keyboard; the Buxheim examples show a later development of the keyboard idiom, clearly now practiced as a high art.

Of the several collections and isolated manuscripts of keyboard music from the fifteenth century, the Buxheim organ book stands out as the most extensive and comprehensive example. Although the inaccuracy of its texts suggests that Buxheim may not have come from the very closest circle around Paumann, it is almost inconceivable that a musician of his stature was not somehow associated with this most significant collection of the age. Two of the *Fundamenta* and a short song are attributed to Paumann, and the similarity of much of the figuration in the anonymous pieces to that cultivated in the *Fundamenta* suggests that his involvement extends well beyond the pieces with direct attribution. The manuscript is written in a notation combining letter-name tablature (tenor and contratenor) with a type of black mensural notation for the discantus (Ill. 4.1). This notation itself suggests something of the way Paumann and his contemporaries conceived of keyboard texture and performance, with the right hand isolated for faster, soloistic figuration. This may also relate to the multiple manuals on many of the larger German organs of the time.

The manuscript seems to fall into two parts: the first, which is earlier (1450s), was written by a single scribe who also wrote an index to this section alone, while the second, containing a somewhat later repertory, was written by several scribes (1470s?; see the introduction to *Music from the Buxheim Organ Book*). In general, the later pieces are the more virtuosic, although sometimes at the expense of the rhythmic subtlety of the earlier pieces. The 256 works divide into liturgical pieces, intabulations of French, German, and Italian songs, teaching pieces (*Fundamenta*), and free preludes. Although it is safe to assume that the liturgical pieces were played on church organs, the secular pieces may have been intended for small positive organs or, judging from sporadic pedal indications, also for the larger church instruments.

The liturgical pieces have much in common with the secular works: they generally adopt the same three-part texture with most of the embellishment in the discantus. Many begin with the characteristic "turn" in the discantus, and there are frequent rhythmic subtleties, such as hocket patterns (Ex. 4.1).[1] Somewhat more austere are the Mass settings,

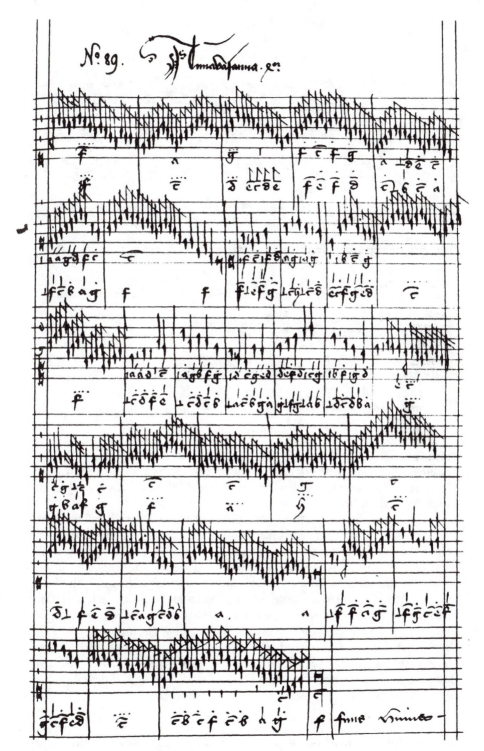

ILLUSTRATION 4.1. Buxheim Organ Book, f. 111. *D-Mbs*, Cim. 352b.
Reproduced with permission.

EXAMPLE 4.1. Buxheim Organ Book, No. 41, "Sequitur Benedicite"

Nos. 150–57, which begin with a rare example in four voices; the text headings throughout the sectional Gloria setting, No. 151, suggest liturgical use, either as substitution for the sung Ordinary or as introduction to the individual lines.

It is impossible to outline here the tremendous variety of methods by which secular songs are transcribed for keyboard; in general the keyboard arrangements seem to demand a tempo slower than the vocal original in order to accommodate the added figuration (although by no means all the settings greatly embellish the original). Although the later works, such as the second intabulation of Dufay's "Se la face ay pale," lack the rhythmic complexity of the works from the earlier part of the manuscript (in which Binchois is one of the most common composers), they show the more continuous patterns of figuration that were to become essential to the keyboard idiom in later years. There is also evidence of fledgling imitation between voices and sequential development of motives (Ex. 4.2).

*   *   *

Another "progressive" element in the collection as a whole is the inclusion of 16 free preludes, the only works, apart from the pedagogical

EXAMPLE 4.2. Buxheim Organ Book, No. 255, "Se la phase pale"

Fundamenta, that are free keyboard works without a vocal origin. Most of the preludes from the earlier portion of the manuscript are very simple affairs beginning with a few patterns of figuration and continuing with a plain chordal texture, presumably a frame for further embellishment. The preludes in the latter portion are generally more extensive, standing on their own as individual pieces. The prelude on F, No. 235, is perhaps most representative of an incipient formal "roundedness." It begins with a free melisma, followed by the standard chordal texture; the central portion of the piece presents a scalar tenor with a variety of sequential figurations in the discantus, rather in the manner of a *Fundamentum* setting; and the piece ends with a long melisma over an organ point on F with its fifth, a return to the style and gestures of the opening.

The preludes are clearly related to the abstract and pedagogical intent of the *Fundamenta;* indeed, some of the latter examples turn into extensive exercises on specific figures and intervals that are indistinguishable from the four *Fundamenta* proper. The main categories of the *Fundamentum* are:

"Ascensus et Descensus," where the tenor rises and falls in scalar, and later, stepwise motion;

"Redeuntes," where the tenor is a reiterated organ point or moves away from and back to its starting note;

"Clausulae," where the tenor presents a cadential pattern (which can be extended sufficiently to form a complete piece);

"Concordanciae," which introduce homophonic, note-against-note harmony.

In all, these exercises present a remarkably comprehensive introduction to keyboard composition and performance, somewhat analogous to the celebrated Italian vocal methods in improvised counterpoint and diminution a century later. The "Concordanciae" introduce what would later be described as first-species counterpoint, and the other exercises constitute a methodical course in diminution and elaboration. Moreover, the given tenors, which often begin in scalar motion and then work through progressively wider intervals, are themselves embellished with

EXAMPLE 4.3. Buxheim Organ Book, No. 189, *Incipit Fundamentum M.C.P.C.*

their own repertory of ornamental formulas. The overwhelming majority of ornamental figures in the discantus, particularly in the earlier exercises of each set, are short four-note scales and turns; triplet motion
and cadence formulas are also quite common. All of these devices are
demonstrated in a succinct example from the first *Fundamentum* (Ex. 4.3,
attributed to Paumann). The rubric describes the basic pattern of the
tenor, e–f–g; g–f–e.

The last two *Fundamenta,* from the latter portion of the manuscript,
show further development of the same ideas. The exercises are more
complex and demanding, now almost all in three-part texture with
much crossing between tenor and contratenor. Paumann's second *Fundamentum,* the last and most extensive in the manuscript, follows a somewhat different format, beginning with short three-voice "cells" that are
developed into increasingly extended pieces. This method seems to cultivate a sense of form, rather than merely one of abstract texture, so that
the player learns to elaborate a simple cell into a sizable paragraph, primarily by extending the ambitus of the tenor to delay its return to the
opening note, and later also by augmenting the tenor notes to allow for
more extensive melismas in the discantus.

The Early Sixteenth Century
Hofhaimer (1459–1537), Schlick (c. 1460–1521), and Buchner (1483–1538)

The turn of the sixteenth century marked a period of considerable
transition in German keyboard music: vocal music was moving toward a
more linear, multivoiced, and imitative texture; indigenous keyboard
music was developing along lines conditioned by the instrumental
medium rather than merely by mimicking vocal practice; and organs
were being built so that the registers could be used separately and in
new combinations, thus allowing for an extremely varied differentiation

of musical lines. Arnolt Schlick's *Spiegel der Orgelmacher* of 1511, the first published German treatise on organ building, was thus a landmark, an attempt to codify and unify the diverse practices of the age.

Schlick's preface gives a useful picture of the general conceptions of music of the time. He justifies music, according to its classical origins, as a mirror of cosmic unity and concord, and also with regard to its use within the Jewish tradition at the time of David, when music was considered a powerful influence on the emotions. Although such statements (often termed "laus musicae") are common in music treatises of the Renaissance and beyond, this is the first instance in a treatise related to keyboard music:

> Music according to the statements of all teachers is justly to be honored because of its inventors, splendid people, also for the sake of those nine talented female personages, the Muses, among whom it is said to have originated and further is to be honored for its nature, for as Boethius says, it is a true friend of unity and concord, a foe of dissension and discord.
>
> Music is also to be justly and highly honored because of its effectiveness in the service of God, adding earnestness and entertainment to the holy services. According to David, it encourages joy, in war, slaughter and truce; it quickens and delights, it makes the angry calm, brings again to the senseless their reason. (Schlick 1980, 13–15)

Schlick's comments on the organ itself are also interesting, since he sees its supreme virtue as lying in the opportunities it affords for multiple-part writing. Here we see reflected the fundamental shift in musical style from the predominantly three-part texture of the mid-fifteenth century to a concern for greater polyphony; in other words, the very capabilities of the organ medium suddenly placed it at the center of the prevailing musical culture:

> This booklet is based upon much experience, and on reasons stemming from the basis of music, and brings together some rules for the building and improving of organs. This is the pre-eminent instrument of music, since the greatest number of voice parts, as many as six or seven, may be controlled by one man. It is customarily used in churches for the praise of God, to facilitate choral singing, and to refresh human spirits and vexations. (Schlick 1980, 17)

The remainder of Schlick's text is an illuminating picture of the state of organ building of the time, its issues ranging from the most fundamental considerations of positioning the instrument to matters of registration and tuning.

Of the surviving music of the age, the handful of pieces by Paul

Hofhaimer, court organist to Emperor Maximilian, represent a transitional stage:[2] the music is in the old-fashioned three-part texture and much of the ornamental figuration, primarily turns and scalar motives, superficially resembles that of the Buxheim repertory. However, the rhythmic complexity of the latter is generally absent, or at least simplified; there is much more of a feeling of a continuous pulse throughout each piece, with a clearer sense of several metrical levels; there is also far less crossing of parts, and each line tends to appropriate a specific range. A short extract from Hofhaimer's "Tanndernack"—preserved in no fewer than four tablatures of the early sixteenth century—demonstrates two essential elements of his style: sporadic imitation between the free voices and frequent movement in thirds (Ex. 4.4).

Schlick's own music is represented primarily by his *Tabulaturen etlicher Lobgesang und Lidlein* for organ and lute (Mainz, 1512), the first example of printed organ tablature. All nine of the works for organ show a new conception of polyphony: the multiple independent lines that Schlick thought so well suited to the organ (four voices being as common in these pieces as the traditional three); a predilection for linear, conjunct motion; and imitation between the free voices. Ornamental figures (other than basic passing notes) are kept to a minimum, imparting a sense of a "pure" contrapuntal idiom, which remained central to German compositional technique well up until the time of Bach two centuries later (Ex. 4.5; Ill. 4.2).

A manuscript collection of Schlick's keyboard compositions, prepared around the time of the coronation of Charles V in 1520, contains

EXAMPLE 4.4. Paul Hofhaimer, "Tanndernack" (Kleber version)

EXAMPLE 4.5. Arnolt Schlick, "Salve regina"

eight versets on the sequence "Gaude Dei genitrix," which, rather in the manner of Hofhaimer, include much parallel movement in thirds. According to a note by the composer, each verset is constructed according to its own character and rules; certainly the layered texture of the fourth verset, with the outer parts moving in thirds and the inner parts moving in parallel sixth chords, is unusual in any era of keyboard composition

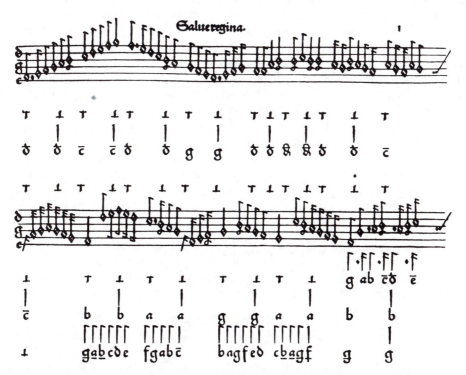

ILLUSTRATION 4.2. Arnolt Schlick, *Tabulaturen Etlicher lobgesang und lidlein uff die orgeln und lauten* (Mainz, 1512): "Salve regina."

before the twentieth century. Most remarkable of all is the second of two settings of the antiphon "Ascendo ad patrem meum," a massive work in ten voices, four of which are to be taken by the pedals. Never before or since have so many independent voices been demanded of one player (Ex. 4.6).

Although Schlick's music betrays a strong interest in the new conventions of polyphonic composition, the rules and methods of High Renaissance counterpoint on the keyboard were most thoroughly codified and exemplified by Hans Buchner, Hofhaimer's most distinguished pupil. Educated at the court of Maximilian I and organist of Konstanz Minister from 1506, Buchner would have come into contact with Heinrich Isaac. Indeed, his liturgical music for organ may well have been written as a keyboard analogue of Isaac's *Choralis constantinus*, part 2, also written for Konstanz.

Buchner's larger surviving *Fundamentum* is one of the most important documents of the age, not only showing a far wider range of topics than the earlier examples from the Paumann circle, but also illuminating many of the important changes in taste and methodology. Immediately evident is the fact that Buchner outlines rules for the subject at hand before giving his examples (Paumann apparently taught by examples alone). The first of the three sections is one of the earliest tutors on keyboard performance. Although Buchner's priority here is to establish a system of correct fingering, he is careful to affirm that his rules are only guidelines that can be modified in the light of more experience. His foremost precept—that each finger should be chosen with the demands of the next note in mind—sounds sensible enough, although, of course, it does not determine any particular style of fingering or articulation. The subsequent rules show that he tends to finger conjunct passage work with two alternating fingers ("paired fingering"); fingers 2 and 4 are the "good" fingers (i.e., those appropriate to the odd-numbered divisions of the beat) in the right hand; consecutive fingers are applied to four-note turn figures, thus mirroring the inherent grouping of the notes. Most alarming for the modern keyboard player might be Buch-

EXAMPLE 4.6. Arnolt Schlick, "Ascendo ad Patrem meum"

ner's prescriptions for consecutive thirds and sixths: these are to be played by fingers 2 and 4 and 2 and 5 respectively, with no change of fingers. Buchner provides a short piece with model fingering to show how these rules work in practice.

The second part deals with the method of intabulation, and the third—historically perhaps the most important—provides the first extant rules for composing with a cantus firmus for keyboard, beginning with the rules of consonance, dissonance, and correct voice leading (he particularly favors contrary motion between tenor and discantus). The two remaining topics give an illuminating view of Buchner's compositional priorities: imitation between voices at the beginning of each section, and the introduction of divisions (coloration) on the free lines, as exemplified by tables of the Paumann type. Thus we see the survival of the Paumann *Fundamentum*—and indeed the four-note turn remains the most popular ornament—but it is to be studied only with the hindsight of the rules of counterpoint.

Buchner's liturgical music is remarkable for its thorough provision of pieces for the Ordinary, Propers, and Offices. Indeed, it represents the first comprehensive collection of German liturgical music, with enough pieces to constitute several Ordinary cycles. Furthermore, the larger pieces, with their succession of various cantus firmus settings and techniques such as imitation and canon, are in some ways precursors of the large chorale fantasias of the seventeenth century. The opening of the short "Kyrie penultimum," No. 7d,[3] shows several interesting features of Buchner's style (Ex. 4.7): first, the chant provides the head-motive for all five voices, and second, the short turn-figures provide the primary coloration (something surviving from the music of the previous century). In m. 2 the turns in the bottom two voices seem to answer each other, but they come at different points in their respective points of imitation. Thus, they almost seem to constitute a secondary level of imitation, one that, for a short while, runs obliquely to the fundamental imitation. Two other features seem to anticipate developments in the seventeenth century: sporadic *style brisé* writing ("Osanna in excelsis,"

EXAMPLE 4.7. Hans Buchner, "Kyrie penultimum"

EXAMPLE 4.8. Hans Buchner, "Gloria patri in la quarti toni"

No. 15d) and monodic textures that favor the topmost voice (No. 29, Ex. 4.8).

*   *   *

Three other figures of Buchner's generation—Hans Kotter (c. 1485–1541), Leonhard Kleber (c. 1495–1556), and Fridolin Sicher (1490–1546)—are significant for their compilation of large tablature collections of contemporary keyboard music. The format of Kleber's tablature (finished in 1524) provides an interesting insight into the musical priorities of the time. It is divided into two basic groups, the first comprising music for manuals only, the second music for both manuals and pedals. Kleber obviously was compiling two distinct repertories here, perhaps for domestic and church use; however, other than the obvious expansion of texture afforded by the pedals, the stylistic and generic differences are not great. We can sense a particular function for the preludes, introducing the tone for a set of intabulations or cantus firmus pieces; indeed, the first pieces in the volume are clearly ordered in the sequence ut–re–mi–fa–sol–la. The repertory, somewhat analogous to the Buxheim collection, is strongly tethered to the vocal music of the day, with works by Ockeghem, Josquin, Obrecht, and Isaac. However, there is a significant representation of composers who were concerned specifically with keyboard music, notably Hofhaimer and Buchner. The appearance of a single Protestant piece, "Kum hayliger gaist," must rank as one of the earliest traces of the Lutheran Reformation in keyboard sources.

Kotter's tablatures (prepared for Bonifacius Amerbach, a humanist and lawyer of Basel) contain significant examples of dance music. Several are described as "Spanish"—homophonic pieces in triple time with

EXAMPLE 4.9. Hans Buchner, "Dantz Moss. Benczenauer"

ornamented upper voices and, in some cases, a hemiola structure in the bass. One of these is attributed to Buchner, as is an interesting dance in duple meter ("Dantz Moss. Benczenauer"). The latter is notable not only for its duple meter; it falls into binary form, with each half repeated. The opening gestures of each are similar and return during the course of their respective sections. Although there is no sense of overall tonal unity—the first half is in C, the second in F—each half modulates to the other's "key" in the middle (Ex. 4.9). The piece concludes with what would, later in the century, be termed a "Nachtanz"—the most ostensively dance-like section with short repeated cadential phrases, presumably played at a faster tempo.

The Later Sixteenth-Century Tablatures
Elias Nicolaus Ammerbach (c. 1530–97)
and Bernhard Schmid (1535–92)

The latter half of the sixteenth century represents a curious and somewhat isolated era in German keyboard music. The free forms of the earlier part of the century—particularly the preludes—are all but absent, as are equivalents to those being developed in Italy and Spain (e.g., ricercar, tiento). Like the keyboard music of a century before, the emphasis is on transcriptions of sacred and secular compositions; however, the most striking difference, even from tablatures from the earlier part of the sixteenth century, is the significantly larger body of dance music. Clearly much of the published material was designed for domestic use, and organists in all likelihood continued to improvise preludes within a liturgical context.

Ammerbach, as organist of the Thomaskirche, Leipzig, demonstrates the spread of keyboard culture to central Germany (the majority of the composers earlier in the century were centered around south Germany and Switzerland). Furthermore, his *Orgel oder Instrument Tabulatur* of 1571 (Ill. 4.3) is the first published example of new German organ tablature, a notation employing letter names for the entire texture. This publication was reissued in a revised and expanded form in 1583, and another volume of polyphonic transcriptions was published in 1575. The later publications show considerably less added diminution, suggesting either that the "Coloraturen" were now to be added by the performer, or that there had been a change in fashion (Ex. 4.10).[4] However, if the later tablatures of Schmid, Paix, Löffelholtz, and Nörmiger are representative of the age, the taste for added coloratura continued to grow during the later decades of the sixteenth century. Ammerbach's 1571 edition presents the pieces in order of increasing difficulty, with progressively more diminution, suggesting a specific pedagogical intent that was not so important in the later publications. There are no pedal indications, and none of the music entails the same technical difficulties as the

ILLUSTRATION 4.3. Elias Nicolaus Ammerbach, *Orgel oder Instrument Tabulatur* (Leipzig, 1571), directions for fingering.

EXAMPLE 4.10. Ammerbach, *Tabulaturbuch:* "Petercken sprack tho Petercken"

music from the first half of the century (other than the sheer awkward-ness of much of the part writing; see, for example, the end of m. 3 in Ex. 4.10, 1571 version).

Continuing the tradition established by Buchner, Ammerbach be-gins his *Tabulaturbuch* with a short introduction to the art of the organ. After explaining the notation of the tablature, Ammerbach includes a detailed introduction to fingering. The close similarities to Buchner's system suggest that both authors represent a keyboard practice that ob-tained throughout Germany for much of the century. The only signifi-cant difference is Ammerbach's prescription of consecutive fingers (4–1, repeated as necessary) for ascending scales in the left hand. Rather than give a single polyphonic example for fingering, as Buchner had done, he provides an extensive table of various sequential patterns. Apart from the obvious predilection for paired fingering, Ammerbach shows very clearly how the fingering is to be adapted to the figural pattern involved, the most common of which, predictably, is the turn.

The *Tabulaturbuch* opens with simple homophonic settings of reli-gious songs. Some of the writing is astoundingly crude, which might suggest that Ammerbach was aiming for a specifically domestic, amateur flavor (Ex. 4.11). On the other hand, given that his introduction contains

EXAMPLE 4.11. Ammerbach, *Tabulaturbuch:* "Ehr lob und danck mit hohem fleis" no rules of counterpoint (in contradistinction to Buchner), it is possible that Ammerbach was simply not fully trained as a composer. Within the context of the present study, such an instance may seem a rarity, but this is because modern historical surveys tend to concentrate on the major figures, those whose music has survived the course of several centuries. However, Ammerbach—like some of the compilers of other tablatures in succeeding years—may be more representative of the general level of keyboard performers at the time: someone skilled in execution and embellishment, but minimally adept as a vocational composer.

Of the secular songs, one in particular ("Ein Henlein weis mit grossem fleis") is specifically pictorial, perhaps the earliest in a long line of hen parodies. Of the dances, the most common to be named are the passamezo and saltarello (apparently interchangeable with the galliard). On the whole, these are collected into groups of a single type rather than paired or formatted as "suites." The only regular grouping is that of a duple-meter dance and its closely related "Nachtanz" in triple time. Many of the dances show the same crudity of voice leading evident in the song settings. However, Ammerbach certainly has a taste for piquant cross-relations, even if these are hardly the result of legitimate voice leading (Ex. 4.12). One interesting rubric in the 1583 edition refers to the last repetition of "Ein pollnischer Dantz," which should be played as fast as possible ("Spile Diese letzte *Repetition* uff den kürtzisten tact")— one of the earliest verbal references to a tempo change.

The "domestic" intentions behind Ammerbach's collection are also suggested by some of the headings (notably for the dances), which seem almost designed to entice the consumer: "Ein ander kurtzer Dantz," "Ein ander lustiges Dentzlein," "Ein ander hübscher Dantz." The composers Ammerbach chose (only a few of whom he actually credited) may thus be those who were most fashionable in the latter sixteenth century. Some from the turn of the century (Hofhaimer, Isaac, and Josquin) were still evidently popular, although rather more examples are found for later composers, such as Senfl, Clemens non Papa, and Lassus.

Another major keyboard publication that appeared a few years after Ammerbach's first publication, Bernhard Schmid's two-part *Tabulatur Buch . . . auff Orgeln und Instrumenten zugebrauchen* (Strasbourg, 1577), gives a similar picture of the age. Lassus is by far the most popular

EXAMPLE 4.12. Ammerbach, *Tabulaturbuch:* "Ein ander kurtzer Dantz"

composer of the sacred intabulations that constitute the first part. The second part, containing songs and dances, also includes works by Lassus (with both German and French titles); other significant figures include Ferrabosco (an example of whose work is also found in Ammerbach) and de Rore. Schmid, like Ammerbach, gives optimistically enticing titles to many of his dances. The pairing of dances is rather more pronounced: the "Passomezo" is often followed by "Il suo saltarello" in triple time; pieces of the "Nachtantz" type are often titled "Proportz" (i.e., a triple-time version), "Hupfauff," or "Hopeldantz" (i.e., hopping dance). There are also some more modern dances: the "Alemando novelle. Ein guter neuer Dantz"—an extremely lively piece comprising short repeated phrases with "open" and "closed" endings—and a pair of apparently royal dances, "La volte du roy" and the triple-time "La corante du roy." The latter pair is, incidentally, a rare example of two dances paired to-gether, yet unrelated harmonically or melodically.

Several more tablatures from the latter sixteenth century continue these trends (all the following examples are taken from Merian 1927, which includes an anthology). Jacob Paix's *Orgel Tabulaturbuch*, pub-lished in 1583, includes an interesting introduction informing the pur-chaser that more *Coloratur* can be added by judiciously fingering the holding parts in order to leave one hand free, and that one should not be too concerned with parallel octaves or fifths since these are often un-avoidable in a "fürgearbeit Werck." The collection opens with a section of motets (with a typical bias toward Lassus) arranged for various feasts of the church year, while the latter half is the "secular" section contain-ing "songs," some of which are intabulations of quite complex and highly ornamented madrigals and dances. Among the latter are an inter-esting "Passomezo" and "Saltarello," comprising a sequence of 16-bar variations. To the ever-increasing list of European national dances is an "Ungarescha," a simple mixolydian piece that would not seem out of place in one of Bartók's beginners' albums (Ex. 4.13). Löffelholtz's man-uscript of 1585 (see Merian 1927, 167–95) begins with dances and sacred pieces interspersed. The increase in the number of sacred pieces with German titles is noticeable, something that is also evident in an anony-mous tablature of 1593 (Merian, 196–219). The latter contains a fully worked setting of "Allein Gott in der Höhe sey Ehr" and the incipits to a large number of chorales. One rarity for a source of this provenance is a short binary "Fuga" with a canzona-like subject.

The two remaining significant sources show, respectively, the begin-nings of the Lutheran and Catholic keyboard schools of the seventeenth century. August Nörmiger's manuscript of 1598 (Merian 1927, 220–58) begins with a veritable chorale-book for keyboard, providing elegant harmonizations for each of its 77 chorales. The style and sequence of settings, covering the church's year and ending with chorales for the

EXAMPLE 4.13. Paix, *Tabulaturbuch:* "Ungarescha"

Catechism, the German Mass, Psalms, and other hymns significant in Lutheran practice, is astonishingly similar to J. S. Bach's "Orgelbüchlein" and *Clavierübung* III, written well over a century later. The secular portion includes two apparent suites of contrasting pieces, each entitled "Mummerey Tantz." As organist of the Dresden court, Nörmiger exemplifies the rich development toward the end of the century of music that was specifically Lutheran—the precondition for the greatest flourishing of Lutheran organ music during the coming decades.

With the publication of the *Tabulaturbuch* (see Ill. 4.4) of Bernhard Schmid the younger (Strasbourg, 1607), we see superficially a sequel to his father's publication. However, there is a radical change in repertory—testimony to the tremendous vogue for the "modern" Italian style in Germany at the turn of the seventeenth century.[5] The book opens with works specifically designed for keyboard from the Italian tradition (preludes on the 12 modes and toccatas by Andrea and Giovanni Gabrieli), followed by intabulations of motets and madrigals by "modern" composers such as G. Gabrieli, Hassler, Marenzio, Morello, and de Rore. The collection ends with 12 canzonas, 2 variation passomezi, and 12 galliards—the repertory that remains closest to the earlier German tabulatures. This publication thus marks the watershed between the sixteenth and seventeenth centuries, a period when radically new styles lived side by side with selected earlier idioms. With its inclusion of relatively new "free" keyboard works, it also marks the end of a period of seeming isolation in south Germany and the inauguration of the environment that fostered composers of Froberger's generation.

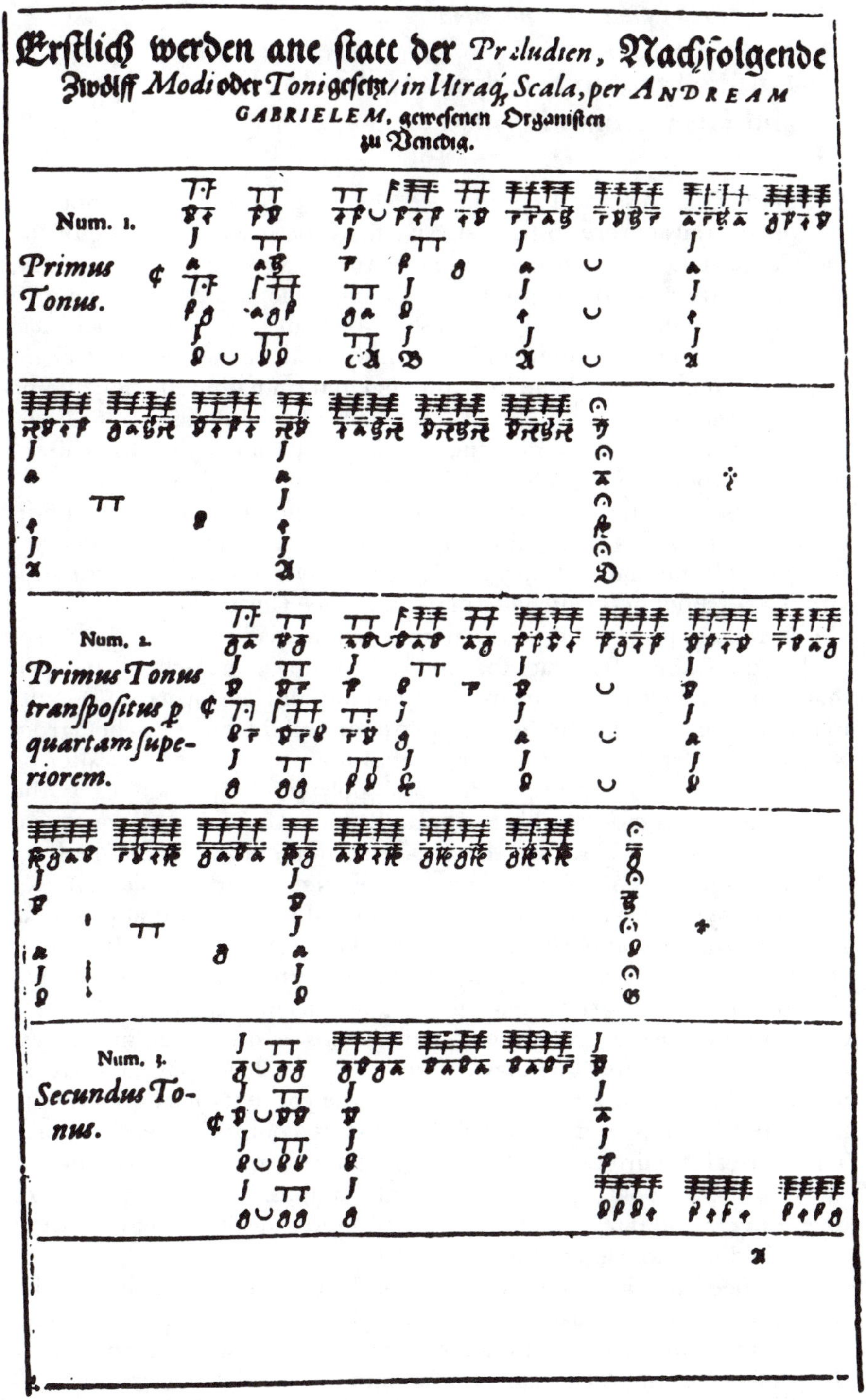

ILLUSTRATION 4.4. Bernhard Schmid, *Tabulatur Buch* (Strasbourg, 1607): opening page of music.

Jan Pieterszoon Sweelinck (1562–1621) and His German Pupils

Sweelinck's historical significance would be assured even if not one note of his music were to have survived. As the teacher of some of the most important German composers of the early seventeenth century, Sweelinck transmitted the glorious tradition of Flemish polyphony into a culture that valued music as both a skilled art and a powerful rhetorical language. While the "Alteration" (the move from Catholicism to Calvinism) of 1578 must have been instrumental in terminating the polyphonic tradition within the Netherlands, Sweelinck's upbringing as a Catholic had ensured him a thorough education in polyphonic style. His achievements as a vocal composer are easily forgotten in the light of the enthusiastic reception of his keyboard music, but his mastery of vocally conditioned polyphony is essential to the quality of all his output. Moreover, he was instrumental in transmitting the motivic idioms of the English virginalist school into Dutch/German usage (see Curtis 1969/87).

It is not merely the German connection that accounts for Sweelinck's significance. The fact that he was a renowned teacher—and primarily in the fields of keyboard composition and performance—points to the pivotal nature of his historical position. All the great teachers from the previous centuries, those composers who were most sought after by their own contemporaries, were vocal polyphonists (Josquin's is the name that comes most readily to mind). But in Sweelinck we have a composer who not only absorbed the vocal tradition but also established the keyboard idiom as a viable pedagogic tool. Not only does this point toward the increasing legitimacy of instrumental music, but it also reflects something of the compositional thinking of the early Baroque. If composition can be taught within keyboard study—rather than as a somewhat abstract polyphonic art—the incipient composer will acquire a different conception of the nature of music. This is most easily sensed in the new convention of the thoroughbass, which condensed polyphonic textures into chordal motion and brought with it the conception of a hierarchy between the lines and between the pitches comprising each chord. There are also more practical and empirical consequences of combining the study of keyboard performance with composition: the capability of one's fingers and one's skill in improvisation will inevitably play a part in the unfolding and elaboration of musical ideas.

We need to sound a note of caution before addressing Sweelinck's surviving keyboard music, since very little is found in Dutch sources close to the composer. What we know of Sweelinck's output is colored by the preferences of his German copyists and pupils, by the works they decided to keep as notated examples of their teacher's skill, and—presumably—by the works he allowed them to copy. While they may not necessarily correspond to what Sweelinck played or even to what he himself valued most highly about his musical achievement, they may nonetheless give us a good idea of what he considered most suitable for those dedicated to learning his art.

The question of improvisation and "what Sweelinck actually played" introduces another consideration relating to Sweelinck's historical significance: the opportunities for performance in the context of the post the composer held for his entire career as organist of the Oude Kerk in Amsterdam. A curious corollary to the Calvinist "Alteration" was the secularization of church property that was turned over to the municipal authorities; although services (the musical component of which was largely unaccompanied psalm singing) were still held on Sundays, the churches were maintained as public, secular buildings. With the incredible success of Amsterdam as a center of commerce and the tremendous advances in Dutch organ building, the daily public recitals by the town organist became an important symbol of municipal pride. While princely courts had employed musicians as status symbols for centuries, the idea of a public musician representing the rising middle classes was quite new. Thus Sweelinck can be seen as one of the major figures in the historical development of the modern concert tradition.

On the other hand, it would be a mistake to categorize Sweelinck as a "modern" musician who viewed music as an autonomous, aesthetically based art. The fact that both Sweelinck's father and his own son held the same position as organist of the same church points to a concept of the musician that is entirely foreign to that of the autonomous genius-musician of later ages. Music was a craft that could be categorized, learned, and studied and, like many other crafts, passed down from one generation to the next.

Frits Noske has made a useful attempt to understand Sweelinck's music in a way that avoids those modern conceptions of musical quality that belittle his achievement (Noske 1988, 121–29). He recommends that we view the music as *forma formans*, "the form forming itself," rather than as "formed form," that which is a fixed aesthetic object. This also enables us to view music as a product of both composition and performance, in which the music is notated as a process in time rather than as a whole standing outside temporal perception. Sweelinck's music, like much music before the eighteenth century, can be thought of as "music in process" (or even "music in progress"), music that could have exploited different directions, combinations, and variations, but that the composer left in a particular state (just as a performer might have made certain interpretative decisions during the course of a single performance).

While it is impossible to do justice here to all the keyboard genres within which Sweelinck worked—the fantasias, the echo fantasias, toccatas, sacred and secular variations—some of the larger fantasias can be viewed as compendiums of compositional techniques found in all these fields of composition. Fantasia No. 4 in the Opera Omnia edition by Leonhardt, Annegarn, and Noske (henceforth L4) is just such an example, one that has not been widely discussed in the existing literature but that contains many of the procedures and details typical of Sweelinck's finest works. Noske observes that many of the fantasias are cast in a tripartite form with the proportions 2:1:1, the first section exploits various contrapuntal combinations with the subject, the second is an exposition of the subject in twofold augmentation, and the third an exposition in twofold diminution (Noske 1988, 86–87). This format is applicable to L4, in which the proportions (in measures) amount to 158:75:72. While this suggests a precompositional idea behind pieces of this kind, there is also a strong sense of spontaneity and invention within the imposed bounds. Indeed, Sweelinck seems to have deliberately obscured some of these divisions in the sounding process of the piece: a distinct break is made in m. 124, where a completely new exposition begins. On the other hand, the "proportional" junction at m. 159 (where the subject begins in twofold augmentation), although heralded by a fast run of thirty-seconds, continues the movement in eighths and sixteenths, which had recently been established in the preceding section (Ex. 4.14a). Furthermore, the introduction of triplet quarters for the first time in m. 217 detracts somewhat from the "proportional" junction at m. 234 (twofold diminution).

One of the factors that contributes to the success of a fantasia of such large proportions is the interest and potential offered by the subject itself. While a "neutral" subject can often engender many contrapuntal possibilities and opportunities for variation (as in the celebrated "Hexachord Fantasia," L5), the subject of L4 has particular potential in its own right (Ex. 4.14b). The first three repeated notes and their dactylic rhythm (long–short–short) imply several generative possibilities: the repetition of pitches is ideal for stretto (first realized in m. 68), and the rhythm establishes a pattern of strong and weak measures, thus generat-

EXAMPLE 4.14a. Sweelinck, Fantasia L4, mm. 156–160

EXAMPLE 4.14b. Sweelinck, Fantasia L4, mm. 1–11

ing a momentum from the start. The sequential movement in minor thirds is the motivic seed of much of the passagework (most notably the second countersubject beginning in m. 35, the *bicinium* beginning in m. 159, and the triplet quarter notes of m. 217) and establishes the concept of sequence as an important means of extending the form.

By far the most interesting aspect of the subject is the chromatic close, which effects the fall back to the initial note a'. The imaginative listener, like the composer, immediately anticipates how this will work in stretto to generate a fully chromatic texture (first fulfilled in mm. 71–72). Indeed, all chromatic notes, with the exception of g sharp, are used several times within the first section (mm. 1–158; this omission makes d the obvious point of rest, the "tonic," rather than a). The chromatic tail is severed from the rest of the subject and sequentially developed in its own right in mm. 264–67, again introducing all the chromatic notes but g sharp. The ear is also drawn to any chromatic material because of its initial association with cadential gestures; thus it is quite striking to hear the subject in a "dechromaticized" form in mm. 101–5 and particularly in mm. 277–92. These two points come after the two sections of most intense chromaticism; clearly they are devised to diffuse the tension, but they also serve to prolong the musical fabric before major cadences (mm. 123–24 and the conclusion of the piece) by removing that marker that is specifically cadential.

Finally, there is the pitch structure of the subject itself. In the first entry the pitch a is sounded in five of the ten notes, which immediately gives the subject a center of gravity, seemingly a point of repose to which the sequential movement and the chromatic tail provide a challenge. All but one of the five remaining notes sound above the a, so that from the start there is a sense of gravity, of falling back to important pitches. That Sweelinck was aware of this upper weighting of the thematic material is immediately evidenced by the beginning of the first countersubject, mm. 7–10, which comprises the five notes *below* the "key" note and the keynote itself (now d″) in ascending scalar order (Ex. 4.14b). It is no accident that it begins on f', the highest point in the subject (in its "answer" position, on d), thus acting as a complement to the subject (ascending, conjunct, and nonchromatic motion, filling in precisely those scalar pitches that are absent from the subject itself). In m. 23 the six ascending notes of this countersubject enter in the bass *before* the subject (soprano), establishing its importance as a theme in its own right, the true counterbalance to the central subject of the piece. (Ex. 4.14c). They are followed by a dactylic rhythmic figure (quarter and two eights, m. 25), which becomes the principal ornamental device for the entire first section and can also be heard as a twofold diminution of the opening rhythm of the subject itself.

Already we can imagine Sweelinck the composer/performer gauging the potential of his subject as an object of research and invention—the term "ricercar," more commonly used in Italian music of this period, seems particularly apt here. The contrapuntal devices, elaborative strategies, and ornamental figuration of his age could be considered a grammatical paradigm to which this particular subject may be applied; the compositional process would thus be a process of trial and error, a calculation of those functions that work with this material and those that do not. If this were thought of as the "science" of composition, the "art" would lie in the ability to construct a syntagmatic chain—a satisfactory sequence of events drawn from the workable functions that sustains the listener's attention and creates some sense of variety and intensification. Finally there is the duality that gives so much Baroque music its potential energy: the interplay of "neutral" contrapuntal necessity and "expressive" rhetorical gesture.

The first section (mm. 1–158) could be thought of as the most formal section of the piece, that is, the area in which the composer experiments with the potential of the subject and its countersubjects. This idea is common to most of Sweelinck's fantasias and plays on the fact that the listener's attention will be most acute at this time; it also establishes a seemingly "neutral" musical discourse against which rhetorical, expressive elaboration can later take place. Nevertheless, these latter features already begin to appear within the first section. The stretto beginning mm. 67–68 is immediately repeated an octave lower. The antiphonal effect is arguably the first rhetorical device in the piece, something that is not necessitated by contrapuntal development but that takes the piece into the realms of human speech and the art of persuasion. This device is essential to Sweelinck's four echo fantasias, although there the repeated passages are much shorter. Sweelinck similarly exploits the ca-

EXAMPLE 4.14c. Sweelinck, Fantasia L4, mm. 23–26

EXAMPLE 4.14d. Sweelinck, Fantasia L4, mm. 81–83

dential leading-tone figures (mm. 82, 95, 100, Ex. 4.14d), which enhance the chromatic intensification at the end of each stretto. While such clashes might happen in traditional Renaissance style, particularly as a result of the application of simultaneous rules of musica ficta, here they become more a rhetorical device, something to be emotionally savored and exploited. There is a certain degree of indulgence in applying the device to successive cadences on d, g, and c.

We begin to have a sense of the "performing" aspects of the piece taking over—the improviser's experimentation with figures of diminution and the display of his dexterity. With the second section and its official topic, "augmentation," we might feel that the augmentation is really a pretext for other things. The bicinium (m. 159) opening the augmentation section begins with another echo device that motivically coheres with earlier events, with the emphasis of the minor third and the dactylic rhythm now heard as an eighth and two sixteenths (Ex. 4.14a, m. 160). The melodic content could also be related to the "ornamental" groppo figures for the cadence of m. 157. One of the most fascinating aspects of a piece of this kind is the way in which these ornamental, apparently secondary, devices suddenly become the topics of discussion; the division between ornament and "primary" musical material becomes deliciously blurred. Contrapuntal devices are not entirely absent, however. Particularly important is the small-scale imitation of short figures, most prominently the upbeat pattern mm. 196–217, with its brief stretto-like contraction in m. 201. However, the imitation is now a factor of "play" rather than research.

After the diminution of the subject in the final section (beginning in m. 234), the piece ends with two statements of the subject restored to its original values (mm. 289–99), with a final countersubject in whole notes. The latter is an ascending passage of five notes that alludes to the ascending nature of the first countersubject. In all, there is a sense of a return to order and to the spirit of the opening expositions. This is quite common in extended keyboard works of this time, and, with the return to polyphony, it might be analogous to the "Amen" section at the end of vocal works.

The various figures of ornamentation and diminution applied by Sweelinck have been examined in detail by Curtis, who reveals the origin of many of these in the repertory of English keyboard music (Curtis 1987, 126–33). Certainly some such figures, notably the "alberti" figures and arpeggiations, do seem indigenous to keyboard music, since they are so aptly designed to fit under the fingers. Other ornamental devices typical of Sweelinck's keyboard music are the repeated notes (m. 181), the arpeggios (mm. 182–84), and the triplet diminution (mm. 193–95). Nowadays there is a tendency to view the "unsingable" elaboration of instrumental music as essentially instrumental and the "pure" *notation* of polyphonic vocal music as archetypically singable. But the preponderance of treatises on vocal diminution in Italian (and later German) sources suggests that virtuosity was often as much as imitation of current vocal practice as the development of a distinct "nonvocal" idiom.[6] Sweelinck's keyboard music thus needs to be seen in the light not only of the Flemish polyphonic tradition (i.e., notated counterpoint) and the English keyboard tradition, but also of some of the vocal ornamental practices of his age.

The question of contemporary performance practices brings us to one further aspect of Sweelinck's activity as composer and performer: the indications of fingering found in several pieces. These include the Echo Fantasia L14 and the toccatas L15, L18, L19, L21, and L22, all of which are found in the same manuscript, the "Lübbenauer Orgeltabulaturen,"[7] dating from approximately two decades after Sweelinck's death, and probably of south German provenance. It is impossible to determine whether the fingering dates back to Sweelinck himself, but this possibility is not to be entirely excluded. Certainly the fingering seems fairly typical of Germanic and English sources from the first half of the century, so we could speculate that it corresponds roughly to Sweelinck's own system.

The first observation concerns the general propensity toward paired fingering of conjunct eights and sixteenths; this could be thought of as a natural extension of the principle of the tactus. The music is based on a hierarchy of strong and weak pulses, which, at the slower levels, is crucial to the preparation and resolution of dissonances. At the quicker levels—where the fingering is most usually found—it governs the conventions of unaccented passing notes and neighbor notes. This *compositional* principle is thus mirrored in the style of performance, just as it is in the necessary conditions of violin bowing, woodwind tonguing, and syllabic singing. This generalization aside, the "Sweelinck" fingerings do tell us one thing about the practice of their scribe: the variability of those fingers that are "good," those that play the strong pulses, and their subdivisions. Although there is a slight bias toward fingers 3 (RH) and 2 (LH), the actual choice of good fingers often seems dependent on context. Furthermore, consecutive fingerings are also a possibility for sixteenths (L14, mm. 115–16 RH; L19, m. 100 LH) and for eights (L18, m. 25 RH—almost a modern fingering [see Ex. 4.15] L19, m. 27). In

EXAMPLE 4.15. Sweelinck, Toccata L18

other words, the "good-bad" hierarchy does not always need to be observed strictly, and some of the faster good notes can be deemphasized, presumably for the sake of flow.

The last important point to draw from the early fingering is its significance for the various ornaments of diminution. In L14, mm. 109–10, the fingering follows the paired neighbor-note figure exactly; especially interesting is the passage in mm. 112–13 in which the fingering consistently follows the offbeat grouping (see Ill. 4.5). This suggests that there is a case for keeping the fingering consistent with each repetition of the figure; L21, mm. 66/69 LH and 67/70 RH, provides a particularly good example of this, where an entire measure is repeated in sequence for each hand, with almost exactly the same fingering (see Ex. 4.16). In some cases the fingering might purposely be changed, for example, L14, mm. 115–16, where the descending pattern is fingered alternately with paired and consecutive fingers, as if to differentiate the second and fourth beats of each measure, but there are few instances in which the fingering is radically different. In other words, the rule might be to keep the fingering consistent, if it is physically convenient.

The fingering of diminution patterns suggests again that their performance is closely related to their compositional role. They add layers of movement over and above the "natural" hierarchy of the meter; sometimes they mirror the meter, sometimes they work against it. Thus they are not automatically blended into the background grammar, and

EXAMPLE 4.16. Sweelinck, Toccata L21

ILLUSTRATION 4.5. Jan Pieterszoon Sweelink, Echo Fantasia (No. 14 in Leonhardt's edition), mm. 110–29. *D-B* MS. Lynar A1, p. 154. Reproduced with permission.

they often serve to constitute discrete planes of sound that work at an angle to the central lines—glittering exceptions that perhaps make the "rules" worthwhile.

Samuel Scheidt (1587–1654) and Heinrich Scheidemann (c. 1595–1663)

It is almost impossible to avoid following a discussion of Sweelinck with a study of his two most important German pupils—those who were perhaps the most significant keyboard composers of their age in eastern and northern Germany respectively. After studying with Sweelinck (c. 1607–8?), Samuel Scheidt spent virtually all his career in Halle, as court organist and later Kapellmeister to the Margrave of Brandenburg and, for a time, as *Director musices* at the Marktkirche (Ill. 4.6). While the latter post was specifically created by the city council, which clearly desired a "modern" municipal director of music, it was closely connected with the long and venerable tradition of the cantorate, an academic school post that carried some musical duties. This situation—a "professional" musician in an "academic" post—led to disastrous conflicts with the Rektor of the Gymnasium, precipitating Scheidt's resignation in 1630. Scheidt's fortunes were continually affected by the Thirty Years' War, and his moves from court to municipal employment and back

ILLUSTRATION 4.6. View of Halle (lithograph by J. Mellinger, c. 1572), showing the Marktkirche with its five towers ("Unser lieben Frawen Pfarkirch") dominating the scene.

again to court life in 1638 show that he was ready to adapt to the musical fortunes of his age. Like Sweelinck, he seems to have eschewed the servile elements of traditional careers in music. Indeed, his publication of *Tabulatura nova* (1624) in the impractical format of open score might be seen as a move toward exemplary, autonomous music, which—as he suggests in the preface—could be transcribed into convenient German tablature for the purposes of performance. Another feature in common with Sweelinck is Scheidt's considerable skill as a vocal composer, which undoubtedly helped to foster the rich polyphony of his keyboard writing. His close association with Michael Praetorius (honorary Kapellmeister for the Margrave until his death in 1619) and Heinrich Schütz must have cultivated his awareness of the most recent Italian idioms, particularly chordal harmony, monody, and textual declamation. In short, with these biographical points in mind, we might expect some of the most spectacular and cosmopolitan music of the age.

Heinrich Scheidemann seems to be a more conservative figure. He studied with Sweelinck for a substantial period (1611–14), and took over his own father's position as organist of the Catharinenkirche in Hamburg. Most of his significant output is music specifically for the organ. While the remarkable breadth of manuscript sources copied in his own age testifies to his contemporary fame as a composer, one would expect his music to be far less progressive than Scheidt's. Scheidemann's reputation today was precipitated in the 1960s by Gustav Fock's discovery of the Zellerfeld organ tablature—a manuscript that contained several hitherto unknown works.[8] Nevertheless, he has often been slighted in much of the modern literature.

Scheidt's *Tabulatura nova* was a landmark in its own time, not least because of the "new" notation, five-line staves rather than organ letter-tablature or the six-line staves common in English and Flemish keyboard sources (see Ill. 4.7). Scheidt's debt to Sweelinck is not difficult to perceive: the rich polyphony and chromatic countersubjects of the "Fantasia à 4 Voc. super Io son ferito lasso" (based on the opening of a madrigal by Palestrina) are immediately reminiscent of Sweelinck's fantasias. Moreover, many pieces follow ideas similar to Sweelinck's: for example, the "Fantasia super ut, re, mi, fa, sol, la" and variation sets on the same secular melodies (e.g., "Est-ce Mars" and "Soll es sein"). There is also a similar attention to detail and unity of material; in "De resurrectione Christi—Hymnus vita sanctorum, decus angelorum" (Book 3), the opening minor third of the hymn becomes the subject of much of the figural imitation during the course of the piece.

If anything, Scheidt develops some of Sweelinck's characteristics to an even greater extent; the six-part pieces with double pedal closing Book 3 present an extremely rich texture, and the canons at the end of Book 1 similarly show a marked interest in the abstract skills of counterpoint. What is especially characteristic of Scheidt's style (and indeed of

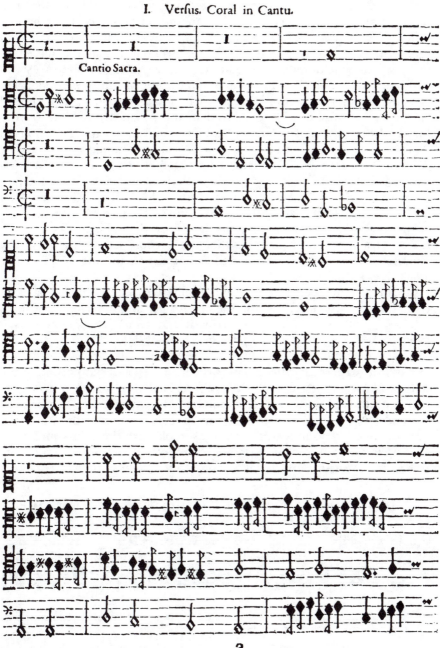

ILLUSTRATION 4.7. Samuel Scheidt, *Tabulatura nova* (1624), opening page of music ("Wir gläuben all an einen Gott").

much subsequent German keyboard music) is his relentless pursuit of ornamental figures. These often give his music much superficial interest, but sometimes he exploits them to a tedious degree (see Ex. 4.17). The sixth variation of the "Passamezzo" is an amusing essay on the *groppo* (a cadential trill, a figure that was very popular in early Baroque Italian music). Dotted rhythm is another device essential to Italian ornamentation,[9] which Scheidt tends to use in most of his pieces in "modern" style.

Many of Scheidt's textures are reminiscent of the newly emerging instrumental sonata genre developed by Italians such as Marini and Castello and most notably displayed in the sonata from Monteverdi's Marian Vespers of 1610. Among Scheidt's most successful emulations of that style are those that seem to imitate a duet between two violins or cornetti: for example, "Vater unser im Himmelreich," verse 7; "Warum betrübst du dich, mein Herz," verse 10. Perhaps the most striking example is the "Echo ad manuale duplex, forte & lene" from Book 2. While the echo idea is somewhat overworked in comparison with Sweelinck's examples, the piece is a virtuoso display of a variety of instrumental gestures. The repeated chords of the first section seem close to Monteverdi's *stile concitato*—that agitated style that was to portray a war-like affect (Ex. 4.18).

Scheidt's interest in exploiting the imitative capacity of keyboard instruments is most clearly exemplified by his use and description of slurs, "Imitatio Violistica" (imitation of string instruments). This device is used extensively for sixteenth-note passages in Books 1 and 2. The fact that the slurs generally cover four notes in the first book and two in the second might suggest that the specific articulation is not as important as the style of playing (but see Kenyon 1989). As Scheidt remarks in his explanation at the end of Book 1, this imitation of string slurring can be used to great effect on light-touched organs, regals, harpsichords, and other instruments.[10] The most interesting examples are those in which slurs are applied only to certain passages within otherwise similar figuration. In the final measures of the toccata on "In te Domine speravi" (Book 2),

EXAMPLE 4.17. Scheidt, "Wir gläuben all an einen Gott," verse 2, mm. 53–58

EXAMPLE 4.18. Scheidt, "Echo ad manuale duplex, forte & lene"

slurs are applied to the repetition of passages, presumably to create an articulative echo—in imitation of separate bows followed by slurred bowing (Ex. 4.19).

The other imitative device that Scheidt employs is the "Bicinium imitating the tremulant of organs with two fingers on one and the same key, in right and left hands"[11] ("Ach du feiner Reiter," variation 5; repeated eighth notes). Presumably such secular variation sets were played more often on harpsichord than on organ, but Scheidt may also have expected performance on the organ. In any case, these repeated-note figures would create an interesting parody of a specific organ mannerism. When it is considered that the organ tremulant was originally designed as an imitation of the human voice, there is an interesting "nested parody" here. Similarly, much of the newly emerging instrumental music of this period was designed to imitate the expression and rhetoric of vocal performance (believed to be the most "authentic" human expression), so Scheidt's keyboard adoption of instrumental idioms takes this process one stage further.

Scheidt's writing has much to commend it: the sparking variation sets with their slick dovetailing of successive variations; the pioneering chorale fantasias (such as "Ich ruf zu dir" from Book 1), which combine fore-imitation, cantus firmus techniques, and figural play; the stricter liturgical settings of Book 3, which show that the "old style" was still flourishing; and finally the sheer virtuosity of the writing, which must be a testimony to the skill of Scheidt as a player, setting his peers and pupils tasks that he doubtlessly discovered with his own fingers. On the other hand, much of the music is rhythmically uninteresting; there is very little of what Curtis describes in his study of Sweelinck (1969/1987)

EXAMPLE 4.19. Scheidt, Toccata on "In te domine speravi"

as "contrametric rhythm"—figures that cut across the metrical divisions. Ornamental figures are often exploited ad nauseum and the interest in some of the longer pieces is barely sustained.

Scheidemann's writing often seems of an altogether different quality. The music can be as fine as Sweelinck's, but it does not stick rigidly to the idioms of the older master; indeed, it shows a highly satisfactory synthesis of the polyphonic integrity of earlier music with newer innovations. Scheidemann left organ works in a wide range of genres, from the succinct "character" elaborations of chorales (e.g., "Herzlich lieb hab ich dich," No. 1/13;[12] "Jesu, wollst uns weisen," No. 1/19; "O Gott, wir danken deiner Güt," No. 1/26—2 verses) to the massive fantasias on "Jesus Christus, unser Heiland" (No. 1/16) and "Wir glauben all an einen Gott" (No. 1/34). The opening of the latter also shows Scheidemann's mastery of the instrumental-duet style so typical of Scheidt. Similarly, the second verse of the Magnificat on the third tone (No. 2/3) can well be compared with Scheidt's "Echo ad manuale duplex" (see p. 178), with its echo effects and *concitato* style. But Scheidemann's example shows a far superior sense of timing, momentum, and variety. Among the free works are several concise preludes, including an excellent essay in chromaticism (No. 3/6), toccatas, and a canzona (No. 3/18) that seems to testify to Scheidemann's knowledge and assimilation of the Italian keyboard style.

Scheidemann's most interesting development is the supremely vocal monodic style he employs at some point in most of his larger chorale settings (and indeed in some of the toccatas, such as No. 3/21). Standing as models for a long and renowned tradition of ornamented organ chorales that stretches well into the second half of the eighteenth century, these examples are patently formulaic. Indeed, the ornamental figures could almost have been derived from an instruction book in diminution. Scheidemann shows his mastery in the way he weaves these together to create lyrical lines that somehow supersede, or at least comment on, the original chorale lines—a sense of "metamelody," perhaps.

The analysis of one extensive piece, the fantasia on "Jesus Christus, unser Heiland" (No. 1/16), will show not only Scheidemann's monodic techniques but also how he integrates several elements to form a work that holds the interest for over 230 measures. Works of this kind in Scheidemann's oeuvre share something of the groundplan of Sweelinck's fantasias: the piece is articulated by various themes or contrapuntal techniques, and each section, particularly the final one, is marked by an intensification of movement or device. In the case of Scheidemann's fantasia, the four lines of the Lutheran chorale provide the themes for the three basic sections (lines two and three, being nearly identical, are combined into a single section). The fourth line is repeated in augmentation in the concluding section, accompanied by echo devices (the background of Sweelinck's fantasias is difficult to ignore here). The proportions of the sections are somewhat looser than Sweelinck's, but each is roughly the same length, lasting 88, 74, and 77 measures, respectively.

Perhaps the most arresting feature of Scheidemann's style is the blending of polyphonic and monodic writing. Each section of the work (i.e., each line of the chorale) begins with an imitative exposition. While there is little of the regular countersubject material that might be encountered in Sweelinck's fantasias, certain gestures, such as the cadential motive in m. 6 (Ex. 4.20), recur frequently. The free voices also "play" more at an early stage in the piece (e.g., mm. 11–18), taking up fragmentary points of imitation. In the opening section the fourth entry (the "subject" beginning on d') is the first solo melodic line, to be played on the *Rückpositiv*—the organ division that is closest to the listener. This entry takes exactly the "correct" number of measures (if compared with the first complete entry of the subject in the tenor, mm. 4–11), but the line is greatly embellished with figures of diminution (Ex. 4.21b). This soprano entry is immediately answered by a similarly embellished entry of the same line in the tenor (Ex. 4.22). Three points are interesting here: first, the diminution follows similar lines but the figuration is completely different; second, the pedal enters with the "answer" in m. 33, as if working in stretto with the figured tenor line; finally, the solo line itself is expanded by a further measure. The ensuing soprano entry (m. 39) is likewise followed by a pedal entry in quasi-stretto, but this time the monody is expanded, and after m. 44 its melody is independent of the framework of the chorale line. From now on the music is a free improvisation that retains the superficial characteristics of imitative and monodic writing. Only in the pedal is the original chorale line retained, but even here it is extended and modified. In the closing measures of the first section the chorale returns as the basis of the monody (mm. 80–87), but the triplet rhythm is new, creating a further metrical level in the piece as a whole.

The actual content of Scheidemann's diminution deserves some comment. The first monodic line (see Ex. 4.21b) follows the rules of diminution manuals quite closely: the diminution always returns to the principal notes, and on the correct beats. Technically, then, its main service is to fill in the gaps between the original notes, just as an improvising singer might have done. However, the figuration seems to develop on its own terms. The opening *tirata*, which fills in the opening fifth of the chorale, generates important scalar passages in mm. 21–22. Moreover, the scalar figuration of m. 22 allows a wonderful expansion of

EXAMPLE 4.20. Scheidemann, "Jesus Christus, unser Heiland"

EXAMPLE 4.21. Scheidemann, "Jesus Christus, unser Heiland"
(a) first line of chorale

(b) embellished solo line

register; a compound melody is generated inside the figuration that spells out the chorale line in both its original register and an octave higher (see arrows above and below the staff in Ex. 4.21b). This sense of registral expansion is taken one step further with the ensuing tenor monody, in which the register of the chorale is expanded an octave on either side (Ex. 4.22). The later monodic entries not only expand the initial length and register dictated by the chorale lines, they ultimately become completely free.

In all, Scheidemann's art is subtle and often elusive. While it is easy to marvel at the contrapuntal ingenuity of Sweelinck's music, since the stricter aspects of imitation and inversion are easily followed, Scheidemann generally avoids regular countersubjects, canonic writing, and inversion of material. He is clearly a child of the "new" Baroque style in which counterpoint seems more a choice of texture than the fundamental fabric of the work. In some ways it is the *illusion* of counterpoint that is important. For instance, the idea of "imitation" is the subject of the final section of "Jesus Christus," the topic rather than the essence of the writing. The texture can switch from imitative writing to chordal monody almost without any noticeable change in sound. Thus the simpler texture of thoroughbass supporting monody works side by side with traditional polyphonic thinking. The success of this music might lie in its multiple dimensions: polyphony, instrumental small-scale imitation and

EXAMPLE 4.22. Scheidemann, "Jesus Christus, unser Heiland"

echo techniques, ornamental monody, and cantus firmus setting work together to form a highly ingenious musical discourse. Just as the polyphony effortlessly merges into soloistic monody, so do the lines of the chorale provide at one moment a strict basis for the material and length of the lines, but at the next merely the starting point for free elaboration and extension.

The Mid-Seventeenth Century
The Influential Froberger (1616–67)

If many recent writers conclude that the influence and historical significance of Johann Jacob Froberger are even more important than his actual music, such an opinion is a backhanded compliment only in light of modern notions of original musical genius. For Froberger's art in some ways established a new conception of notated music in seventeenth-century Germany and Austria. As one of the most cosmopolitan composers of the age, he rapidly became familiar with the diverse styles of Italy, northern Europe, and France, and with his assimilation and synthesis of all these genres he demonstrated a new sense of stylistic criticism. One may almost feel that he wrote music at one remove from his elder (and at least one younger) contemporaries—music about other musics.

It was this very trait that made him especially significant during the last decade of the century, when the majority of the early publications of his music appeared (posthumously). For in this period the general musical consciousness caught up, as it were, with Froberger's outlook. National traits were now widely discussed and disputed, and German composers often saw themselves as synthesizing the finest aspects of the seemingly opposed Italian and French styles. It is no accident that the High Baroque German composers of the early eighteenth century used keyboard genres that are central to Froberger's oeuvre: toccatas, free fugues, fugues in ancient style, and dance suites. Froberger's approach to composition can also be seen as quintessentially German; contrapuntal thinking underlies even the most informal of textures, and motives are tightly organized into a foreground layer of contrapuntal argument.

Froberger's cosmopolitan nature also renders the traditional division of German keyboard music into north and south (and therefore, roughly, Protestant and Catholic) somewhat lame. He was born in Stuttgart of a family from Halle, spending much of his life in the court at Vienna and traveling widely to Italy, France, the Spanish Netherlands, and England. As a Catholic convert, Froberger wrote music distinguished from that of his more northern contemporaries by its complete lack of Protestant components—most notably the Lutheran chorale. However, with the exception of his two toccatas *alla levatione,* his music does not relate directly to the Catholic liturgy either. Furthermore, though the suites obviously belong to the harpsichord repertory, much of his music seems equally suited to organ and stringed keyboard instruments. If, nevertheless, the unmeasured preludes of Louis Couperin really do reflect the performance of some of Froberger's toccatas (by which they are said to be strongly influenced), the harpsichord would seem more suited to these works as well.[13]

It is fortunate that nearly half of Froberger's surviving works are preserved in three autograph manuscripts—the first two dedicated to Ferdinand III (1649 and 1656), the remaining one to Ferdinand's successor, Leopold I (c. 1658). The recent publication of these three presentation manuscripts, together with two prints from the 1690s, in facsimile with excellent commentaries, has rendered Froberger's character much more accessible (SCKM, 3 and 4). The composer shows an inclination to group works by genre, as if to give an exhaustive anthology of each (a practice he probably inherited from Frescobaldi). Each of the first two volumes contains six toccatas, fantasias or ricercars, canzonas or capriccios, and suites, while the third (a much less lavish production) presents only capriccios and ricercars.

Especially striking is Froberger's use of different notations for each style, which underlines both the stylistic (and, to a certain extent, national) differences and the playing techniques involved. As Robert Hill has remarked in his introduction to the facsimile edition (SCKM, 3), the Italian notation for the toccatas (six lines for the upper staff, RH, and seven for the lower, LH) gives very precise instructions as to which hand plays which notes; this generates a specific style of fingering and articulation (Ill. 4.8). The polyphonic pieces, like Scheidt's *Tabulatura nova,* are notated in open score, which, although requiring developed score-reading ability, ensures that the player internalizes the independence of the voices (Ill. 4.9). Finally, the suites employ French notation (the two five-line staves that subsequently became standard for keyboard music), and here there is no precise direction as to which hand plays which notes (Ill. 4.10). This is perhaps well suited to the rather free part writing of the French style, strongly influenced as it is by lute performance and composition. An all-too-precise style of performance would counteract the intentional ambiguity of the inner voices.

Froberger's ricercars are easily compared with the stricter fantasias of the north German and Dutch schools, pointing to the ubiquity of the *prima prattica,* or at least various seventeenth-century interpretations of it, throughout the Germanic lands. The toccatas, on the other hand, show the absorption of later, more improvisatory Italian styles developed by Merulo, Frescobaldi, and Rossi. While Froberger's debt to his teacher, Frescobaldi, is obvious, Apel was the first modern scholar to note the even closer resemblance to Froberger's Roman colleague Michelangelo Rossi. This newer type of toccata is less rhapsodic, with

ILLUSTRATION 4.8. Johann Jacob Froberger, Toccata opening 1649 collection.
A-Wn, Mus. Hs. 18706, f. 3. Reproduced with permission.

ILLUSTRATION 4.9. Johann Jacob Froberger, Fantasia from the 1649 collection.
A-Wn, Mus. Hs. 18706, f. 22. Reproduced with permission.

ILLUSTRATION 4.10. Johann Jacob Froberger, Allemande from the 1649 collection. *A-Wn*, Mus. Hs. 18706, f. 84. Reproduced with permission.

fewer sections and an alternation of free and fugal sections (Apel 1972, 552). As Buelow has observed, the toccatas that come closest to Frescobaldi are the two elevation toccatas ("da sonarsi alla Levatione"), with their daring and unpredictable shifts of texture and harmony (Buelow 1985, 162).

If Froberger's notated toccatas sometimes appear to lack the flair of their Italian precedents, we must always remember his reputation as an extremely spontaneous and expressive player. According to the patroness of his last years, Princess Sibylla of Württemburg-Montbéliard, no players could interpret his music well if they had not heard the master himself.[14] The radically different, unmeasured notation of Louis Couperin's preludes should also be borne in mind (see p. 128). But like much German music of the Baroque, the notated toccatas show the composer's skill in unifying diverse ideas on paper, an activity that he may have relished independent of immediate performance considerations.

While preserving the distinction between "free improvisatory" and fugal sections, Froberger delighted in blurring some of their respective characteristics. One striking example is the sixth toccata from the 1656 autograph: in the opening section the ornamental flourish in m. 4 is subjected to imitation in the following measure; the first fugal section begins in m. 10, but the figuration matches that which went before so closely that it is some time before the listener is aware of the junction. The merging of the ornamental and the thematic is especially acute in the move from

EXAMPLE 4.23. Froberger, Toccata 6, *Libro quarto* (1656)

"improvisation" to fugal writing in mm. 27–28: the ornamental dactyl
that ends one section becomes the principal motive of the next (Ex. 4.23).

A brief analysis of Toccata 4 from the 1649 autograph may elucidate
some of the typical features of Froberger's compositional method. The
first eight measures (numbered according to Schott's edition of the
Oeuvres complètes, which contains twice as many measures as the autograph) present a simple chordal frame that moves from C to the dominant of D minor. Virtually every measure is adorned with some form of
imitation of the "free" ornamental gesture in m. 2 (Ex. 4.24a), a texture
that could perhaps elusively be described as "imitative homophony."
The remainder of the opening "improvisatory" section, mm. 9–16,
moves back to the tonic, with a faster and more regular harmonic
rhythm. The imitation, too, is quicker and more exact, occurring on
every half measure (or rather every quarter measure in the original).
Thus, the imitation (based again on the opening motive) sounds more
formal and could indeed be mistaken for a fugal section (Ex. 4.24b).
However, the unaccompanied entry of a new and apparently unrelated
theme in m. 17 signifies the first "official" fugal section (Ex. 4.24c),
which merges back into free style for the cadence of mm. 28–30 (the
upward-rising fourth in the tenor recalling the opening gesture). The
next section typically displays the fugal theme in compound meter
(Ex. 4.24d), which is again arrested by two measures of free cadential
material (mm. 43–44).

The closing section draws together many of the ideas in the piece.
This begins in m. 45 with a further elaboration of the fugal theme, now
passed from voice to voice and accompanied by quarter-note motion (Ex.
4.2e). This is not only a return to the "imitative homophony" of the opening "improvisatory" section, but the upbeat rhythm (*suspirans,* in the terminology of Wolfgang Caspar Printz; see n. 19) is a direct allusion to the
ornamental theme heard at the outset of the piece (m. 2). Thus here we
have the ultimate synthesis both of the improvisatory and fugal textures,
and of the themes that mark each of these sections. The last five measures
of the piece introduce continuous, linear sixteenth-note figuration—a direct outgrowth of the preceding imitations that, in effect, produce continuous sixteenth notes. Descending fourths recall a further feature of the
opening figuration, and the final cadence, with its characteristic twist to

EXAMPLE 4.24. Froberger, Toccata 4, *Libro secondo* (1649)

(a)

(b)

(c)

(d)

(e)

the minor, mirrors the ending of the first "improvisatory" section (m. 16). In all, then, the piece displays something of an arch-shaped symmetry, coupled with a sense of progressive development: the improvisatory material is steadily rationalized, the fugal themes are researched in progressively smaller note values, and finally, the opposition between the two basic components—improvisatory and fugal—is resolved.

Froberger's suites have often caused much excitement in the history books. While his French contemporaries Chambonnières and Louis Couperin generally collected dance pieces first of all by tonality, Froberger (together with his contemporary Kindermann) grouped them into suites. This may mark a move toward a typically Germanic sense of abstraction, where each suite profiles the generic differences of popular dances while unifying them by key. Several provisos are necessary here. Froberger apparently did not invent the standard eighteenth-century grouping of allemande–courante–sarabande–gigue. While this is evident in the Amsterdam publication, *10 Suittes de Clavessin,* of 1698/1710, Mortier's pirated edition of 1710 adds the title "Mis en Meilleur ordre," presumably to show that the dances have been grouped with contemporary tastes in mind.[15] Froberger's own collections of 1649 and 1656 present the dances in the order allemand–courante–sarabande (with a gigue at the end of suite 2) and allemande–gigue–courante–sarabande, respectively. Furthermore, although the dances clearly fall into suites, Froberger does not draw attention to this in his autograph; he merely provides titles for each successive dance (as was common practice for seventeenth-century keyboard suites).

Froberger's dances are generally fuller-voiced than those of Chambonnières, particularly the allemandes, which seem the most abstracted from the original dance function. Although the harmonic rhythm is often regular, the phrase lengths are frequently unpredictable and the meter is obscure. It is almost as if Froberger has taken something of the improvisatory toccata style of his Italian models and transformed it into a French *style brisé*. This lute-derived style undoubtedly appealed to a composer with an interest in contrapuntal subtlety: a chord can be spread to sound both like a single arpeggiated voice and like several voices sounding in turn. It was from this technique that much of the idea of compound melody—so important in High Baroque German music—was born (Ex. 4.25). The gigues similarly offer much contrapuntal opportunity, being a forum for fugal texture (not unlike the canzona), but integrated into a binary form.

Froberger's toccatas have often been associated with the unmeasured preludes of Louis Couperin (see p. 128). A similar association can be made for some of the dance movements. Certain pieces may indeed have provided models for the younger French composer, for example, the allemande and courante from the fourth suite and the sarabande of the fifth suite of the 1649 collection (see Nos. 82, 84, and 87 in the Louis Couperin edition cited in note 12). Couperin used the prevailing four-part texture of Froberger, but wrote pieces that were even more sumptuous and contrapuntally developed. Their added ornamentation (both in notation and symbols) may provide a clue toward Froberger's own performance of his suites, as is the case with the unmeasured notation of the preludes.

Froberger's interest in the abstract compositional potentials of the

EXAMPLE 4.25. Froberger, Allemand, Suite 4, *Libro secondo* (1649)

allemande relates to one further aspect of his achievement: character pieces with descriptive titles, most of which take the place of the allemandes in his suites. Here we have pieces that portray a specific affect (generally laments) and also contain symbolic gestures. The laments for both Ferdinand III and IV end with ascending passages that represent the respective monarch's soul ascending to heaven; almost by compensation, the lament for M. Blancrocher ends with a depiction of the hapless victim falling down the stairs. While these works represent the beginnings of this genre within German keyboard music,[16] they seem to be symptomatic of a wider movement, particularly in the Austrian capital. Johann Heinrich Schmelzer wrote a famous lament for strings on the death of Ferdinand III, and Biber's pictorial and symbolic violin music ranks among the most vivid instrumental music of the seventeenth century.

One of the most significant Viennese keyboard composers of the next generation, the Italian immigrant Alessandro Poglietti (d. 1683), took the trend almost to an extreme, and was perhaps the first to refer to the pictorial genre in a pedagogical treatise. Among his many programmatic works is the collection of pieces depicting the events of a revolution in Hungary in 1671, one of the first of the genre to contain a protracted narrative element. In 1677 he presented a cycle of pieces to Emperor Leopold I, "Rossignolo" ("The Nightingale"), which not only contains examples of a toccata, canzona, and dance movements, but also an "Aria Allemagna" with variations imitating a plethora of national habits and musical instruments. Like Froberger, he also showed an intense interest in "pure" contrapuntal composition, as exemplified in his significant manuscript treatise of 1676 on keyboard performance and composition.

North German Figures of the Midcentury
FRANZ TUNDER (1614–67), MATTHIAS WECKMANN (C. 1616–74), AND JOHANN ADAM REINCKEN (1623–1722)

Although none of the north German composers of the midcentury was as well traveled as Froberger, they were all exposed to the latest Italian works and performers. Franz Tunder first encountered Italian music though his teacher, Johann Heckelauer, and may have met Frescobaldi during his youth (NG 1980, 19: 253–54). As organist of the Marienkirche in Lübeck his responsibilities included not only playing the organ for the liturgy but also presenting evening concerts at certain times of year ("Abendmusiken"). As "Werckmeister"—church accountant and general administrator—he rose above the social position generally held by an organist; in many ways he rivaled the cantor, who was traditionally responsible for the concerted music during services. The "Abendmusiken," standing outside official church services, became an important environment for newer, perhaps even experimental, music and works written specifically for concert performance.

Tunder's vocal works show the strong influence of all the latest German and Italian styles; indeed, one of his works is an arrangement of a motet by Rovetta. What comes as a surprise is that his organ music is considerably more conservative in style, preserving much of the idiom and texture of Scheidemann's music. Here, then, we see a division in style between keyboard and ensemble music (defining categories of style was, after all, a particularly popular pastime among German compositional theorists). Although much of what was notated of Tunder's organ music was doubtless prepared for concert (rather than liturgical) performance, it does seem that Tunder saw his role as an organist as tradition bound, while as a composer of texted music he could afford to be more up-to-date. Historical narratives often give the impression that past ages developed their arts in an even, linear path of evolution. But much of the Baroque period seems to be characterized by the survival of older and newer styles side by side, with apparently equal status. What counted was the appropriateness of each work for the specific function for which it was intended; not all such functions demanded music of the most progressive kind.

Nevertheless, it would be a mistake to see Tunder's preludes as a mere facsimile of Scheidemann's works. They also take something from the loose-limbed form of the Frescobaldi/Froberger toccata, with the freer sections standing on either side of fugal material. In this respect Tunder is an important link between the south European toccata tradition and the monolithic preludes of Buxtehude. On the whole, though, Tunder's preludes lack the pungency and subtle textures of Froberger, and his single surviving canzona is one of the lamest examples of the genre.

It is Tunder's large chorale fantasias that have brought him most renown. They take over much of the vocally inspired monodic style of Scheidemann, and echo effects (so beloved in the Sweelinck school) are employed to an almost unprecedented degree (see especially "Christ lag in Todesbanden"). In all, though, the pieces lack much of the carefully paced intensification of Sweelinck or Scheidemann. They verge on being autonomous essays (i.e., with little close affective relationship with the chorale texts) on many of the common figures in organ music of the age—a play of musical signs, some melancholy, some extroverted, that originated in the texted dramatic music of the early Baroque.

Matthias Weckmann is one of the most fascinating, but also most frustrating composers active during the mid-seventeenth century. He is fascinating on account of the number of important figures with whom he was closely associated; educated in Dresden and Hamburg, he studied with Schütz, Kittel, and J. Praetorius (a Sweelinck pupil) and also had contact with Scheidemann. In 1655 he took over as organist at the Jacobikirche and in 1660 formed an exceedingly influential *Collegium musicum*. Despite a celebrated musical duel between Weckmann and Froberger, the two became close friends and Weckmann was instrumental in introducing elements of Froberger's toccata and suite style to north Germany. He also learned something of Froberger's style of playing, since the latter sent him a copy of a suite with all the ornaments included (according to Mattheson). Another close friend and associate was the important composer/theorist Christoph Bernhard, who also worked in both Dresden and Hamburg.

The frustrations surrounding Weckmann concern the authenticity of his music. While some late-nineteenth-century scholars credited him with an enormous body of keyboard works, several musicologists of the 1960s dismissed a large proportion of these works both on stylistic grounds and on doubts concerning the authenticity of some of the sources. More recently, a careful reexamination of the manuscripts (Silbiger 1989), new editions of the free keyboard works and a scholarly recording of the complete organ works (see the Guide to Literature and Editions, p. 221) have suggested restoration of many of these works to the Weckmann canon. The history and the ideologies behind these disputes are interesting in themselves, not least the alternating desires to "purify" and "expand" the oeuvre of an important figure. It is certainly not to be disputed that Weckmann is a composer of the utmost talent and versatility. Nevertheless, we should guard against treating each composer of this era as an isolated, identifiable genius; much of the music is generic, written for traditional functions, and not necessarily designed to flaunt the talents of a single composer.

Weckmann's chorale-based works are traditional in style, concerned with the cantus firmus form developed by Scheidt rather than the more "modern" chorale-fantasia forms of Scheidemann and Tunder. The free keyboard works mark an important development of the *stylus phantasticus,* that dramatic idiom most commonly associated with the preludes of Buxtehude. The "Praeambulum Primi toni a.5" in D (No. 1),[17] with its opening free section and its two related fugal passages, has much in common with the toccatas of Froberger, although its compass is greatly enhanced by the versatile pedal division of the north German organ. The *manualiter* toccatas (for harpsichord?) can also be compared with Froberger's; Nos. 4 and 7 and (to a lesser extent) No. 8 contain passages of fast sequential chords, early examples of the circle-of-fifths harmonic sequences so prevalent in the closing years of the seventeenth century (Ex. 4.26). No. 8 has the distinction of being one of Weckmann's wildest works, containing perhaps more changes of mood, style, and figuration in a short space of time than any other German work of its kind.[18]

One of the most interesting figures of the entire Baroque era is the near-centenarian Johann Adam Reincken. He was acquainted with both Scheidemann and Bach. Like many of the great organists of the German Baroque, Reincken hardly confined his musical activities to the organ loft of St. Catharine's church in Hamburg; indeed, he was instrumental in the founding of the celebrated Hamburg opera in 1678, and his instrumental suites show his close relationship with the burgeoning *collegium musicum* tradition. Thus, he would have been continually exposed to the most fashionable music in German culture. His remarkably small surviving output suggests that he had close links with the Froberger school (e.g., his keyboard suites and his variations on the "Mayerin" theme, used by Froberger).

Reincken's most celebrated work, the enormous fantasia on "An Wasserflüssen Babylon," can hardly be ignored; virtually no other keyboard piece from the mid-seventeenth century provides such a compendium of all the styles, techniques, and figurations available to a German composer of the time. The suave chorale style of Scheidemann is alloyed with the quicksilver dramatic movement of the sacred concerto and opera. As with Tunder, the virtuosity of the player takes precedence over the affective connotations of the text; indeed, we can see this writing as evidence of yet another development of Sweelinck's concert tradition.

Reincken's compositional (or perhaps improvisational) procedure is to introduce a new technique, or series of techniques, with each line of the chorale melody; in this sense the piece has something in common with variation forms, although, of course, the "theme" changes with each variation. The latter half of the piece contains the most extreme contrasts and the fastest note values, but beyond this Reincken does not seem to have been concerned with a large-scale formal architecture.

The opening lines of the chorale are treated in Scheidemann's monodic manner, providing a compendium of the contrapuntal and imitative idioms of the age, from the rich polyphony of the motet (with a delineation of the uppermost line) to free fugal and duet textures. Next

EXAMPLE 4.26. Weckmann, Toccata in D

(from m. 137) Reincken turns to a play of short figures—those melodic and rhythmic motives that so often provide the basic building blocks of Baroque music. Indeed, within the space of one chorale line, Reincken often provides what could almost be a tailor-made example for the figural theories of Printz and Bernhard.[19]

Two more important points can be drawn from a study of "An Wasserflüssen Babylon." First, there is the generation of extraordinary harmonic sonorities by following through the linear movement of the voices (mm. 222–24; see Ex. 4.27a). This sort of experimentation is relatively common in Spanish and English music of the mid-seventeenth century but is unusual in German music. Second, there is the influence of operatic idioms, most notably recitative style and sudden changes of character. This occurs most prominently in the penultimate line of the chorale, especially mm. 264–91. Initially there are contrasts between a measure of scalar motion that sounds almost like a short instrumental ritornello and three measures of expressive monody (mm. 264, 268; see Ex. 4.27b). Then this "ritornello" passage is alternated with what sounds

EXAMPLE 4.27a. Reincken, "An Wasserflüssen Babylon," mm. 222–24

EXAMPLE 4.27b. Reincken, "An Wasserflüssen Babylon," mm. 264–69

EXAMPLE 4.28. Reincken, Suite in C, Sarabande

like the fragments of a dance in triple time (mm. 272–80). Finally we have what could be a sequence of rhetorical questions (mm. 281–84), followed by a virtuosic scalar passage, culminating in an extravagant trill (mm. 285–91). The scalar passage, which is essential to both the opening "ritornello" and the concluding coloratura passage, could be considered the subject of an oration—something that could be explained by the rules of rhetoric, so beloved by certain German theorists. This section could be explained equally well as an operatic narrative following the contrasts of event, character, or thought.

Reincken's "secular" music (presumably mostly for harpsichord) has been somewhat slighted in existing literature. The recent publication of a new edition by Klaus Beckmann has not only served to remind us of the existence of these pieces, but also has uncovered some hitherto unknown works in the form of five more suites.[20] Although the surviving sources give little clue as to the dating of these works (a particularly difficult task in the case of a life span such as Reincken's), all the suites, as transmitted by the extant sources, follow the standard Baroque sequence of allemande-courante-sarabande-gigue. A comparatively late date of composition may be implied by the close relationship between the allemande and courante of each suite.

Style brisé is a particularly prominent element in Reincken's suites. Indeed, the sarabandes often consist entirely of broken chords where the occasional stepwise passing note helps to provide the hint of a melody (C-major suite, Beckmann 3; see Ex. 4.28). The most developed movements are the gigues, which are usually on a larger scale than Froberger's; sometimes there might be a witty inversion of the subject in the second half (C-major suite; see Ex. 4.29), and although little room is left for episodic contrast,[21] the sequential elements of subjects are often extended beyond their original length.

EXAMPLE 4.29. Reincken, Suite in C, Gigue

The Later Seventeenth Century
Dietrich Buxtehude (c. 1637–1707)

The task of surveying Buxtehude's keyboard music in a study of this kind is daunting. Of all the German composers concerned, Buxtehude has been most accepted as a precursor of the "common practice" repertory. The work of nineteenth-century Bach scholar Philipp Spitta profiled Buxtehude as the most important influence on Bach's organ music, and certain preludes have become standard works in the organist's repertory. No other composer in this survey has been so extensively studied, and the comprehensive life-and-works study by Kerala Snyder (1987) all but renders a further study (at least of the keyboard works) redundant. Furthermore, given Buxtehude's proximity—indeed, his contribution—to the early stages of "common practice" tonality, his music has been the object of developed forms of both historical and theoretical analysis.

Buxtehude's career as organist of the Marienkirche in Lübeck follows directly on that of Tunder. With the responsibilities as *Werckmeister* in addition to organist (see p. 191), Buxtehude was the most prestigious and highly paid musician in the city. He combined the traditional and progressive roles of the musician (both trends having been evident throughout the course of this chapter): as an organist he was the traditional servant of the liturgy, but his renowned "Abendmusiken," financed by the business community, rendered him a more autonomous composer, writing for the musical marketplace. The organ preludes perhaps come somewhere between these two functions—music that may literally have been created as an interface between the Vesper service and the Abendmusik.

His friendship with the Hamburg circle of musicians, notably Reincken and Theile, meant that he was in close contact with the most progressive forms of north German musical life and thought (see Ill. 4.11). His acquaintance with Weckmann must have been an important link with south German music, in particular the work of Froberger (Snyder 1987, 246). The close attention given to his organ music since the nineteenth century has somewhat eclipsed his other compositional achievements, but his sacred works and the published (and manuscript) collections of sonatas rank among the highest achievements in the whole of seventeenth-century music.

One work is sufficiently compact and adventurous to serve as a model example of Buxtehude's free style: the Praeludium in F-sharp Minor, BuxWV 146. Here we see a further development of the Froberger toccata model, with more strongly profiled distinctions between fugal and free sections. Among the many approaches that seem appropriate for this kind of work, perhaps the most obvious involves a consideration of the *stylus phantasticus*. Snyder has eloquently shown that

ILLUSTRATION 4.11. Johannes Voorhout, "Domestic Music Scene," Hamburg 1674 (Hamburg, Museum für Hamburgische Geschichte; reproduced with permission). The painting shows Johann Adam Reincken at the harpsichord, together with Dietrich Buxtehude (with music on his lap) and, probably, Johann Theile to the left, playing the gamba.

this term is slightly problematic. As coined by the polymath Athanasius Kircher (and thus directly applicable to the music of his close acquaintance Froberger), it seems to refer to highly developed contrapuntal writing that demonstrates the skill and "freedom" of the composer. Mattheson's definition, drawing on Kircher's, slants it much more toward the concept of fantasy, the unexpected, and the bizarre. In a consideration of BuxWV 146, a work that sits squarely between the ages of Kircher and Mattheson, it may be productive to see both definitions of the *stylus phantasticus* at work. The two central fugues show Buxtehude's complete mastery of "modern" counterpoint; the regular countersubject of the first fugue is largely invertible, and the outlines of a second countersubject are even evident. The countersubject of the second fugue is designed to dovetail with the subject, thus generating an uninterrupted play on the neighbor-note *suspirans* figure (B in Ex. 4.30a); before long this motive is all that remains of the subject, like the lingering smile of Lewis Carroll's Cheshire cat.

Turning now to the "fantastic" aspect of the *stylus phantasticus*, it is possible to isolate two elements. First there is a notion of the improvisation and bravura of the performer. We may easily imagine a performer spontaneously creating the opening statement (Ex. 4.30b) and

EXAMPLE 4.30. Buxtehude, Praeludium in F-sharp Minor, BuxWV 146
(a)

(b)

the recitative section following on from the fugues. Nevertheless, the tonal direction of the piece and its remarkable cohesion suggest the work of a "modern" composer—one who sees the notated work as a rounded whole, complete in itself. The player's perspective (i.e., the "free" virtuoso improvisor) is assimilated to some degree within the notation. Another obvious element is the influence of Baroque dramatic music, particularly the rhetoric of the recitative and the more mercurial sacred concertos.

One further way of viewing the piece—which can, to some degree, integrate several approaches—is to attempt an analysis along the lines of the structure of classical rhetoric. Much has been written on the application of rhetorical principles to German music of the Baroque; many theorists concerned themselves with these issues in an age when music was so often conceived as an art of persuasion. On the other hand, few significant composers mentioned their reliance on rhetorical principles, and although most would have studied rhetoric at school, it is by no means certain that they would have learned composition according to its principles.[22] Thus, the following analysis is undertaken in the belief that rhetorical thinking was part of the flavor of Buxtehude's age, although not a hard and fast recipe; it may legitimately be used as a method of analysis provided it is not taken to reflect a putative creative process.

Different theorists give different versions of the list of headings constituting an oration; the following list represents the most common titles (drawn, as they are, from the conventions of classical rhetoric).[23]

| *Exordium* | The introduction to the oration, designed to prepare the listener for what is to come: mm. 1–13, the basic introduction and survey of the tonic and the introduction of figure A as the motivic basis of much of the piece |

Narratio	The recapitulation of previously known facts: mm. 14–29, another approach to the definition of F-sharp minor, with a concise survey of the chordal areas available within its ambitus (similar circle-of-fifths movement is used later in the piece, but generally in much slower motion)
Propositio	The central thesis of the oration: mm. 29–50, the first fugue, with its contrapuntal discussion, providing the weightiest argumentation of the piece
Confirmatio	A reworking and confirmation of the central thesis: mm. 50–78, a reworking of the fugal theme and the introduction of the new "issue," figure B; increasingly daring modulations, but always returning to the tonic
Confutatio	A survey of opposing and erroneous views: mm. 78–90, the freest section, largely devoid of either figure A or B, the widest and, in terms of temperament, wildest departure from the tonic. Buxtehude the orator turns his point to his advantage, though, since the G-sharp minor leads directly to the dominant chord of the tonic
Conclusio/Peroratio	The satisfactory conclusion of the argument: mm. 91–129, the final confirmation of F-sharp minor, the integration of figures A and B. Return to the idiom of both the *Exordium* (e.g., mm. 111–113) and the *Narratio* (e.g., the circle-of-fifths mm. 96–99)

Among the remaining free organ works of Buxtehude, the three ostinato works deserve special mention (the Passacaglia in D Minor, BuxWV 161, and the two ciacconas in C Minor and E Minor, BuxWV 159 and 160). The ostinato form, like the praeludium, derived from the south German tradition, and thus represents a new direction in north German organ music. We should also not forget the remarkable ostinato movements in Buxtehude's sonatas for violin and viola da gamba, such as that opening the sonata in B flat, BuxWV 255. There was doubtless much mutual influence between these and the works for organ, although the latter are exclusively triple-time dances with bass themes moving from tonic to dominant.

Evidently these works cannot explore the ambitus of the tonic to the same degree as the praeludia; contrasts and overall shaping are generally achieved with a subtle pacing of the variations. Only the Passacaglia in D Minor admits modulation, wherein the two central sections present the theme in F major (the relative major) and in A minor (the dominant). In all, this is an extremely symmetrical work, with seven variations to every key area (between each of which there is a short modulatory transition). Buxtehude's approach to varying the figuration throughout the Passacaglia is subtle, breaking away from the standard practice of introducing a new figuration for each variation. Indeed, in passages such as mm. 45–50, the figurations completely overlap with the underlying repetitions of the ground, yielding no clue to their presence. Thus there is a sense of overall direction that transcends the events of each successive variation.

Snyder's study of Buxtehude's chorale fantasias shows them to be among the most remarkable pieces of their genres, works that exploit the expressive potential of multiple manuals (Snyder 1987, 259–66). In this respect, fantasias such as "Nun freut euch, lieben Christen gmein," BuxWV 210, and the "Te Deum laudamus," BuxWV 218, make little sense outside their original performing environment of the Baroque organ. Only in the twentieth century have composers consistently considered instrumentation and timbre to be as essential to the musical work as melody, harmony, and rhythm, but here we see an essential point that is often overlooked in earlier music. The original instruments not only give us a clue as to how the music can be performed today, they also give us not a little insight into how the work came to be created in the first place.

In their synthesis of the chorale fantasia with the *stylus phantasticus*, Buxtehude's extensive chorale works lie in the same tradition as Reincken's great fantasias. After Buxtehude there are virtually no more examples of this genre, although the famous anecdote about Bach improvising to Reincken on "An Wasserflüssen Babylon" (Snyder 1987, 259) suggests that some organists still practiced such arts. Here we may be witnessing an important division between improvisatory forms and notated music. While later composers such as Bach were wont to improvise extended chorale fantasias that crossed many stylistic and formal boundaries, the music they committed to paper was considerably more cautious. In other words, notated music was becoming regarded as an individual "work," with its own internal coherences—something that was not necessarily coextensive with music that was performed, or, rather, improvised.

Buxtehude's shorter chorale preludes belong to a tradition that continued well into the next century. Indeed, with his vocally inspired monodic elaboration of the chorales, Buxtehude could be seen as a crucial link between Scheidemann and Bach. While a few of his works are multiverse settings, suggesting that he may have improvised between the verses of the congregational chorale, the majority of his preludes point toward the well-documented practice of improvising introductions to the chorale, setting the pitch, mode, and mood for what was most likely unaccompanied singing (Snyder 1987, 98). The notation of such chorale preludes may have been desirable for a number of reasons: first, for performance on special occasions when the organist may have wished to "perfect" what he otherwise would have improvised; second, to provide a model for students; and finally, to preserve an especially successful improvisation.

Many writers assume that all composers of chorale preludes intimately depict the words of the text in their compositions, and frequently point to complex levels of allegory and interpretation. In the case of Buxtehude, as with so many of his contemporaries, there is clear evidence of word-painting in the widest possible sense. "Durch Adams Fall ist ganz verderbt," BuxWV 183, contains much chromatic motion, pointing to the "spoiling" of God's creation by mankind, and the prominent leaps in the pedal assure us of the reality of the fall. However, in general, Buxtehude's style of elaboration and ornamentation is relatively consistent. There are, of course, turns of phrase that, by analogy with operatic music, could be considered expressive, and the composer might outline the general affect of a chorale, but thereafter his work is an elaboration of the original melody with ornamental and "expressive" figures—a play of expression that has no immediate verbal corollary.

South Germany

In some ways the customary division between north and south German schools of keyboard composers is somewhat artificial, since there was obviously so much mutual influence, particularly from south to north. The division is perhaps most evident in the split between Lutheran and Catholic practice. In the north the composers tended to remain in one place, since the organist positions were generally stable, if not lucrative and musically stimulating. In the Catholic south, on the other hand, the organ was less important (and indeed the instrument was less developed, with a smaller pedal division); thus keyboard composers were often more involved in court life and regularly traveled to other—particularly Catholic—lands.

JOHANN CASPAR KERLL (1627–93)

Johann Caspar Kerll enjoyed a cosmopolitan career that took him from his native Saxony to Brussels, Munich, Vienna, and Rome. His background and musical personality are not unlike Froberger's, studying as he did with Carissimi, and enjoying privileges in some of the major courts of central Europe. Although his dramatic works (as Kapellmeister at the Munich court he wrote more than ten operas) and church music show him to be a composer of greater overall range than Froberger, his keyboard oeuvre is more limited, with far fewer examples of the suite genre; furthermore, his toccatas follow the Frescobaldi model more closely.

Most significant for the context of the later seventeenth century is his publication of organ versets on the Magnificat tones, *Modulatio organica* (1686). This concise collection sums up some of the major (and sometimes conflicting) issues concerning keyboard music at the end of the period under discussion. First, the pieces show the survival of the organ as a functional part of the Catholic liturgy; these pieces could hardly be material for recitals or even postludes. Indeed, the first verset of each tone is incomplete without the chant incipit. The modal orientation of the pieces and their miniaturized representation of Frescobaldi's stricter and freer styles show that late-seventeenth-century music (particularly for the church) still admitted older styles. The collection has a didactic quality that Kerll himself stressed in his dedication: "In a nutshell, it contains the *Iliad* of the organ's art: variety, so that it may delight, and brevity, so that it will not fatigue."[24] He later outlines his concern for the "rules of the art," specifically the laws of counterpoint and mode, to which he seems to attribute an eternal, nonhistorical validity, as if they were a logical extension of the laws of natural science.

Another facet of Baroque musical life is represented by the fact that the collection was designed for presentation to Maria Antonia, Archduchess of Austria, on the occasion of her wedding to the Elector of Bavaria. While Kerll states in his dedication that he intended this music to be performed upon the arrival of the Princess, it is clear that, with his engraving of the collection, he intended it as presentation material, a sort of musical souvenir.

While these issues reflect the backward-looking and essentially traditional nature of the collection, other elements place Kerll in the progressive camp; comparison of the surviving examples of the engraving shows that he was continually revising the collection, improving what most of his contemporaries would have considered minor details.[25] Furthermore, in his preface to the reader he admonishes those players who adapt and embellish the music according to their own whims: "Food properly cooked is bad when cooked again" (SCKM, 5, vii). Thus there is a sense of the music fixed by the notation, which the player realizes without adding anything to the compositional process. To take the culinary analogy further, the player's role is to unwrap and present the food, rather than to turn the knobs on the stove.

This sense of the emerging notion of the "musical work" goes hand in hand with the conception of the composer as an individual character with specific intentions and precepts. The most striking evidence of this newer attitude is Kerll's inclusion, at the end of the publication, of incipits to his other keyboard works. Others had apparently appropriated many of these works as their own, and this thematic catalog—possibly the first in the history of music—reestablishes the composer's authorship of a specific, almost canonic, oeuvre.

Georg Muffat (1653–1704)

Georg Muffat pursued a career analogous to that of Froberger several decades earlier. Born in Savoy of German-French parentage (of Scottish origins), and considering himself a German, Muffat lived in Alsace, Paris, Salzburg, Rome, and Passau. No other composer did more to

EXAMPLE 4.31. Muffat, Toccata 1, *Apparatus musico-organisticus*

synthesize the increasingly delineated French and Italian styles, and he was closely associated with both Lully and Corelli, the figureheads of their respective nations of residence. One factor common to virtually all these German composers is their expertise in other musical fields. Muffat is justly best known for his orchestral suites and concertos, and for his introduction of the French style of bowing into Germany.

Muffat's keyboard writing is best represented in the *Apparatus musico-organisticus,* which he had printed and presented to Emperor Leopold in 1690. As the composer states in his preface, the music is not unlike Frescobaldi's of 70 years before, but it reflects the integration of many later idioms. Although he notes his experience of the great organists of Germany, France, and Italy, the publication also betrays the influence of the instrumental music of these lands. To Muffat's great credit, very little of this music could be mistaken for that of Frescobaldi or of any of the "modern" Italian and French composers. Nevertheless, the 12 toccatas constituting the majority of the volume continue the Frescobaldian model of loosely linked free and imitative sections. Several of the fugal sections are based on subjects that would have been common in Frescobaldi, such as the canzona-like theme in Toccata 4, m. 24, and the chromatic subject in Toccata 7, m. 72.

Much of the figuration is also superficially reminiscent of the earlier Italian style, notably the "Lombardic" rhythms (Toccata 1, mm. 55–56, Ex. 4.31; Toccata 3, mm. 42–47). However, the harmonic thinking is usually more cadentially directed, with many long sequences. The influence of Corelli's string writing is evident in several "moto perpetuo" sections. In Toccata 5, mm. 7–14, we can almost imagine a dialogue between violin and violoncello, complete with chains of suspensions. Most striking in this respect is Toccata 8, m. 71, a passage that perhaps comes closest to the Corellian model (Ex. 4.32). This figuration returns for the

EXAMPLE 4.32. Muffat, Toccata 8, *Apparatus musico-organisticus*

EXAMPLE 4.33. Muffat, Toccata 9, *Apparatus musico-organisticus*

final section, m. 104, now marked "Presto." The *cantabile* style of the late Italian Baroque is also evident in certain pieces, most notably the Adagio in Toccata 9, m. 56 (Ex. 4.33).

The influence of French style is equally apparent throughout the collection. There is the proliferation of ornament symbols, including various versions of the trill sign and the standard French signs for the "tierce coulée" and "port de voix." Several toccatas open with expansive slow sections in up to five parts. Most obviously French are those that allude to the Lullyan overture, such as the dotted grave opening Toccata 7 and the opening of Toccata 10, with its sweeping upward scales. Toccata 11 also contains French influences—the adagio at m. 39 begins like a French chaconne, and the white notation of the ensuing allegro seems to be an immediate allusion to French practice.

The remaining works in the collection consist of a chaconne, passacaglia, and the "Nova cyclopoeias harmonica," which comprises a short aria and a pictorial hammer-and-anvil piece, "Ad malleorum ictus allusio." The passacaglia begins very much in the style of a French passacaille, with an opening statement that returns at various points in the course of the piece. However, before long (from m. 35) the variations progressively introduce figures of diminution that would not be out of place in variation movements of Italian or German origin. The piece is thus an interesting synthesis of national styles, something that becomes typical of German music during the first half of the eighteenth century.

JOHANN CASPAR FISCHER (C. 1670–1746)

Johann Caspar Fischer is another German composer who transmitted the Lullyan style to Germany; the details of his early life are extremely vague, but his most prestigious and productive employment was as Kapellmeister to the Baden court, for which he wrote much instrumental and theatre music. Of his celebrated published keyboard collections, the first two are relevant to the period of this study: *Les pièces de clavessin*, 1696 (later published as the *Musicalisches Blumen-Büschlein*, 1698) and *Ariadne musica neo-organoedum*, 1702.

The title page of the *Musicalisches Blumen-Büschlein* immediately strikes a new tone for keyboard publications. First, it describes the music as a collection of "various *Galanterien*," in other words, fashionable secular dances, many of which were associated with the French court. Although the traditional allemande, courante, sarabande, and gigue are not discarded, there is particular emphasis on the more modern dances, such as the bourrée, gavotte, menuet, rondeau, and passepied. Lully had been the first composer to group together such dances from his dramatic works, and Fischer (together with Kuhnau; see p. 215) was instrumental in introducing similarly "modern" suites to the keyboard in Germany. Other phrases on the title page are also significant: the collection is designed specifically for "Liebhaber" and thus seems to target the wealthy amateur—someone who might play for pleasure and delight ("Ergötzlichkeit") rather than for the cultivation of one's profession. Moreover, although the original title page specifically refers to the "Clavessin," Fischer's German dedication states that the pieces ("Partheyen"—a new title for the suite, similar to Kuhnau's "Partien") are to be played on the "Clavicordium, oder Instrument" (i.e., harpsichord). This mention of the clavichord again points to the intimate, domestic intention behind the music, which, as Fischer states, shows his "deeper reverence" for the dedicatee, the wife of the Margrave of Baden. There might even be a sense of gender modeling here: the musical amateur is specifically conceived as a woman—someone with time, money, and a taste for the most fashionable "trifles."

The style of writing is greatly different from that of most previous harpsichord music: the *style brisé* is now the exception rather than the rule (appearing mostly in the preludes) and, for the most part, even the lightest dances preserve linear part writing. A comparison with contemporary instrumental dances, in particular Fischer's own *Le journal du printemps* of 1695, shows that these pieces directly mimic the voice leading of instrumental music; indeed, there is the possibility that some might be transcriptions. We can see this as part of a general trend in keyboard music during the last decade or so of the seventeenth century: a studied absorption of recent instrumental idioms and less reliance on traditional, indigenous keyboard figuration (see, for instance, Muffat's assimilation of Lully and Corelli, p. 203). One particular reason may have been the "amateurization" of the keyboard medium. Published music, in particular, may have been directed at (or even demanded by) those who wished to experience public and professional orchestral music at home.

The most idiomatic and original keyboard pieces are the preludes that open each partita (none, incidentally, is modeled on the French overture, with which Lully would have begun his orchestral suites). With their brevity and frequent pedal points, these preludes seem to be descendants of the south German verset preludes, but their broken chords and *style brisé* texture place them firmly in the repertory for stringed keyboard instruments. They include miniature essays on short figures that, through imitation, create the illusion of a polyphonic texture within a chordal frame (not unlike Froberger's "imitative homophony"; see p. 187); essays in broken and block chords; and examples of the *stylus phantasticus* with rapid mood swings and virtuoso passage work. In all, these preludes are much more massive and musically challenging than their modest proportions betray.

The traditional four dances are represented incompletely in Partitas 1 and 4, completely only in Partita 6; the majority of the movements are the "modern" dances. Menuets appear in all but two of the partitas, and that of the seventh partita is played in alternation with a trio; here the influence of the instrumental trio is particularly striking, with two melody instruments pitted against an agile bass instrument (Ex. 4.34).

Perhaps the most remarkable of the movements are those that employ the variation principle, especially the aria and variations of Partita 5. The idea of introducing a song-like piece into keyboard writing is analogous to the interest in instrumental textures, and its popularity in the 1690s is evidenced by similar examples by Böhm, Pachelbel, and Kuhnau. Here we have a binary song-form with a strong melodic profile, which is clearly more "modern" than the traditional chorale (Ex. 4.35a). The melodic shape is preserved, rather than obscured, in the succeeding variations; the first variation, for instance, shares the melody between two voices that, in imitation of one another, reinforce the intervallic gestures of the original (Ex. 4.35b). Some of the motivic material would not be out of place in one of Sweelinck's variation sets; the repeated notes of the final variation are an obvious example, although it is likely that Fischer also took his cue from string ensemble writing.

Fischer's *Ariadne musica* of 1702 presents a somewhat different view of keyboard music, one that clearly favors the organ and its liturgical traditions over "secular" stringed keyboard instruments. The composer's mission is more serious, and—in view of his dedication of the work to a cleric—has something of the character of religious observance. As his preface suggests, Fischer wishes to introduce the organist to the difficul-

EXAMPLE 4.34. Fischer, Trio from Partita 7, *Musicalisches Blumen-Büschlein*

EXAMPLE 4.35. Fischer, Aria from Partita 5, *Musicalisches Blumen-Büschlein*
(a)

(b)

ties and pitfalls of the new tonal system. In the collection of 20 paired preludes and fugues he covers no fewer than 19 keys (E minor appears twice, as a phrygian and transposed dorian mode) organized in ascending order, with the minor mode preceding the major.

Fischer is perhaps the first composer to devise the prelude-fugue pairing on a regular basis (as opposed to the looser praeludia of both north and south German schools), and there is not normally a thematic connection between the two. It seems that the idea of the prelude and fugue (in Germany, at least) was directly contemporaneous (and indeed associated) with the first experiments in organizing the keys of the tonal system—an association that Bach clearly recognized two decades later. The preludes, with their frequent pedal points, are clearly descendants of the south German organ verset tradition, and although sometimes similar in texture to the preludes opening the suites of the *Musicalisches Blumen-Büschlein,* they are generally more concise. Given that both preludes and fugues are usually musical miniatures, there is no sense in which the prelude acts as a "light" preparation for the "weightier" material of the fugue; both movements can have dense contrapuntal and motivic textures.

North Germany at the End of the Seventeenth Century

NICOLAUS BRUHNS (1665–97)

Nicolaus Bruhns, like his near-contemporary Purcell in England, died at a tragically early age and left enough music to suggest that he could have developed into one of the most significant German composers of the late Baroque. As organist of the church in Husum, near his

EXAMPLE 4.36. Bruhns, Praeludium in E Minor

place of birth, his career was relatively unremarkable. However, two factors seem particularly important: Buxtehude apparently regarded him as his favorite pupil, and his fame as a violinist was almost as great as his achievement on the organ. Indeed, Mattheson relates the anecdote that he played the two instruments at the same time (NG 1980, 3, 375). The German virtuoso school of violin playing (evidenced in the remarkable works of Biber, J. J. Walther, and Westhoff) is often ignored in general histories of music; however, it not only played a major role in the development of the violin and its repertory, but also influenced other instrumental media.

Of Bruhns's five surviving organ works (12 excellent vocal works are also preserved), the longer Praeludium in E Minor stands out as something striving beyond a routine imitation of Buxtehude. With its loose, multisectional form it is a supreme example of the *stylus phantasticus*, admitting little overall formal organization with no hint of the unifying concerns of early eighteenth-century composers. Its immediate significance lies in its shock value: not only are the changes of mood and tempo entirely unpredictable, but the very subject matter is unusual, most notably the second fugue subject, which challenges the metrical sense of both performer and listener (Ex. 4.36).

What may be unique about this piece in the history of German keyboard music is the probable influence of the German virtuoso violin school. The aforementioned fugue subject would certainly be easier to play on the violin, given the dynamic nuancing afforded by bowing. And the opening gesture of the prelude, with its striking chromatic compound melody, may also reflect the thinking of a composer accustomed to unaccompanied violin playing. There are obvious string techniques, such as the "harpeggio" section, mm. 95–111, and the broken chords, mm. 126–29. Most important, there is throughout a fluid interplay of monophony and real and implied polyphony, especially evident in the second fugue, where the countersubjects, like the subject, are of a fragmentary nature (Ex. 4.36). The gigue from J. P. Westhoff's first suite for unaccompanied violin (1696) provides a suitable analogue (Ex. 4.37).

EXAMPLE 4.37. J. P. Westhoff, Gigue, Suite 1 for Solo Violin

EXAMPLE 4.38.

(a) Westhoff, Sarabande, Suite 1 for Solo Violin

(b) Bruhns, Praeludium in E Minor

The sarabande from the same suite also comes from a world similar to that of the chordal section in Bruhns's Praeludium, mm. 112–19 (Ex. 4.38a and b).

GEORG BÖHM (1661–1733)

The keyboard works of Georg Böhm are preserved only in copies, and most of these are of central rather than north German origin. Beckmann has shown how the copyists changed many details of the notation and were probably responsible for transcribing the pieces from tablature into modern notation.[26] Williams, too, has shown how the copyists may have distorted the structure of one of Böhm's chaconnes, owing to their unfamiliarity with the French conventions (which would have been obvious to a composer from the cosmopolitan cities of north Germany; see Williams 1989, 43–54).

Beckmann's concern with restoring the keyboard music of Böhm to its "original" version through a process of notational "purification" reflects a particular attitude toward early repertories that has prevailed for over 30 years. The assumption is that the "original" is the most authentic version, from which—by its very nature—we learn and experience the most. The identity and intentions of the original composer are also placed at a premium, although this attitude is strictly applicable only to composers of a much later age. Nevertheless, some composers we have encountered in the course of this study do indeed show a possessive attitude toward their oeuvre (e.g., Froberger and Kerll), which could be considered analogous to the later conceptions of individual genius.

We must be conscious of the general nature of music in the German Baroque. Composers appropriated diverse styles, idioms, and even works; their creative activity seems primarily directed toward producing music appropriate for their environment, for which they utilized new and old elements almost without discrimination. In this sense, the transcriptions of Böhm's Thuringian followers are no less important than his (lost) original manuscripts, since the latter, in turn, would have reflected a compositional process that was hardly unique or easily separable from the general musical culture of the age.

Böhm's œuvre is particularly significant in showing how a north German composer could make generic innovations similar to those of Fischer and Kuhnau. In other words, we can sense that the time was ripe for the newer "galant" keyboard suite and for lyrical keyboard arias (with or without sets of variations). While the majority of Böhm's suites are traditional, his Ouvertüre in D Major is definitely of the more modern kind, going even one step further than Fischer by opening with a French overture. Its single transmission—in the "Andreas Bach-Buch," which was compiled in the circle of J. S. Bach's elder brother Christoph during the first decade of the eighteenth century—gives us no clue as to whether it postdates Fischer's publication of 1696. The most significant difference from Fischer's writing, at least as implied by the surviving manuscripts, is Böhm's looser attitude to voice leading; while some movements, such as the minor Trio of the Rigaudon, strictly preserve a three-part texture, most admit a flexible number of voices (e.g., the opening of the Rondeau, Ex. 4.39).

Böhm has been greatly celebrated as the innovator of the chorale partita, a variation form that applies to the chorale techniques normally used for secular melodies. The shape and phrasing of the melody are retained throughout, and the elaborated textures are predominantly homophonic rather than contrapuntal. Clearly Böhm's innovation (which may, in any case, be shared by Pachelbel) reflects the trend during the last decade of the seventeenth century toward introducing more lyrical *cantabile* airs for keyboard (see p. 213). Indeed, one of Böhm's partitas is based on a "modern" sacred aria rather than a traditional chorale ("Jesu, du bist allzu schöne"). The intimate nature of these works, and the fact that they may be just as suited to home use on the harpsichord as to public performance on the organ, may relate to the fashion for domestic devotional songs at the end of the seventeenth century, something actively encouraged by the Lutheran Pietist movement.[27]

EXAMPLE 4.39. Böhm, Rondeau from Ouvertüre in D

Central Germany at the End
of the Seventeenth Century

JOHANN PACHELBEL (1653–1706)

Johann Pachelbel lived and worked long enough in the state of Thuringia to be counted as a central German figure. However, he was born in Nuremberg, the Bavarian city to which he returned in 1695, and he spent some time in Vienna during his early 20s. As a Protestant organist, his exposure to the predominantly Catholic repertories of the south is particularly significant. His surviving vocal and instrumental music shows him—like the majority of the finest composers for keyboard—to have been fully conversant with the wider field of German music; moreover, the course of his education suggests a composer who was deeply concerned with intellectual issues.

Pachelbel, as organist at the Predigerkirche in Erfurt (1678–90), was required to give a yearly recital to demonstrate his continuing and improving skills (Williams 1984, 50). His duties in providing preludes to the chorales were also carefully outlined in his contract (NG 1980, 14: 46). In all, then, we can see that much of Pachelbel's output was conditioned by the contingencies of his employment, and that the quality of the product was under continual attention. Moreover, his systematic exploitation of virtually every chorale genre of the age and his comparatively large number of publications[28] suggest that he may also have been concerned with amassing a body of pedagogic material—music that could be a model for his younger contemporaries.

The chorale genres espoused by Pachelbel have been too well covered to warrant a close study here. He provides examples of the genres of the Scheidt/Scheidemann era, including bicinia, polyphonic songs, and ornamented monodic settings. Although a monodic work like "Wir glauben all an einen Gott" contains virtually all the same figures of diminution found in Scheidemann, the work is far more compact, with little space between ornamented lines. This development could reflect both the demands of Pachelbel's post (i.e., short introductions to congregational chorales rather than solo recital pieces) and the later seventeenth-century trends toward cohesion and efficiency of invention (q.v. the epigrammatic fugues of Fischer). The "classic" Pachelbel chorale prelude is that in which the chorale is presented in long notes, with each line preceded by fore-imitation—an efficient, somewhat mechanical structure that serves the dual purposes of introducing the melody clearly and presenting a unified musical whole. The pieces beginning with a more extended fugue on the opening phrase of the chorale are perhaps the most impressive (e.g., "Durch Adams Fall ist ganz verderbt").

The overall impression is certainly one of compositional competence and a strong awareness of the various categories. However, there

EXAMPLE 4.40. Pachelbel, Magnificat Fugue in G Minor (No. 25)

is little that is daring, either in terms of the mixing of genres and styles, or in terms of text painting; Pachelbel barely exploits common expressive devices and seems almost to be committed to a "neutral" compositional style. Rather more interesting from this point of view are the works that he was required to perform at his last post at St. Sebald, Nuremberg. Here there was a far stronger residue of the Catholic rite within the Protestant liturgy, and Pachelbel's primary duty was to provide fugues as intonations to the Magnificat at vespers.

Like the chorale settings, Pachelbel's Magnificat fugues seem to bear no relation to any conceivable implications of the text, and they show a similar tendency toward providing a comprehensive account of the genre. In this respect they are as historically important as Fischer's fugues in offering us a thorough picture of the fugal styles available to a German composer at the close of the seventeenth century. While the majority show Pachelbel's predilection for concise, unified forms, those that mix styles and introduce seemingly contradictory elements are perhaps the most interesting. The most common instance of this is Pachelbel's occasional resort to *style brisé*. Fugue No. 25, for instance, is essentially a short, tautly controlled fugue exploiting a small number of repetitive motives.[29] However, the last six measures constitute a coda of an entirely different style and nature, which almost suggests a move from organ to harpsichord/clavichord style (Ex. 4.40).

In many cases the interest lies in Pachelbel's choice of subjects, since these often determine the entire motivic and harmonic course of the piece. Most fascinating of all is perhaps the subject of Fugue No. 95, which sounds like the unison ritornello of an Italian concerto (Ex. 4.41). Although Pachelbel manages to maintain a three-part texture throughout, much of the writing is necessarily homophonic and, given the repetition in the subject, tonally static. The "inappropriate" subject notwithstanding, the piece is short enough to work well as a curious fugal experiment.

EXAMPLE 4.41. Pachelbel, Magnificat Fugue in G Major (No. 95)

With the exception of the church-related genres of the chorale prelude and the Magnificat fugue, Pachelbel's greatest interest seems to have lain in the variation form. Some of his larger chaconnes, particularly the F-Minor Ciacona for organ, match those of Buxtehude for their dramatic pacing and control of figuration. Variation form is central to the *Musicalische Sterbens-Gedancken* of 1683: four chorale partitas, similar in style and structure to those of Böhm. Each set contains one variation in a chromatic, "pathetic" style—perhaps an allusion to the presumed unhappy catalyst for the publication, the death of Pachelbel's wife and child in a plague of 1681. The summit of Pachelbel's achievement in the variation genre is the *Hexachordum Apollinis,* published in 1699: six variation sets for organ or harpsichord on the popular genre of the keyboard aria.

The modest scale and range of these pieces does not belie their subtlety and quiet virtuosity. The music is finely worked and finished to a degree seldom experienced in Pachelbel's chorale writing. The opening of the fourth aria and the first variation provides a succinct example (Ex. 4.42): a lyrical line is created by the intertwining of the two upper parts and the tonal direction of the bass line. In other words, the "melody" is a fluid amalgam of elements rather than a single line. This impression is even stronger in the first variation, in which every line of the original three-part texture is preserved but ornamented in a delicate *style brisé.* Not only does this create further implied lines, but the opening *anapaestic* rhythm in the right hand (an adaptation of the opening gesture of the aria) is subtly developed to form the main "idea" of the variation.

EXAMPLE 4.42. Pachelbel, *Hexachordum Apollinis,* Aria Quarta

JOHANN KUHNAU (1660–1722)

A study of seventeenth-century German keyboard music is perhaps no better concluded than with Johann Kuhnau, since he epitomizes most of the trends of the High Baroque while anticipating many developments of the early eighteenth century, most notably the achievements of J. S. Bach and Handel. Perhaps his very proximity to these two composers (both geographically and stylistically) accounts for his comparative neglect in most recent studies; his output understandably suffers if judged according to the styles and values of the Bach era.

Kuhnau is arguably the last "Renaissance man" in the field of musical composition. Having received his early musical education in one of the greatest centers of German musical culture, Dresden, he subsequently studied ancient and modern languages, cultivated an interest in mathematics, became a successful practicing lawyer, and, with the publication in 1700 of his satirical novel *Der musicalische Quacksalber*, showed himself to be a talented and humorous writer. In 1684 he became organist of the Leipzig Thomaskirche and in 1701 took over the post of cantor and *Director musices* for the major Leipzig churches. All four of his keyboard publications appeared between the years of 1689 and 1700.

Not surprisingly, Kuhnau is also a major compositional theorist of his age, and the prefaces to his keyboard publications are almost as significant as the music they introduce. The first two publications (1689, 1692) are entitled *Clavier-Übung*,[30] and the prefaces show that they had several aesthetic and pedagogic purposes: the partitas are to provide "refreshment for spirits fatigued by other studies" but are also to edify those who make a profession of music. In the preface to the second volume Kuhnau further notes his inclusion of more fugues, especially those with countersubjects, specifically for the edification of the connoisseur. Kuhnau's instruction is informative indeed, since in both volumes he includes a remarkable quantity of ornaments, notably of the one-note *accentus* type. There is no reason to doubt that Kuhnau reflects much of the practice of his age with this notation; indeed, as he states in his preface, it is in the application and realization of ornamentation that the skill of a player is recognized. Kuhnau's instructive examples are a useful reminder to the modern player that performance of Baroque music does not consist merely of the accurate reading of the notation (Ill. 4.12).

The prefaces to the second volume of the *Clavier-Übung* and to the subsequent publication, the *Frische Clavier-Früchte* of 1696, show Kuhnau's concern that his innovative music not be seen to violate the traditional rules of counterpoint; for instance, dances allow a freer approach to part writing, and apparent parallel octaves can be justified as the product of voice exchange. In the latter publication Kuhnau takes great pains to explain that the numerous figures of diminution have their root in the art of oratory—figures that give to common flowers a strange and beautiful color.

ILLUSTRATION 4.12. Johann Kuhnau, *Neuer Clavier Uebung erster Theil* (Leipzig, [1689]); Sarabande from Partita 1, showing double-dash (shake and single-dash (accentus) ornaments.

The music of the two volumes of *Clavier-Übung* and of *Frische Clavier-Früchte* falls into two genres, the keyboard suite and sonata. The partitas follow the standard format for the late seventeenth century, with the four usual dances introduced by a prelude. However, both volumes of *Clavier-Übung,* particularly the second, do admit some extra movements, such as the double, bourrée, chaconne, menuet, gavotte, and aria. In this respect Kuhnau anticipated Fischer's introduction of "modern" dances by several years. Kuhnau similarly employs the more linear style of part writing, as necessitated by instrumental music; this doubtlessly satisfied his conscience as a connoisseur of the theory of musical composition. Nevertheless, the music is seldom stiff, and the notated voice leading often results in a *style brisé* texture. Furthermore, the plethora of ornaments guarantees a constant diversion for player and listener alike.

In the preface to *Clavier-Übung* II, Kuhnau explains the sonata appended to the volume. He asks rhetorically why the keyboard cannot play the same type of music as the other instruments use, particularly since no other instrument allows such completeness of texture. Kuhnau's apparent invention of the German keyboard sonata seems almost the inevitable product of the growing tendency for keyboard composers in the closing decades of the seventeenth century to appropriate the genres and styles of other media. Kuhnau's prototypical sonata opens with a broad walking-bass movement, followed by a fugue and two dance-like movements, and ends with a return of the opening. This multimovement work is not unlike traditional German keyboard praeludia and toccatas, with their alternation of strict and free sections, but the new title at least shows the intention to rejuvenate the keyboard medium with new forms and idioms.

The *Frische Clavier-Früchte* of 1696 presents seven further "fresh fruits" of the sonata genre. Immediately evident is the tightly controlled motivic texture pervading movements in an astonishing variety of forms and styles: inventions on a small collection of figures, fugues with strongly profiled subjects, expressive arias, rhetorical recitatives, and dance movements (which conclude each sonata). Kuhnau's development of the episodic passages in his fugal movements—exploiting existing motives, usually within lyrical sequences—is perhaps his primary contribution to the historical development of fugue as an extended form. Several concerto-like movements (the fast movements in Sonatas 1, 5, and 6) also show the development of fledging ritornello forms. Although Kuhnau spoke out against modern operatic style in his later years as Thomaskantor (his position was, for a time, greatly threatened by the activities of the young upstart Telemann), there are many dramatic gestures here, such as the recitatives in the first, second, fourth, and seventh sonatas, and the curious *Bebung* section of the sixth sonata. The most lyrical movements (the second section of Sonata 3, the openings of Sonatas 4 and 7) present a rich polyphonic texture with motivically integrated inner voices. Most of the closing dance movements cultivate a lighter texture, as if to give the listener relief after the relentless fugues and allegro movements.

Kuhnau's final publication, the *Musicalische Vorstellung einiger biblischer Historien* of 1700, is the work for which he is most renowned today. Although Kuhnau points to the obvious precedent of Froberger in the writing of program music, these sonatas are the first keyboard works to present a detailed narrative verbal program (with the exception of one sonata by Poglietti) and, as such, are virtually unparalleled before the nineteenth century. Kuhnau's preface is a fascinating study of the power and effect of music: on the one hand, he believes in the mathematical structure of music as something that directly parallels and affects the human emotions; on the other, he admits that much is conditioned by the particular humor and character of the listener, and that the words in texted music make the primary emotional impression on the listener. His verbal programs are thus indispensable in elucidating the symbolic and allegorical content of the music; only when they have been assimilated will the music have its full effect on the listener.

Despite the necessary asymmetry of most of these sonatas (since so much depends on the dramatic pacing of the biblical stories from which they draw their narratives), it is remarkable how closely the general formats resemble the sonatas of *Frische Clavier-Früchte:* most end with a long dance-like section and many contain fugal movements. Thus, Kuhnau's programs might give us a useful narratological guide by which to understand many of the multimovement forms in German keyboard music. It would be wrong to invent a story for every example of the *stylus phantasticus,* but it might be productive to view such works from the perspective of narrative, a sequence of events not unlike that of an opera.

Perhaps the most outstanding movement in the entire collection is the opening of the second sonata: the depiction of Saul's sadness and madness. Here we find a tantalizing blend of recitative and snatches of regular figuration; there is perhaps no finer precedent for the *Empfindsamkeit* of many of C.P.E. Bach's keyboard works written more than half a century later. The ensuing fugue is even more impressive, since "madness" is somehow communicated within the structure of a relatively strict fugue, complete with countersubject. First, the subject itself is striking for its almost anarchic implied modulations (covering G minor, D minor, and C minor within its first three bars; Ex. 4.43a); and second, frenzied runs begin to disrupt the basic process of the fugue (Ex. 4.43b). In other words, the steady dislocation of the fugue gives us a particularly vivid impression of Saul's madness, now perhaps even more disturbing than the "stream of consciousness" of the opening movement. With Kuhnau, as with so many of his immediate predecessors, we may be seeing the emergence of one of the most striking aspects of later German musical culture; within the cultivation of formalized, seemingly abstract structures, the German composer seems to communicate the greatest depth of emotion, creating the most disturbing or the most sublime metaphors for human experience.

EXAMPLE 4.43. Kuhnau, Suonata seconda, *Musicalische Vorstellungen einiger biblischer Historien*

(a)

(b)

Guide to Literature and Editions

Paumann and the Buxheim Organ Book

For a thorough study of the earliest German preludes, in the most important tablature before Buxheim (by Adam Ileborgh), see Richter 1981. Information on the Buxheim tablature is found in the prefaces to the two editions, *Das Buxheimer Orgelbuch* (Wallner) and *Music from the Buxhelm Organ Book* (Thomas). Thomas's edition covers only a selection of the Buxheim pieces, but presents them in a more playable format than Wallner's edition. It is also less "diplomatic," in that Thomas corrects obvious errors and implausible readings in the original manuscript. The two most thorough studies of the music are Southern 1963 and Zöbeley 1964; for some recent observations placing Paumann and the collection in a wider German context, see Strohm 1993, 489-93.

The Early Sixteenth Century: Hofhaimer, Schlick, and Buchner

Schlick's writings on the organ are closely examined in Barber 1975 and in Barber's edition of the *Spiegel der Orgelmacher* (Schlick 1980). Meeùs 1975 provides an essay on organ pitch before the time of Schlick. The most up-to-date study of Schlick's style and the context of contemporary instrumental music is Keyl 1989. For a short study of Hofhaimer, see Valder-Knechtiges 1987. For a consideration of temperaments of the early sixteenth century, see Lindley 1974.

The Later Sixteenth Century and the Tablatures of Ammerbach and Schmid

The most thorough study of German keyboard tablatures from the latter part of the sixteenth century is Merian 1927, which also contains many incipits and several complete transcriptions. Much information is also available in Brown 1967. The most recent and thorough study of Ammerbach and his environment is the introduction to Jacobs's edition of his *Orgel oder Instrument Tabulaturbuch* (1984).

Sweelinck and His Pupils

The most comprehensive and up-to-date survey is Dirksen 1997, which also provides a detailed study of the questionable works in Sweelinck's oeuvre, giving complex arguments for reattribution and disattribution on the grounds of both stylistic and source evidence. Two earlier books also provide illuminating and detailed surveys of Sweelinck's keyboard music. Curtis 1969/1987 lays emphasis on the English precedents for Sweelinck's style, with a thorough examination of the contacts between England and the Netherlands at the time; Noske 1988 offers a comprehensive study of Sweelinck's entire oeuvre, thus placing the keyboard music within a wider context. The musical analyses are particularly illuminating and include some interesting proposals as to how this, music can be aesthetically appreciated. Snyder 1980, a study of the theoretical context for Buxtehude, contains some important observations on a theoretical tradition that can be traced back to Sweelinck. For studies of other Dutch composers of Sweelinck's age, see Williams 1969 and (specifically on Peter Cornet) Walther 1982.

The edition in the Sweelinck *Opera omnia* (1968) remains the most comprehensive and reliable. Several later editions provide shorter and useful selections, but do not present superior readings. A selection of other Netherlandish music from the sixteenth and seventeenth centuries, much of it anonymous, can be found in the anthology *Nederlandse Klaviermuziek* (1961).

Scheidt's keyboard music has been well covered in recent writings, partly because of the 400th anniversary of his birth in 1987. Breig 1969 provides a detailed source study of the manuscript transmission of Scheidt's song-variations (later work on this general repertory is found in Newman 1980). Greene 1987 gives a general survey of the *Tabulatura nova*, outlining its function within the liturgy at Halle. Another useful birthday offering, including biographical and contextual information, is Stolze 1987. The latest consideration of the function, form, and significance of Scheidt's works is found in Bush 1990. For a survey of Scheidt's later publication, the *Görlitz Tablature* of 1650, and its relation to a chorale collection from the late eighteenth century, see Dahlberg 1988. Performance practice, especially the function of the slurs labelled "Imitatio violistica," is addressed by Kenyon 1989. Scheidt's work as an organ examiner is surveyed in Koch 1992, giving us insight into his attitude and tastes as an organist.

The most recent edition of the *Tabulatura nova* is Vogel's (1994–2002), which provides an excellent introduction to the sources and performance practices. Complete editions can also be found in *Werke* (Mahrenholz, 1953) and in the old *Denkmäler deutscher Tonkunst* series (Seiffert/Moser, 1958), which is still adequate, at least for consultation.

Scheidemann

Recent work on Scheidemann's style and sources includes Kinder 1988, a study of a newly discovered variation set, and Dirksen 2000 on Scheidt and Scheidemann; a monograph by Pieter Dirksen on the chronology and transmission of the keyboard music is forthcoming. Scheidemann's intabulations have excited particular attention in recent years, demonstrating that this often-neglected genre is an important facet of the seventeenth-century keyboard literature, and that Scheidemann's examples rank among the finest of the entire tradition. This repertory has been rendered accessible in a modern edition by Cleveland Johnson (1990); the foreword gives a concise and illuminating introduction to the genre and its functions. The same author (Johnson 1989) provides the most comprehensive survey to date of the genre of German intabulations, 1550–1650; Dirksen 1987 studies a hitherto unknown intabulation. Belotti 1995 and 1998 contributed further work on Scheidemann's intabulations. In addition to the four editions listed under Scheidemann's name (including a recent one by Dirksen [2000] of the little-known harpsichord music), his works can also be found in Böcker's edition of *Celler Clavierbuch*.

Froberger

Froberger has been the object of many studies conducted from a variety of angles, but the most comprehensive survey of his life and works can be found in the prefatory notes to the third volume of Siegbert Rampe's edition of the complete works (1993–). The final volume of this edition (vol. 6), still in preparation, will include as an appendix a catalogue of Froberger's complete works. Among the older studies, Leonhardt 1968 is particularly illuminating, placing Froberger in the larger context of the musical life of his time. A useful summary is Rasch 1992, supplemented by an updated and annotated worklist in Rasch and Dirksen 1992. For a general study of the Italian influence on German keyboard music of the entire Baroque see Riedel 1968; this is updated with a study of Frescobaldi's influence on seventeenth-century German composers in Riedel 1987. Silbiger 1980 offers a closer study of the Roman Frescobaldi tradition, with particular reference to Froberger's visit to Rome from 1637 to 1641; new information on Froberger's Roman sojourns is presented in Annibaldi 1995. For a basic survey of his toccatas and their types, see Kosnick 1982. Froberger's suites of dance movements are examined in Starke 1972, and the larger field of the Baroque "tombeau" is the subject of Vendrix 1987. Silbiger 1993 is a recent study on various aspects of the keyboard works and their sources.

Questions of performance practice in the toccatas are addressed in a penetrating essay by Moroney (1976) on the unmeasured preludes of Louis Couperin; Moroney also discusses the relationship between the two composers in his edition of Couperin's keyboard music (see p. 128 and n. 13). Pfeiffer 1979 examines the influence of the French unmeasured prelude on the larger German tradition, stretching from Froberger to Bach and Handel.

Two fine new editions of Froberger's complete keyboard works, one by Howard Schott, recently completed (1979–92), and the comprehensive critical edition by Rampe, (1993–), currently in progress, will render all earlier editions obsolete (including a recent partial reprint of the old Guido Adler edition by Dover [1994]).

Tunder, Weckmann, and Reincken

Tunder's life and works have been the object of several shorter surveys, such as Hudson 1977. Perhaps the most useful survey is Snyder 1987, with its illuminating study of the social and musical contexts of both Tunder and Buxtehude.

Weckmann's connections with Froberger have recently been examined by Rampe 1991 and 1997. The latest studies of the sources are found in Silbiger 1989, the prefaces to Rampe's Weckmann edition of 1991, and Silbiger's introduction to the facsimile of Lüneburg KN, 147 in SCKM, 9. Davidsson 1991, supplemented by the liner notes in his recording *Matthias Weckmann: Das Orgelwerk* (Motette DCD, 11461 [1991]), offers a penetrating survey of Weckmann's cultural context, and includes hypothetical analyses of the organ works according to German rhetorical theories.

Weckmann's keyboard works have recently become available in several good editions: the choral variations in Breig's edition (1979), and the remaining works in either Rampe's (1991) or Davidsson's (1991) edition; the latter does not include the suites.

Reincken's associations with Buxtehude and the discovery of a new portrait are covered in Snyder 1979. The double-pedal tradition of both composers is the subject of a recent study by Belotti (1990). Several authors have concentrated on the influence of Reincken on J. S. Bach, the most recent of which is Wolff 1986a.

Apel's edition of Reincken's works (1967) is still useful and generally accurate, although Beckmann's editions (1974 and 1982) benefit from newer research regarding attribution and sources. Moreover, they present the pieces in a more readable format.

Buxtehude

With the publication of Snyder 1987, its comprehensive Buxtehude bibliography, and a further annotated bibliography in German in Wettstein 1989, a detailed bibliography is redundant here.

Interpretation of the existing sources for Buxtehude's organ music is notoriously difficult, since no primary sources survive and many secondary ones contain obvious corruptions; most modern editions obscure these problems and give the appearance of a "clean text." The most recent studies to discuss these issues are Lücker 1979, Beckmann 1986, Archbold 1987, Kenyon 1988, and Williams 1989. The related issue of chronology in the free organ works was examined most recently by Beckmann (1990), who also makes use of Snyder's hypothesis that the organs in Lübeck were "well-tempered" in 1683 and thus rendered capable of playing in hitherto unusable keys.

Buxtehude's organ works have been analyzed in great detail and from a variety of angles, a situation shared by no other seventeenth-century German keyboard composer. Sponheuer (1990) examines the ostinato works for organ with regard to their seemingly opposed elements of fantasy and order; Wurm (1984) examines one of these works from a hermeneutical/numerological standpoint; Defant (1989) looks at the wider issue of the *stylus phantasticus* and its relation to principles of order. Benitez (1989) analyzes one representative toccata with respect to its rhythmic and metrical background.

For a comprehensive analysis of the toccatas from several viewpoints, including a Schenkerian approach, see Archbold 1985. Riedel 1990 examines some of the toccatas in the light of modal theory, and Wolff 1990 from the standpoint of string writing. The monodic chorale-based works and their historical place are the subject of Breig 1990, while Edler 1990 covers the chorale fantasias. Archbold 1990 is a spirited advocate of the expressive chorale preludes, attempting to counteract the bias of the critical literature toward the free praeludia.

The Dover reprint of the old edition by Spitta and Seiffert (1988) provides a useful and inexpensive overview of Buxtehude's organ works, and Hedar's edition of 1952 sometimes gives viable alternative readings, but the serious student should consult more recent editions: Beckmann's (1972/80), Albrecht's (1994–98), and those in the new collected edition of Buxtehude's music now in progress (Belotti, 2001).

Kerll, Muffat, and Fischer

For a study of the French influence on German composers of the late seventeenth century, especially Muffat and Fischer, see Audbourg Popin 1986. Radulescu 1980 provides a general study of Muffat's toccatas and their performance; Kube 1993 deals with their formal structure and aesthetic goals. Performance practice (and its relation to notation) is also covered by Wagner 1980. Monson 1972 is an interesting study of a newly discovered source for later versions of two of Muffat's toccatas, showing that the composer became more cosmopolitan and less directly dependent on Italian styles. Fischer's life and works are the subject of Walter 1990.

Of the editions of Muffat's *Apparatus musico-organisticus*, the one by Radulescu (1982) is the most accurate, with the music well presented. For Kerll, the *Collected Works for Keyboard* edited by Harris (1995) and the *Sämtliche Werke* edited by O'Donnell (1994) will no doubt supersede the old Sandberger edition (1901).

Böhm, Bruhns, Pachelbel, and Kuhnau

Bruhns's life and works are covered by Geck 1968; his Toccata in E Minor is the object of Sponheuer's study of the north German organ toccata and the *stylus phantasticus* (1985–86). Hartmann 1987 examines the newly discovered manuscript of *Pachelbel's Musikalische Sterbens-Gedanken*. Sarber's dissertation (1983) places Pachelbel's organ works in the historical traditions of Frescobaldi and of southern Germany. Wolff 1986b provides a fascinating study of the transmission of Pachelbel's music and his use of tablature.

Arbogast 1983 is a full-length, systematic monograph on the keyboard style of Kuhnau. Schroeder 1983 offers an analysis of the narrative and affect of sections of Kuhnau's *Biblische Historien,* in accordance with the various figures and gestures she perceives in the music. Kellner 1980 offers a short hypothesis regarding Kuhnau's use of number alphabets in these sonatas.

The editions of Pachelbel's organ works by Fedtke (1987) and by Gurgel (1982, 1985) present the music in the cleanest and most usable texts. However, they do not cover all the works, so the comprehensive edition by Mathaei, Stockmeler, and Zászkaliczky (1928–74) is indispensable for certain pieces. The earlier volumes of this edition are unfortunately marred with many editorial suggestions regarding phrasing and fingering, and some of the later volumes contain registrational suggestions that should not be regarded as didactic. Earlier editions of Kuhnau's keyboard works are now superseded by the *Collected Works for Keyboard* prepared by Harris (2003).

General Literature on Seventeenth-Century German and Dutch Keyboard Music

General and specific problems of authenticity in north German organ music are addressed in Beckmann 1989. For a study of lost lateseventeenth-century sources that have recently been discovered on microfilm, see Joelson-Strohbach 1987b. Webber 1986 examines a specific source of north German provenance that evidences the spread of south German and Italian styles in the north.

Wolff's (1986b) study of the Eckelt tablature book gives a fascinating view of the sort of music organists and composers collected at the end of the seventeenth century. It also works as a good introduction to the use of tablature around this time. Hill 1985 gives an account of the sort of keyboard notebooks that would have formed the early training of Bach and Handel. His 1990 study gives a performer's perspective of the interpretative implications of tablature and of how much is lost by the use of "modern" staff notation.

On the subject of the problems and definitions of genre, see Edler 1988, a study of the fantasia in German Baroque theory and composition, with an examination of chorale fantasias by Buxtehude and Reincken; see also Teepe's study of the development of the fantasia (1990). Edler's (1990) article on the relation between organ music and the social structure of north German cities produces an unusual combination of social and musical analysis. Walker 1985–86 examines the theory of fugue from the period of Sweelinck to Buxtehude. Riedel 1980 surveys cyclic fugal compositions from the time of Froberger to Albrechtsberger, with particular attention to south German and Italian composers. Bradshaw 1972 outlines the origins of the toccata and its development throughout the entire seventeenth century. Dehmel 1989 provides perhaps the most comprehensive modern study of the organ toccata and praeludium throughout the entire seventeenth century, including a thorough survey of the concept of *stylus phantasticus.*

Several writings are concerned with the anonymous *Wegweiser,* published repeatedly from 1689, virtually the only German organ instruction book for the entire century: see Beechey 1972, Gleason 1972, and Barber 1987. A recent (1989) translation of Niedt's keyboard treatises dating from 1700 is an important contribution to our knowledge of the keyboard art; the preface gives a particularly damning view of the average organist at the end of the seventeenth century.

Notes

1. Numbering and music text from Wallner's edition of the Buxheim organ book (1958–59), with correction in m. 5.

2. Paracelsus thought highly of Hofhaimer, asserting that he was to the organ what Dürer was to painting (Valder-Knechtiges 1987).

3. Numbering from Schmidt's edition of Buchner's organ works (1974).

4. Transcriptions of Ammerbach from Jacobs's edition of his works (1984).

5. As witnessed by Michael Praetorius in his renowned introduction to the "new Italian style," *Syntagma musicum,* vol. 3 (Wolfenbüttel, 1619). Interestingly, this new influence was particularly important for Lutheran vocal music.

6. See, for example, Frederick Neumann, *Ornamentation in Baroque and Post-Baroque music* (Princeton, 1978), 525–43.

7. *D-B* MS. Lynar Al. For an appraisal of this and related sources, see Breig 1968.

8. See Fock's Introduction to vol. 1 of Scheidemann's *Orgelwerke* (1967).

9. See, for example, Giulio Caccini's suggestions in the introduction to his *Le nuove musiche* (Florence, 1601), ed. Wiley Hitchcock (Madison, 1970).

10. "Wo die Noten / wie allhier / zusammen gezogen seind / ist solches eine besondere art / gleich wie die Violisten mit dem Bogen schleiffen zu machen pflegen. Wie dann solche Manier bey fürnehmen Violisten Deutscher Nation /nicht ungebreuchlich / gibt auch auff gelindschägigen Orgeln / Regalen / Clavicymbaln und Instrumenten / einen recht lieblichen und anmutigen *concentum,* derentwegen ich dann solche Monier [sic] mir selbsten gelieben lassen / und angewehnet"; see the facsimile in Seiffert and Moser's edition of Scheidt's *Tabulatura nova,* 1957, 126.

11. "Bicinium imitation Tremula Organi duobus digitis in una tantum clave, manu tum dextra, tum sinistra."

12. Numbering refers to the three volumes of Scheidemann's *Orgelwerke* (1967–71).

13. See Davitt Moroney's essay on Couperin's unmeasured preludes in Louis Couperin, *Pièces de Clavecin,* ed. Paul Brunold, rev. Davitt Moroney (Monaco, 1985), 12.

14. See Schott's edition of Froberger's *Oeuvres complètes* (1979), vol. 1, p. vi.

15. For a different interpretation, see Rasch 1992, 138.

16. On the earlier French lute tradition of the lament and *tombeau,* see Vendrix 1987.

17. Numbering refers to Rampe's edition of Weckmann's *Sämtliche freie Orgel und*

Clavierwerke (1991).

18. Weckmann's authorship of the *manualiter* toccatas is not securely established (see Silbiger 1989).

19. Bernhard's treatises are available in translation, in Walter Hilse, "The Treatises of Christoph Bernhard," *The Music Forum* 3 (New York, 1973), 1–196; Printz's theories are most thoroughly described in *Phrynis Mytilenaeus oder Satyrischer Componist*, vol. 2 (Quedlinburg, 1676–77; reprinted Dresden/Leipzig, 1696); *Musica modulatoria vocalis* (Schweidnitz, 1678).

20. However, Beckmann attributes the celebrated fugue in G minor to Heinrich Buttstett; see the notes to his edition of Reincken's *Sämtliche Werke für Klavier/Cembalo* (1982).

21. Something that, incidentally, Bach saw fit to add to Reincken's fugues; see Ulrich Siegele, *Kompositionsweise und Bearbeitungstechnik in der Instrumentalmusik Johann Sebastian Bachs* (Neuhausen, 1975), 11–22.

22. For a perceptive and candid discussion of these issues within German culture and music theory, see Arno Forchert, "Musik und Rhetorik im Barock," *Schütz-Jahrbuch* 7/8 (1985/6): 5–21.

23. This recipe was compiled by Jacobus Kloppers, *Die Interpretation und Wiedergabe der Orgelwerke Bach* (Frankfurt, 1966), 57–58.

24. See the facsimile of *Modulatio organica*, SCKM, 5, vi.

25. See Harris's introduction to the facsimile, ibid.

26. See Klaus Beckmann's introduction to Böhm's *Sämtliche Werke für Klavier/Cembalo* (1985).

27. J. A. Freylinghausen, one of the most important collectors of devotional songs, was a direct associate of the Pietist leader A. H. Francke.

28. See, e.g., *Musicalische Sterbens-Gedancken* (Erfurt, 1683); *Acht Choräle zum Praeambulieren* (Nuremberg, 1693); *Hexachordum Apollinis* (Nuremberg, 1699).

29. Numbering according to Zdszkaliczky's edition of Pachelbel's *Ausgewählte Orgelwerke* (1928).

30. Kuhnau appears to be the first to employ the nomenclature "keyboard-practice," which was widely used by German composers of the early eighteenth century, most notably J. S. Bach.

Selected Bibliography

EDITIONS

Ammerbach, Elias Nikolaus. *Orgel oder Instrument Tabulaturbuch* (1571/83). Ed. Charles Jacobs. Oxford, 1984.

Böhm, Georg. *Sämtliche Orgelwerke*. Ed. Klaus Beckmann. Wiesbaden, 1986.

——. *Sämtliche Werke für Klavier/Cembalo*. Ed. Klaus Beckmann. Wiesbaden, 1985.

The Brasov Tablature (Brasov Music Manuscript 808): German Keyboard Studies 1680–1684. Ed. John H. Baron. Recent Researches in the Music of the Baroque Era, 40. Madison, WI, 1982.

Bruhns, Nicolas. *Sämtliche Orgelwerke*. Ed. Klaus Beckmann. Wiesbaden, 1972.

Buchner, Hans. *Sämtliche Orgelwerke*. Ed. Jost Harro Schmidt. Das Erbe deutscher Musik, 54–55. Frankfurt, 1974.

Buxheim Organ Book. Facsimile edition. Ed. Bertha Antonia Wallner. Documenta

Musicologica. Series 2, vol. 1. Kassel, 1955.

Das Buxheimer Orgelbuch. Ed. Bertha Antonia Wallner. Das Erbe deutscher Musik, 37–39. Kassel, 1958–9.

Buxtehude, Dietrich. *Neue Ausgabe sämtlicher Orgelwerke.* 5 vols. Ed. Christoph Albrecht. Kassel, 1994–98.

——. *Organ Works.* Ed. P. Spitta and M. Seiffert. New York, 1988.

——. *Sämtliche Orgelwerke.* Ed. Klaus Beckmann. Wiesbaden, 1972.

——. *Sämtliche Orgelwerke.* Ed. Josef Hedar. Copenhagen, 1952.

——. *Sämtliche Sulten und Variationen für Klavier/Cembalo.* Ed. Klaus Beckmann. Wiesbaden, 1980.

——. *The Collected Works* 15, Part 1, Keyboard Works. 2 vols. Ed. Michael Belotti. New York, 2001.

Celler Clavierbuch; Ausgewählte Stücke für ein Tasteninstrument (Cembalo, Orgel, Klavier). Ed. Martin Böcker. Wiesbaden, 1990.

Cornet, Peeter. *Collected Keyboard Works.* Ed. Willi Apel. CEKM, 26. 1969.

——. *Complete Keyboard Works.* Ed. Pieter Dirksen and Jean Ferrard. Monumenta Musica Neerlandica, 17. Utrecht, 2001.

Early German Keyboard Music: An Anthology. 2 vols. Ed. Howard Ferguson. Oxford, 1970.

Faber Earl Organ Series: The Netherlands and Northern Germany. Vols. 10–12. Ed. Henrick Glahn and Haakon Elmer. London, 1986.

Faber Early Organ Series: Southern Germany and Austria. Vols. 13–15. Ed. Susan Wollenberg. London, 1986.

Fischer, Johann Kaspar Ferdinand. *Sämtliche Werke für Klavier und Orgel.* Ed. Ernst V. Werra. Leipzig, 1901; New York, 1965.

Freie Orgelwerke des norddeutschen Barocks. Ed. Klaus Beckmann. Wiesbaden, 1984.

Froberger, Johann Jacob. *Diverse...Partite, 2 parts (Mainz, Bourgeat, 1693, 1696); 10 Suittes de Clavessin (Amsterdam, Mortier, n.d.).* Facsimile edition. Introduction by Robert Hill. SCKM, 4. New York, 1988.

——. *Neue Ausgabe sämtlicher Werke.* 6 vols. Ed. Siegbert Rampe. Kassel, 1993.

——.*Œuvres complètes pour clavecin.* 3 vols. Ed. Howard Schott. Paris, 1979–92.

——.*Organ Works.* [Ed. Guido Adler.] New York, 1994.

Hofhaimer, Paul. *Salve Regina, Recordare, Tanndernack.* Ed. Michael Radulescu. Vienna, 1973.

Kerll, Johann Kaspar. *Ausgewählte Werke.* Ed. Adolf Sandberger. Denkmäler der Tonkunst in Bayern. Series III, Jg.II/2. Leipzig, 1901.

——. *The Collcted Works for Keyboard.* 2 vols. Ed. C. David Harris. The Art of the Keyboard, 2. New York, 1995.

——. *Modulatio organica.* Ed. Francesco Di Lernia. Vienna, 1991.

——. *Modulatio organica super magnificat octo eccleslasticis tonis respondens.* Fascimile edition. Introduction by C. David Harris. SCKM, 5. New York, 1987.

——. *Sämtliche Werke für Tasteninstrumente.* 4 vols. Ed. John O'Donnell. Diletto musicale, 1203–1206. Vienna, 1994.

Keyboard Music from the Andreas Bach Book and the Möller Manuscript. Ed. Robert Hill. Cambridge, MA, 1991.

Kleber, Leonhard. *Die Orgeltabulatur des Leonhard Kleber.* Ed. Karin Berg-Kotterba. Das Erbe deutscher Musik, 91–92. Frankfurt, 1987.

Krieger, Johann Philipp and Johann Krieger. 2 vols. *Sämtliche Orgel- und Clavierwerke.*

Ed. Siegbert Rampe and Helene Lerch. Kassel, 1999.

Kuhnau, Johann. *Klavierwerke.* Ed. Karl Päsler, rev. Hans Joachim Moser. Denkmäler deutscher Tonkunst. Series I/4. Leipzig, 1901/1958.

———. *The Collected Works for Keyboard.* Ed. C. David Harris. The Art of the Keyboard, 6. New York, 2003.

Lübeck, Vincent. *Keyboard Music from Swedish Sources.* Ed. Pieter Dirksen. Stockholm, 2000.

Lümeburg, Ratsbucherei, Mus. Ant. Pract. 1198. Facsimile edition. Introduction by Bruce Gustafson. SCKM, 22. New York, 1987.

Muffat, Georg. *Apparatus musico-organisticus.* Facsimile edition. Ed. Karl F. Wagner. Dokumente zur Aufführungspraxis alter Musik, 1. Innsbruck, 1979.

———. *Apparatus musico-organishcus.* 4 vols. Ed. Michael Radulescu. Vienna/Munich, 1982.

———. *Apparatus musico-organisticus.* Ed. Rudolf Walter. Suddeutsche Orgelmeister des Barock, 3. Altötting, 1968.

Music from the Buxheim Organ Book. Vol 1: Chanson Intabulations and *Basse Danse* Settings. Ed. Bernard Thomas. London, 1981.

Nederlandse Klaviermuziek uit de 16e en 17e Eeuw. Ed. Alan Curtis. Monumenta Musica Neerlandica, 3. Amsterdam, 1961.

Ottobeuren, Benediktiner-Abtei, Bibliothek und Musik-Archiv, Ms Mo 1037. Facsimile edition. Introduction by Robert Hill. SCKM, 23. New York, 1988.

Pachelbel, Johann. *Ausgewählte Orgelwerke.* 6 vols. Ed. Karl Matthaei, Wolfgang Stockmeier, and Tamás Zászkaliczky. Kassel, 1928–1974.

———. *Hexachordum Apollinis.* Ed. Hans J. Moser and Traugott Fedtke. Kassel, 1958.

———. *Magnificat-Fugen für Orgel.* Ed. Anne M. Gurgel. Leipzig, 1985.

———. *Musikalische Sterbensgedanken; vier Choralpartiten für Orgel/Cembalo/Klavier.* Ed. Traugott Fedtke. Frankfurt, 1987.

———. *Orgelwerke.* Ed. Traugott Fedtke. Frankfurt, 1972.

———. *Orgelwerke.* Ed. Anne M. Gurgel. Leipzig, 1982.

Praetorius, Jacob. *Choralbearbeitungen für Orgel.* Ed. Werner Breig. Kassel, 1974.

———. *Drei Praeambula: Magnificat-Bearbeitungen für Orgel.* Ed. Michael Belotti. Stuttgart, 2000.

Reincken, Johann Adam. *Collected Keyboard Works.* Ed. Willi Apel. CEKM, 16. 1967.

———. *Sämtliche Orgelwerke.* Ed. Klaus Beckmann. Wiesbaden, 1974.

———. *Sämtliche Werke für Klavier/Cembalo.* Ed. Klaus Beckmann. Wiesbaden, 1982.

Scheidemann, Heinrich. *Complete Harpsichord Music.* ed. Pieter Dirksen. Wiesbaden, 2000.

———. *Orgelwerke.* 3 vols. Ed. Gustav Fock and Werner Breig. Kassel, 1967–71.

———. *Sämtliche Motettenkolorierungen: für Orgel.* Ed. Klaus Beckmann. Wiesbaden, 1992.

———. *12 Orgelintavolierungen.* 3 vols. Ed. Cleveland Johnson. Wilhelmshaven, 1990.

Scheidt, Samuel. *Das Görlitzer-Tabulaturbuch aus dem Jahre 1650: 100 vierstimmige Choräle für die Orgel.* Ed. Fritz Dietrich. Kassel, 1987.

———. *Tabulatura nova.* Ed. Harald Vogel, 3 vols. Wiesbaden, 1994–2002.

———. *Tabulatura nova, Werke.* Vol. 6. Ed. Christhard Mahrenholz. Hamburg, 1953.

———. *Tabulatura nova für Orgel und Clavier.* Ed. Max Seiffert, rev. Hans Joachim Moser. Denkmäler deutscher Tonkunst, 1. Wiesbaden, 1958.

Schlick, Arnolt. *Hommage à L'Empereur Charles-Quint–Dix versets pour Orgue.* Ed.

Macario Santiago Kastner. Barcelona, 1954.

——. *Tabulaturen etlicher Lobgesang und Lidlein uff die Orgeln and Lauten.* Ed. Gottlieb Harms. Hamburg, 1957.

Schmid, Bernhard. *Tabulatur Buch.* Facsimile in Bibliotheca Musica Bononiensis 4/52. Bologna, 1969.

Sweelinck, Jan Pieterszoon. *Acht Choralbearbeitungen für Orgel von Jan P. Sweelinck und seine Schule.* Ed. Pieter Dirksen. Utrecht, 1991.

——. *Opera omnia.* Vol. 1: *The Instrumental Works.* Ed. Gustav Leonhardt, Alfons Annegarn, and Frits Noske. Amsterdam, 1968.

——. *6 Echo-Fantasien.* Ed. Rudolf Walter. Mainz, 1987.

Tunder, Franz. *Sämtliche Orgelwerke.* Ed. Klaus Beckmann. Wiesbaden, 1974.

——. *Zwei Choralfantasien.* Ed. Klaus Beckmann. Wiesbaden, 1991.

van Noordt, Anthoni. *Tabulatuur-boeck van Psalmen en Fantasyen.* Ed. Max Seiffert. Vereniging voor Nederlandse Muziekgeschiedenis, Uitgave, 19. Amsterdam, 1957.

Vienna, Minoritenkonvent, Klosterbibliothek und Archiv Ms XIV 714. Facsimile edition. Introduction by Robert Hill. SCKM, 24. New York, 1988.

Vienna, Österreichische Nationalbibliothek, Musiksammlung Mus. Hss. 16560 18706 18707. Facsimile edition. Introduction by Robert Hill. SCKM, 3. New York, 1988.

Weckmann, Matthias. *Choralbearbeitungen für Orgel.* Ed. Werner Breig. Kassel, 1979.

——. *Lüneberg, Ratsbücherei, Mus. Ant. Pract. KN 147.* Facsimile of partial autograph. SCKM, 9. New York, 1988.

A Practical Edition of the Free Organ Works. The Interpretation of his Organ Music. Vol. 2. Ed. Hans Davidsson. Stockholm, 1991.

——. *Sämtliche freie Orgel- und Clavierwerke.* Ed. Siegbert Rampe. Kassel, 1991.

LITERATURE

Annibaldi, Claudio. "Froberger in Rome: From Frescobaldi's Craftmanship to Kircher's Compositional Secrets." *Current Musicology* 58 (1995).

Arbogast, Jochen. *Stilkritische Untersuchungen zum Klavierwerk des Thomaskantors Johann Kuhnau (1660–1722).* Regensburg, 1983.

Archbold, Lawrence. *Style and Structure in the Praeludia of Dietrich Buxtehude.* Ann Arbor, 1985.

——. "Towards a Critical Understanding of Buxtehude's Expressive Chorale Preludes." In *Church, Stage and Studio: Music and Its Contexts in Seventeenth-Century Germany,* ed. Paul Walker, 87–106. Ann Arbor/London, 1990.

——. "Why Are There So Many Buxtehude Editions?" *The American Organist* 21 (May 1987): 87–91.

Audbourg Popin, Marie-Danielle. "Bach et le 'goût français.'" *Revue de Musicologie* 72 (1986): 271–77.

Barber, Elinore. "Riemenschneider Bach Institute Vault Holdings, Facsimile series: . . . Wegweiser . . . die Kunst die Orgel recht zu schlagen: A Seventeenth-Century Organ Instruction Book–Part I" *BACH* 18, 1 (1987): 25–36.

Barber, Elizabeth Berry. "Arnolt Schlick, Organ Consultant, and His 'Spiegel der Orgelmacher and Organisten.'" *Organ Yearbook* 6 (1975): 33–41.

Beckmann, Klaus. "Der authentische Text der Orgelwerke Buxtehudes: ein Streitobjekt?" *Musik und Gottesdienst* 40 (1986): 1–10.

——. "Echtheitsprobleme im Repertoire des hanseatischen Orgelbarocks." *Ars*

Organi 37 (1989): 150–62.

———. "Zur Chronologie der freien Orgelwerke Buxtehudes." In *Dietrich Buxtehude und die europäische Musik seiner Zeit: Bericht über das Lübecker Symposium 1987*, ed. Arnfried Edler and Friedhelm Krummacher, 224–34. Kassel, 1990.

Beechey, Gwilym. "A 17th-Century German Organ Tutor." *Musical Times* 113 (1972): 86–89.

Belotti, Michael. "Buxtehude und die norddeutsche Doppelpedaltradition." In *Dieterich Buxlehude und die europäische Musik seiner Zeit: Bericht über das Lübecker Symposium 1987*, ed. Arnfried Edler and Friedhelm Krummacher, 235–44. Kassel, 1990.

———. *Die freien Orgelwerke Dietrich Buxtehudes: Überlieferungsgeschichtliche und stilkritische Studien.* Frankfurt, 1995.

———. "Die Kunst der Intavolierung: Über die Motettenkolorierungen Heinrich Scheidemanns." *Basler Jahrbuch für historische Musikpraxis* 22 (1998): 91–101.

———. "Peter Philips and Heinrich Scheidemann, or the Art of Intabulation." In *Proceedings of the Göteborg International Organ Academy 1994*, ed. Hans Davidsson and Sverker Jullander, 75–84. Göteborg, 1995.

Benitez, Vincent P., Jr. "Rhythm and Meter in Buxtehude's Toccata in D Minor, BuxWV 155." *The Diapason* 80 (July 1989): 14–16.

Bradshaw, Murray C. *The Origin of the Toccata.* Dallas, 1972.

Breig, Werner. "Die Claviermusik Sweelincks und seiner Schüler im Lichte neuerer Forschungen und Editionen." *Die Musikforschung* 30 (1977): 482–92.

———. "Die geschichtliche Stellung von Buxtehudes monodischem Orgelchoral." In *Dietrich Buxtehude und die europäische Musik seiner Zeit: Bericht über das Lübecker Symposium 1987*, ed. Arnfried Edler and Friedhelm Krummacher, 260–74. Kassel, 1990.

———. "Die Lübbenauer Tabulaturen Lynar A1 and A2. Eine quellenkundliche Studie." *Archiv für Musikwissenschaft* 25 (1968): 96–117, 223–36.

———. "Zu den handschriftlich überlieferten Liedvariationen von Samuel Scheidt." *Die Musikforschung* 22 (1969): 318–28.

Brown, Howard Mayer. *Instrumental Music Printed Before 1600.* 2d ed. Cambridge, MA, 1967.

Buelow, George J. "Froberger." In *The New Grove North European Baroque Masters,* 151–70. New York, 1985.

Bush, Douglas E. "The Sacred Organ Works of Samuel Scheidt: Their Function, Form and Significance." In *Church, Stage and Studio: Music and Its Contexts in Seventeenth-Century Germany,* ed. Paul Walker, 43–65. Ann Arbor/London, 1990.

Curtis, Alan. *Sweelinck's Keyboard Music: A Study of English Elements in Seventeenth-Century Dutch Composition.* Leiden/New York, 1969. 3rd ed. 1987.

Dahlberg, Josef "Das Görlitzer Tabulaturbuch 1650 von Samuel Scheidt und das Allgemeiner Choral-Melodienbuch 1793 von Johann Adam Hiller: ein Vergleich." *Musik und Kirche* 58 (1988): 22–28.

Davidsson, Hans. *Matthias Weckmann: The Interpretation of His Organ Music.* Vol. 1. Göteborg, 1991.

Defant, Christine. " . . . ad ostentandum ingenium, abditam harmoniae rationem, ingeniosumque . . . contextum docendum": Aspekte des Stylus phantasticus in den Orgelwerken und der Kammermusik Dietrich Buxtehudes." *Schütz-Jahrbuch* 11 (1989): 69–103.

Dehmel, Jörg. *Toccata und Prädudium in der Orgelmusik von Merulo bis Bach.* Kassel,

1989.

Dirksen, Pieter. "Der Umfang des handschriftliche überlieferten Clavierwerkes von Samuel Scheidt." In *Schütz-Jahrbuch* 13 (1991), 91–123.

———. "Eine unbekannte Intavolierung Heinrich Scheidemanns." *Die Musikforschung* 40 (1987): 338–45.

———. "New Perspectives on Lynar A 1." In *The Keyboard in Baroque Europe*, ed. Christopher Hogwood. Cambridge, 2003.

———. "Scheidemann, Scheidt, und die Toccata." In *Schütz-Jahrbuch* 22 (2000), 29–47.

———. (ed.). *Sweelinck Studies*. Utrecht, 2002.

———. *The Keyboard Music of Jan Pieterszoon Sweelinck: Its Style, Significance and Influence*. Utrecht, 1997.

Edler, Arnfried. "Buxtehude und die norddeutsche Choralfantasie." In *Dietrich Buxtehude und die europäische Musik seiner Zeit: Bericht über das Lübecker Symposium 1987*, ed. Arnfried Edler and Friedhelm Krummacher, 275–88. Kassel, 1990.

———. "Fantasie and Choralfantasie: On the Problematic Nature of a Genre of Seventeenth-Century Organ Music." *Organ Yearbook* 19 (1988): 53–66.

———. "Organ music Within the Social Structure of North German Cities in the Seventeenth Century." In *Church, Stage and Studio; Music and Its Contexts in Seventeenth- Century Germany*, ed. Paul Walker, 23–41. Ann Arbor/London, 1990.

Geck, Martin. *Nicolaus Bruhns: Leben und Werk*. Cologne, 1968.

Gleason, Harold. "A Seventeenth-Century Organ Instruction Book." *BACH* 3 (1972): 3–12.

Hartmann, Günter. "Johann Pachelbels 'Musicalische Sterbens-Gedanken': Ein im Modenhauer-Archiv (Spokane) aufgefundenes Autograph." *Neue Zeitschrift für Musik* 148 (1987): 16–21.

Hill, Robert. "'Der Himmel weiss, wo diese Sachen hingekommen sind': Reconstructing the Lost Keyboard Notebooks of the Young Bach and Handel." In *Bach, Handel, Scarlatti Tercentenary Essays*, ed. Peter Williams, 161–72. Cambridge, 1985.

———. "Tablature Versus Staff Notation: Or, Why Did the Young J.S. Bach Compose in Tablature?" In *Church, Stage and Studio; Music and Its Contexts in Seventeenth-Century Germany*, ed. Paul Walker, 349–59. Ann Arbor/London, 1990.

Hudson, Frederick. "Franz Tunder, the North-Elbe Music School and Its Influence on J. S. Bach." *Organ Yearbook* 7 (1977): 20–40.

Ishii, Akira. "The toccatas and contrapuntal keyboard works of Johann Jacob Froberger: a study of the principal sources." Ph.D. dissertation, Duke University, 1999.

Joelson-Strohbach, Harry. "Ein bisher unberücksichtigter Notendruck mit deutscher Cembalomusik um 1710 (Georg Böhm, Johann Adam Reincken, Johann Pachelbel et alii)." *Die Musikforschung* 40 (1987a): 242–49.

———. "Nachricht von verschiedenen verloren geglaubten Handschriften mit barocker Tastenmusik." *Archiv für Musikwissenschaft* 44 (1987b): 91–140.

Johnson, Cleveland. *Vocal Compositions in German Organ Tablatures 1550–1650: A Catalogue and Commentary*. New York and London, 1989.

Kellner, Herbert A. "Diskussionen: Welches Zahlenalphabet benütze der Thomaskantor Kuhnau?" *Die Musikforschung* 33 (1980): 124–25.

Kenyon, Paul. "How Baroque was Buxtehude? Some Possible Corruptions Examined." *Organists' Review* 74 (1988): 127– 30.

———. "'Imitatio violistica' in Scheidt's Tablatura Nova." *Musical Times* 130 (1989):

45–47; for further correspondence regarding this issue, see the same journal, 1989: 197 and 1989: 384–85.

Keyl, Stephen. "Arnolt Schlick and Instrumental Music circa 1500." Ph.D. dissertation, Duke University, 1989.

Kinder, Katrin. "Ein Wolfenbütteler Tabulatur-Autograph von Heinrich Scheidemann." *Schütz-Jahrbuch 10* (1988): 86–103.

Koch, K. P. "Samuel Scheidt als Orgelgutachter." *Musik und Kirche* 62 (1992): 198–208.

Koopman, Ton. "Dietrich Buxtehude's Organworks: A Practical Help." *Musical Times* 132 (1991): 148–53.

Kosnick, James W. "Froberger's Toccatas." *The American Organist* 16 (July 1982): 38–44.

Kube, Michael. "Motivische Verknüpfungen und äesthetisches Urteil: Zu Georg Muffats *Apparatus musico-organisticus.* " *Schütz Jahrbuch* 15 (1993): 63–75.

Leonhardt, Gustav. "Johann Jakob Froberger and His Music." *L'Organo* 6 (1968): 15–38.

Lindley, Marc. "Early 16th-Century Keyboard Temperaments." *Musica Disciplina* 28 (1974): 129–51.

Lücker, Martin. "Dietrich Buxtehudes Orgelwerke: Fragen an eine Neuausgabe." *Musik und Kirche* 49 (1979): 20–25.

Marshall, Kimberley. "From Motet to Intabulation." In *Proceedings of the Göteborg International Organ Academy 1994,* ed. Hans Davidsson and Sverker Jullander, 44.

Meeùs, Nicolas. "Some hypotheses on the History of Organ Pitch Before Schlick." *Organ Yearbook* 6 (1975): 42–52.

Merian, Wilhelm. *Der Tanz in den deutschen Tabulaturbüchern.* Leipzig, 1927.

Monson, Craig A. "Eine neuentdeckte Fassung einer Toccata von Muffat." *Die Musikforschung* 25 (1972): 465–71.

Moroney, Davitt. "The Performance of Unmeasured Harpsichord Preludes." *Early Music* 4 (1976): 143–5 1.

Musch, Hans. "Praeludium *In organo pleno.*" *Basler Jahrbuch für historische Musikpraxis* 22 (1998): 9–38.

Newman, Carol D. "Keyboard Dances and Variations in Turin, Biblioteca Nazionale, MS Foà 8." Ph.D. dissertation, University of North Carolina, 1980.

Niedt, Friederich E. *The Musical Guide* (Parts 1, 1700/10; 2, 1721; 3, 1717). Trans. Pamela L. Poulin and Irmgard C. Taylor. Oxford, 1989.

Noske, Frits. *Sweelinck.* Oxford and New York, 1988.

Pfeiffer, Christel. "Das französische Prélude non mesuré für Cembalo: Notenbild-Interpretation-Einfluß auf Froberger, Bach, Handel." *Neue Zeitschrift für Musik* 140 (1979): 132–36.

Radulescu, Michael. "Die 12 Toccaten von Georg Muffat." In *Die süddeutschösterreichische Orgelmusik im 17. und 18. Jahrhundert,* ed. Walter Salmen, 169–84. Innsbruck, 1980.

——. "The *Apparatus musico-organisticus* of Georg Mufat." In *The Organist as Scholar: Essays in Memory of Russell Saunders,* ed. Kerala J. Snyder, 133–49. Stuyvesant, NY, 1994.

Rampe, Siegbert. "Das 'Hintze-Manuskript': Ein Dokument zu Biographie und Werk von Matthias Weckmann und Johann Jacob Froberger." *Schütz-Jahrbuch* 19 (1997): 71–111.

——. "Matthias Weckmann und Johann Jacob Froberger: Neuerkenntnisse zu

Biographie und Werke beider Organisten." *Musik und Kirche* 61 (1991): 325–32.

Rasch, Rudolf. "Johann Jakob Froberger and the Netherlands." In *The Harpsichord and Its Repertoire: Proceedings of the International Harpsichord Symposium Utrecht 1990,* ed. Pieter Dirksen, 121–41. Utrecht, 1992.

——. "The Travels of Johann Jacob Froberger 1649–1650." In *The Keyboard in Baroque Europe,* ed. Christopher Hogwood, Cambridge, 2003.

——. and Pieter Dirksen. "Eine neue Quelle zu Frobergers Cembalosuiten." In *Musik in Baden-Württemberg–Jahrbuch 2001* (Stuttgart, 2001), 133–153

Richter, Lukas. *"Praembeln und Mensurae:* Studien zur Orgeltabulatur des Adam Ileborgh." *Beiträge zur Musikwissenschafft* 23 (1981): 265–308.

Riedel, Friedrich W. "Buxtehudes Toccaten im II. Ton: Eine vergleichende Betrachtung." In *Dietrich Buxtehude und die europäische Musik seiner Zeit: Bericht über das Lübecker Symposium 1987,* ed. Arnfried Edler and Friedhelm Krummacher, 245–59. Kassel, 1990.

——. "Der Einfluß der italienischen Klaviermusik des 17. Jahrhunderts auf die Entwicklung der Musik für Tasteninstrumente in Deutschland während der ersten Hälfte des 18. Jahrhunderts." *Analecta Musicologica* 5 (1968): 18–33.

——. "The Influence and Tradition of Frescobaldi's Works in the Transalpine Countries." In *Frescobaldi Studies,* ed. Alexander Silbiger. Durham, 1987.

——. *Quellenkundliche Beiträge zur Geschichte der Musik für Tasteninstrumente in der zweiten Hälfte des 17. Jahrhunderts.* 2d ed. Munich, 1990.

——. "Die zyklische Fugen-Komposition von Froberger bis Albrechtsberger," in *Die süddeutsch-österreichische Orgelmusik im 17. und 18. Jahrhundert,* ed. Walter Salmen, 154–67. Innsbruck, 1980.

Sarber, V. Gayle. "The Organ Works of Pachelbel as Related to Selected Organ Works by Frescobaldi and the South and Central German Composers." Ph.D. dissertation, University of Indiana, 1983.

Schlick, Arnolt. *Spiegel der Orgelmacher und Organisten* (1511). Trans. Elizabeth Berry Barber. Bibliotheca organologica, 113. Buren, 1980.

Schneider, Matthias. "Spüren des Tombeau in der norddeutschen Tastenmusik des 17. Jahrhunderts." In *Tod und Musik im 17. un 18. Jahrhundert, XXVI. Internationale Wissenschaftliche Arbeitstagung Michaelstein, 12. bis 14. Juni 1998,* ed. Günter Fleischhauer et al., 217–32. Michaelstein, 2001.

Schott, Howard M. *A Critical Edition of the Works of J. J. Froberger.* Ph.D. dissertation, University of Oxford, 1977.

Schroeder, Dorothea. "Johann Kuhnau's 'Musikalische Vorstellung einiger biblischer Historien': Versuch einer Deutung." *Hamburger Jahrbuch für Musikwissenschaft* 6 (1983): 31–45.

Siedentopf, Henning. *Johann Jakob Froberger: Leben and Werk.* Stuttgart, 1977.

——. *Studien zur Kompositionstechnik Johann Jakob Frobergers.* Tübingen, 1978.

Silbiger, Alexander. "The Autographs of Matthias Weckmann: A Reevaluation." In *Heinrich Schütz und die Musik in Dänemark zur Zeit Christians IV,* ed. Anne Ørback Jensen and Ole Kongsted, 117–44. Copenhagen, 1989.

——. "The Roman Frescobaldi Tradition, c. 1640–1670." *Journal of the American Musicological Society* 33 (1980): 42–87.

——. "Tracing the Contents of Froberger's Lost Autographs." *Current Musicology* 54 (1993): 5–23.

Snyder, Kerala J. "Buxtehude's Organ Music: Drama Without Words." *Musical Times*

120 (1979): 517–2 1.

——. *Dietrich Buxtehude: Organist in Lübeck.* New York and London, 1987.

——. "Dietrich Buxtehude's Studies in Learned Counterpoint." *Journal of the American Musicological Society* 33 (1980): 544– 64.

Southern, Eileen. *The Buxheim Organ Book.* Brooklyn, 1963.

Sponheuer, Bernd. "Die norddeutsche Orgeltoccata und die 'höchsten Formen der Instrumentalmusik': Beobachtungen um der grossen e-moll Toccata von Nicolaus Bruhns." *Schütz-jahrbuch* 7–8 (1985–6): 137–46.

——. "Phantasik und Kalkül: Bemerkungen zu den Ostinato-Kompositionen in der Orgelmusik Buxtehudes." In *Dietrich Buxtehude und die europäische Musik seiner Zeit: Bericht über das Lübecker Symposium 1987*, ed. Arnfried Edler and Friedhelm Krummacher. Kassel, 1990.

Starke, David. *Frobergers Suitentänze.* Darmstadt, 1972.

Stolze, Wolfgang. "Samuel Scheidt (1587–1654): Zum 400. Geburtstag." *Musik und Kirche* 57 (1987): 126–36.

Strohm, Reinhard. *The Rise of European Music, 1380–1500.* Cambridge, 1993.

Teepe, Dagmar. *Die Entwicklung der Fantasie für Tasteninstrumente in 16. und 17. Jahrhundert: eine gattungsgeschichtliche Studie.* Kassel, 1990.

Valder-Knechtiges, Claudia. "Paul Hofhaimer Monarcha Organistarum." *Concerto* 11–12 (1987): 15–16.

Vendrix, Philippe. "Le Tombeau en musique en France à l'époque baroque. *Recherches sur la musique française classique* 25 (1987): 105–38.

Wagner, Karl F. "Die Originalnotation des Apparatus musico-organisticus von Georg Muffat und ihr aufführungspraktischer Informationswert." In *Die süddeutsch-österreichische Orgelmusik im 17. und 18. Jahrhundert,* ed. Walter Salmen, 185–200. Innsbruck, 1980.

Walker, Paul. "From Renaissance 'Fuga' to Baroque Fugue: The Role of the 'Sweelinck Theory Manuscripts.'" *Schütz-Jahrbuch* 7–8 (1985–6): 93–104.

Walter, Rudolf *Johann Caspar Ferdinand Fischer: Hofkapellmeister der Markgrafen von Baden.* Frankfurt, 1990.

Walther, Paul. "Peeter Cornet's Music." *Diapason* 73 (June 1982): 11–14.

Webber, Geoffrey. "New Evidence Concerning the Transmission of Styles in Seventeenth-Century German Organ Music: MS Berlin Amalien Bibliothek 340." *Organ Yearbook* 17 (1986): 81–88.

Wettstein, Hermann. *Dietrich Buxtehude (1637–1707): Bibliographie zu seinem Leben und Werk.* Munich and New York, 1989.

Williams, Peter. "Buxtehude's Organ Works: The Snares and Delusions of Notation." *The American Organist* 21 (May 1987): 68–71; also published in *Organists Review* 72 (1987): 301–7.

——. "A Chaconne by Georg Böhm: A Note on German Composers and French Styles." *Early Music* 17 (1989): 43–54.

The Organ Music of J.S. Bach. Vol. 3: *A Background.* Cambridge, 1984.

"Sweelinck and the Dutch School." *Musical Times* 110 (1969): 1286–88.

Wolff, Christoph. "Buxtehudes freie Orgelmusik und die Idee der 'imitatio violistica'." In *Dietrich Buxtehude und die europäische Musik seiner Zeit: Bericht über das Lübecker Symposium 1987*, ed. Arnfried Edler and Friedhelm Krummacher, 310–19. Kassel 1990.

——. "Conrad Paumanns Fundamentum organisandi und seine verschiedenen

Fassungen." *Archiv für Musikwissenschaft* 25 (1968): 196–222.

——. "Johann Adam Reinken and Johann Sebastian Bach: On the Context of Bach's Early Works." In *J. S. Bach as Organist,* ed. George Stauffer and Ernest May, 57–80. Bloomington, IN, and London, 1986a.

——. "Johann Valentin Eckelts Tabulaturbuch von 1692." In *Festschrift Martin Ruhnke: zum 65. Geburtstag,* 374–86. Neuhausen-Stuttgart, 1986b.

——. "Orgelmessen aus dem 16. Jahrhundert in einer wenig bekannten deutsch-italienischen Handschrift." 39–51. *Basler Jahrbuch für historische Musikpraxis* 22 (1998): 39–51.

Wurm, Karl. "Christus Kosmokrator: Ein hermeneutischer Versuch zu D. Buxtehudes Passacaglia in d BuxWV 161 und zu J. S. Bachs Präludium und Fuge C-dur BWV 547." *Musik und Kirche* 54 (1984): 263–71.

Zöbeley, Hans. *Die Musik des Buxheimer Orgelbuchs: Spielvorgang, Niederschrift, Herkunft, Faktur.* Tutzing, 1964.

CHAPTER FIVE

Italy

Robert Judd

Music for keyboards held an important place in the cultural life of the loose collection of city-states that formed Italy in the period prior to 1700. Among the principal musical employees of sacred establishments were organists and harpsichordists whose duties included performing, teaching, and composing. Music printing was a sizable industry in Italy and many keyboard composers published "authorized" keyboard prints that reflect a considerable tradition. Italy also dominated European manufacture of quilled instruments in the sixteenth century (and produced many in the seventeenth as well). Another prominent seventeenth-century musico-cultural export, opera, found an important place in London, Paris, Vienna, and other major European cities. By 1700 it had become *de rigueur* to travel to Italy to view cultural artifacts or enjoy its musical tradition. Schütz and Handel (and later Mozart) were among the most famous of those who came to finish their musical education. Reciprocally, Italians themselves traveled abroad and found secure employment as well as receptive musical audiences, and Italian publications were widely disseminated. The "Italian style" was known and heard from Moscow to Dublin.

During the period from 1500 to 1700 these forces and others were in play, making for a complex reticulum of threads that is sometimes hard to unravel, but the developments can be summarized with a handful of personalities and concepts. The first important artifact is the production of organists from St. Mark's Venice, a considerable body of music that is best examined with the actual basilica in mind (Ill. 5.1). Its grand and highly decorative space exudes majesty; the organ music from two instruments that reverberated here aimed at equal grandeur. Andrea Gabrieli and Claudio Merulo represented the pinnacle of that achievement.

ILLUSTRATION 5.1. St. Mark's Venice (interior). Lengthwise section, showing organ placement and giving some indication of the size of the building compared to the size of the organs. Reproduced with permission from Renato Lunelli, *Studi e documenti di storia organaria Veneta* (Florence, 1973).

About the same time, farther south at the court of the Este family in Ferrara, a different style with lasting ramifications emerged, evidenced in the work of Luzzasco Luzzaschi and Ercole Pasquini (with the probable influence of masters of the madrigal like Cipriano de Rore). Carlo Gesualdo, prince of Venosa (near Spanish-dominated Naples) and megalomaniac, found the Ferraran musical scene immensely stimulating during his sojourn and marriage there in 1594; in his retinue were composers with Spanish-oriented training who must have both shared their own music and taken with them features of Luzzaschi and Pasquini's "experimental" style, exemplified most clearly in pieces called *stravaganze* (extravagances) or *durezze e ligature* (harshnesses and suspensions). Thus, the "Neapolitan school" was established, a separate tradition as important as that of the Venetians. From Ferrara also came the single most important master of the period, Girolamo Frescobaldi (1583–1643). He left Ferrara at the devolution of the court in 1598 and was soon established at St. Peter's in Rome, the premier sacred establishment of the peninsula; apart from a few months in Mantua and a six-year stay in Florence, he remained in Rome until his death.

It is possible to view the period after Frescobaldi's death as one of decline in terms of keyboard music; after all, the extraordinary rise in popularity of both opera and violin music drew composers away from keyboard idioms. The loss of interest in *stile antico* (old-style polyphonic) composition and the rise of *basso continuo* keyboard music, a kind of compositional shorthand, are indicative of changes in compositional goals during the seventeenth century that some contemporaries viewed as artistic decline. On the other hand, despite the relative dearth of keyboard music in the period from about 1650 to 1700, much remains that is of high quality. Bernardo Pasquini (1637–1710) is the most prominent of a number of keyboard composers active toward the end of the century.

Finally, significant keyboard music by Giulio Cesare Aresti and his colleagues originated in Bologna, the center of ensemble music late in the century. The cavernous San Petronio Basilica (with a reverberation span of over 12 seconds) proved to be an amenable location for sonatas in a new style related to that of Pasquini. But before examining these musical developments more closely, it will be helpful to consider some of the wider cultural issues of the period, as well as the role of instruments and liturgy in music making at the keyboard.

Political Considerations

Unlike the musical cultures of France and England, that of Italy never revolved around a single nucleus. No doubt this was a reflection of its political fragmentation; the peninsula was united as a nation only in 1870. The lay of the land formed a number of discrete regions (Ill. 5.2); especially significant for our topic are Tuscany (Florence), Lazio (Rome), Campania (Naples), and the Po valley (including Venice, Milan, Bologna, and Ferrara). Their boundaries were hardly impenetrable, notwithstanding the discomfort of sea, horse, and coach travel; diplomats and legates as well as musicians and artists traveled across most of Italy (and indeed Europe) with surprising frequency. Nevertheless, we find quite different styles of music in the cities of these regions.

Political preoccupations of the sixteenth and seventeenth centuries influenced keyboard players and their music primarily as obstacles to be overcome or avoided. Overriding concerns were the turmoils of Reformation and Counterreformation; initiation of the Inquisition and concomitant stifling of creative impulse; the cataclysm of the Thirty Years' War (1618–48), which had reverberations in Italy despite the region's lack of full involvement; and the daily concerns of subsistence. This was not an age of social justice, and the life of the peasant was short and hard. Famine and plague took a heavy toll on society; we know, for example, that in 1648 pardons were offered to thieves who brought grain to Rome. Despite the misery surrounding them, the wealthy acknowledged the importance of music making, and they (as well as the Church) supported many performers and composers.

The principal political entities of Italy were either smaller cities ruled by landed nobility (e.g., Ferrara or Mantua) or quasi-imperial city-states (e.g., Venice, Naples, or Rome). The Spanish dominated politics in

ILLUSTRATION 5.2. Map of Italy, c. 1600.

the two centuries under consideration, and their political power base on the Italian peninsula was the Kingdom of Naples, seat of the viceroy. The French, based in the northwest, counteracted the Spanish and helped maintain a balance of power; apart from Rome, the city-states that we have come to regard as important artistically—Venice and Florence— had more limited political influence and often used alliances creatively to maintain stability. Venice was second only to Rome, with an empire extending eastward to Cyprus and in 1650 a population of well over three million. Courtly society at the centers of Italian political life— Rome, Venice, Naples, Florence, and Milan—provided a foundation for artistic culture. But to these centers we must add those from the second political tier, duchies such as Ferrara and Parma that were in a sense a holdover from medieval fiefdoms. In small, out-of-the-way towns, nobility occasionally established courtly life on a grand scale, enabling artistic patronage to a greater degree than even the most powerful political centers, and providing a stable setting for the production of keyboard music at a high artistic level. One might view the smaller duchies as emulating the courtly culture of the major cities, most notably Mantua, home of the Gonzagas and Monteverdi. Although Mantua's keyboard musicians left no music, two similar duchies had musicians who left substantial legacies: Ferrara, ruled by the Este and home of Luzzaschi and Frescobaldi; and Parma, ruled by the Farnesi and home of Merulo.

Problems of Documentation

In attempting to survey keyboard music of Italy before 1700, we are bound to an extent by the vagaries of history and must rely on surviving documentary evidence. Keyboard playing was overwhelmingly an improvised art and little music played by professionals would have been written down; the keyboard music that *was* written down is often "merely" music for amateurs and beginners. Although the situation began to change around 1590 with the publications of Merulo and Andrea Gabrieli, several organists known by contemporary descriptions to have played fine music have left little trace of their art. Documentation of keyboard composition in Italy is much greater than in most of Europe, and one can actually speak of two separate traditions, but even here, what we have is a dim reflection of an extensive oral tradition.[1]

The documentary remnant largely corresponds with the political scenario, with some important provisos. Until about 1600, Venice tends to overbalance the scene because of its flourishing publishing industry; Florence and Rome had outstanding performers, but their music is lost. After 1600, Rome achieved prominence through Frescobaldi, while in Venice there is a lack of music from all but a few players; organists at St. Mark's like Giovanni Gabrieli (1557–1612) and Francesco Cavalli (1602–76) left little keyboard music.

Instruments

Keyboard instruments may be classified according to whether they produce sound with wind or with strings; the former include church and domestic organs and regals; the latter, instruments such as harpsichords, virginals, and clavichords. Most share a compass of about four octaves (either C–c‴ or F–f‴).

Organs

The Italian organ was almost always one manual, with perhaps a few pull-down pedals. Unlike the practice in Spain, divided stops were not employed. Musically this means that solo-accompaniment texture was rare, and antiphonal effects were achieved only through octave changes. The prevalence of two (or more) instruments in large churches or cathedrals meant that "polychoral" organ music similar to that for instrumental ensembles was possible, and the practice is reported, although no music is extant.

Another notable feature of organs is their independence of ranks: each rank of the ripieno, or principal chorus, was drawn independently. Table 5.1 gives an indication of a typical ripieno-dominated instrument, that of Lorenzo da Prato in San Petronio Bologna (1474–77; see Ills. 5.3 and 5.4). The instrument is quite small, and has only one stop outside the ripieno. Other instruments of the period have more flute ranks, and later the undulating *voce umana* or *fiffaro* (8′ principal-type stop) was quite common. Only occasionally is a reed stop encountered (often a "regale," i.e., a short-resonator stop). The sound of Italian organs is often described as sweet and gentle, but it is worth remembering that such apparently small specifications were sufficient to fill the vast spaces of St. Mark's in Venice or San Petronio in Bologna. Registration recommendations by Costanzo Antegnati and Girolamo Diruta confirm a quite limited instrument primarily founded on principals and flutes.

TABLE 5.1
Specification of the da Prato organ,
San Petronio, Bologna

Principale	16
Ottava (octave)	8
Quintadecima (fifteenth)	4
Decimanona (nineteenth)	$2\frac{2}{3}$
Vigesimaseconda (twenty-second)	2
Vigesimasesta (twenty-sixth)	$1\frac{1}{3}$
Vigesimanona (twenty-ninth)	1
Trigesimaterza (thirty-third)	$\frac{2}{3}$
Trigesimasesta (thirty-sixth)	$\frac{1}{2}$
Flauto in XV (Flute: fifteenth)	4

Stringed Keyboard Instruments

Harpsichords and clavichords were common by the mid-sixteenth century. The earliest surviving instrument, by Jerome of Bologna

ILLUSTRATION 5.3. Da Prato organ, San Petronio, Bologna. Built 1471–75; restored by Tamburini, 1982. Reproduced by courtesy of Oscar Mischiati.

(1521), is shown in Illustration 5.5. One can see the typical characteristics of Italian building here, particularly its thin inner case (which would have been placed in a heavy outer case). There are no signs that two-manual instruments were built in Italy in the period under consideration. The traditional view that harpsichords normally were made with two 8′ registers has been refined through the research of Barnes (1971) and Wraight (1989), who have shown that typical instruments from

ILLUSTRATION 5.4. Keyboard of da Prato organ, San Petronio, Bologna. Note the split keys for A flat / G sharp. Reproduced by courtesy of Oscar Mischiati.

ILLUSTRATION 5.5. Harpsichord by Jerome of Bologna (1521). The earliest surviving domestic keyboard instrument. Reproduced by courtesy of the Board of Trustees of the Victoria & Albert Museum.

Venice prior to 1600 had one 8' and one 4' register; only in the later seventeenth century did two 8' registers become prevalent. Their characteristic sound has a sharp attack and somewhat rapid decay, so that Frescobaldi, for example, found it necessary to remind performers "not to leave the instrument empty," in other words, to restrike notes as necessary when playing his toccatas. Smaller instruments survive, including richly decorated *spinettinas* (some at 4' pitch); these probably were used in the home for improvised popular song and dance arrangements.

Unusual Instruments

Italians seem to have been fascinated by complexities in their instruments: the *cembalo cromatico* (Ill. 5.6) and *archicembalo* (Ill. 5.7), instruments with from 19 to 31 notes per octave, were unparalleled elsewhere in Europe, and enabled distinctions between enharmonic equivalents like G sharp and A flat or D sharp and E flat and the extension of meantone and other noncyclical tunings to remote keys. The *archicembalo*, which was made to play experimental music in imitation of ancient Greek *genera*, must have been an extraordinary auditory experience; Luzzaschi is said to have been proficient at it. Signs of decadence become evident later, with toy stops on organs such as drums, birds, and bells common by the end of the seventeenth century, but even the *arpitarrone*

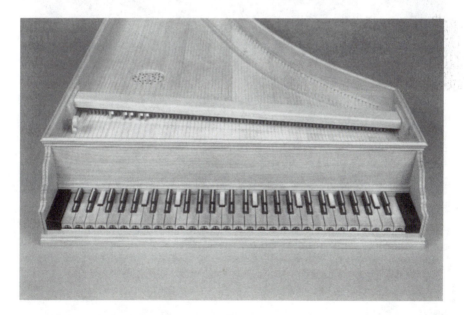

ILLUSTRATION 5.6. Cembalo cromatico (Denzil Wraight 1988). Nineteen-note harpsichord following sixteenth-century Venetian style (none has survived to copy).

ILLUSTRATION 5.7. Archicembalo (Trasuntino 1606). Experimental instrument built to perform music according to ancient Greek diatonic, chromatic, and enharmonic genera. Reproduced by courtesy of the Musei Civici d'Arte Antica, Bologna.

(apparently a virginal-like instrument strung with gut) and *claviorganum* (combination of harpsichord and organ) indicate a predilection for the unusual or bizarre. Michele Todini's organ/harpsichord/spinet (Ill. 5.8) is the outer limit of keyboard novelty for its own sake; tourists made a point of visiting this extraordinary creation on their travels. (See Williams 1966, 205, for other oddities: instruments of paper, alabaster, and other unusual materials.)

The Liturgy

Since the use of the organ in church provided the impetus for most keyboard music played in Italy, it is important to grasp the liturgical forms into which the organ music fit. ("Church" here refers to the Roman Catholic Church, for Protestantism and other Reformation movements had little impact on Italian Christianity of the period.) The liturgy of the Roman Catholic Church falls into forms according to time of both year and day. In Advent and Lent (the preparation seasons for

Christmas and Easter, respectively), use of the organ in liturgy was restricted; within the liturgical day, the organ was employed primarily in mass and vespers. Most often, however, only services on feast days and Sundays had organ music. Mass and vespers have a regular repetitive form in which some elements occur at every instance (the "Ordinary") and some elements change according to specific days and seasons (the "Proper"). Almost any part of the service could be sung or played on the organ (along the lines, for example, of the French format shown in Table 3.1). Evidence of liturgical practice is exemplified in Frescobaldi's *Fiori musicali* (1635), where antiphonal versets for the Kyrie are brought together with toccatas, canzonas, and ricercars to be played as substitutes for other parts of the mass. A particularly noteworthy genre arose specifically in Italian liturgical practice: the toccata for the elevation of the sacred host. Banchieri (1605/1969) gives a few brief instances of what it might have been like, and Diruta (1609/1983) documents it; the earliest instances are the *durezze e ligature* of Ercole Pasquini, de Macque, and Trabaci. Similar works by Frescobaldi and others are found throughout the seventeenth century, although not in the Venetian tradition. Another character piece, the *Battaglia*, must have been popular, to judge from its many manifestations throughout Europe; from Banchieri (see below) we learn that it was appropriate for Easter in depicting "Christ's victory over Death." Organ *Pastorale* with long pedal notes and repetitive bucolic atmosphere also became popular after the publication of Frescobaldi's in 1637.

The Organ and alternatim *Practice*

Antiphonal performance between organ and choir (termed *alternatim* performance) probably dates from the earliest use of the organ in church. It took firm root, for we find well-developed organ music for such performance in the early source of keyboard music Faenza 117; by the sixteenth century it was ubiquitous, often listed in churches' instructions for performance. Although antiphonal organ performance was common for both Ordinary and Proper, it is the Ordinary for which the most music survives. Adriano Banchieri's important lists of when organists were to play during mass and vespers (1605/1969) clearly demonstrate how much the instrument was used; other writers, notably Biagio Rossetti (1529; see Lynn 1973, 19), confirm that the organ was an important part of the entire liturgy.

Thus, much music survives for *alternatim* performance of the Mass Ordinary (Kyrie, Gloria, Credo, Sanctus, Agnus Dei); organ music was also used during vespers in alternation with chant for the Magnificat and hymns. A number of sources for liturgical practice suggest that it was common to substitute instrumental works, sometimes based on highly secular songs, for items of the proper in both mass and vespers; we find that canzonas and ricercars may have been used at the Gradual, Offertory, Elevation, Communion, and at the end (Benedicamus Domino/Deo Gratias) of mass, and in place of Magnificat antiphons and psalms of vespers.

Liturgical books describing ceremonial often comment critically on *alternatim* practice; authorities were concerned that every word of the sacred rite be voiced. A particularly sensitive issue in this regard was the Credo; its *alternatim* settings disappear after 1614. There was also a continual proscription of dance music in ceremonials, indicating that it, too, formed a part of liturgical usage, to the dismay of those concerned for propriety in church.

The Music
The Earliest Evidence

Italian organ building is documented in the early fourteenth century; the earliest organist to gain wide renown was the blind Florentine Francesco Landini (c. 1325–99), portrayed on his tombstone with a portative organ on his lap. But only a few keyboard manuscripts from before 1500 are extant, the most important of which is Faenza 117. About 50 pieces, most intabulations of vocal music, are preserved in this source, which was compiled around 1420 and includes music from the late fourteenth century of both Italian and French provenance. All the music is notated on two staves in two voices (the upper usually embellished), and its repertory corresponds with what we know from documentation was played at the keyboard: motet and song intabulations, a dance, and *alternatim* settings of Kyries, Glorias, and other works, the lower voice consisting of Gregorian chant cantus firmus, the upper part embellished.[2] A good instance of idiomatic writing is found in No. 25, a Benedicamus Domino. A pair of excerpts (Ex. 5.1) serves to show the extraordinary two-hand dialogue used extensively in this piece; the lower part's restrikings in these examples replace long notes found in most pieces of the manuscript. The writing in Faenza 117 is often virtuosic in the extreme (rhapsodic figurations and colorful dissonance treatment abound), and probably shows how a master would have performed.

The Early Sixteenth Century

After Faenza 117, virtually no music is extant until the first keyboard print in 1517, although from the similarity of the repertory of Faenza 117 to that of the early sixteenth-century sources we assume it to be indicative of what was played in the interim. The sources that survive from the period 1517 to 1540 show that intabulation was still an important part of keyboard playing; that dance music for keyboard was

EXAMPLE 5.1. Faenza 117, No. 25: Benedicamus Domino I, mm. 15–17, 23–24

common; that sacred intabulations and organ masses conceptually similar to Faenza 117 continued to be composed, now for all parts of the Mass Ordinary; and, most significantly, that idiomatic, rather free pieces expressly designed for keyboard, called ricercars, were now being created.

INTABULATIONS

Intabulations include Andrea Antico's 1517 milestone in printing, *Frottole intabulate da sonare organi*, and about 25 other works in manuscripts and prints of the period (such as 6 works in Marc' Antonio Cavazzoni's 1523 collection *Recerchari motetti canzoni*, whose titles indicate vocal origins, although only one vocal model survives). We will look at a sampling from Antico as representative of the genre. This volume of 26 intabulations of secular songs is the first print exclusively devoted to keyboard music; intabulations for lute similar to these had been published extensively prior to this volume by Ottaviano Petrucci. Antico's arrangements are unpretentious but often beautiful works, formally and texturally regular, like their vocal models. One finds several idiomatic changes throughout the volume that indicate keyboard arrangement: the use of parallel thirds in diminutions, cadential ornaments, scale diminutions, octave shifts, and a certain freedom regarding the voice leading of the inner parts. Also noteworthy are the variations found in written-out repeats. Here we find signs of variation technique that must have been common at the time, although there are few overt sets of variations from the period. Example 5.2, from No. 15 (Marco Cara's "O che aiuto o che conforto [Ah, who can help, who can comfort?]") shows

EXAMPLE 5.2. Antico, *Frottole*, No. 15 (Cara, "O che aiuto"), mm. 1–6, 14–19, and vocal model

several of these features. The vocal original shows the process of intabulation.

EARLY DANCES

The earliest collection of dances for keyboard comes down to us in a little manuscript (Venice 1227) containing 39 short pieces, all anonymous, dating from c. 1530. Here we encounter dance types common later, as well as typical harmonic and rhythmic styles. Rhythmically lively 4-measure phrases are coupled in groups of two or three, a formal pattern that many later dance forms adopted. The type leads to the binary forms that dominate dances after about 1600.

The manuscript includes dances such as the passamezzo (duple meter), pavane (duple), and saltarello (triple). These employ harmonic patterns around which performances were improvised, not unlike modern jazz bass patterns. The most common are the passamezzo antico and passamezzo moderno (Ex. 5.3), but all the dances and dance songs reflect similar harmonic style. Example 5.4 provides an instance. Called *"Todero, over: Tuo tene mamina"* (your dear little mother),[3] the harmony is a close approximation of that of the passamezzo antico pattern, and the interplay between effectively triple and duple meters is its most salient and delightful feature; such pieces doubtless regularly accompanied dance.

Another collection of dance music is found in the Castell' Arquato manuscripts (c. 1540), which contain 13 works that show the tradition of suites, variations, and passacaglias in Italy in their early stages: three-movement protosuites made up of pavana–saltarello–ripresa (or coda). The pavanes and saltarellos are based on the passamezzo antico and passamezzo moderno, with 8-measure patterns nearly always repeated, thus supplying the earliest variation sets in Italy (although variation as a structural goal was apparently not important to the anonymous composer[s]). The ripresas are similar to later ciacconas or passacaglias, usually based on 2-measure dominant-tonic harmonic patterns. While the music is simple, its organizational logic is indicative of things to come.

When playing these and other sixteenth-century dances, it is important to bear in mind how they were understood in Italy. The best guides are dance manuals such as Fabritio Caroso's *Il Ballarino* (1581) and *No-*

EXAMPLE 5.3. Harmonic patterns
(a) *passamezzo antico* (minor)   (b) *passamezzo moderno* (major)

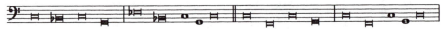

EXAMPLE 5.4. Venice 1227, *Todero*

biltà di Dame (1600). These books contain a great deal of information on dance etiquette, as well as many workaday dance settings for lute and keyboard and instructions for coupling pieces together and repeating patterns. In certain dances, 8- or 16-measure patterns were intended to be repeated up to ten times. The practical significance is that modern performers may design dance suites according to lengthier series of pieces than suggested in musical sources of the period; for example, since Caroso's "Barriera" consists of a duple section played seven times, a "Grave sciolta" (in triple meter) played twice, a saltarello, duple section, and galliard, one might construct such a suite from unordered material in the sources (with appropriate embellishment of repeats).

SACRED MUSIC

Although a wide variety of music was probably used liturgically, some is overtly intended for such use, especially *alternatim* settings for mass and office. Jeppesen (1960) averred that the organ mass by Jacques Brumel found in Castell' Arquato contains the most interesting music of the entire set of manuscripts; in terms of freedom of texture and dissonance treatment, the music is indeed extraordinary, and nothing like it is to be found in subsequent organ masses by Girolamo Cavazzoni, Merulo, or Andrea Gabrieli. On the other hand, the versets in Munich 9437, a recently discovered manuscript roughly contemporaneous to

Brumel, are rather skeletal. Another piece in this source entitled *Intonazione* is the earliest appearance of that genre designation: a brief introductory work that also functions as a means of giving the pitch to the choir. The piece includes directives to use pedals, the first such instructions found in Italian keyboard music.

THE EARLY RICERCAR

The term "ricercar" is identical to the word used today for research, and the two are related in that ricercars are the most intellectually oriented instrumental music. The term also means "to seek out" or "extract," and one senses this kind of "searching" in lute ricercars from the early sixteenth century. Its use as a genre title furthermore indicates music without text or specific function ("absolute" or "abstract"). Stylistically, two types of ricercars may be seen in early Italian keyboard music, differentiated according to their use of imitation: the earlier type uses imitation infrequently, whereas the later type, which dominated ricercar composition from about 1540, employs imitation pervasively. The earlier ricercar is stylistically related to the toccata, first heard of in a lute source from 1536. Ricercars are among the first Western art music to eschew reference to words and to rely entirely on sound in order to be appreciated. One might expect these attempts to be somehow inadequate or experimental, but such is not the case; the best ricercars are carefully crafted and formally logical. Marc' Antonio Cavazzoni, the first to publish keyboard ricercars, gives two fine examples of the mostly nonimitative type.

MARC' ANTONIO CAVAZZONI (C. 1490–C. 1560)

Cavazzoni's 1523 print stands quite apart from later keyboard publications (no more were to be issued for 20 years). Its ricercars each precede a motet of the same key, and thus appear to be preludial in function, although in terms of balance they outweigh the motets in length and substance. Several features in the ricercars suggest an improvisatory approach to composition: sequence plays an important structural role; imitation is limited to brief expository points and cadential figures; there is a lack of formal cohesion; and the entire keyboard range is employed, although not in a structurally significant way. Cavazzoni must have been an exuberant performer, if the ricercars reflect his own playing. There is a continual sense of reaching for the extremes in the ricercars; freedom of dissonance treatment, form, range, and texture prevails. Example 5.5, an internal section of 15 measures from the second ricercar (150 measures long), gives a sense of Cavazzoni in full flight. What appears to be a leap of a ninth in the upper voice, mm. 54–55, is actually the entry of a new voice; the G "ought" to sound on the downbeat of m. 55 (and aurally one senses its presence). The adding or dropping of voices almost arbitrarily is often encountered in tablature notations of the period. The

EXAMPLE 5.5. Marc' Antonio Cavazzoni, *Recerchari motetti canzoni*, Ricercar 2, mm. 53–66

dissonances in mm. 58–59 are also remarkable; the logical voice leading results in striking clashes. The range of the ricercars (which extends to f‴) is extraordinary: no other pieces of the period go much higher than a″, and extant instruments do not go beyond c‴ (although there are indications that instruments with the present range C–c‴ may have been altered from F–f‴).

1540 to 1620

Most genres of Italian keyboard music are evident in the music examined thus far: intabulations continued to be made until the end of the seventeenth century, albeit infrequently; closely related are canzonas, or canzoni alla francese (songs in the French style), which rose to great popularity in the early seventeenth century and provided a form for lively imitative writing. Canzonas were at first intabulated directly from French chansons, but soon took on a life of their own; the variation canzona became particularly popular. Variation canzonas achieve thematic unity across several sections by varying an initial subject, often ingeniously. They are occasionally punctuated with contrasting material in interposed sections.

We have encountered the roots of toccata style in Marc' Antonio Cavazzoni's work: it avoids imitation to a large extent, including instead much figuration and passagework. The word "toccata" is used with reference to keyboard music in the 1560s, although the earliest printed toccatas date from the 1590s. Dances continued to be written throughout the period, and assumed greater importance in the late seventeenth century, when ordered suites also appeared. The corrente and gagliarda tend to dominate the dance output for keyboard. Variations on bass themes also play a prominent role; in addition to passamezzos are patterns like the Ruggiero, Romanesca, and Folia. In the realm of sacred music, *alternatim* versets were common throughout the period. Indications for using canzonas and toccatas in the liturgy appear regularly, but no new musical forms for the liturgy were devised.

The only major genre that has no pre-1540 parallel is the imitative ricercar. In the late 1530s some composers apparently made a conscious decision to employ pervasive imitation among voices in a polyphonic texture; independent lines with imitative "subjects" became the norm for vocal music during this time. Its earliest instrumental appearances are in Venice, where in 1543 Marc' Antonio Cavazzoni's son Girolamo published his first book of organ music, including four ricercars in the new style. Its novelty is reflected in the title of the first collection of imitative ricercars to be published, the *Musica nova* ("New music") for instrumental ensemble of 1540.[4] Imitative textures remained prominent in keyboard writing until the onset of basso continuo in 1600, and continued to play an important part in much of the music beyond.

Composers worked with these genres in varied ways, of course, but it is possible to define regional traditions; our examination thus focuses on the first important centers—Venice, Ferrara, and Naples—as well as cities that later assumed prominence (Rome) or were more peripheral (Milan, Brescia).

VENICE

Venice, capital of the Italian music-printing industry, was also home to numerous organists whose music was published. Foremost among them by virtue of both quantity and quality are Claudio Merulo and Andrea Gabrieli, whose music appeared around 1600, but prior to their prolific activity several important events took place that set the stage for future developments. The most significant step was the move to the imitative ricercar by Girolamo Cavazzoni.

Imitative ricercars use one or more subjects as building blocks, the manner of their employment defining each piece. Compositional artifice in the treatment of subjects was highly regarded (as it generally has been in musical circles throughout history), and thus we see many instances of "learned devices" such as stretto, augmentation and diminution, invertible counterpoint, *inganno*,[5] and the combining of subjects. Perhaps the most noteworthy compositional device is progressive variation, the evolution of thematic material across multiple imitative sections. While this is not found in all ricercars of the period, the concept was prevalent, and composers could fairly be said either to take it up or consciously do its opposite—devise subjects for successive sections with highly contrasting material.

It would be natural to assume that if the treatment of subjects is the essence of ricercars, the invention of subjects would be important to composers, but such is not the case. Composers took pride in developing complex musical works with predetermined material and apparently had little interest in writing melodies for their own sake. This attitude is directly descended from an aesthetic of vocal music common to Ockeghem and Josquin, where the most arbitrary of musical material— such as writing a subject based on a textual phrase by extracting the musical syllables—was used to create fine musical works. Perhaps the most famous instance is Josquin's *Missa La sol fa re mi*: it was conceived, so the story goes, from the phrase "lascia fare mi [leave it to me]," a put-off from one of Josquin's employers who continually procrastinated after Josquin asked him a favor! The subject "la sol fa re mi" was also popular with keyboard composers, as we shall see. A "hidden" facet of ricercar composition in the sixteenth and early seventeenth centuries is the striving for ingeniousness in devising the manipulations of various subjects. Girolamo Cavazzoni deserves pride of place as the first to publish such music for the keyboard.

GIROLAMO CAVAZZONI (C. 1525–AFTER 1577)

We know little of Girolamo Cavazzoni's life, and include him in our discussion of Venice primarily because his two volumes of keyboard music were published there (1543 and after 1549). His four imitative ricercars each include four or more points of imitation and one section of rapid passagework; they average about 100 measures in length. One sees in these works consistent progressive thematic variation. Cavazzoni's deployment of variation in the second ricercar can be seen by studying Example 5.6 together with a schematic of the piece showing thematic areas proportionally (Ill. 5.9). Subject A is varied in a clear way only in subject D (m. 40); subject E "progresses" with further diminution; G cancels the diminution and drops the first note; and H varies G with

EXAMPLE 5.6. Girolamo Cavazzoni, Ricercar 2, subjects

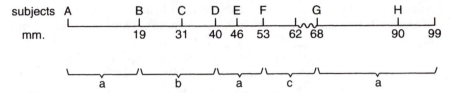

ILLUSTRATION 5.9. Girolamo Cavazzoni, Ricercar No. 2, deployment of subjects.

diminution and extension. A well-conceived formal plan for the piece as a whole is thereby revealed, with sections based on the opening material occurring at the beginning, middle, and end of the work.

In the realm of the canzona, too, Girolamo Cavazzoni merits recognition. He published two, based on "Faulte d'argent" and "Il est bel et bon." They are not intabulations but independent works with thematic allusion to popular tunes. To move away from intabulation is a significant step, although we have already seen that devising new subjects was not a particularly high priority, and thus Cavazzoni's approach is perhaps logical. Be that as it may, it seems not to have been taken up again until Andrea Gabrieli did so 20 or 30 years later.

The organists Jacques Buus, Annibale Padovano, and Sperindio Bertoldo were active in Venice during the period following Girolamo Cavazzoni's publications. The ricercar was important to all three: Buus is notable for his lengthy essays as well as the first monothematic ricercar, while Padovano's 1556 collection suggests refinements to the concept of the genre. Two ricercars attributed to Bertoldo in a 1591 print are in fact versions of Padovano works from 1556. Both Padovano and Bertoldo wrote toccatas that were published posthumously. These composers must remain secondary in importance, however, to Claudio Merulo and Andrea Gabrieli.

CLAUDIO MERULO (1533–1604) AND ANDREA GABRIELI (1533–85)

Merulo and A. Gabrieli both competed for a position at St. Mark's in 1557; Merulo prevailed. After Padovano left Venice in 1565, Andrea took the post of second organist, and he and Merulo were colleagues for 18 years until 1584, when Merulo was lured to Parma for a lucrative court position. Their performances at St. Mark's were primarily improvised, as we know from the St. Mark's audition records. Girolamo Diruta, a pupil of Merulo whose treatise *Il Transilvano* (1593) is considered below, described their playing as "dueling": "They were answering each other with such invention and gracefulness that I was almost carried away."

No compositions for their antiphonal playing have survived, but a significant amount of fine solo music by both is extant, more than by any other composers of the period. Merulo's works were published in six volumes between 1567 and 1611, Gabrieli's in six volumes between 1593 and 1605. A comparison of their printed output is given in Table 5.2.[6] Their quantitative output reflects their most significant achievements: for Merulo the toccata, for Gabrieli the ricercar. Our consideration focuses on these aspects of each.

TABLE 5.2
Published Output for Keyboard of Merulo and A. Gabrieli

Genre	Merulo	A. Gabrieli
ricercars	8	17
		4 parody ricercars
organ masses	3 masses	3 masses
	3 Credos	2 Credos
toccatas	19	4
		8 intonations
canzonas	20	4 "ricercari ariosi"
		1 "canzon ariosa"
		1 "fantasia allegra"
intabulations	4	13 chansons
		3 madrigals
		1 motet
variations	—	1 set on the passamezzo antico

MERULO AND THE TOCCATA

As we have seen, the toccata style is evident as early as 1523 in Marc' Antonio Cavazzoni's ricercars, and although toccatas are conspicuously absent in Girolamo Cavazzoni's work, there is evidence to suggest that these kinds of works were played throughout the period before 1591, the year the first keyboard toccatas (by Bertoldo) were published. Bertoldo's and other earlier toccatas (including some of those published in Diruta's 1593 treatise, as well as those by Andrea Gabrieli and Padovano) are rather unremarkable and occasionally tedious in their use of stereotyped scalar figures with chordal accompaniment in alternating right and left hands. Merulo himself wrote at least one of this type, published by Diruta. A second stage of development, artistically more successful, may be seen in Merulo's two volumes of toccatas published in 1598 and 1604.[7] Their sumptuous presentation, every page beautifully copper-engraved, is matched by their musical quality (see Ill. 5.10).

Merulo's 19 toccatas in these two books are arranged according to mode, suggesting perhaps a liturgical preludial function; their grand

ILLUSTRATION 5.10. Merulo, *Toccate* (1598), p. 16 (Toccata 4, first page). Copper engraving by Simone Verovio. Reproduced by courtesy of the Music Division, Library of Congress.

solemnity certainly accords with performance at St. Mark's or other large churches. One can see a new approach to virtuosity in these works, presaged in Diruta's treatise but otherwise not encountered. Ornamentation is quite heavy, but different from that of other Venetians in that elaborate rhythms and shorter note values dominate. Merulo also approaches texture quite differently from his earlier contemporaries: the toccatas have a constant polyphonic contrapuntal underpinning, rather than the chords and figuration of the earlier type. In addition, the forms in which Merulo writes show signs of close attention to detail. While historians of the toccata have noted Merulo's use of "five-part toccata form" in anticipation of toccatas by Buxtehude and J. S. Bach, it would be an oversimplification to assume a direct connection, despite certain outward resemblances. We do see, however, that Merulo shifted from heavily embellished to virtually unembellished "sections" (often not demarcated by cadences) as a way of formally planning his works.

His ninth toccata from Book I is a particularly fine work and can serve as representative of the set. Its 55 measures fall loosely into three parts according to the plan in Table 5.3. Mm. 1–5, 14–17, and 40–43 are shown in Example 5.7. The three "sections" are by no means rigidly demarcated; the subtlety with which Merulo moves between textures is significant and hardly seen in toccatas by contemporaries.

This interaction of embellishment, texture, and form in Merulo's toccatas is not matched in his other works, but his canzonas are remarkable and worthy of consideration. Merulo did not write works based on thematic borrowing in the mold of G. Cavazzoni, but appears simply to have intabulated vocal or instrumental arrangements. The intabulations are transformed by Merulo's sophisticated and mannered embellishments. Unlike the somewhat mechanical intabulations of Andrea

TABLE 5.3
Merulo, Toccata No. 9 (Book I)

Section	Mm.	Comments
Introduction	1–4	Polyphonic opening with imitation, figurations, cadence on D
Imitative	14–43	Two imitative ideas: the first, an ascending scalar third at m. 15, is hinted at in the introduction; the second, m. 32. They are separated by a nonimitative "interlude," mm. 22–32, during which (mm. 28–29) reference is again made to the introduction. The section cadences on D, m. 43
Conclusion	43–55	Scales and figurations; virtuosic figurations (m. 50): "codetta," mm. 53–55

EXAMPLE 5.7. Merulo, Toccata 9 (1598), mm. 1–5, 14–17, 40–43

(a) mm. 1–5

(b) mm. 14–17

(c) mm. 40–43

EXAMPLE 5.8. Merulo, "Susanne un jour," opening (with vocal model)

Gabrieli, Merulo's are valuable additions to the keyboard literature by virtue of their ornamental artistry. The opening of his arrangement of "Susanne un jour" together with its vocal model gives an indication of Merulo's approach (Ex. 5.8). Diruta made regular reference to Merulo's embellishment technique in the canzonas, and this example bears out his testimony to Merulo's remarkable technique.

ANDREA GABRIELI

Andrea Gabrieli's output for keyboard (all published posthumously) was the largest prior to Frescobaldi. Like Girolamo Cavazzoni, his most notable achievements were in ricercar and canzona composition. Although embellishment is an important surface element in many of his works, it never attains Merulo's level of virtuosity, and sometimes leads to their downfall, as in the overladen intabulations alluded to above. In his ricercars and canzona-like original compositions, however, the flaw is avoided and the works succeed remarkably. In his ricercars Gabrieli favored the use of few subjects: five are monothematic, and only one uses more than three subjects. The three monothematic ricercars that open the 1595 collection are perhaps the most impressive; his use of fourfold augmentation in combination with the subject in all three lends a wonderful air of majesty to the works. He never combined inversion with monothematicism (i.e., he did not try to supplement the limited material with variants); augmentation and stretto are preferred contrapuntal techniques. Example 5.9 shows mm. 45–56 of Ricercar 2 ("primo tono alla quarta alta"), the registral high point of the work, with fourfold augmentation in the bass combined with other entries (marked "A"). The variety of scale within the ricercars is also remarkable: five are about 120 measures in length, yet three are only 50. Learned devices and embellishment are found in abundance; progressive thematic variation is also a common feature of the polythematic ricercars. Gabrieli's sixth from the 1596 collection is one his finest of the latter. Its 118 measures may be parsed into three sections, one per subject (they are never combined): subject B enters in m. 26, subject C in m. 64 (thus the final subject is set

EXAMPLE 5.9. Andrea Gabrieli, Ricercar 2 (1595), mm. 45–56

forth in nearly twice the space as the first two). The subjects are given in
Example 5.10 (diminutions of the original are removed beneath to clarify
thematic profiles). Subject C is a version of A with the fourth note omitted; subject B retains the scalar third of A, but is further removed than C.

Gabrieli's canzonas appear in three volumes. The most interesting
are nine pieces stylistically similar to canzonas, called by such names as
"Fantasia alegra," "Canzon ariosa," and "Ricercar arioso," in addition to
three "ricercars" based on French chanson melodies. These last are directly related to G. Cavazzoni's canzonas, as they also take thematic material and work it in ways quite unrelated to the models. The "Canzon
ariosa," though not based on a vocal model, is representative of
Gabrieli's canzona style at its best: its contrasting sectional design is clear
(AABCCDD); the initial subject (Ex. 5.11a) was popular and used by G.
Cavazzoni and others. The polychoral effect of section C is achieved successfully through registral shift (Ex. 5.11b).

EXAMPLE 5.10. Andrea Gabrieli, Ricercar 6 (1596), subjects

EXAMPLE 5.11. Andrea Gabrieli, "Canzon ariosa"
(a) subject A

(b) registral shift, mm. 20–23

DANCE MUSIC IN VENICE

A line of "low-art" tradition distinct from the "high art" of Buus, Padovano, A. Gabrieli, and Merulo, following on from Venice 1227 and Castell' Arquato, may be drawn through prints issued in Venice that are made up primarily of dances: an anonymous set published in 1551 by Gardane, and a volume each by Marco Facoli (1588), Giovanni Maria Radino (1592), and Giovanni Picchi (1621). They show a trend in this repertory that is taken up only partially in later Italian variation and dance sets; like the parallel high-art tradition, much of it appears to evaporate with the decline of keyboard music printing in Venice after Picchi's volume. None of these composers gained particular renown in their day, a symptom of a certain stigma that appears to have accompanied dance music in Venice (it was a genre notably snubbed by Diruta). Andrea Gabrieli's fine set of passamezzo variations is the only allusion to dance music by a St. Mark's organist. We may look briefly at the most notable features of these four volumes, which move in chronological order from least to most highly developed.

Gardane's short book of 25 dances is modest in ambition and demands little technical expertise. It contains a passamezzo antico and a passamezzo moderno, each with three variations, and other common types of popular dance songs. There is a stylistic unity of detail to the works, perhaps most notably the penchant for shifting between B flat and B natural, giving a piquant and modally ambivalent tinge to the several works in G minor. Facoli's volume contains a large set of variations on the passamezzo moderno and accompanying saltarello, as well as other dances and twelve *arie* for accompanying dance songs. In the latter works the instrument quietly accompanies the verse, with more lively music for ritornelli (which would have been danced). The variations, arias, and two *tedesche* (i.e., allemandes) are notable as some of the earliest of their types.

EXAMPLE 5.12. Giovanni Picchi, *Passamezzo 1*, mm. 9–16

Radino had his set of dances issued in both lute and keyboard notation in 1592. The most interesting works are the two variation sets, both
based on the passamezzo moderno. There is consistent figural development and motivic unity in each variation; figurations occur that are also
found in Merulo's toccatas (and that resemble works for *viola bastarda*).
Giovanni Picchi's *Intavolatura di balli d'arpicordo* (Venice, 1621) is noteworthy both for its virtuosic contents and because it is the last volume of
such music for keyboard to be typeset and published in Venice. It contains an astonishing wealth of interesting, sometimes bizarre, figuration.
The opening piece, a set of six passamezzo antico variations, is particularly fine for its fiery and exciting display; Picchi is able to shift mood remarkably by changing the *affetto* of each variation. Example 5.12, the
second half of the first variation, gives a taste of some of his brilliance.
The final embellishment is unparalleled in the literature. Picchi's manuscript passamezzo sets are equally engaging, and his exotic "polacha"
dance also presents extraordinary figuration and harmonic twists. Although one gets the impression from his foreword that he might have
been a difficult man to work with, his keyboard music is remarkable indeed.

BANCHIERI, DIRUTA, AND ASOLA

Our survey of music in Venice around 1600 concludes with consideration of two complementary theoretical works by Girolamo Diruta and

Adriano Banchieri, together with a slender but influential volume by Giovanni Matteo Asola. These need not be tied too closely to Venice, as they were all applicable to practice throughout the peninsula. Adriano Banchieri's *L'organo suonarino* (1605) is the most important volume of the period for liturgical use of the organ, but Girolamo Diruta's Part II of *Il Transilvano* (1609) also presents a detailed discussion with numerous music examples. Both were reprinted frequently, and both acknowledged each other's contributions to the field. Banchieri's is the more down to earth, Diruta's the more scholarly. Asola published a cantus firmus book in 1592 that went through at least seven printings and must have provided many organists with material for the improvising of organ versets.

Banchieri's title, understood more readily by his initial readers than by us, is a pun referring to books called *cantorino*, which had been published since the early sixteenth century. They typically presented rudiments of singing for clerics; Banchieri himself prepared one in 1622. The *suonarino* is similarly a book of rudiments for beginning organists. Its chapters are called *registri*, again punning on the term used to describe organ stops. The various editions contain a number of short pieces of minor interest; more important are his wide-ranging comments on performance practice. In his tables for when to play at mass and vespers we see that *alternatim* practice dominates, but also that canzonas, motet intabulations or ricercars, and toccatas would have been regularly used.

In another theoretical work Banchieri made remarks worth quoting about the activities of organists:

> As for the *basso seguente* [i.e., basso continuo], so much in use these days: I wish that this were not the case; since it is an easy thing to do, many organists are successful at ensemble playing, but, being overcome by vanity [in this success], do not take the trouble to learn improvisation and playing from open scores. . . . In short, we will soon have two classes of players: those who are proper organists, i.e., those who use open scores and improvise well; and on the other hand the *bassisti*, who, overcome by laziness, are satisfied merely to play [from] the bass. Beyond that they will be "like an ass with a lyre." (Adriano Banchieri, *Conclusioni nel suono dell'organo* [Bologna, 1609], 24 [translation by the author])

What Banchieri saw soon transpired. Open scores, although strongly advocated by Frescobaldi, fell from use, and basso continuo (and its variants) came to be a common means for notating solo keyboard music in the latter part of the seventeenth century. The developments need not be interpreted too negatively, however, since playing basso continuo well is actually closely related to skilled organ improvisation. Indeed, a large amount of basso continuo solo music from around

1700 by Bernardo Pasquini and others attests to its usefulness and potential (although its quality is utterly dependent upon the performer's skill in presentation).

Girolamo Diruta's treatises were oriented to different issues from those of Banchieri, but are equally valuable documents for contemporary performance practice. He published *Il Transilvano* in two parts (1593 and 1609). The first is important for technical details of keyboard performance such as touch, fingering, ornamentation, and hand position; it includes an appendix of 13 toccatas—some of high quality—from Venetians like Merulo and Gabrieli as well as the Ferraran Luzzaschi and the Roman Quagliati. In the second part, Diruta gave instructions for arranging music from partbooks into a keyboard score, discussed more ornamentation, considered counterpoint and other musical fundamentals, and gave versets and plainchant cantus firmi for liturgical use. His directions for registration are mood oriented, but useful for indicating combinations of stops; for example, "The eighth tone makes the harmony charming and delightful. One can accompany this tone with the flute alone, with the flute and octave, or with the flute and fifteenth [i.e., flute 8' alone, or flute 8' and octave 4'; or flute 8' and fifteenth 2']" (*Seconda parte*, Libro IV, 22).

Asola's work is in a sense as significant as Banchieri's and Diruta's, in view of its publishing history, although it contains no directions or descriptions for use. A page is reproduced in Illustration 5.11. Organists typically would simply have taken these chants as subjects for their improvised versets; examples on chants given here abound in the literature (see also Ill. 3.1, p. 93).

FERRARA

Sixty miles southwest of Venice, in the heart of the Po valley, lies Ferrara, a city with a long and distinguished history of music making and the arts, thanks to the patronage of the ruling family, the Este. During the sixteenth century it was the home of several renowned keyboard musicians, who established a tradition related to but distinct from that of Venice. The first organist to leave his mark on Ferrara was the French *émigré* Jacques Brumel, who served as court organist from 1532 to a few years before his death in 1564. He was succeeded by Luzzasco Luzzaschi, who served until the departure of the Este court in 1598 (Ferrara reverted to the papacy upon the death of Duke Alfonso II, who left no suitable heir). The last generation of Ferrarese organists, Ercole Pasquini and the young Girolamo Frescobaldi, made their way to Rome.

Recent research into the Ferraran school has raised the interesting possibility that here lie the origins of the Neapolitan school, that Brumel, Luzzaschi, and E. Pasquini may have influenced Giovanni de Macque and his pupils Mayone and Trabaci. But the exact lineage of influence is still unsettled. A number of ricercars tentatively attributed to Brumel (in

ILLUSTRATION 5.11. Asola, *Canto fermo sopra messe* (1596 ed.), p. 3: chants for the Kyrie "Cunctipotens genitor," Mass for the Apostles. Organists typically improvised service music from such works. Reproduced by Courtesy of the Civico Museo Bibliografico Musicale, Bologna.

the Bourdeney Codex)[8] do indeed augur certain features in the music of some Neapolitan composers as well as of Frescobaldi (but not Pasquini), although some of Brumel's more positively identified music is quite different in style.

LUZZASCO LUZZASCHI (C. 1545–1607)

The 16 instrumental works by Luzzaschi that have come down to us are not as suggestive as one would wish, considering reports of his abilities. They include two pedagogical ricercars and a short toccata in Diruta's *Il Transilvano*, an instrumental canzona, and a set of 12 ricercars. The latter (dating from 1578) show a fondness for the use of many subjects, often paired in successive sections and employing progressive thematic variation. They differ from the Venetian style, although No. 3 is monothematic; neither do they employ combinations of subjects as Trabaci and Frescobaldi were to do. There is no idiomatic keyboard writing in these works. The toccata is too short to suggest much, but its figuration and harmonic procedure more closely resemble those found in the Venetian toccatas than those of the Neapolitans or Ercole Pasquini. The latter has left the most exciting keyboard music to come from Ferrara.

ERCOLE PASQUINI (C. 1540–BEFORE 1620)

Pasquini's output gives us a better sense of the atmosphere in Ferrara. His 30 extant compositions reflect a number of innovations in toccatas, *durezze*, canzonas, variations, and dances; despite the lack of contemporaneous publication of his works, Pasquini deserves to be named among the most important keyboard composers around 1600. His six short toccatas reflect some Venetian influence, but may be the earliest works to explore the harmonically affective style also taken up by Mayone, Trabaci, Rossi, Frescobaldi, and others. Characteristics such as abrupt harmonic shifts, figuration of originality sometimes approaching the bizarre, and changes of texture and figuration are found in these toccatas. Some of these features may be seen in the opening section of Toccata S6 (Ex. 5.13). ("S" numbers refer to Pasquini's *Collected Keyboard Works*.) The upper-voice trill, mm. 1–2, is surely intended to be freely increasing in speed from the leisurely beginning, and the section increases in activity and pace to the cadence.

Pasquini's canzonas explore progressive thematic variation sufficiently to designate them variation canzonas. There is little doubt that at least one canzona (S16) was well known by Frescobaldi and other masters, since it appears in no less than seven manuscripts of the period. Three versions (all given in his *Collected Keyboard Works*) together with Canzona S14 (which employs the same opening subject) provide an interesting means for studying the compositional working out and developing of material.[9] Example 5.14 presents the versions of the subject that Pasquini develops in three sections over 60 measures. Its

EXAMPLE 5.13. Ercole Pasquini, Toccata S6, mm.1–11

essence, two falling fourths a third apart, is one of the most frequently
encountered motives in keyboard music of the seventeenth century.

Pasquini also wrote *durezze* and correntes, a fine madrigal intabulation, and five sets of variations, the most developed being the Ro-

EXAMPLE 5.14. Ercole Pasquini, Canzona S16, subject and variations

EXAMPLE 5.15. Ercole Pasquini, *Durezze* S8, mm. 48–64

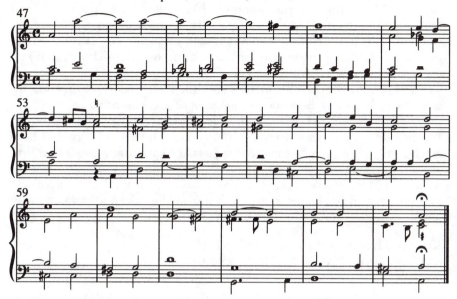

manesca (S24), with 13 well-ordered variations. The conclusion of his second *durezze* (Ex. 5.15) gives a taste of the "harshness" of dissonance in these and similar works by Neapolitans and Frescobaldi—dissonance that undoubtedly was intended for the elevation of the mass, of which Diruta wrote that the organ should "imitate the bitter and harsh torments of the Passion."

NAPLES

Naples, Italy's largest city in the sixteenth century and the third largest in all of Europe, was the seat of the Spanish viceroy and thus heavily under the influence of Spanish culture. Still, Italians played an important role in musical developments. The court of the viceroy and the chapel of the Chiesa della Santissima Annunziata provided the setting for organists Giovanni de Macque, Giovanni Maria Trabaci, and Ascanio Mayone. These composers form the core of what has become known as the "Neapolitan school," although they were preceded by Antonio Valente and Rocco Rodio. Neapolitan music owes little to the Venetian style, and is by and large more virtuosic, idiomatic, harmonically adventurous, and original than even the best of Merulo and Andrea Gabrieli. The fact that the Venetians published keyboard volumes according to genre while the Neapolitans mixed genres in volumes of "collected works" is indicative of a fundamentally different outlook. Harpsichord (and harp) were alluded to regularly in Neapolitan prints, while the Venetians eschewed all but organ (although much of their music is well suited to stringed keyboard instruments). Technically difficult music is also more prevalent in Naples. We have Rodio's virtuosic writing as early as 1575 in the first publication of Neapolitan keyboard music, and Mayone's nearly unplayable toccatas are flamboyant in the extreme, whereas Merulo's virtuosity is more rooted in vocal style. It is the break with vocal style, the pride in idiomatic writing for harpsichord, that sets the Neapolitans apart from the Venetians.

The origins of the chromatic experiments in this repertory so emblematic of the early Baroque *seconda prattica* are somewhat obscure, but the coincidence of such writing and the music of Gesualdo is suggestive. It is possible to trace a lineage beginning in Ferrara with Rore and Luzzaschi, who were greatly admired by Gesualdo and the Neapolitans, but an underestimated influence may well have been Giovanni de Macque, teacher of Mayone and Trabaci and mentor of Gesualdo. Even before de Macque arrived in Naples, however, a distinct keyboard idiom was thriving, as evidenced in the music of Rodio and Valente.

Rocco Rodio (c. 1535–after 1615) and Antonio Valente (fl. 1565–80)

Although little is known of Rodio, his 1575 volume of five ricercars and four cantus firmus pieces betrays no signs of inexperience. His ricercars are imitative and include much figuration and idiomatic keyboard writing. The fifth, monothematic, is distinct from the others in that its subject, the famous *la sol fa re mi*, appears as an *obbligo*, a constant part of the piece.[10] Probably most surprising about Rodio's collection is the technical demands it makes; the coda from the first ricercar proves a challenge indeed (Ex. 5.16).

Soon after Rodio, Valente's two volumes of keyboard music, remarkably free from northern influence, were published. The first, the *Intavolatura de cimbalo* (1576), employs a unique notation related to Spanish number tablature; it contains canonic ricercars, variation sets, and other works, most of which seem rather rudimentary in comparison with

EXAMPLE 5.16. Rodio, Ricercar 1, coda

(continued)

Rodio. His second volume, 43 *Versi spirituali* (1580), is unusual as well, but of much higher quality. These fine miniatures are organized into seven sets of six (plus one extra), each set named not according to tone but to solmization step from *ut* to *la*, with a set in B flat and a single verse in E flat. No authentic-plagal distinction is made, and there are no references to specific plainchants. Although nearly all are imitative (the sixth of each set is canonic), they present a wide variety of character and mood. The verses could have been used generically in the liturgy at mass or vespers wherever *alternatim* organ was required.

GIOVANNI DE MACQUE (C. 1550–1614)

Giovanni de Macque came to Naples in about 1585, after a peripatetic youth; he was born in Flanders, served as a choirboy in Vienna, and lived in Rome from 1574. He steadily rose in the musical community and took the premier post of Naples, head of the viceregal chapel, in 1599, remaining there until his death. Unlike his pupils Mayone and Trabaci, he published no keyboard music, but over 30 works attributed to him are extant in manuscripts, including *durezze*, canzonas, capriccios, variations, and dances. The capriccios and *durezze* are his finest pieces. In his *Capriccio sopra re fa mi sol*, a sectional work based on a hexachordal subject, de Macque sets forth a bold opening (Ex. 5.17a);[11] its six sections are filled with imaginative writing, including remarkable embellishment like the cadence of the second section (Ex. 5.17b). Two sections introduce imitative ideas with no recognizable connection to the main subject (Ex. 5.17c). Although the final section begins somewhat anticlimactically (a 20-measure elaboration of Ex. 5.17d), the last few measures make for a dramatic finish (Ex. 5.17e).

In de Macque's pieces named *stravaganze*, we find a *durezze* style similar to that seen in Ercole Pasquini, although with more figuration and fewer smooth lines, suggesting an earlier date of composition.[12]

EXAMPLE 5.17. De Macque, *Capriccio sopra re fa mi sol*
(a) mm. 1–5

(b) mm. 35–37

(c) subjects, mm. 25, 70

m. 70

(d) mm. 87–88

(e) mm. 104–7

EXAMPLE 5.18. De Macque, *Seconda S[t]ravaganza*, mm. 11–16

Example 5.18 gives a portion of the second *stravaganza* reminiscent of the chromaticism of Wagner.

De Macque published two sets of 12 ricercars; both are lost, but one set survives in manuscript.[13] Scholars have observed in these works, which like Luzzaschi's have no keyboard figuration, frequent thematic variation, as well as free and *inganno*-based rhythmic and melodic variations of the subjects. De Macque is the first to present all thematic material at the beginnings of his ricercars, combining three or four subjects.[14] De Macque's Ruggiero variations, although included in Watelet's edition of his keyboard music, appear to be intended for performance on the harp; the last variation, at any rate, is unplayable at the keyboard. While music for the two instruments was to a large degree interchangeable, it is important to acknowledge the harp as medium of performance for this and, indeed, much of the Neapolitan repertory.

GIOVANNI MARIA TRABACI (C. 1575–1647)
AND ASCANIO MAYONE (C. 1565–1627)

Some of the finest music to emerge from the Neapolitan sphere of influence is found in four books of keyboard music published between 1603 and 1615 by the viceregal organists Ascanio Mayone and Giovanni Maria Trabaci. Like Merulo and Andrea Gabrieli in Venice, they are contemporaneous and produced similar outputs; also like their counterparts, each has distinguishing stylistic characteristics. Trabaci's best music is oriented to the ricercar and canzona and is the more influenced by polyphonic ideals, while Mayone's best music is more idiosyncratic, virtuosic, and oriented to the toccata and toccata-like elements of other genres. These tendencies may be related to the men's life experiences: Mayone was a renowned harpist as well as organist, but wrote little polyphonic vocal music; Trabaci began as an organist but advanced to the directorship of the viceregal chapel on the death of de Macque in 1614, and published a large quantity of vocal music.

Trabaci's two keyboard volumes contain about 165 pieces, many still awaiting publication in a modern edition. While the relative neglect of his music is undeserved, Trabaci's offputting posturing has not helped endear him to readers. The introductions to his volumes include self-inflating comments that blame players and listeners if they do not appreciate his music sufficiently—it is their own fault for not having studied it properly, or for their poor taste. Nevertheless, he makes many interesting analytical points, especially in the ricercars of Book II (where he describes in detail how thematic material is deployed). His 24 ricercars (two sets of 12) and 7 canzonas are noteworthy for their progressive thematic variation; as we shall see shortly, the canzonas are treated in a figurational way that is typically Baroque, wherein textural lines gain independence through diminutions at the quarter-, eighth-, or sixteenth-note level.

Trabaci's ricercar "in the fourth tone with three subjects and *inganni*" (1603) is a fine piece that amply demonstrates his approach to counterpoint; like most of his ricercars (and those of de Macque and Mayone), it is based on multiple subjects stated at the outset, unlike those by Girolamo Cavazzoni or Andrea Gabrieli, which are more sectionally oriented and rarely combine subjects. Mm. 1–9 set forth the thematic material (Ex. 5.19a). The subjects (which stem from a single "neighbor note" cell) are all varied both intervallically and rhythmically in the course of the work. Although not by any means the only variation technique, *inganno* was important enough for Trabaci to put in his title. This is intervallic variation according to hexachordal syllables: for example, *fa mi re mi fa* might represent the pitches CBABC (in the "hard" hexachord, built on G), but they might also represent the pitches FEABC (in a combination of the hard and the "natural" hexachord, built on C). An *inganno* version of subject 3 that uses this variation is given in Example 5.19b; note also the rhythmic variation at the end of this subject statement. As befits a composition whose goal is combining subjects, this ricercar ends with two statements of all three combined. The second, from the final measures of the piece, is shown in Example 5.19c.

Trabaci's canzonas also reflect contrapuntal concerns. Two (Nos. 2 and 4) include homophonic interjections in addition to thematic variations and (unlike the ricercars) virtuosic idiomatic writing. Canzona 2 is made up of five sections, the first of which begins with resonant homophonic statements (Ex. 5.20a, p. 278). The second and third sections, both in triple meter, are not closely related to the opening thematically, but the fourth section varies the opening effectively in diminution (Ex. 5.20b). The final section begins with an augmentation of the previous one (subject in treble) with diminutional figuration in the lower voices (sixteenth notes) (Ex. 5.20c), then reverts to a simple repetition (m. 31 = m. 44) with a rhapsodically embellished final cadence. The final repetition seems strangely out of place here, an archaic holdover from a typically French formal feature that was dropped from Italian canzonas after about 1600.

EXAMPLE 5.19. Trabaci, Ricercar 4 (1603)
(a) mm 1–9

(b) *inganno*

(c) conclusion

Trabaci's most famous pieces are perhaps not his best: two *durezze* from Book I. They are similar to pieces by Ercole Pasquini and de Macque that we have already seen, and although Trabaci's may predate them (dating in de Macque and Pasquini is uncertain), it seems more likely that Trabaci's teacher provided him with models. It is also possible that Trabaci was influenced by Bernardo Clavijo del Castillo, a Spaniard who visited Naples in the 1580s. Again we cannot be entirely sure of who influenced whom, and it is entirely possible that Clavijo himself was under the influence of de Macque when he wrote his only extant organ work, a *tiento* in the *durezze* style.[15] Trabaci also incorporated this chromatic style into his toccatas, like Pasquini, but his are somewhat less well developed (with the possible exception of his essay for chromatic harpsichord) than those of his contemporary Mayone. Even more than Trabaci, Mayone's toccatas show the *durezze* influence.

Each of Mayone's two volumes of keyboard music (1603, 1609) con-

EXAMPLE 5.20.   Trabaci, Canzona 2 (1603)
(a) opening

(b) section 4

(c) section 5

tains ricercars, canzonas, a madrigal, toccatas, and variations. In contrast
to Trabaci, Mayone's output adds up to only about 30 compositions. The
ricercars, although well crafted, appear to be a gesture to those who desired *stile antico* compositions. Mayone wrote only nine (four in the first
book, five in the second); the last three of Book II are cantus firmus
works harking back to Rodio (one is for harp). His eight canzonas also
display considerable contrapuntal artifice, to which is added much virtuosic figuration. They are sectional variation canzonas with more idiomatic writing for the keyboard than those by Trabaci. Several present
straightforward repetitions of sections: Book II, Nos. 1 and 2, suggest
ABA forms, the latter distinguished by an extraordinary set of roulades
in its middle section.

     Mayone's ten toccatas surpass those of Ercole Pasquini and Trabaci
in length and quality. Five conclude with a clear ricercar-like section (as
those of the Venetian Annibale Padovano, though the resemblance is
probably coincidental), and four are figurational throughout. The figurations depend on intriguing varieties of trills, including, for example,
series of ascending thirty-second-note triplet neighbor notes. Harmonically the toccatas employ the *durezze* style as a matter of course. The most
imposing toccata, Book I, No. 5, shows many of these features. The
opening (mm. 1–12) is a lovely *durezze* introduction with typically Ma-
yonian embellishment; it sets forth the thematic material of the work, the

subject AAEFE (Ex. 5.21a). In basing the toccata on a subject, Mayone in
a sense combines the figurational with the imitative. The work falls into
four parts, the second and fourth of which are fiery and heavily embellished. They are separated by imitative treatment of the motive (mm.
19–23). The embellishment of mm. 29–30 (Ex. 5.21b) is an indication of
Mayone's extreme approach (note the motive in the lower voice), well
suited to harpsichord performance.

EXAMPLE 5.21. Mayone, Toccata 5 (1603)
(a) opening

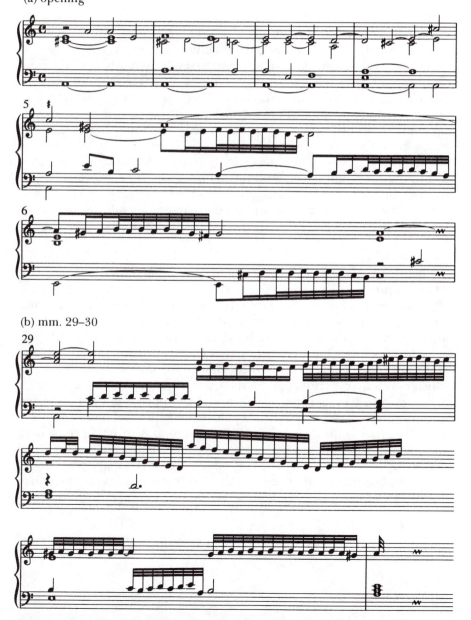

(b) mm. 29–30

Both Mayone and Trabaci wrote extended and impressive variation sets; both even treated the same bass themes (Ruggiero and Fidele), suggesting a certain competition. These and similar variation themes were also set by Frescobaldi, Storace, and others over the course of the century.

We must pass over a number of other works by Neapolitan composers found in a manuscript copied by Luigi Rossi (Rossi MS), including a *Canzon francese del Principe*, doubtless a work by Gesualdo himself, and as idiosyncratic as one might expect.

MILAN

Milanese organists never achieved the stature of the Neapolitans and Venetians. The music we have, although competent, is of secondary importance. Giovanni Paolo Cima, for example, published a collection (in open score) in 1606, consisting of ricercars, canzonas, and transposition exercises, but the music has little keyboard figuration and much of it would sound equally well in ensemble performance. His seventh ricercar contains an ostinato *obbligo* in one voice, which may have had some influence on later composers of ostinato ricercars; his canzonas include variation types. Other composers who reflect a style similar to Cima's include Francesco Porta and Francesco Bianciardi, both of whose music survives only in manuscript; a number of volumes of ensemble music written by Milanese organists also survive, suggesting a focus away from keyboard music.

BRESCIA

In Brescia, 50 miles east of Milan, important music for keyboard was composed, including the canzonas of the organist Florentio Maschera and ricercars and canzonas by Costanzo Antegnati. The latter, a member of the most important family of organ builders in Italy, wrote idiomatic music for keyboard in his ricercars (including works with progressive variation), but Maschera's set of 21 canzonas was certainly the more popular. They were printed at least six times (one edition, of which only a manuscript copy survives, was apparently in open score for organists) and served as models for literally hundreds of similarly styled canzonas in the following 20 years. Their thematic treatment is remarkable, for in addition to thematic development and variation (including *inganno*), Maschera treats the same subject developmentally across several works (e.g., Nos. 1, 2, 3, 4, 7, 8, and 9 all have related opening subjects). While triple sections are few and keyboard-style canzona features are not prevalent, there can be no doubt that Maschera's pathbreaking set was highly influential on later keyboard musicians and composers.

ROME

Little evidence remains of a Roman keyboard tradition in the sixteenth century apart from a toccata by Paolo Quagliati in Diruta's *Il Transilvano*. We know that de Macque worked in Rome before moving to Naples, that Ercole Pasquini moved to Rome after the demise of the Este in Ferrara, and that Merulo's two books of toccatas were printed there in around 1600 (Merulo participated in the Roman Farnese retinue as well as the Parmesan). We are uncertain of dates for Pasquini's music, so it is possible that some of his extant music was written during the Rome years; even so, it is clearly a transplanted offshoot from Ferrara. Not until Frescobaldi does the situation change in Rome.

Girolamo Frescobaldi (1583-1643)

After a visit to Rome in 1639, the French gambist and diarist André Maugars wrote, "It is not without cause that Girolamo Frescobaldi has acquired so much fame in Europe" (Hammond 1983, 91). After an unprecedented quantity of keyboard publications and a lifetime of public performance at St. Peter's, it is small wonder that near the end of his life Girolamo Frescobaldi was virtually a household name among keyboard players. Frescobaldi was above all a player; as Maugars noted, "Although his printed works give sufficient witness of his ability, in order to judge his profound knowledge it is necessary to hear him improvise toccatas full of contrapuntal devices and admirable inventions" (Hammond 1983, 91-92). Fortunately Frescobaldi, more than any of his contemporaries, took a great interest in publishing his own music, especially concerning himself with details of performance practice and notational means of effecting the best possible performances. A number of his volumes have extensive prefaces outlining their purposes and goals. This music clearly succeeds in revealing much of that improvisational artistry to which Maugars alluded.

Frescobaldi was born in Ferrara, where he was raised in the full flush of that duchy's musical activities; he repeatedly acknowledged a debt to his teacher Luzzaschi. Like Pasquini, evidently he left Ferrara after the departure of the Este court. We cannot be sure of his whereabouts until 1607, when he took up service for a noble Ferrarese family and immediately journeyed to Brussels as part of his patron's retinue (his only trip outside Italy). He returned in 1608 after publishing his first volume, a collection of madrigals, in Antwerp. On his way back he stopped in Milan for at least a month and attended to his first keyboard publication, the *Fantasie*; before he reached Rome he was elected to take Ercole Pasquini's place at St. Peter's. He remained there until his death, except for two interruptions: to Mantua in 1615 for a few months, and to Florence from 1628 to 1634. He was active in other venues in Rome as well, particularly at the palaces of noble patrons and at the Oratorio del Crocifisso.

Frescobaldi dominated the publication of keyboard music from 1615 to 1645; only one other Roman, the violinist Michelangelo Rossi, published anything comparable in this period.[16] In several instances Frescobaldi supervised the publication of his keyboard music personally; in addition, a large amount of manuscript music bears his name in attribution. Our survey must of necessity consider in detail only a small fraction of Frescobaldi's output, which numbers well over 150 pieces in prints alone; we will concentrate on the beginnings of his output and on his most characteristic music, the toccatas.

Fantasie (1608). Frescobaldi owes little to any known precursors in this remarkable first effort, some of which must have been written well before he reached the age of 25. As a genre the fantasia is allied to the ricercar tradition, and Frescobaldi's set is contrapuntally complex, containing little idiomatic keyboard writing. It follows the practice of Luzzaschi, de Macque, Trabaci, and others in collecting 12 works together, but is organized in two ways: according to number of subjects and by mode. There are four sets of three fantasias each, according to one, two, three, or four subjects, and there is one piece per mode. Unlike Trabaci's or any other composer's ricercars, these works are written in distinct sections, suggesting a conceptual blend with the variation canzona; in subject treatment there are similarities with the combinative techniques of Trabaci's and Mayone's ricercars, particularly in Frescobaldi's use of *inganno* and thematic variation. Although these techniques make their presence felt throughout the volume, the additional use of augmentation, diminution, and inversion make resemblances to the Neapolitans only slight. Frescobaldi is consciously clever to the point of precocity, as if he were proving a point with this contrapuntal virtuosity that he perhaps regretted later; unlike his ricercars and capriccios, equally challenging contrapuntally but in a sense more human, he never had the fantasias reprinted. Still, these works represent some of the high points of the *artificioso* Italian style, and were considered valuable enough by no less a master than Bernardo Pasquini to copy them 60 years after their publication. It is ironic that despite his continual demonstration of such contrapuntal virtuosity, Frescobaldi acquired an undeserved reputation for a lack of intelligence; Doni's famous comment that "all his knowledge is at the ends of his fingertips" hardly accords with the intellectual demands of these works.[17]

Frescobaldi's next two publications were both issued in 1615, and firmly established his reputation. Each presents a facet of his personality also reflected in notation. The intellectual comes through in ricercars and canzonas in open score, the emotional through toccatas and variations in engraved keyboard score. The ricercars belong to the same world as the *fantasias,* but the toccatas are entirely new creations and contain some of the finest music of the era for any medium.

Recercari et Canzoni (1615). There can be no doubt that Frescobaldi thought carefully about the ricercars published in this collection; in a sense they represent a summing up of activity in Italy from his vantage point. Like the *Fantasie,* they are ordered according to mode, but their stylistic ordering is more disguised. Two ricercars reflect the Neapolitan style, two the Venetian style, one the Ferraran; the remaining five are Frescobaldi's own. The plan is given in Table 5.4.

This evaluation is misleading in that the "foreign" works might best be viewed as only allusions to those styles. The typical Trabaci ricercar resembles Nos. 1 and 9, but would include more idiomatic keyboard figuration than found here. The typical Andrea Gabrieli ricercar is not as clearly laid out as Nos. 3 and 5, and none combines three subjects. Luzzaschi's 12 ricercars of 1578 reflect a fondness for pairing successive subjects (Nos. 1,

TABLE 5.4
Organization in Frescobaldi, *Recercari et Canzoni* (1615)

No.	Style	Comments
1	Neapolitan	3 *soggetti*
2	Ferraran	hexachordal inversion, paired subjects
3	Venetian	3 sections, three themes: A, B+A, C+B+A
4	Frescobaldian	hexachord *obbligo* subject (migrating)
5	Venetian	5 sections, 3 themes: ABC, A, B, C, A+B+C
6	Frescobaldian	hexachord *obbligo* subject (in alto; allusion in other voices)
7	Frescobaldian	hexachord *obbligo* subject (in tenor; no allusion in other voices)
8	Frescobaldian	*obbligo* to avoid all stepwise motion
9	Neapolitan	4 *soggetti, conclusione**
10	Frescobaldian	hexachord *obbligo* subject (in soprano, pervasive in other voices)

Conclusione is the technical term for combining all subjects at the end of a contrapuntal work.

2, 7, 8, 10, 11, and 12), and hexachordal inversion is prominent in No. 1, which may have served as a conceptual model in this instance.

Such stylistic allusion perhaps indicates Frescobaldi's "rite of passage" from journeyman to master; his "own" compositions all share *obbligo* tendencies seen almost to excess in his *Fantasie*. Here they are more evenly balanced and varied, and include considerable free material in accompanying voices. In these pieces the *obbligo* consists of setting the subject in one voice with no other material, forming so-called "ostinato ricercars" (Nos. 6, 7, and 10), or forbidding stepwise motion (No. 8). The former technique is found as early as 1549 in the music of Giuliano Tiburtino, but the latter has no precedent. The wry character of much of this writing becomes outright humorous here, as in, for example, the final measures of No. 8 (Ex. 5.22).

Toccate, Book I (1615). Frescobaldi here continued his vision of musical poetics at the keyboard; the toccatas were well received from their first printing, and remain a monument in the history of keyboard music. Several features of Frescobaldi's first book of toccatas must have surprised its original purchasers before they ever played a note: its elegant (and costly) engraved format, not seen since Merulo's works of 1604 (compare Ills. 5.12 and 5.10); its scope, a set of 12 works ordered modally (following a tradition associated with ricercars); the omission of the organ as performing medium on the title page (it was included in later editions); and most important, Frescobaldi's modest but insistent preface, outlining in detail how he wanted various aspects of the music played.[18] It is tempting to search for stylistic antecedents to this volume,[19] but in so doing it is important to remember that purchasers' initial reactions of surprise probably continued, along with wonder and delight, after studying and hearing the music within. Like much great

EXAMPLE 5.22. Frescobaldi, Ricercar 8 (1615), mm. 63–70

ILLUSTRATION 5.12. Frescobaldi, *Toccate* (1615) p. 1 (Toccata 1, first page).
Copper engraving by Nicolo Borbone. Reproduced by courtesy of the Music
Division, Library of Congress.

art, this music operates both as summation and prophecy, to which no genealogy can fully do justice.

The toccatas' chief features include frankly unpredictable but well-ordered overall structure; adoption of the *durezze* style as a fundamental element; a variety of figuration set forth in discrete sections, some of which the composer paradoxically acknowledged could be deleted if the performer so chose; and, not least, a high level of virtuosic technical demands. Most of these features can be found throughout the volume; while some, such as Nos. 2, 5, and 6, open with more *durezze* than others, none entirely eliminates these characteristic harmonic explorations that so clearly distinguish Frescobaldi's from the Venetian toccatas. Toccata 10 may serve as a representative of these features; its formal design is given in Table 5.5.

Frescobaldi begins with arpeggiation in place of a *durezze* opening (Ex. 5.23a), foreshadowing the viola bastarda-style figuration to follow (Ex. 5.23b). Music for viola bastarda is full of such chordal/arpeggiated figures, and although a direct relation cannot be established, the similarity of this opening to that style supports the description. The three motivic elements that follow are successively more energetic and push forward to the cadence in m. 18. Here, at the midpoint of the toccata, a formal articulation is made and the *durezze* style introduced (Ex. 5.23c). The second half of the toccata similarly has three concluding sections, the outer two of which again recall the bastarda style. Example 5.23d shows the shift over sections 6b and 6c, giving some indication of the way Frescobaldi literally propels his motive forward and over a sectional articulation.

The last two toccatas of Book I suggest organ more strongly than do the others: No. 11 begins with pedal points, and No. 12 is a *durezze* piece

TABLE 5.5
Sections in Frescobaldi,
Toccata 10 (1615)

Section	Mm.	Description
1	1–6	introduction
2	6–8	"bastarda" solo
3a	8–11	motivic i
3b	11–15	motivic ii
3c	15–18	motivic iii
4	18–20	*durezze*
5	20–24	motivic
6a	24–29	"bastarda" solo
6b	29–33	motivic interlude
6c	33–39	"bastarda" solo

EXAMPLE 5.23. Frescobaldi, Toccata 10 (1615)
(a) opening

(b) mm. 6–7

(c) mm. 18–19

(d) mm. 31–33

that eschews ornamentation and virtuosic figuration entirely and is thus suggestive of the elevation toccatas of the *Fiori musicali* (1635). The volume was reprinted almost immediately, with several noteworthy changes: its variation sets were revised, and four correntes were added.

This revised edition was reprinted twice by 1628 and once more, with further additions, in 1637, making five editions in all.

Capricci (1624). There is much that is capricious in the *Capricci*, such as the whimsical subject of the cuckoo-call DB as ostinato in the top voice (No. 3), the *obbligo* to resolve all suspensions the "wrong way" or up (No. 8), and the *obbligo* to have the performer sing a fifth ostinato part (No. 11). The dominance of sectional works in the collection indicates that Frescobaldi was preoccupied with variation at several levels: No. 10 is a variation canzona in all but name and No. 7 a set of five variations on "Or che noi rimena" (the piece, based on the tune also known as "Aria del balletto" or "More palatino," was removed from reprints, suggesting recognition that it did not belong with the capriccios); nearly all the works were oriented to sectionalized variation of their respective starting points.

Toccate, Book II (1627). This volume is in several ways an expansion into territory first claimed in Book I. Like the earlier work it contains a set of toccatas (a madrigal intabulation representing the twelfth), variation works, and dances; here Frescobaldi adds liturgical versets for vespers, canzonas, and the first true keyboard passacaglia sets to appear in print. In these toccatas, as in Book I, the variety of figuration, virtuosity, and imaginative variation over the span of both short sections and longer designs is remarkable. A few examples must suffice to show some of these, as well as the changes from the previous collection.

Four toccatas are expressly designated for organ—two for elevation, two with pedal parts. The ecstatic opening of the elevation toccata No. 4 (Ex. 5.24a) is one of the great moments of the collection, although the harmonic explorations of the remainder of the toccata are equally inspired. Similar openings with prominent descending minor sixths are found in the *durezze* capriccio (1624) and the fifth toccata of Book I, but here the "harshnesses" are more tempered and subtle. The opening of Toccata 5 from Book II is also magnificent, for different reasons; one can imagine the grandeur of this pure G-major triad with the simple but profound chromatic inflection resonating in St. Peter's (Ex. 5.24b). The conclusion of this work provides a mesmerizing instance of a notable trait of several toccatas in the collection, the insistent repetition of a short figure, almost like a stutter; indeed, one feels palpable relief at its resolution in the final chord (Ex. 5.24c).

For sheer virtuosity, however, Toccata 9 is unmatched. This is Frescobaldi's most technically demanding toccata; at its conclusion he wrote the aphorism "not without effort does one reach the end"—with a smile, one senses. It begins innocently enough, with a typical introduction (mm. 1–4), but the cadence of the following section (m. 11) serves notice of technical difficulties to come (Ex. 5.25a). And come they do, with an unparalleled amount of virtuosic writing, including the proportional labyrinths of mm. 11–16 (Ex. 5.25a) and the final cadence (not

EXAMPLE 5.24. Frescobaldi, from *Toccate* (1627)

(a) Toccata 4, opening

(b) Toccata 5, opening

(c) Toccata 5, conclusion

EXAMPLE 5.25. Frescobaldi, Toccata 9 (1627)
(a) mm. 9–16

(b) mm. 50–52

shown). Among nearly a dozen distinct figurations, that of mm. 50–51 (Ex. 5.25b) is a dazzling instance of effective writing for harpsichord.

THE VARIATION SETS AND CANZONAS

One senses a certain amount of dissatisfaction on Frescobaldi's part with his variation sets as they appeared in two editions of Book I, Book II, and a supplement to the retrospective reprint of both books (1637). The first edition's variations were revised immediately, another set strayed into the *Capricci*, and in the supplement he reworked the passacaglias of Book II into the *Cento partite sopra passacagli* ("hundred settings of the passacaglia"). The variations are characterized by stylistic shifting throughout, and they rarely restrict themselves to one idea per variation as did those by Mayone and Trabaci. Frescobaldi's finest set, the 14 Romanesca variations (in the revised version of 1615), is un-equaled. Its variety of affective writing runs the gamut from toccata style to mannerist chromaticism, virtuosity, and elegant simplicity. The bravura twelfth variation is followed by two simple settings that quietly but effectively refute any ostentation suggested by the preceding py-rotechnics.

Frescobaldi's fascination with variation is also manifest in his can-zonas of 1615, 1627, and 1635. We can see an increasing concern for the variation canzona and the intricacies of progressive thematic variation in the 1627 works, which continue the trend of subtlety established in the earlier set. All six of the 1627 canzonas employ variation to some degree (two of the 1615 set do not); the most subtle example, Canzona 4, virtu-ally combines toccata and canzona style in one work. Its thematic varia-tion is given in Example 5.26. The scalar fourth of the opening is taken for section B; this in turn is rhythmically modified, then transformed to an anacrusis-motive (C.1 and C.2). The motive of C.2 is modified for sec-tion D, accompanied by the line labeled "z," providing material for the final section, which bears little indication of the point of departure.

EXAMPLE 5.26. Progressive thematic variation in Frescobaldi, Canzona 4 (1627)

Fiori musicali. Frescobaldi's last work to be published in his lifetime is the Fiori musicali (1635), a collection for liturgical use at mass that includes versets, canzonas, ricercars, elevation toccatas, and two capriccios on secular tunes. Its purpose is partly pedagogical, as Frescobaldi himself acknowledged in its important preface, but he transcended mere pedagogy in each of the genres he took up, particularly the canzonas and capricclos. The versets demonstrate how he might have improvised at St. Peter's; the short toccatas and Kyrie versets are miniatures of variety and imagination. In his preface he also stressed the importance of learning to use open score at the keyboard, an overriding concern throughout his life and probably one of the reasons for publishing this collection. The canzonas, most of which employ variation, are noteworthy for the frequent shifts in tempo (usually marked "adasio-alegro") that demarcate sections. Rather than proceeding without break between sections, little cadential flourishes soften the otherwise sharp corners.

The two capriccios, Bergamasca and Girolmeta, are sectional and contrapuntal, like those of the 1624 collection, but seem less abstract, perhaps because of their folk-tune bases. Frescobaldi's note at the head of the Bergamasca, "whoever plays this will learn not a little," indicates its complexity. It is based on a popular four-phrase melody set in seven clearly articulated sections, including languorous chromatic and virtuosic triplet-dominated styles. Most of the texture is derived from the four melodic phrases, but here Frescobaldi is not tied to rigid contrapuntal premises and simply delights in combining the exuberant little melodies in myriad ways.

THE MANUSCRIPT CORPUS

A quantity of music nearly equal to Frescobaldi's published output is extant in manuscript form; we are fortunate that most of the manuscripts have now been made available in facsimile and provide us with considerable context for evaluating the attributions. Silbiger's assessment (1980b) after having studied the matter closely is sensible: only a few works can be positively confirmed as Frescobaldi's, and considering the care Frescobaldi took over his publications, the unpublished corpus must remain secondary. Among the most important of the manuscript works as probable indicators of Frescobaldi's stylistic development after 1627 are three toccatas in Chigi 25 (published in Frescobaldi 1968) and eleven canzonas in London 40080.

1630 to 1700

Frescobaldi left his mark on later generations in several ways. His most famous pupil, Johann Jacob Froberger, was sent by the Austrian emperor to study with him. German-speaking lands seem to have been as much influenced by Frescobaldi's work as Italy; one sees some of the fantastic element of the toccatas as well as much of the learned style of the ricercars in a number of later German composers, including J. S. Bach, who as a teenager copied the *Fiori musicali*. In the seventeenth century the Italian "learned style" was exemplified more by Frescobaldi than by Palestrina.[20] French and English composers, too, were well aware of Frescobaldi's musical legacy. Even eighteenth- and nineteenth-century musicians studied and arranged Frescobaldi's contrapuntal masterpieces.

More immediately, his toccatas, canzonas, ricercars, variations, and dances were unavoidably models to follow (or react against) for successors in Italy. But only a handful of Italian composers had keyboard music published after Frescobaldi's death, and only one was received with anything approaching the response accorded Frescobaldi: Michelangelo Rossi. Ironically, Rossi played the instrument that eclipsed the keyboard and all others in popularity after 1650, the violin. Coinciding with the drop in publication of keyboard music were the extraordinary rise in popularity of opera (and its relatives cantata and oratorio) and the increasing appearance of music for violin-based ensembles. There is little evidence in Italy of transcription of opera selections for keyboard (a popular genre in France at the time)—a curious lacuna, since opera is a genre prominent in the output of both Rossi and the most prolific keyboard composer of the late seventeenth century, Bernardo Pasquini.

MICHELANGELO ROSSI (1602–56)

Recent research (Silbiger 1983) suggests that a rivalry may have existed between Frescobaldi and Rossi, rather than, as has often been proposed, a master-pupil relationship. In addition to being an outstanding violinist, Rossi was an opera composer and madrigalist in the Gesualdo tradition; although he served for some time as organist in a Roman church, his printed keyboard output consists of only one volume of toccatas and correntes, probably published in the early 1630s (the exact date is not given in the publication). It was reprinted at least three times (the last reprint perhaps as late as the 1660s), a sign of its continued popularity. The toccatas are fine works, although they lack the variety of style and affect found in Frescobaldi. Nine of the ten are about the same length, with often similar, sequentially based imitative sections. In this regard Rossi departs from the example of Frescobaldi, whose imitative sections appear less frequently and tend to be briefer. There is plenty of bold chromaticism and creative figuration, however. Toccata 7 is famous for its conclusion, a chromatic section that includes a long succession of parallel chromatic major thirds, but other works are equally striking. The conclusion of Toccata 6 (Ex. 5.27a), with its virtuosic left-hand part, is reminiscent of the "bastarda" figurations of Frescobaldi's Toccata 10

EXAMPLE 5.27. Rossi
(a) Toccata 6, mm. 66–71

(b) Toccata 10, mm. 1–5

(Book I); the opening section of Rossi's Toccata 10 evokes the harmonic juxtapositions of Gesualdo (Ex. 5.27b).

LITURGICAL WORKS

Banchieri, Diruta, and Asola continued to be reprinted during Frescobaldi's lifetime. Later, Antonio Croci (1642) and the southerner Giovanni Battista Fasolo (1645) wrote books of liturgical organ music more or less emulating Frescobaldi's *Fiori musicali*. Croci's music is intended for beginners, tellingly including a few works for those unable to span an

EXAMPLE 5.28. Fasolo, *Fuga quarta sopra Ut re mi fa sol la,* mm. 77–80

octave with one hand. Fasolo's collection is larger and better. It consists of a number of versets for *alternatim* performance from both proper and ordinary, and concludes with eight ricercars and canzonas (one per mode) and four *fughe* based on popular tunes. While not quite up to the standards of the *Fiori musicali,* the music in this collection is uniformly of high quality and modern in outlook. The larger pieces within the organ masses (a number of variation canzonas but no ricercars) and the sets of unassigned pieces at the end are most interesting. Fasolo's hymns for the liturgical year include directives to play chant melodies an octave above (or below) for clarity, as well as other performance comments. The finest piece of the collection may be the last, *Fuga quarta sopra Ut re mi fa sol la.* It falls into three sections totalling 117 measures, setting the subject with a delightful variety of countermotives; one is shown in Example 5.28.

THE SOUTH: SALVATORE, STORACE, AND STROZZI

It is difficult to speak of a tradition of Neapolitan keyboard music after 1630: most composers from the south were influenced by Frescobaldi at least as much as by Trabaci or Mayone. While we have the works of Fasolo and his contemporaries Del Buono (Palermo, 1641), Salvatore (Naples, 1641), Bernardo Storace (Venice, 1664), and Gregorio Strozzi (Naples, 1687), they are nothing if not widely disparate.[21] Del Buono's is an idiosyncratic set of 14 harpsichord "sonatas," all cantus firmus settings of the hymn *Ave maris stella*; as we have seen, Fasolo is liturgically oriented; Storace's writing is dominated by variation sets; and Strozzi's is the retrospective publication of a septuagenarian. Salvatore and Strozzi follow the Mayone-Trabaci pattern most closely, but even these works have individual quirks that suggest not a tradition but individuals acting relatively independently. We can study the music, much of it attractive and competent, and place it in the general perspective of the period, but the sense of each composer's isolation is hard to dispel.

Giovanni Salvatore (d. c. 1688) wrote a collection similar in content to Trabaci's that contains ricercars, canzonas, toccatas, and mass versets, but variations are conspicuously absent. The ricercars, written on two or three *fughe* (Trabaci's terminology is used rather than Frescobaldi's), are highly reminiscent of Trabaci, but the organ masses (which include settings for all of the Ordinary but the Credo) are unusual for Neapolitan music; the only other southern Italian to include them is Fasolo, and he lays them out quite differently. It is in his canzonas that Salvatore stands above his peers. These four works are uniformly well conceived and written. The last is a series of short movements on the Bergamasca tune used by Frescobaldi; the other three are more generically designed. The second is particularly fine, with a short homophonic motive occurring at its outset and again several times in the course of the work. Its 76 measures include a section in triple meter, mm. 39–57, and a heavily embellished statement of the subject in augmentation at the conclusion. Example 5.29 gives the opening and conclusion of the work.

Bernardo Storace was working in Messina (Sicily) at the time of his *Selva di varie compositioni* (1664), his only known work. It is focused primarily on variations. More than any other successor, he emulated the variation types of Frescobaldi (e.g., Romanesca, Monica, Ruggiero, Folia). Storace's 15 variation sets include 5 on the "passacagli" and "ciaccona," which comprise in total over 300 variations of the 2-measure themes. He also wrote two toccata-canzona pairs, ricercars, and charac-

EXAMPLE 5.29. Salvatore, *Canzone Francese Seconda*, mm. 1–4, 74–79

ter pieces: a spirited *Ballo della Battaglia* full of martial onomatopoeia, and a near-minimalist 250-measure Pastorale consisting of dozens of figurations over a pedal, some repeated as many as four times. The Ciaccona (110 two-measure variations), perhaps the finest piece of the volume, falls into four parts, the first as long as the remaining three. Part two moves from C to F major, and changes to $\frac{9}{8}$; part three moves to B-flat major; part four returns to the home key and meter. There is continual accumulation of tempo and energy, released when sections come to an end. The opening motive returns at two key points, and a fine variety of chromatic and ornamental inflections makes for a very impressive work. Example 5.30 presents its opening.

Gregorio Strozzi's *Capricci* (1688) is an anachronistic volume. He had worked under Trabaci at the Annunziata, and Trabaci's influence is clearly to be seen in the variety of pieces and styles in the collection as well as the occasional writing for *organetto*, *flauto*, harp, and string ensemble. The book begins with three *capricci*, a generic title that denotes pieces as disparate as a lengthy set of variations on *Ut re mi fa sol la* (one of the last on that venerable subject) and a short work rather like a variation canzona. He includes ricercars, "sonatas" (similar to variation canzonas), toccatas, a madrigal intabulation (on Arcadelt's *Ancidetemi pur*, also set by Mayone, Trabaci, and Frescobaldi), a monumental set of Romanesca variations, galliards, correntes, other dances (some in two-part score with figures above or below both voices, some apparently for ensemble), and a "toccata de passacagli." The longer pieces are the most successful: *Ut re mi fa sol la*, the Romanesca, and the passacagli. Strozzi

EXAMPLE 5.30. Storace, Ciaccona, mm. 1–8

builds effective designs in these works and moves beyond the more mundane or outdated writing of some of the ricercars and canzonas.

The Romanesca variations, or "Romanesca con Partite, Tenori, e Ritorn[elli]," as he called them, is the longest work of the volume, over 450 measures; it seems likely that when he wrote it Strozzi had his forebears in mind. The 15 variations are interspersed with four "Tenore" statements (after variations 3, 5, 10, and 13). These are free harmonizations of the Romanesca theme, set with *durezze* chromatic inflections and little embellishment. The "Ritornelli" are placed after variations 1, 4, and 7; like the *tenori* they are short chordal sections free of embellishment. The term "ritornello" is somewhat ambiguous, as each is different; it may indicate performance by string ensemble. The variations proceed from a toccata-like introduction with archaic harmonic and figural extravagances to a wide variety of motivic and technically challenging writing. Variations 11 and 12 include directives for harp or string performance. Variation 14 is a tour de force that might well serve as a finale, but, like Frescobaldi, Strozzi continues simply, with a fifteenth variation that acts as an interlude before the final set of 18 2-measure variations on a given "Ritornelli nel binario" related to the Romanesca bass.

Finally, mention should be made of the Neapolitan composer Alessandro Stradella's sole work for keyboard, a toccata with features that will recur in the toccatas of Alessandro Scarlatti (see Silbiger 1982, 263–64). Its continual motoric (often violinistic) writing propels the work forward with energy and excitement.

THE NORTH: BOLOGNA

The compositional activities of keyboard players in the north are even more obscure than those of their southern counterparts: significantly, virtually no Venetian keyboard music was published after 1620. A new trend may be seen in the growing ensemble output from Venice and Bologna after 1650, for which the founding of the Accademia Filarmonica in Bologna in 1666 was an important milestone. While the few modest publications for keyboard from the same period issued by Bolognese presses are hardly comparable to the ensemble activity, some are noteworthy. Giulio Cesare Aresti, organist at San Petronio for 50 years, produced hymn versets in the pedagogical volume *Modulationi precettive* (c. 1664), and later edited an anthology of "sonatas" by contemporaries like Ziani, Pollarolo, the German Kerll, Giustiniani, and Bernardo Pasquini. These vary in style from somewhat old-fashioned toccata-like or canzona-like works to more modern pieces. An instance of the latter is Carlo Francesco Pollarolo's Sonata in D Minor, an internal section of which is given in Example 5.31. Pollarolo achieved considerable stature as an opera composer, and was head of music at St. Mark's in Venice from 1692 until his death in 1722. The imitative piece is in the canzona tradition, closer to a fugue than a sonata; it emphasizes subject state-

EXAMPLE 5.31. Pollarolo, Sonata in D minor, mm. 26–33

ments beginning with A and D and has "episodes." In this excerpt the subject sounds in the alto (mm. 26–27), followed by a short sequential episode before the next entry (bass, m. 32).

Some manuscript music from the Bolognese sphere awaits detailed evaluation and publication; Silbiger's groundwork[22] suggests that there is much fine music here, perhaps including other works by Pollarolo.

RETROSPECTIVES: BATTIFERRI AND FONTANA

Two collections of ricercars were issued in the post-Frescobaldi era, by Luigi Battiferri (Bologna, 1669) and Fabritio Fontana (Rome, 1677). Both are clearly in the Frescobaldi mold. Battiferri, a Ferraran, included a lengthy preface lamenting the loss of ricercar-type works, naming Ercole Pasquini, Luzzaschi, and Frescobaldi as important Ferrarans who preceded him (he claimed Frescobaldi as a teacher). Fontana, from Genoa, was Frescobaldi's successor at St. Peter's in Rome. Both sets include 12 ricercars. They represent the end of the Italian tradition of *stile antico* keyboard writing, as both composers self-consciously acknowledge. Battiferri's, at least, were known in the north; they were copied by the famous Austrian composer-theorist Johann Fux, among others.

BERNARDO PASQUINI (1637–1710)

The musical environment of Rome in the later seventeenth century was profoundly affected by Arcangelo Corelli and Alessandro Scarlatti, whose output in instrumental chamber music and opera, respectively, can scarcely be overestimated. Bernardo Pasquini was a lesser peer of these two; with them, he was prominent in the Arcadian Academy, a focal point for artists and patrons in Rome. Handel must have encountered Pasquini during his sojourn in Rome in the early 1700s, and in all probability Pasquini taught Scarlatti's son Domenico, one of Italy's most famous keyboard players. At his best, Pasquini is very good indeed, as we may infer from the attention accorded him by contemporaries. Although his level of inspiration and originality may not often reach that of a Frescobaldi or a Domenico Scarlatti, his large and varied output contains much that is well crafted and of considerable charm, establishing him as the most important figure in Italian keyboard music between those two masters.

Pasquini published no keyboard music, but several of his autograph manuscripts are preserved. His oeuvre is considerable; he wrote in all of the familiar genres, including a number of interesting variation sets and toccatas. He also wrote many dances and collected them in suites—the first Italian to do so in a significant way. While Pasquini was certainly aware of Frescobaldi (he copied the 1608 *Fantasie* as a student and modeled a few of his own works directly on those by Frescobaldi), his stature as a prolific and able opera composer in indicative of entirely different compositional foundations. The *durezze* style and a wide variety of motivic figuration are apparent in his earlier or older-style works, but later pieces reflect the lyricism and simplicity of the eighteenth-century galant. Model inflections are replaced in the dances and arias by tonal harmony. Pasquini also left a number of curious half-compositions: 28 "sonatas" (more properly suites) evenly divided for one and two harpsichords, for which Pasquini wrote only the figured basses; and a similarly constructed set of over 100 versets (not published in the modern edition but available in facsimile).

Suites. Although Pasquini's 15 suites are counterparts to violin suites of the period by Corelli and his predecessors, they are modest in scope and hardly resemble Corelli's *Sonate* in variety or ambition. They are also quite distinct from the suites of the French or of Froberger, and set forth material simply, with pleasant and unaffected grace. They may be divided into about five each of two, three, and four movements, most containing forms of alemanda, corrente, gavotta, and giga, in that order, although the dance-type is not always identified. The corrente from the Suite in B flat (No. 26 of his collected keyboard works) is indicative of Pasquini's style (Ex. 5.32a) and displays the characteristic harmonic procedures of classical binary form. The giga to the same suite is typical of most, with imitative writing in the first part matched by imitation of the inversion in the second (Ex. 5.32b).

Toccatas. Much fine writing is to be found in Pasquini's 30-odd toccatas,[23] although there is a sense (as in much of his music) that he repeats himself from piece to piece. Yet there is a wide variety of striking

EXAMPLE 5.32. B. Pasquini, Suite in B flat

(a) corrente

(b) giga theme and inversion

figuration in the works when taken separately, including pedal toccatas, arpeggio writing, motivic interplay, and lively violinistic counterpoint. In general, the notion of unity over the course of a toccata is not particularly important to Pasquini, although a few, such as No. 88, reflect this ideal. Like some of his predecessors, Pasquini apparently puts great stock in startling openings for his toccatas, most of which are imaginative and colorful. One of the most effective is given in Example 5.33.

Variations. Pasquini clearly enjoyed this genre, and composed ten large sets as well as four passagagli of more modest dimensions. In these works he distinguished between themes of his own invention and those with traditional themes, and is thus notable as one of the first to write variations on his own themes (although Frescobaldi preceded him with the "Aria detta La Frescobalda"). He usually distinguished between the two in titles: the old themes he called partite, the new variationi. One of the most interesting sets is the Variationi d'inventione (No. 53), which, despite its title, might be viewed as an homage to Frescobaldi. It consists of 11 variations, 4 of which refer to dances, thus suggesting a kind of crossbreed with the suite also found in Storace variation sets: Nos. 5 to 7 are styled "in corrente," No. 11 "gagliarda." The theme resembles Frescobaldi's "Aria detta La Frescobalda," and variations following refer more or less clearly to Toccata 9 from Book II, correntes from Books I and II, and other works.[24] The final, "gagliarda," variation (for which no reference has been determined) may serve to indicate Pasquini's attractive and rhythmically intriguing approach (Ex. 5.34).

Pasquini's first Folia and Bergamasca *Partite* (Nos. 61 and 64) also deserve to be singled out for their fine writing, which includes violinistic

EXAMPLE 5.33. B. Pasquini, *Tastata 92*, mm. 1–6

Example 5.34. B. Pasquini, *Variatione d'inventione,* var. 11, MM. 1–10

figuration, much rhythmic and metric variety, chromatic *affetti,* and virtuosic *passaggi.* This is exciting music that rewards careful study.

ALESSANDRO SCARLATTI (1660–1725)

Scarlatti left a large quantity of keyboard music, somewhat surprising for one so intimately linked to opera. The extant toccatas and other works, about 40 in all, probably date from after 1700 and receive only brief consideration here. They are quite distant from the style of Pasquini and many have distinct movements. They consist primarily of rapid and volatile violinistic ideas, both imitative and figurational; rhapsodic, recitative sections (some written out, some simply with figured bass long notes); and a variety of additional movement types, including fugues and dances. These are virtuosic works that contain much fiery energy, not always under complete formal control. The occasional extended sequences, for example, betray hasty writing. The most noteworthy toccata is the last, an extended multimovement work that finishes with a set of 29 variations on the Folia, perhaps the last to be written for the harpsichord.

Guide to Literature and Editions

The best general overview of the Italian milieu and keyboard music to the first half of the seventeenth century is Hammond 1983, which provides a thorough background for Frescobaldi and his music. It is supplemented by Hammond 1988, which has wide coverage and contains much useful information. A good encyclopedic survey of the subject is found in Apel 1972, although it is sometimes difficult to draw the strands of his work together. Also valuable for background to the period are Strohm 1993 for the pre-1500 era, Bianconi 1987, a general overview of the seventeenth century with emphasis on Italy, and Allsop 1992, a study of the Italian trio sonata.

For instruments, the general books by Russell (1959/1965) and Williams (1966) provide excellent introductions. Studies on Italian organs are dominated by Lunelli (1956), supplemented by numerous studies in the journal *L'organo*, especially by Oscar Mischiati. For harpsichords, Wraight's work (1989) is important. Arnold 1931/1965 is a model of clarity and full of insight into continuo practice of the period. Brown 1976 is an easy-to-use and thorough consideration of sixteenth-century embellishment technique. Diruta's treatise, one of the most important documents we have concerning performance practice at the keyboard, is available in facsimile (1593, 1609/1983) and translation (1984), although the latter does not compete with the thoroughness of Soehnlein's dissertation (1975). Silbiger 1980b is the most important work on the manuscript material, essential for correcting previous misconceptions on the subject in Apel and elsewhere. His introductions to the SCKM volumes (1987–89) supplement and occasionally correct the earlier work. Three collections of articles include much recent research: Silbiger 1987, Durante and Fabris 1986, and D'Alessandro and Ziino 1987. The first two deal with Frescobaldi, the latter with Neapolitan music.

Much of the music considered here has been the subject of dissertations. The most important are Boncella 1991 (the Venetian toccata), Cannon 1968 (the organ mass), Jackson 1964 (Trabaci), Ladewig 1978 (Frescobaldi and his circle), Lynn 1973 (organ music for propers), McDermott 1979 (Merulo's canzonas), Moore 1993 (Michelangelo Rossi), Panetta 1991 (Hassler and the Venetians), Schaefer 1985 (liturgical practice), Slim 1960 (the early ricercar), Soehnlein 1975 (Diruta), and Judd 1989 (a survey of Italian keyboard music from the perspective of notation). Most also contain editions of music otherwise difficult to obtain.

Many specific topics are covered by articles in the secondary literature; a good place to start exploring the field is through literature cited in Hammond 1988 or Judd 1989. A few key authors may be mentioned here: Annibaldi 1990 on Frescobaldi; Bonta 1969 on liturgy and music; Darbellay 1987, 1988 on aspects of Frescobaldi performance; Ladewig 1987 on the variation canzona; and Silbiger on Michelangelo Rossi (1983) and the post-Frescobaldi era (1980c and 1982). The Italian section of Caldwell 1986 contains many insights. Additional articles are cited below as representative of the best recent work.

Editions

Most Italian keyboard music from before 1700 is available in modern editions. The CEKM series includes more than 20 volumes of Italian music, including editions of selections from the Frescobaldi manuscripts, the Chigi manuscripts (mostly from the Frescobaldi circle), Castell' Arquato (sixteenth century), the Luigi Rossi manuscript (Neapolitan composers c. 1600), and the works of the two Pasquinis, as well as volumes devoted to Antegnati, Battiferri, Cima, Facoli, Merulo, Picchi, Salvatore, Storace, and Strozzi. Editorial control among CEKM volumes has varied considerably, and some editions are crippled by errors and omissions (those for Bernardo Pasquini and the Chigi manuscripts perhaps more than most). A series published by Zanibon includes excellent editions of works of de Macque, Mayone, Michelangelo Rossi, Valente, and Frescobaldi. In recent years, several Italian publishers have started new series with editions of both unpublished and previosuly published keyboard music by Corradini, Frescobaldi, Andrea Gabrieli, Luzzaschi, Merulo, Bernardo Pasquini, Quagliati, Trabaci, and others; several of the new editions are listed below. *Studi per edizzioni scelte* (Florence) has published an extensive series of facsimiles of Italian keyboard prints, including music of Frescobaldi, Merulo, Rossi, Strozzi, and Trabaci. Forni (Bologna) has also issued many facsimile reprints of early keyboard editions, including the Venetian publications of the Gabrielis and their circle. Garland (New York) has published facsimiles of many important manuscript sources of seventeenth-century Italian keyboard music, with useful introductions by Alexander Silbiger (SCKM).

Editions of the early repertory are found in Jeppesen 1960 (Castell' Arquato MSS, Marc' Antonio Cavazzoni's *Recerchari motetti canzoni*), *Keyboard Music at Castell' Arquato* (1975–), *Balli antichi veneziani* (1962), and Antico, *Frottole intabulate* (1984); a recently unearthed manuscript (Munich 9437) is now available in *Eine neue Quelle zur italienischen Orgelmusik* (1982). Ricercars from Ferrara are available in recent editions: *Ricercars of the Bourdeney Codex* (199 1) and Luzzaschi, It *secondo libro de ricercari* (198 1). Most of the works of Merulo are available; Andrea Gabrieli's works are available through Kalmus reprints of the editions by Pidoux, but see Panetta 1991 for consideration of his manuscript output (most of which must remain doubtful); and through a new edition by Clericetti (1997). Many of Frescobaldi's works have been published in excellent editions by Darbellay as part of the still unfinished *Opere complete*. Another complete edition has been initiated by Bärenreiter to replace their old and in many ways unsatisfactory edition by Pidoux. Its first volume, with the *Recercari et canzoni* (1615) is edited by Christopher Stembridge, who also provides a lengthy preface on performance practice. For those works not yet included, the earlier edition by Pidoux serves adequately in the interim, but Pidoux's editions of the two books of toccatas and the capricci are now obsolete. Rossi's works are available in an excellent edition by Gilbert, which supersedes that of White (CEKM). Alessandro Scarlatti's toccatas are now available in a critical edition by Macinanti (2000). Most of Alessandro Scarlatti's works have long been available in Shedlock's edition. Even the most serious gaps can be filled with little effort: the Trabaci edition, begun in the 1960s, remains incomplete, but the facsimile is available, as is Jackson's complete edition in his dissertation (1964); most of the unpublished pieces by Frescobaldi, Ercole Pasquini, and Bernardo Pasquini, as well as a large quantity of anonymous repertory, are available in facsimile in the SCKM series.

Notes

1. Indeed, the relative wealth of volumes of keyboard music from prior to 1700 (well over 100) has proved an embarrassment of riches, and other documentary evidence in more piecemeal forms (letters, payrolls, etc.) has not yet been fully tapped; one task of future historians is to sift this evidence for what it can tell us about keyboard music and playing.

2. McGee (1986) suggested that Faenza was used by two lutes, but Strohm (1993, 92) effectively refuted his assertion (see also chap. 1, n. 4).

3. "Todero" is probably related to the French dance-type tordion.

4. The title page of this volume declares that the music is suitable for *organi* (organs), although publication in partbooks means that its use at the organ was dependent on intabulation.

5. The alteration of the shape of a subject through change of hexachord; see Ex. 5.19 for a specific instance in the music of Trabaci.

6. Music attributed to Merulo and A. Gabrieli extant only in manuscript form is not tabulated here because many of the attributions are questionable; see Panetta 1991.

7. One might question whether the works are truly Venetian since Merulo had moved to Parma in 1584 and the volumes themselves were published in Rome, but stylistically they are closer to the composers named above than to the Romans.

8. David Pinto ("Correspondence," *Music & Letters* 76 [1994]: 659–60) has identified a concordance with a *tiento* of Cabezón in these works: the third Bourdeney ricercar ("Altra fantasia di Giaches") appears in Cabezón's 1578 volume, ff. 57–59, as "Tiento del 3. Tono, fugas al contrario."

9. For a detailed discussion see Ladewig 1987, 247–52; on the versions and editions of this piece, see also Silbiger 1980, 183–86.

10. An *obbligo* is a predetermined compositional restriction, frequently encountered in contrapuntal learned-style works.

11. This opening is alluded to directly in a capriccio by Trabaci; see Silbiger 1980b, 168.

12. See Silbiger 1980b, 170–74, where an otherwise unpublished version of one of de Macque's *durezze* is given and discussed.

13. Newcomb (1990) tentatively proposed that a set of anonymous ricercars in a Regensburg manuscript is a copy of de Macque's other lost book.

14. Stembridge's edition of 12 ricercars from a Florence manuscript was published too recently for me to consider. I rely here on discussions in Ladewig 1978 (where three are edited), Ladewig 1987, Wiering 1992, and Newcomb's introduction to *The Ricercars of the Bourdeney Cordex* (1991).

15. See the discussion of Aguila de Heredia in chapter 6 for consideration of the Spanish branch of the *durezze* tradition.

16. We may pass over the somewhat derivative canzonas and ricercars of Antonio Cifra published in 1619 in both score and part-book formats, which in any case are oriented toward instrumental ensemble.

17. See Newcomb NG 1980, 6: 828, who noted that Doni had an ax to grind.

18. Both Trabaci and Mayone included prefaces, but Frescobaldi's deference to the reader and the close detail of his performance suggestions distances him from the Neapolitans.

19. See, e.g., the writings of Apel, Hammond, and Newcomb.

20. Claudio Annibaldi's 1998 study of manuscript *I-Rvat* MS Chigi Q.IV. 19, a source that contains Frescobaldi's copies of works by Palestrina and Victoria, neatly links Frescobaldi to

the *stile antico* tradition of the later seventeenth century.

21. Although the Fasolo and Storace volumes were published in Venice, both composers worked in the south.

22. See Silbiger's introduction to SCKM, 10.

23. Sometimes he referred to them as "tastatas."

24. See Silbiger, introduction to SCKM, 7, viii, for a more detailed catalog of references.

Selected Bibliography

EDITIONS

Antico, Andrea, publ. *Frottole intabulate da sonare organi libro primo*. Ed. Christopher Hogwood. Tokyo, 1984.

Aresti, Giulio Cesare, coll. and ed. *Sonate da organo di varii autori*. Ed. Traugott Fedke. Frankfurt, 1978.

Balli antichi venezzani [Venice 12271. Ed. Knud Jeppesen. Copenhagen, 1962.

Banchieri, Adriano. *L'Organo suonarino* (selctions). Ed. Raimund Schächer. Stuttgart, 2000.

Berlin, Deutsche Staatsbibliothek, MS L. 215 [Bernardo Pasquini Autograph]. SCKM, 7. New York, 1988.

Bologna, Civico museo bibliografico musicale, MS DD/53. SCKM, 10. New York, 1987.

Cavazzoni, Girolamo. *Orgelwerke*. 2 vols. Ed. Oscar Mischiati. Mainz, 1959.

Cavazzoni, Marc' Antonio. *Recerchari motetti canzoni*. See Jeppesen 1960, vol. 2.

Corradini, Nicolò. *12 ricercari (1615) per organo o clavicembalo*. Ed. Daniele Salvatore and Giovanni Torlontano. Bologna, 1998.

An Early Fifteenth-Century Italian Source of Keyboard Music: The Codex Faenza, Biblioteca comunale, 117. Facsimile edition. Musicological Studies and Documents, 10. 1961.

Frescobaldi, Girolamo. *11 Canzonas and 1 Toccata from the unsigned manuscript "Fioretti del Frescobaldi" London, British Library, Ms. Add. 40040*. Ed. Andrea Marcon and Armin Gaus. Musica antiqua nova arte scripta 1. Zimmern ob Rottwell, 1994.

——. *Fiori musicali*. Ed. Andrea Macinanti and Francesco Tassini. Bologna, 2000.

——. *Fiori musicali di diverse compositioni: toccate, kirie, canzoni, capricci e ricercari, in partitura a 4* [modern edition in open score]. Ed. Christopher Stembridge. Padua, 1997.

——. *Keyboard Compositions Preserved in Manuscripts*. 3 vols. Ed. W. Richard Shindle. CEKM, 30. 1968.

——. *Neue Ausgabe sämtlicher Orgel- und Clavierwerke–New Edition of the Complete Organ and Keyboard Works*. 1 vol. to date. Ed. Kenneth Gilbert and Christopher Stembridge. Kassel, 2003–.

——. *New Edition of the Complete Organ and Keyborard Works*. 1 vol. to date. Ed. Kenneth Gilbert and Christopher Stembridge. Kassel, 2003–.

——. *Opere complete*. 4 vols. to date. [*Toccate*, vols. 1 and 2; *Capricci, Fantasie*]. Ed. Etienne Darbellay, Alda Bellasich. Milan, 1977–.

——. *Opera Strumentale. Toccata, Canzone, Ricercare e Fantasie intavolati per Organo o Clavicembalo*. Ed. Daniele Borghi. Bologna, 1998.

——. *Il primo libro delle Fantasie a quattro*. Ed. Daniele Borghi. Bologna, 2001.

——. *Orgel- und Klavierwerke*. 5 vols. Ed. Pierre Pidoux. Kassel, 1949–54.

Gabrieli, Andrea. *Le composizioni vocali in intavolature per tastiera e liuto*, 1 (L'intavolatura di Torino). Ed. Dinko Fabris. Edizione nazionale delle opere di Andrea Gabrieli, 17. Milan, 1993.

——. *Orgelwerke*. 5 vols. Ed. Pierre Pidoux. Kassel, 1952.

——. *Sämtliche Werke für Tasteninstrumente*. 6 vols. Ed. Giuseppi Clericetti. Vienna, 1997.

Keyboard Music at Castell'Arquato. Ed. H. Colin Slim. CEKM, 37. 1975–.

Keyboard Music of the late Middle Ages in Codex Faenza 117. Ed. Dragan Plamenac. Corpus mensurabilis musicae, 57, 1972.

London, British Library, MS Add. 30491 [Rossi, MS]. SCKM, 11. New York, 1987.

London, British Library, MS Add. 31501 [Bernardo Pasquini, partial autograph]. SCKM, 8. New York, 1988.

London, British Library, MS Add. 40080 ["Fioretti del Frescobaldi"]. SCKM, 2. New York, 1987.

Luzzaschi, Luzzasco. *Il secondo libro de ricercari a quattro voci 1578*. Ed. Michelangelo Pascale. Rome, 1981.

Macque, Giovanni de. *Ricercari sui dodici toni*. Ed. Christopher Stembridge. Milan, 1994.

——. *Werken voor Orgel*. Ed. Joseph Watelet. Monumenta Musicae Belgicae, 4. Antwerp, 1938.

Maschera, Florentio. *Libro primo de canzoni ... a quattro voci.* Ed. Robert Judd. Italian Instrumental Music of the Sixteenth and Early Seventeenth Centuries, 9. New York, 1995.

Mayone, Ascanio. *Primo libro di diversi capricci per sonare.* Ed. Christopher Stembridge. Padua, 1981.

——. *Secondo libro di diversi capricci per sonare.* Ed. Christopher Stembridge. Padua,1984.

Merulo, Claudio. *Canzoni d'intavolatura d'organo.* Ed. Walker Cunningham and Charles McDermott. Recent Researches in the Music of the Renaissance, 90–1. Madison, WI, 1992.

——. *Messe d'intavolatura d'organo.* Ed. Robert Judd. CEKM, 47/5. Neuhausen-Stuttgart, 1991.

——. *Ricercare d'Intavolatura d'Organo.* Ed. J. Morehen. Recent Researches in the Music of the Renaissance, 122. Madison, WI, 2000.

——. *Toccate d'Intavolatura d'Organo.* 2 vols. Ed. Umberto Pineschi. Pistola, 2000–2001.

——. *Toccate per organo.* 3 vols. Ed. Sandro Dalla Libera. Milan, 1959–6 1.

Neapolitan Keyboard Composers, ca. 1600 [Rossi MS-excerpts]. Ed. Roland Jackson. CEKM, 24. 1967.

Eine neue Quelle zur italienischen Orgelmusik des Cinquecento [Munich 9437]. Ed. Marie Louise Göllner. Münchner Editionen zur Musikgeschichte, 3. Tutzing, 1982.

Opere per organo (Staatsbibliotek Preussischer Kulturbesitz, Manuscript. N. Mus. ant. pract. 21) [incl. works by Pallavicino and Stivori] 2 vols. Ed. Armando Carideo. Bologna, 1999, 2001.

Pasquini, Bernardo. *Collected Works for Keyboard.* 7 vols. Ed. Maurice Brooks Haynes. CEKM, 5. 1964–68.

——. *Opere per tastiera,* 2 vols. to date. Ed. Armando Carideo and Francesco Cera. Tastature; Musiche intavolate per strumenti da tasto; Istituto dell'Organo Storico Italiano, 2 and 5. Colledara, 2002–.

Pasquini, Ercole. *Collected Keyboard Works.* 3 vols. Ed. W. Richard Shindle. CEKM, 12.1966.

The Ricercars of the Bourdeney Codex: Giaches Brumel [?], Fabrizio Dentice, Anonymous. Ed. Anthony Newcomb. Recent Researches in the Music of the Renaissance, 89. Madison, WI, 1991.

Quagliati, Paolo. *Toccata; ricercari e canzoni.* Ed. Armando Carideo. Colledara, 2000.

Rossi, Michelangelo. *Toccate e correnti.* Ed. Kenneth Gilbert. Padua, 1991.

Scarlatti, Alessandro. *Toccate (Biblioteca del Conservatorio di Napoli ms. 9478) per organo o clavicembalo.* ed. Andrea Macinanti, Francesco Tasini. Bologna, 2000.

Seventeenth-Century Keyboard Music in the Chigi Manuscripts of the Vatican library. 3 vols. Ed. Harry B. Lincoln. CEKM, 32. 1968.

Trabaci, Giovanni Maria. *Cento versi sopra li otto finali ecclesiastici.* Ed. Nicola Ferroni. Bologna, 1996.

——. *Composizioni per organo e cembalo.* 2 vols. Ed. Oscar Mischiati. Brescia, 1964–69.

——. *Toccate per organo o cembalo.* Ed. Edoardo Bellotti. Pistola, 1996.

Valente, Antonio. *Intavolatura de cimbalo (Naples 1576).* Ed. Charles Jacobs. Oxford, 1973.

Vatican, Biblioteca Apostolica Vaticana, MS Chigi Q.IV.25 [attributed to Frescobaldi]. SCKM, 1. New York, 1988.

Vatican, Biblioteca Apostolica, MSS Chigi Q.IV.24, 26–29, and Q.VII1.205–206. SCKM, 15. New York. 1989.

LITERATURE

Allsop, Peter. *The Italian 'Trio' Sonata: From Its Origins Until Corelli.* Oxford, 1992.

Annibaldi, Claudio. "Musical Autographs of Frescobaldi and His Entourage in Roman Sources." *Journal of the American Musicological Society* 43 (1990): 393–425.

——. "Palestrina and Frescobaldi: Discovering a Missing Link." *Music & Letters* 79 (1998): 329–345.

Arnold, F. T. *The Art of Accompaniment from a Thorough-bass.* 2 vols. 1931. Reprint. New York, 1965.

Attacciati, Cesare. "La notazione dei trilli nelle musiche frescobaldiane per tastiera." *Rivista italiana di musicologia* 25 (1990): 61–99.

Banchieri, Adriano. *L'organo suonarino.* 1605. Reprint. Amsterdam, 1969.

Barnes, John. "The Specious Uniformity of Italian Harpsichords." In *Keyboard Instruments: Studies in Keyboard Organology 1500–1800,* ed. Edwin M. Ripin, 1–10. Edinburgh, 1971.

Benvenuti, Giacomo. *Andrea e Giovanni Gabrieli e la musica strumentale in San Marco.* 2 vols. Istituzioni e monumenti dell'arte musicale in Italia, 1–2. Milan, 1932.

Bianconi, Lorenzo. *Music in the Seventeenth Century.* Cambridge, 1987.

Boncella, Paul Anthony Luke. "The Classical Venetian Organ Toccata (1591–1604): An

Ecclesiastical Genre Shaped by Printing Technologies and Editorial Policies." Ph.D. dissertation, Rutgers University, 1991.

Bonta, Stephen. "The Uses of the *Sonata da Chiesa.*" *Journal of the American Musicological Society* 22 (1969): 54–84.

Borgi, Daniele. "Affetti, intenzioni e colori cangianti: I ricercari di Luzzaco Luzzaschi, maestro di color che sanno." *Arte organaria e organistica* 5 (1998): 42–45.

Brown, Howard M. *Embellishing Sixteenth Century Music.* London, 1976.

——. *Instrumental Music Printed Before 1600: A Bibliography.* Cambridge, MA, 1965.

Caldwell, John. "Keyboard Music: 1630–1700." In *Concert Music (1630–1750),* ed. Gerald Abraham, 505–89. New Oxford History of Music, 6. Oxford, 1986.

Cannon, Clawson Y. "The 16th- and 17th-Century Organ-Mass: A Study in Musical Style." Ph.D. dissertation, New York University, 1968.

Carideo, Armando. "Wiederentdeckte Kompositionen von Francesco Stivori und Germano Pallavicino." *Basler Jahrbuch für historische Musikpraxis* 22 (1998): 53–67.

Cera, Francesco. "Sessanta versetti e una pastorale di Bernardo Pasquini scoperti in una fonte sconosciuta." *Ricercare* 12 (2000): 111–20.

D'Alessandro, Domenico Antonio, and Agostino Ziino. *La musica a Napoli durante il Seicento.* Rome, 1987.

Darbellay, Étienne. "Forme, temps et mémoire: l'intrigue comme modèle d'unité chez Girolamo Frescobaldi (1583–1643)." in *Musicus perfectus: Studi in onore di Luigi Ferdinando Tagliavini.* Ed. Pio Pellizzari. Bologna, 1995, 203–36.

——. "Tempo Relationships in Frescobaldi's *Primo Libro di Capricci.*" In *Frescobaldi Studies,* ed. Alexander Silbiger, 301–26. Durham, NC, 1987.

——. *Le Toccate e i Capricci di Girolamo Frescobaldi: Genesi delle edizioni e apparato critico.* Milan, 1988.

Diruta, Girolamo. *Il Transilvano.* 1593, 1609. Reprint. Buren, 1983.

——. *The Transylvanian (Il Transilvano).* 2 vols. Ed. Murray C. Bradshaw and Edward J. Soehnlen. Henryville, 1984.

Durante, Sergio, and Dinko Fabris, eds. *Girolamo Frescobaldi nel IV centenario della nascita.* Florence, 1986.

Hammond, Frederick. *Girolamo Frescobaldi.* Cambridge, MA, 1983. Revised Italian edition translated by Roberto Pagano. Palermo, 2002.

——. *Girolamo Frescobaldi: A Guide to Research.* Garland Composer Resource Manuals, 9. New York, 1988.

——. "Girolamo Frescobaldi and the Hypothesis of Neapolitan Influences." In *La musica a Napoli durante il Seicento,* ed. Domenico Antonio D'Alessandro and Agostino Ziino, 217–36. Rome, 1987.

——. "The Influence of Girolamo Frescobaldi on French Keyboard Music." *Ricercare* 3 (1991): 147–68.

——. *Music and Spectacle in Baroque Rome: Barberini Patronage under Urban VIII.* New Haven, 1994.

——. "*Préludes non mesurés* and the tradition of improvisation in French and Italian keyboard practice during the 17th and 18th centuries." In *Giacomo Francesco Milano e il ruolo dell'aristocrazia nel patrocinio delle attività musicali nel secolo XVIII.* Ed. Gaetano Pitarresi. Regio Calabria, Italy, 2001, 145–156.

——. and Alexander Silbiger. "Frescobaldi, Girolamo." *NG 2001,* 9: 238–52.

Harper, John. "Frescobaldi's Early *Inganni* and Their Background." *Proceedings of the Royal Musical Association* 105 (1978–79): 1–12.

Jackson, Roland John. "The Keyboard Music of Giovanni Maria Trabaci." Ph.D. dissertation, University of California, Berkeley, 1964.

Jeppesen, Knud. *Die italienische Orgelmusik am Anfang des Cinquecento.* 2d edition. 2 vols. Copenhagen, 1960.

Johnson, Calvert. "Early Italian Keyboard Fingerings." *Early Keyboard Journal* 10 (1992): 7–88.

Judd, Robert. "The Use of Notational Formats at the Keyboard." Ph.D. dissertation, University of Oxford, 1989.

Kinkeldey, Otto. *Orgel und Klavier in der Musik des 16. Jahrhunderts: ein Beitrag zur Geschichte der Instrumentalmusik.* 1910. Reprint. Hildesheim, 1968.

Klein, Heribert. *Die Toccaten Girolamo Frescobaldis.* Mainz, 1989.

Krummacher, Friedhelm. "Phantastik und Kontrapunt: zur Kompositionsart Frescobaldis."

Judd, Robert. "The Use of Notational Formats at the Keyboard." Ph.D. dissertation, University of Oxford, 1989.

Kinkeldey, Otto. *Orgel und Klavier in der Musik des 16. Jahrhunderts: ein Beitrag zur Geschichte der Instrumentalmusik.* 1910. Reprint. Hildesheim, 1968.

Klein, Heribert. *Die Toccaten Girolamo Frescobaldis.* Mainz, 1989.

Ladewig, James L. "Frescobaldi's *Recercari, et canzoni franzese* (1615): A Study of the Contrapuntal Keyboard Idiom in Ferrara, Naples, and Rome, 1580–1620." Ph.D. dissertation, University of California, Berkeley, 1978.

————. "The Origins of Frescobaldi's Variation Canzonas Reappraised." In *Frescobaldi Studies,* ed. Alexander Silbiger, 269–83. Durham, NC, 1987.

Lunelli, Renato. *Der Orgelbau in Italien in seinen Meisterwerken vom 14. Jahrhundert bis zur Gegenwart.* Mainz, 1956.

Lynn, Robert Burgess. "Renaissance Organ Music for the Proper of the Mass in Continental Sources." Ph.D. dissertation, Indiana University, 1973.

Macey, Patrick. "Frescobaldi's Musical Tributes to Ferrara." In *The Organist as Scholar: Essays in Memory of Russell Saunders,* ed. Kerala J. Snyder, 197–231. Stuyvesant, 1994.

McDermott, Charles M. "The *Canzoni d'intavolatura* of Claudio Merulo: A Guide to the Art of Improvised Ornamentation." Ph.D. dissertation, University of California, Berkeley, 1979.

McGee, Timothy J. "Instruments and the Faenza Codex." *Early Music* 14 (1986): 480–90.

Monson, Craig. "Elena Malvezzi's Keyboard Manuscript: A New Sixteenth-Century Source." In *Early Music History* 9 (1989): 73–128.

Moore, Catherine Janet. *The Composer Michelangelo Rossi: A "Diligent Fantasy Maker" in Seventeenth-Century Rome.* New York, 1993.

Newcomb, Anthony. "Frescobaldi, Girolamo." In *The New Grove Dictionary of Music and Musicians,* ed. Stanley Sadie, vol. 6, 824–35. London, 1980.

————. "Frescobaldi's Toccatas and Their Stylistic Ancestry." *Proceedings of the Royal Musical Association* 111 (1984–85): 28–44.

————. "When the 'Stile Antico' was Young." In *XIV Congresso della Società Internazionale di Musicologia, Bologna-Ferrara-Parma 1987,* ed. Angelo Pompilio et al., vol. 3, 175–81. Turin, 1990.

Panetta, Vincent Joseph, Jr. "Hans Leo Hassler and the Keyboard Toccata: Antecedents, Sources, Style." Ph.D. dissertation, Harvard University, 1991.

Russell, Raymond. *The Harpsichord and Clavichord: an Introductory Study.* 1959. Reprint. New York, 1965.

Sachs, Barbara, and Barry Ife, ed. and trans. *Anthology of Early Keyboard Methods.* Cambridge, 1981.

Sartori, Claudio. *Bibliografia della musica strumentale italiana stampata in Italia fino al 1700.* 2 vols. Florence, 1952, 1968.

Schaefer, Edward E. "The Relationship Between the Liturgy of the Roman Rite and the Italian Organ Literature of the 16th and 17th Centuries." D.M.A. dissertation, Catholic University of America, 1985.

Schulenberg, David. "La toccata del primo barocco e l'avvento della tonalità," *Rivista italiana di musicologia* 27 (1992): 103–23.

Silbiger, Alexander. "Imitations of the Colascione in 17th-Century Keyboard Music." *Galpin Society Journal* 33 (1980a): 92–97.

————. *Italian Manuscript Sources of 17th Century Keyboard Music.* Ann Arbor, 1980b.

(1983): 18–38.

——. "On Frescobaldi's Recreation of the Ciaccona and the Passacaglia." In *The Keyboard in Baroque Europe*. Ed. Christopher Hogwood, Cambridge, 2003.

——. "Passacaglia and Ciaccona: Genre Pairing and Ambiguity from Frescobaldi to Couperin." *Journal of Seventeenth-Century Music* 2 (1996), <http://www.sscm-jscm.org/jscm/v2no1.html>

——. "The Roman Frescobaldi Tradition." *Journal of the American Musicological Society* 33 (1980c): 42–87.

——. ed. *Frescobaldi Studies*. Durham, NC, 1987.

Slim, H. Colin. "Keyboard Music at Castell' Arquato by an Early Madrigalist." *Journal of the American Musicological Society*, 15 (1962): 35–47.

——. "The Keyboard Ricercar and Fantasia in Italy, c. 1500–1550, with Reference to Parallel Forms in European Lute Music of the Same Period." Ph.D. dissertation, Harvard University, 1960.

——. "Some Puzzling Intabulations of Vocal Music for Keyboard, c. 1600, at Castell'Arquato." In *Five Centuries of Choral Music: Essays in Honor of Howard Swan*, ed. Gordon Paine, 127–51. Stuyvesant, NY, 1989.

Soehnlein, Edward John. "Diruta on the Art of Keyboard-Playing: An Annotated Translation and Commentary of *Il Transilvano*, Parts I (1593) and II (1609)." Ph.D. dissertation, University of Michigan, 1975.

——. "Diruta and His Contemporaries: Tradition and Innovation in the Art of Registration *c*1610." *The Organ Yearbook* 10 (1979): 15–33.

Stembridge, Christopher. "The *cimbalo cromatico* and Other Italian Keyboard Instruments with Nineteen of More Divisions to the Octave: Surviving Specimens and Documentary Evidence." *Performance Practice Review*, 6 (1993): 33–59.

——. "Music for the *Cimbalo Cromatico* and Other Split-Keyed Instruments in Seventeenth-Century Italy." *Performance Practice Review*, 5 (1992): 5–43.

——. "Italian Organ Music to Frescobaldi." In *The Cambridge Companion to the Organ*. Ed. Nicholas Thistlethwaite and Geoffrey Webber. Cambridge, 1998, 148–63.

Strohm, Reinhard. *The Rise of European Music, 1380–1500*. Cambridge, 1993.

Tagliavini, Luigi F. "The Art of 'Not Leaving the Instrument Empty': Comments on Early Italian Harpsichord Playing." *Early Music* 11 (1983): 299–308.

——. Varia frescobaldiana." *L'Organo* 21 (1983; publ. 1987): 83–128.

Towne, Gary. "Music and Liturgy in Sixteenth-Century Italy: The Bergamo Organ Book and its Liturgical Implications." *Journal of Musicology* 6 (1988): 471–509.

Vartolo, Sergio. "Girolamao Frescobaldi: annotazioni sulla musica per strumento a tastiera." *Nuova Revista Musicale Italiana*, 28 (1994): 620–63.

Wiering, Frans. "The Ricercars of Macque and Trabaci: A Case of Musical Competition?" *Muziek & Wetenschap* 2 (1992): 179–200.

Williams, Peter. *The European Organ 1450–1850*. London, 1966.

Wraight, Denzil. "Harpsichord [Italy]." In *Early Keyboard Instruments*, ed. Stanley Sadie, 9–25, 66–71, 83–85. New York, 1989.

MANUSCRIPT SHORT TITLES

Berlin 215	*G-Bds* MS L. 215
Bologna 53	*I-Bc*, MS DD/53
Bourdeney	*F-Pn* Rés. Vma. 851.
Castell' Arquato	*I-CARc* (ten fascicles with no call numbers)
Chigi 25	*I-Rvat* MS Chigi Q.IV.25
Faenza 117	*I-FZc* MS 117
London 40080	*GB-Lbl* Add. 40080
Munich 9437	*G-Mbs* MS Mus. 9437
Rossi MS	*GB-Lbl* Add. 30491
Venice 1227	*I-Vm* MS Ital. IV. 1227

CHAPTER SIX

Spain and Portugal

Robert Parkins

The "golden age" of Iberian keyboard music extended from the middle of the sixteenth century to the turn of the eighteenth century, its major figures beginning with Antonio de Cabezón and ending with Juan Cabanilles. Music in Spain and Portugal was by no means untouched by outside influences, but it remained somewhat insular and remarkably conservative, especially in the seventeenth century, and never completely escaped the ethos of the Renaissance. Even performance practices did not seem to change radically, some still following the guidelines of a sixteenth-century aesthetic in the early 1700s.[1]

To acknowledge a strain of conservatism in this music is not to imply that it is innocuous or uninteresting. True, the contrapuntal idiom can seem unyielding, real chromaticism is rare, and even in the later seventeenth century the developing major-minor tonal system never quite squeezed out the vestiges of modality. But this sometimes austere musical menu is often spiced with pungent items characteristically Iberian: prominent augmented triads, diminished triads in root position, grating simultaneous cross-relations, unorthodox dissonance treatment, and a predilection for certain unusual intervals like falling diminished fourths. At times the counterpoint appears to operate under its own laws, such as intentional hidden fifths or octaves that strongly color the harmony. Even the usually straightforward rhythms can be interrupted by dance-like shifting accents, syncopations, and irregular groupings.

Despite the eventual variegation of forms and styles, the texture of four-voice modal polyphony was a norm from which Iberian composers did not easily depart. The principal musical types—from liturgical versets and hymns to variations and tientos—tended to adhere closely to this framework. Although elements of the free, noncontrapuntal style found in contemporaneous foreign keyboard literature sometimes appeared briefly, there was really no Iberian equivalent to the toccatas of Italian and Germanic composers. The *tiento* (Port. *tento)* was the predominant genre during this entire period, evolving from little more than a simple intabulation of a motet to an array of highly idiomatic subgenres. By the seventeenth century these included extended multisectional pieces based on one or more subjects, motley pastiches of a lighter nature (like *batallas),* serious and reflective *tientos de falsas,* and distinctive works for divided organ stops.

The area we refer to as Spain was not entirely unified at that time, and regional differences were sometimes reflected in the keyboard music. These distinctions become more apparent as our attention shifts from Castile (Cabezón) to Aragon (Aguilera de Heredia), then to Portugal (Coelho)—under Spanish rule from 1580 to 1640—and Andalusia (Correa de Arauxo), and finally to the eastern regions, particularly Valencia (Cabanilles). This broad impression may be a distorted one, for it is based largely on the surviving works of a few composers. Several compilations and publications have disappeared, and we know of instances in which Spanish composers so jealously guarded their keyboard works that many of these never saw the light of day. In addition, the authors of a substantial portion, at least a third, of the seventeenth-century keyboard literature remain unidentified.[2]

Throughout this period, characterized by religious conflict in much of Europe, the Catholic Church retained its power and supremacy in Sp ain and Portugal. Indeed, it was not unusual for organists to be priests as well in this intensely theocratic society. As a corollary, the organ was the instrument for which most pre-eighteenth-century Iberian keyboard music was written, even though a substantial portion could be played on other keyboard instruments. For practice and teaching, the clavichord *(manicordio)* was by far the most popular. Its affordability and portability made it ubiquitous, as evidenced by the writings of theorists like Santa Maria as well as the estate inventories of musicians. Harpsichords, referred to generically as *clavicordios* (more specifically, *clavicímbalos* or some variant thereof), do not seem to have been nearly as plentiful; in fact, very few surviving Iberian harpsichords have been shown to predate the eighteenth century. However, there is evidence of their use at the courts, in churches (especially during Penitential seasons when the organs were silent), and in the homes of professional organists. In addition to instruments produced by native builders, harpsichords were also imported, mainly from Flanders in the sixteenth century and Italy in the seventeenth century. Nonetheless, it appears that before the 1700s all other keyboard instruments in Iberia remained secondary to the organ.

The Iberian Organ

Prior to the early 1500s, organs in Spain no doubt resembled instruments built elsewhere in Europe, particularly in the Netherlands. In addition to the more sizable stationary organs, there were regals and somewhat less movable *realejos,* or positive organs. During the course of the sixteenth century, the larger Spanish organs began to develop an identity all their own (see Ill. 6.1). Most instruments in Castile, except for organs in large churches and cathedrals, possessed only a single manual with a compass of C/E–a″. The rather mild, transparent principals (*flautados*) were supplemented by a chorus of flutes (*nazardos*). A second manual division, if present, usually took the form of a *cadireta,* situated behind the player's back like a Germanic *Rückpositiv,* and was based on 4′ pitch, sometimes with no 8′ stop at all. As in Italian organs, there was no pedal division, at most a few rudimentary pedals or buttons pulling down the lowest octave of manual keys (see Ill. 6.2), sometimes with an independent rank of 16′ flue pipes (*contras*) to reinforce the bass at cadences.

During the latter part of the sixteenth century Castilian builders began to divide certain stops into bass and treble halves. On a single keyboard one could then accompany a distinctive solo sound in one hand

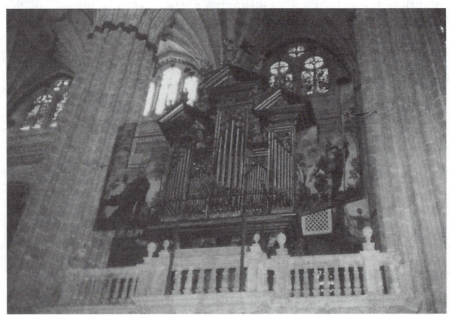

ILLUSTRATION 6.1. Original case of the Epistle organ (1558) in Salamanca's New Cathedral. Shown here is the "exterior" side of the double façade (with horizontal trumpets added much later).

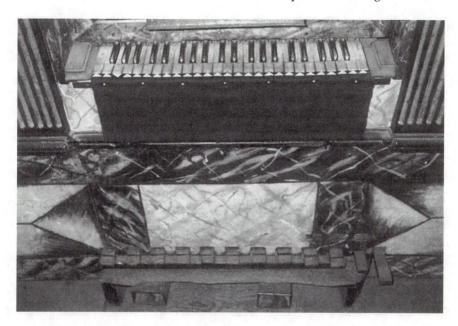

ILLUSTRATION 6.2. Keydesk of the Epistle organ in Salamanca's New Cathedral with eight pull-down pedals for the bottom short octave plus extra pedals for "toy" stops on the right.

with, for example, the subtler *flautado* in the other. The possibility of different tonal colors for the right and left hands on a one-manual instrument would alter significantly the direction of the Iberian organ and its literature. The importance of the half-register, or *medio registro*, cannot be overstated, for it introduced a subgenre of Iberian keyboard literature that was exclusively "organ music": the *tientos de medio registro* could not be played satisfactorily on any other keyboard instrument.

By the early seventeenth century the typical Spanish organ had developed mainly along two paths: (1) an eastern (Catalonian) type with two manuals, undivided stops, and few reed stops (none of the full-length trumpet type); and (2) the mainstream Castilian variety that forsook the *cadireta* in favor of a single manual with divided stops (c′/c♯′), including trumpets and other reeds. The kingdom of Aragon, situated between Castile and Catalonia, produced instruments incorporating both styles, and during the course of the century such regional practices would intermingle widely throughout the entire Iberian Peninsula, Portugal included.

Iberian organs continued to evolve slowly, and by the late 1600s the older keyboard compass had expanded slightly in the treble (C/E–c‴). At about the same time, there occurred the most striking innovation of all: the addition of horizontal trumpets *(clarines)* that projected outward

ILLUSTRATION 6.3. Horizontal trumpets protruding from a pair of opposing organs (1737–38) at Braga Sé (Cathedral) in Portugal.

from the main case, yielding a distinctively brilliant, penetrating sound. Possibly short-resonator reeds were sometimes affixed in a similar manner even in the late sixteenth century, but no solid evidence suggests that horizontal trumpets were built before 1659 (Wyly 1977, 41). As with divided registers, this new fashion first took hold in the central area around Castile and spread later to the more distant regions east and west. By the early eighteenth century horizontal reeds had become the most easily recognizable characteristic of the Iberian organ. Many large churches and cathedrals possessed pairs of organs with batteries of *trompetería* facing each other from both sides of the *coro,* the enclosed choir area often situated toward the middle of the nave (see Ill. 6.3).

The Nascent Literature and the Theorists

The first published keyboard literature from Spain did not appear until the mid-sixteenth century, but it is clear that by then the art of improvisation and composition for organ and other keyboard instruments had reached a rather high level. In addition, more information regarding the performance practice of keyboard music is available from sixteenth-century Spain than from any other country at that time. The earliest treatise to discuss keyboard playing was printed in 1555: Juan Bermudo's *De claración de instrumentos musicales.* Just two years later Luis [Luys] Venegas de Henestrosa published the first anthology in Spain to include keyboard music, compiled some ten years before.[3] The *Libro de cifra nueva para tecla, harpa, y vihuela* (1557), so named for its notation in the relatively "new" Spanish number tablature *(cifra)*, contained some 138 works by well-known and unknown composers, as well as an informative preface. (The subtitle "for keyboard, harp, and vihuela" indicates the relative transferability of music for these "harmonic" instruments. The *fantasías* for vihuela, the Spaniards' preference over the lute, were usually playable—if not always idiomatic—on the organ or clavichord, while most keyboard pieces could be performed by a vihuelist with some adaptation.) The third publication to appear was another theoretical and practical treatise, Fray Tomás de Santa María's *Arte de tañer fantasía, assí para tecla como para vihuela* (1565). Like Bermudo, Santa María did not neglect to insert several of his own keyboard works. This volume remains the most comprehensive and detailed source of information on several aspects of keyboard performance, most notably embellishments, fingering, and rhythmic alteration.

Venegas's *Libro de cifra neuva* includes pieces both sacred and secular, offering a convenient survey of the main genres developed by the middle of the century.[4] Among the exclusively liturgical works are *fabordones* and *himnos*. The *fabordón* was a short harmonization of a psalm tone, either plain *(llano)* or embellished *(glosado)*. The *himnos* were generally more elaborate contrapuntal treatments of commonly used hymns, in two to four voices with the cantus firmus in long notes. Included are settings of three melodies that would appear most frequently in Iberian organ music during the next 150 years: *Sacris solemniis, Ave maris stella*, and especially *Pange lingua*. The Spanish *Pange lingua* was not the familiar Gregorian tune but a popular melody in triple meter of uncertain origin.

Decidedly secular are the *diferencias* (variations) and most of the intabulations. The simple sets of continuous variations on popular tunes do not begin to reveal the refined art of elaboration developed by Spaniards like Cabezón, but the creative embellishment of vocal pieces by such luminaries as Josquin and Crecquillon can be seen in anonymous intabulated versions of several *chansons*.

More significant is the inclusion of a genre that was to predominate in one form or another until the eighteenth century: the keyboard tiento. The first tientos published in Spain had not been intended for keyboard instruments. Earlier in the century, vihuela books by Milán (1536), Mudarra (1546), and Fuenllana (1554) included several rather improvisatory, nonpolyphonic pieces for their instrument with this appellation. The free, preludial style of most of these vihuela compositions reflects one of the literal meanings of the term "tiento," from the verb *tentar*, denoting an "initial attempt" or a preliminary (i.e., tentative) "feeling out" of the instrument as well as the tuning and mode. Early use of the word "tiento" in Spain followed a course quite similar to that of ricercare in Italy; that is, a term first seen in homophonic pieces for lute was somewhat later adopted for keyboard works as well, with imitative polyphony becoming a dominant texture.

Polyphonic works for keyboard instruments with the designation "tiento" first made their appearance in Venegas's *Libro de cifra nueva*. Half (14 of 28) are by Cabezón, ascribed simply to "Antonio," while those by unknown or lesser colleagues (e.g., Vila, Soto, Palero) constitute the other half. Thematic material is occasionally borrowed from preexisting vocal music both sacred and secular, but most tientos are ostensibly original. Many reveal their vocal origins in almost banal simplicity (as in No. 21 in Venegas), while a few tend toward elaborate embellishment, sometimes to the extent of glossing entries even within the first point of imitation (No. 55).

Quite similar in style to the tientos in the *Libro de cifra nueva* are the 24 pieces by Tomás de Santa María published in his *Arte de tañer fantasía*, a work he had begun in the 1530s. The fact that he referred to them as *fantasías* rather than tientos may reflect the usage of contemporary vihuelists, who used the term "fantasía" for imitative works and "tiento" for homophonic pieces with florid interludes.

Of far more significance than Santa María's rather unremarkable compositions is the information he offers on how to perform them and other keyboard music of the time. In addition to providing extensive instruction on improvising *glosas* to embellish melodic lines, he explains that individual ornaments are a normal and necessary part of performing keyboard music. These ornaments—*quiebros* and *redobles*—had been described earlier in much less detail by Bermudo and Venegas, but they were by no means standardized. The underlying ethos is consistent with general ornamentation practices elsewhere during the sixteenth century, and the essential features may be condensed as follows:

1. *Redobles* and *quiebros* are never indicated in the musical text, but the performer is expected to add them.
2. The consonant main note falls on the beat.
3. Longer ornaments tend to decorate longer notes.
4. Longer ornaments favor the upper rather than the lower auxiliary note and may include a short prefix to the trill on the main note.

Bermudo mentions only the term *redoble* and includes double trills (in contrary motion), while Venegas calls his trills *quiebros*. Santa María employs the terms *redoble* and *quiebro reiterado* ("repeated quiebro") for different forms of longer trills, but uses *quiebro senzillo* ("simple quiebro") for the short forms that could be described as equivalent to turns, mordents, or inverted mordents. He adds that in the "very new style" one may elect to begin the trills with the upper note just before the beat. A further twist is his suggestion to hold down the main note of the short

EXAMPLE 6.1. Santa María's Ornaments

Redoble

Quiebro reiterado

Quiebros senzillos

quiebro while quickly touching the auxiliary tone (an effect that sounds better on the clavichord than on the organ). Santa María's suggested ornaments are shown in Example 6.1.

Of no less interest is the discussion on how to play "with good [rhythmic] style" (*con buen ayre*). Santa María remarks that ostensibly equal notes on the page are often subtly inflected rhythmically under the hands of skilled keyboard players, resulting in three basic patterns:

1. Long-short pairs of eighths or quarter notes "for strictly contrapuntal pieces and in long and short *glosas*."
2. Short-long pairs of eighths "for short *glosas* and in pieces such as *fantasías* . . . much more elegant than the aforementioned."
3. Three short eighths plus one long one in a group of four "for short and long *glosas* . . . the most elegant of all."

All three of Santa María's examples feature a *glosa* in eighth notes for the right hand with a simple two-voice accompaniment in the left. Although the first two styles are illustrated by dotted notes, the author cautions that the result should be subtle and the shorter notes "must not go very quickly." As with *notes inégales* in later French music, the beat remains steady as the smaller subdivisions are gently altered.

Perhaps the third item of most interest to keyboard players is Santa María's discussion of fingering, more thorough and detailed than any other sixteenth-century description, and revealing a practice that was comparatively progressive. For linear fingerings, there was a direct connection between the rhythmic values and the number of fingers in a "unit" to be repeated. Consecutive long notes, like whole or half notes, were to be played with one or two fingers (e.g., 33 or 3434), while the faster *glosas* would require three to four fingers (e.g., 234 or 1234). One may deduce from Santa María's remarks that normal touch was at least somewhat detached and that finger substitution was out of the question.

Cabezón (1510–66)

Antonio de Cabezón, one of several illustrious blind organists in the history of music, was undoubtedly the greatest Iberian keyboard master of the sixteenth century. Born in 1510 in Castrillo de Matajudíos (near

Burgos) and educated in nearby Palencia, Antonio received an appointment as organist to the chapel of Queen Isabella while still in his teens (1526). He remained in the service of the royal court after her death in 1539, and by 1548 Prince Philip (later to become King Philip 11) retained Cabezón as his own chapel organist. For the next eight years he traveled with Philip outside Spain to various countries, most notably Italy, Germany, the Netherlands, and England. Cabezón continued in the employ of the royal court in Madrid until his death in 1566.

Virtually all of Cabezón's surviving keyboard compositions are contained in two publications: Venegas's *Libro de cifra nueva* (1557) and the *Obras de música para tecla, arpa y vihuela*, published posthumously in 1578 by Antonio's son Hernando.[5] Notated in numerical tablature like Venegas's anthology, the *Obras de música* includes not only the bulk of Antonio's surviving works but also one or two pieces attributed to his brother Juan and five attributed to Hernando. The prefaces to both of these collections provide instructive remarks on ornamentation and fingering.

Some 40 of Cabezón's works are featured by Venegas in his collection, among them *himnos, versos, fabordones, glosados, diferencias,* and tientos. The tientos evince the heritage of the Franco-Netherlandish motet style, transferred to the keyboard. The quiet motion of imitative polyphony in four voices is occasionally decorated by diminutions, most often in "interludes" in which the subjects do not appear. These episodic sections reveal the composer pulling away from the vocal idiom toward a more idiomatic keyboard style; they often assume the form of a duet, a contrasting homophonic texture, an accompanied *glosa,* or a continuation of the contrapuntal idiom with or without imitation.

Among the most inspired and profound works in the sixteenth-century keyboard repertoire are the 14 tientos chosen by Hernando for publication in the *Obras de música.* Two of them *(Fuga a cuatro* and *Ad dominum cum tribularer clamavi)* are rather specialized types not included among those actually bearing the title "tiento" in the 1578 print. The 12 pieces called tientos seem to be systematically arranged so that those written in the presumably earlier "motet" style alternate with more mature, adventurous ones. The even-numbered tientos (in Anglés's edition of 1966) are cast in the traditional mold of the midcentury tientos in Venegas's *Libro de cifra nueva.* Characterized by overlapping points of imitation in four voices and a seamless *stile antico* texture uninterrupted by figuration, they are imbued with an austere mysticism unmatched in similar works by Cabezón's contemporaries.

The six odd-numbered tientos, ostensibly reflecting a later style of writing, are among Cabezón's most inspired creations. No longer limited to the more abstract "vocal" lines with occasional diminutions that define the midcentury tiento, these half-dozen masterworks forge ahead toward a more elaborate style. To be sure, most of the opening subjects still begin with the white-note rhythmic motion of the motet, but they soon dissolve into figuration more idiomatic to the keyboard. Moreover, these longer subjects possess a more distinctive personality with a sharpened sense of tonal direction.

The third tiento (in mode I) is often regarded as the finest of the group. The opening motive (Ex. 6.2a) is immediately recognizable as that of the *Salve regina*, although this is not acknowledged in the title. The chromatic inflections in subject 1 are not unusual with Cabezón, nor is the fact that they are sometimes inconsistently applied throughout; only the context determines, for example, whether the second note is raised. Highly unusual for this time are the new motives developed from the transformation of subject 1 and subject 2 (Ex. 6.2c), as are the two striking interludes in which they appear (Ex. 6.2b and d). Not until Aguilera de Heredia do we see this technique resurface in Iberian keyboard literature. Just as remarkable is the final section: immediately following an entry of subject 3 with a florid countersubject (Ex. 6.2e) is an extended *glosa* in the bass accompanied by simple chords in the right hand, both springing from the *Salve regina* motive (Ex. 6.2f). By the end of the century this kind of texture would be given a life all its own with the introduction of divided-register pieces.

Also developed to a high degree of refinement by Cabezón were variations, or *diferencias*, a form familiar to the early Spanish vihuelists but little explored by Cabezón's keyboard contemporaries outside the Iberian Peninsula. Only after his death did serious interest in this genre begin to surface elsewhere, particularly in England and Italy. The nine sets of *diferencias* in the *Obras de música*, based on folk tunes and dances, are a high point of sixteenth-century keyboard music. Characteristically Spanish is the conservative four-part contrapuntal texture, cautiously retained even in this secular format. Unlike some later variation sets, Cabezón's *diferencias* are continuous, even overlapping, rather than separate entities. The number of variations ranges from two to eight, each set beginning not with a simple statement of the theme, but with the first variation.

Three sets are based on *Las vacas (O guárdame las vacas)*, a version of the Romanesca; other popular tunes used by Cabezón for variations include *La dama le demanda*, the villancico *¿Quién te me enojó Isabel?*, and *El canto llano del cavallero*. The *diferencias* based on dances include two sets on *La pavana italiana* and one on *La gallarda milanesa*. The tune employed by Cabezón for his *Diferencias sobre la pavana italiana* is almost identical to that of *La dama le demanda*, but the *Discante sobre la pavana italiana* employs another dance tune: the "Spanish Pavane," or *Pavaniglia*, also used by Bull, Sweelinck, and Scheidt.

The *Diferencias sobre el canto llano del cavallero*, based on the love song *Dezilde al cavallero*, are perhaps Cabezón's finest achievement in this genre. The actual metrical structure of the first phrase, obscured by the

EXAMPLE 6.2. Cabezón, Tiento 3
(a) mm. 1–10

(b) mm. 57–60

(c) mm. 77–82

(d) mm. 117–21

(e) mm. 144–49

(continued)

(f) mm. 158–60

regular bar lines as with many popular tunes, is shown in Example 6.3. The division of eight pulses into 3 + 3 + 2 at the conclusion of the phrase is an elongated version of a quicker pattern that was to become a salient rhythmic figure in seventeenth-century Iberian keyboard music.

Typically, the tune is clearly delineated by the top voice in the first variation. It remains in the soprano, slightly ornamented, in variation 2. Variations 3 and 4 feature the theme in the tenor and the alto, respectively. The fifth and last variation is unusual, however, in that until the final cadence the texture is reduced to three voices throughout, with the tune in tenor range functioning as the bass line.

Until recently not regarded as worthy of modern publication are the 44 *glosados*—richly embellished intabulations, mainly of motets and chansons in four, five, and six voices—included by Hernando in the 1578 *Obras*. Although the practice of intabulation seems to have nearly died out in Spain by the 1600s, it is clear that during the preceding century techniques of improvising and writing for the keyboard developed from this practice. The esteem held by Antonio and other Spaniards for the Franco-Netherlandish school of vocal polyphony is evidenced by Hernando's inclusion of numerous works by Josquin, Crecquillon, Clemens non Papa, Gombert, Lassus, Mouton, Verdelot, and Willaert (several of whom had been associated with the Spanish court). There is much to be learned from these intabulations about Antonio's approach to glossing with diminutions. Performers may also discover some useful embellishments—written out in context—that are not mentioned in theorists' descriptions of *quiebros* and *redobles*; one obsessively recurring figure is the inverted turn preceding a repeated long note (Ex. 6.4).

EXAMPLE 6.3. Cabezón, *Diferencias sobre el canto llano del cavallero*, mm. 1–8

EXAMPLE 6.4. Cabezón, *Prenes pitié*, mm. 1–2

Antonio's *glosados* vary rather widely in complexity and difficulty; some remain close to the original model, while others paraphrase it until the source is barely recognizable. In the hands of such a master, many arrangements reveal an idiomatic and creative technique, not at all limited to the stereotyped recipes found in treatises. No less interesting are the four intabulations attributed to Hernando, and it is instructive to compare the *glosados* of father and son based on the same vocal model. In Example 6.5, a brief excerpt from each composer's setting of Lassus's *Suzanne un jour* is shown, with the corresponding passage in the original chanson.

EXAMPLE 6.5.
(a) A. Cabezón, *Susana*, mm. 49–53

(b) H. Cabezón, *Susana un jur*, mm. 76–80

(c) Lassus, *Suzanne un jour*, mm. 38–40

The liturgical works—that is, those pieces specifically intended for use in masses or daily offices—constitute a substantial portion of the *Obras de música*. If the number of surviving hymns and versets is any indication, the organ seems to have played a much more prominent role in the offices than in the mass. Cabezón's hymn settings are for two, three, or four voices, typically with a cantus firmus in long notes in one of the parts. Predictably, the majority are settings of *Ave maris stella* and *Pange lingua*.

The *versos*, intended for *alternatim* performance, include Kyries, versets for psalmody, *fabordones*, and Magnificats. Most are systematically arranged in sets of eight, corresponding to modes I–VIII. The eight groups of *versos* for the psalm tones, like the simpler hymns, have a pedagogical as well as a liturgical purpose. Cabezón designated these beautiful but uncomplicated psalm versets "for beginners," leaving the more highly embellished *fabordones* for those farther along. The plain cantus firmus appears in a different voice for each of the four short *versos* in the group, while the remaining three lines spin out imitative counterpoint.

The *fabordones*, basically accompanied plainchant in four voices, are also grouped in eight sets of four. The first of each set is always plain *(llano)* and homophonic, the second has an embellished *(glosado)* treble voice, the third ornaments the bass, and the last features diminutions in the inner voices. The fourth verse of the *Fabordón del sexto tono* displays a surprising rhythmic curiosity as the bass *glosa* moves from normal eighth notes into quintuplets (Ex. 6.6).

Each of the eight Magnificats includes either six or seven verses only six are necessary, but perhaps Cabezón provided an extra one for use in the Benedictus. There is a wider variety of treatment in these than in the more standardized *versos* mentioned earlier. Especially beautiful are the seven *Versos del cuarto tono*. As in the other Magnificat settings, most of the versets here are treated in ornamented motet style, borrowing motives from the appropriate Gregorian tune; they are, in effect, miniature tientos. The sixth *verso* departs from the motet style with a migrating stream of eighth notes in a *glosa* accompanying the subject (Ex. 6.7a). The final *verso* is in the style of a *fabordón* glossed in the treble voice with the plain cantus firmus in the tenor (Ex. 6.7b).

From these short versets to the more complex and profound tientos, the subtle but intense power of Antonio de Cabezón's art is always

EXAMPLE 6.6. Cabezón, *Fabordón del sexto tono*, verso 4, mm. 18–22

EXAMPLE 6.7. Cabezón, *Versos del cuarto tono [Magnificat]:*
(a) verso 6, mm. 1–5

(b) verso 7, mm. 1–5

present. As a composer of music for keyboard, he had few equals among his contemporaries in other countries, and certainly none in Spain and Portugal. That exquisite balance between contrapuntal mastery and expressive beauty remained unsurpassed by later Iberian composers as well. Hernando wrote in his preface to the *Obras de música* that in exchange for the sight that was denied Antonio, God "gave him a marvelous view of the soul, opening the eyes of understanding for him to master the great subtleties of this art and to arrive at a point no other mortal had reached."

Aguilera de Heredia (1561–1627) and the Aragonese School

Sebastián Aguilera de Heredia was the first important representative of the seventeenth-century school centered around Saragossa in Aragon. In many ways the inheritor of the Cabezón tradition, he was the next figure of real significance after the great Antonio. To be sure, relatively little Iberian keyboard music survives from the period between Cabezón and Aguilera de Heredia; only a smattering of pieces from the hands of composers like Hernando de Cabezón, Jerónimo and Francisco Peraza, Estacio de la Serna (Lacerna), and Bernardo Clavijo del Castillo remains.

Appointed organist at the cathedral of Huesca in 1585, in 1603 Aguilera assumed the more prestigious position of master organist of La Seo in nearby Saragossa, where he stayed until his death. No more than 18 of his keyboard works are known, but among them are several subgenres that would predominate in Spanish keyboard music through the age of Cabanilles: *tientos de falsas*, multisectional tientos, *tientos de medio registro*, and three-voice *Pange lingua* settings. It is fair to say that his compositions served as prototypes for much seventeenth-century Spanish keyboard music.

Aguilera's three *tientos de falsas* are apparently the first works to include the word *falsas* ("false notes," or dissonances) in the title.[6] The dissonant notes in these pieces are nothing extraordinary, but they are brought into relief by the conspicuous absence of *glosas*, or any quick notes at all. The *tientos de falsas* are characterized by a quietly moving texture of long notes and suspensions throughout—similar to the Italian *durezze e ligature*—recalling the calm ambience of tientos in motet style of a half century earlier. A special prominence is reserved for the augmented triad, its jarring dissonance—especially in meantone temperament—standing out in bold relief from the otherwise unadventurous harmony. The longest and most attractive of Aguilera's tientos in this style is the *Tiento de 4º tono de falsas*. A double subject (Ex. 6.8) pervades the entire piece to the extent that there is hardly a measure in which at least one of the two main subjects is not present.

A general tendency to reduce the number of subjects helped foster still another subspecies in the early seventeenth century: the multipartite monothematic tiento. Each new section is usually announced by a change of meter, the subject undergoing various rhythmic transformations, as in some Italian canzonas. Aguilera's *Tiento de 4º tono* (referred to as *Tiento grande* in one manuscript copy) is a good example of a sectionalized tiento with a single subject and its rhythmic variants. It is one of five tientos by Aguilera, excluding the *falsas*, intended for full *(lleno)* register rather than divided stops. In the lengthy first section the subject (Ex. 6.9a) appears not only in its original form but also in diminution and augmentation. The rhythmic drive of the first countersubject sets the tone for the entire passage, and the impetus is picked up later by new motives darting in and out. The triple-meter section at first transforms the subject with a dance-like iambic rhythm (Ex. 6.9b); then, following the cadence in m. 154 a new subsection begins in which the subject is announced in equal long notes (Ex. 6.9c). The third and last subdivision of the passage in triple meter transforms the subject still

EXAMPLE 6.8. Aguilera, *Tiento de 4º tono de falsas*, mm. 1–6

EXAMPLE 6.9. Aguilera, *Tiento [grande] de 4º tono*
(a) mm. 1–7

(b) mm. 130–36

(c) mm. 164–70

(d) mm. 199–202

(e) mm. 223–32

(f) mm. 236–39

again, accompanied by quick triplets (Ex. 6.9d). The return to duple meter is signaled by one final statement of the subject in whole notes, reminiscent of a cantus firmus (Ex. 6.9e). Finally, a flourish of sixteenth notes energizes a typically short but brilliant coda (Ex. 6.9f).

Several elements in the *Tiento de 4º tono* are worthy of attention as hallmarks of Spanish keyboard music (particularly in the east) during the seventeenth century:

1. A melodic diminished fourth in the subject and special emphasis on its harmonic relative, the augmented triad.

2. The introduction of idiomatic figures (sometimes derived from the subject) in imitation and sequence as counterpoint to the subject.

3. A section in triple meter, often emphasizing a strong, even homophonic, short-long rhythm |♩♩|♩♩·.

4. The introduction of triplet figuration not just for occasional variety but also, toward the end of the tiento, as a new rhythmic force.

5. A final free flourish of quicker notes in a brief flirtation with toccata style.

6. A temporary but consistent syncopation in which an ordinary measure of eighth notes is subdivided in the rhythmic pattern 3 + 3 + 2 (Ex. 6.10).[7]

7. An accentual shift in groups of six notes, with a consequent

Example 6.10. Aguilera, *Tiento [grande] de 4º tono*, mm. 80–84

ambiguity between triple and compound meters, as in $\frac{3}{8}\!:\!\frac{6}{8}$ (see Ex. 6.9c). This rhythmic device would become well worn by the end of the century, especially among composers in eastern Spain.[8]

Thirteen of Aguilera's pieces fall under the general heading of tiento (sometimes labeled *obra,* meaning "work"), and four are for divided registers. All four *tientos de medio registro* feature the solo in the bass (*bajo, vajo*; Port. *baixo*), one with two solo voices for the left hand. An infectious rhythm invigorates these *vajos*, incorporating syncopations, triplets, and 3 + 3 + 2 subdivisions. Interludes between solos tend to be short and infrequent, but the solo bass entries are spun out at some length by sequences and transpositions of material at different tonal levels. The solo figuration itself exploits a number of recurring motives, some of them to remain clichés in left-hand *medio registro* tientos throughout the century.

Among the five specifically liturgical organ works by Aguilera are two *Salbes* (based on the *Salve regina)* and a pair of settings on the Spanish *Pange lingua.* The latter are models for what could be described as a stereotypical seventeenth-century subspecies for this particular tune: a three-part texture in which the unadorned cantus firmus may appear in any voice. Figuration in the other two parts is often imitative, sometimes derived from the tune itself, as in Example 6.11. The ABA structure of the melody allows for a recapitulation of the initial section, frequently indicated simply by a sign to repeat.

The tradition established by Aguilera was continued in mid-seventeenth-century Aragon, most notably by Jiménez and Bruna. José Jiménez [Jusepe Ximénez] (1601–72), Aguilera's successor at La Seo in Saragossa, left nearly two dozen surviving organ works, among them 8 tientos (or *obras)* and 11 liturgical works (most of them on the *Pange lingua*). His set of 20 variations on the famous *folía* theme is one of the first of many in the keyboard repertoire. Furthermore, his two *Batallas del 6⁰*

Example 6.11. Aguilera, *La reina de los Pange lingua,* mm. 1–4

tono are among the earliest in a plethora of "battle" pieces to appear in Iberian keyboard literature over the next hundred years.[9] These *batallas* belong to a small but distinct class of keyboard pastiches, like Aguilera's popular *Ensalada (Obra de 8º tono alto),* patterned after earlier vocal works, in several discrete, highly contrasting sections, and usually in a variety of meters. The opening subject (in paired imitation), sectional structure, regularity of phrases, harmonically simple homophonic passages, and dialogues between treble and bass are typical of a genre modeled largely on Janequin's *La guerre.* Jiménez adds his own contributions to a catalog of *batalla* clichés (Ex. 6.12) that would some years later exploit the spectacular horizontal trumpets, echoes, and other dramatic effects featured on Iberian organs.

Pablo Bruna (1611–79), known as "the blind man from Daroca," was undoubtedly the most important composer of Spanish keyboard music between Correa and Cabanilles. Other than liturgical works (versets and *Pange lingua* settings), Bruna's known output consists of some 20 pieces, mainly tientos, most of them for *medio registro.* In many of the tientos he carries Aguilera's monothematic principle to a new level, adding more sections and expanding the use of repetition at multiple tonal levels into chains of "modulatory passages." Possibly Bruna's most beautiful work is his Tiento on the Litany of the Virgin *(Tiento de 2º tono por ge sol re ut sobre la letanía de la Virgen),* intended for divided registers (not explicitly stated but obvious from the careful separation of bass and treble voices). Although labeled a tiento, it is in actuality a loose set of continuous variations generated by the opening subject and its implied harmonic scheme.

Coelho (c.1555–c.1635)

The Portuguese organist and composer Manuel Rodrigues Coelho was born in about 1555 at Elvas, where he received his early musical training. He was appointed temporary organist at the cathedral in Badajoz (Spain) from 1573 to 1577 but later returned to Elvas, where he served as cathedral organist. In 1602 Coelho (or Rodrigues Coelho) accepted his most illustrious appointment, that of court organist in Lisbon. He died around 1635, having retired just two years before.

In 1620 Coelho published his *Flores de música pera o instrumento de tecla & harpa,* the first volume of Iberian keyboard music to be printed since the *Obras de música* of Cabezón in 1578. Unlike the earlier Spanish publications, Coelho's volume was notated in open score (see Ill. 6.4) rather than in numerical tablature. The 24 *tentos* in the *Flores de música* are supplemented by 4 *Susanas* (intabulations on Lassus's famous *Suzanne un jour).* The substantial remainder of the collection consists entirely of liturgical music.

Example 6.12. Jiménez, *Batalla de 6⁰ tono* (two settings)

(a) [2] mm. 1–6

(b) [1] mm. 104–7

(c) [1] mm. 149–53

(d) [2] mm. 24–26

(e) [2] mm. 114–16

The *tento* was the Portuguese counterpart of the tiento, and Coelho included three for each of the eight tones. A brief glance soon reveals an obvious difference between Coelho's *tentos* and the tientos of Aguilera de Heredia and his followers: none of the Portuguese pieces is for divided register, since the practice of the *medio registro* (Port. *meyo*

ILLUSTRATION 6.4. Coelho's *Tento do quarto tom natural* from *Flores de música* (1620), illustrating notation in *partitura* (open score).

registo) had apparently not yet caught on in Portugal. Nor do they sound as characteristically "Iberian" in their harmonies and rhythms; Coelho's music exhibits more foreign influences and recalls Sweelinck and his circle in particular. Although some of the *tentos* exploit a single subject, most are polythematic compositions in several overlapping sections. The principal subject sometimes reappears throughout the piece–as in some of Sweelinck's fantasies–despite the addition of new subjects and motives in succession. Also reminiscent of Sweelinck is Coelho's ability to generate new motives and figuration from a single source. Most of his *tentos* are less unified, however, and resemble updated versions of the old-fashioned polythematic *tentos* by his Lusitanian predecessor António Carreira (c.1525–c.1590). Thus, the design can be open-ended, with numerous sections sewn together like patchwork. The essence is variety rather than large-scale structural unity, and in several cases the procedure leads to compositions of more than 300 measures.

Coelho's *tentos* exhibit characteristics of both traditional sixteenth-century style and the newer fashions of the early seventeenth century. Among the older elements are (1) the usual four-voice contrapuntal texture; (2) construction in dovetailed sections based on a number of different subjects, normally introduced by points of imitation; (3) an opening subject in long notes; (4) occasional modification of a subject with accidentals; and (5) episodes of free counterpoint between thematic entries. The newer characteristics include (1) a later recurrence of the opening subject; (2) more frequent introduction of triplets, dotted notes, and other short rhythmic figures simply for the sake of variety; (3) occasional use of new subjects that are variants of previous ones; and (4) much more idiomatic keyboard figuration, including sequential treatment. Altogether absent is the coda in toccata style favored by Aguilera and other Spaniards. In fact, Coelho's *tentos* often end with a segment in triple meter rather than a return to duple meter.

The *Tento do quarto tom natural* (Ill 6.4) is among the more structurally unified and musically persuasive. Set in the fourth tone untransposed *(natural)*, this *tento* is only 164 measures long and is based on four subjects, all of which begin with the same two notes–a technique preferred by Cabezón. The opening subject, typically in white notes, is balanced by a countersubject that progressively grows more rhythmically active (Ex. 6.13a). Subject 2 (Ex. 6.13b) is, by design or coincidence, an inversion of the core of subject 1 (under the dotted bracket in Ex. 6.13a), and subject 3 (Ex. 6.13c) clearly grows out of the second subject. The fourth and final subject (Ex. 6.13d) seems to be derived from the opening motive in diminution accompanied by an altered (and augmented) version of subject 2. As in Aguilera (and even in Cabezón), ephemeral motives derived from the main subjects appear sporadically in brief episodes of imitation before vanishing.

EXAMPLE 6.13. Coelho, *Tento do quarto tom natural*

(a) mm. 1–9

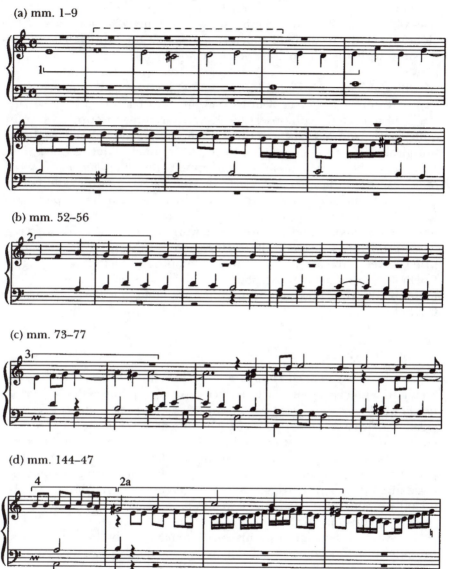

(b) mm. 52–56

(c) mm. 73–77

(d) mm. 144–47

Most of the liturgical music in Coelho's collection consists of hymns, Magnificats, and Kyries (*Kyrios*). Among them are four settings of *Pange lingua,* based on the Spanish tune, but not in three voices. Instead, the unembellished cantus firmus appears in each voice of a four-part texture in successive verses, as with Cabezón. In five of the *Ave maris stella* settings, however, the plainchant is chopped into five segments, each of which serves as a subject for its respective *verso*. Of particular interest are 23 five-voice versets for the Magnificat (one to four *versos* for each of the eight tones), the heading of which specifies that the cantus firmus is "to be sung with the organ: this voice is not played; the four below are played."

Although Coelho's *Flores de música* remained the sole publication of keyboard music in Portugal in the seventeenth century, works by later Portuguese organist-composers have survived in manuscript.[10] Most are quite similar to works by Spanish contemporaries, including specifically liturgical works *(versos, entradas)* in the traditional imitative polyphonic style as well as *tentos* (with a variety of appellations like *obra, fantasia, concerto, concertado, fuga, tenção, exercício)*. The collections from the end of the century include a few of the increasingly popular battle pieces, or *batalhas* (some even supplying hints here and there regarding the use of horizontal reeds), in addition to several works designated for divided registers *(obras de meyo registo)*. Although most of these works remain unidentified, several are ascribed to known composers, including Rodrigues Coelho. A dozen or so are attributed to Pedro de Araújo (fl. 1662–1705), undoubtedly the most significant figure among the Portuguese after Coelho.

Correa de Arauxo (1584–1654)

Just six years after the appearance of Coelho's *Flores de música,* the Spaniard Francisco Correa de Arauxo [Araujo] published his *Libro de tientos y discursos de música práctica, y theórica de órgano intitulado Facultad orgánica* (Alcalá de Henares, 1626). The title makes it immediately apparent that this volume was intended specifically for the organ, unlike earlier publications described more broadly for "keyboard" *(tecla)* and other polyphonic instruments. Not only does the *Facultad orgánica* contain a large number of keyboard works by Correa (notated in *cifra),* but it also includes a valuable treatise with a wealth of information on various facets of performance practice.

The year and location of his birth remained obscure until rather recently, but it is now certain that Correa de Arauxo was baptized in Seville in September of 1584. In 1599 the young musician assumed the position of organist at the Collegiate Church of San Salvador (Seville), and several years later he was ordained to the priesthood. He remained at this post for 37 years, but his tenure was afflicted with personal problems, conflicts with church authorities resulting in lawsuits, and chronic illness in his later years. In 1630 he even instigated a revolt among the church musicians for higher pay, refused to play extra services, and at one point interrupted vespers with loud complaints from the organ gallery. As a result he was incarcerated, and the locks to the organs were changed to block his access to the instruments during the ensuing litigation. Correa finally left Seville to become the organist at Jaén Cathedral in 1636, but remained there only four years. His last position was at Segovia Cathedral, where he arrived in 1640. He died in 1654, having been forced by illness to resign his duties the year before.

As the title *Libro de tientos* implies, nearly all of Correa's works (62 out of a total of 69 pieces) are tientos: 20 for right-hand solo (*de tiple*, including two for two trebles); 16 for left-hand solo (*de baxón*, including three for two basses); and 26 for undivided registers (*registro entero*). Five-voice exceptions to the normal four-part texture include the *medio registro* pieces with two solo voices and one for *registro entero* (No. 62—all tiento numbers correspond to those in Kastner's 1974 edition). Also unusual are three tientos exploiting thirty-second notes (Nos. 58–60) and two in triple meter (Nos. 62–63).[11]

The arrangement of tientos in the *Facultad orgánica* is fairly systematic, but Correa's table of contents does not reflect the actual order. Instead, it is organized according to the difficulty of the pieces (in five grades) as it proceeds to some of the more complex works, labeled *discursos*. Thus, Correa's intention is clearly didactic as well as practical, and his *Libro de tientos* is a compendium of different types (Kastner 1973, 76): (1) monothematic in the traditional imitative style (such as No. 17); (2) monothematic with the subject appearing only inconsistently within *glosas* and figurations (No. 10); (3) polythematic in the old style (No. 24); and (4) polythematic with a preponderance of keyboard figuration (No. 2). The majority of these feature a variety of textures, often within the same piece, that may include simple imitative counterpoint, imitative polyphony embellished by *glosas*, free counterpoint resembling toccata style, *medio registro* style characterized by a *glosa* in one hand versus accompaniment in the other (not necessarily with divided stops), and passages in *falsas* style. Not included are two subgenres favored by composers of the Aragonese school: the multisectional monothematic tiento in which the subject metamorphoses through rhythmic variation and the *tiento de falsas*.

As with Aguilera and Coelho, the typical opening subject of a tiento by Correa de Arauxo is of the *stile antico* type, often pitted against livelier counterpoint. Correa usually prefers to maintain the original form of the subject, rarely indulging in any sort of rhythmic transformation (as in No. 7) or simple alteration (No. 29); occasionally he introduces a double subject (No. 12) or a subject answered in inversion (Nos. 1, 25, 46). Beyond the initial exposition, Correa's tientos are less predictable. Thematic entries are loosely presented and sometimes difficult to hear, often sneaking in unobtrusively through an inner voice. New motives may appear from time to time, but they are rarely derived from one of the subjects. The typically long interludes have less imitative textures and frequently introduce toccata-like passages of sixteenths or triplets. Also not unusual are concluding sections in a similarly flamboyant style.

The 36 *tientos de medio registro* outnumber the others, a sign of the increasing popularity of organs with divided stops, a "famous invention, and very familiar in the Kingdoms of Castile, although not known in others," according to Correa.[12] The majority of his *medio registro* pieces involve more than one subject, the first usually presented twice as a solo, the second entry transposed by a fourth or a fifth. The initial solo entry and sometimes later entries appear only after the other three voices have entered in preimitation of the subject. As in Coelho's full-register *tentos*, the principal subject may return after other subjects have been introduced (Nos. 26, 29, 41).

The episodes between solo entries are often extensive, generally much longer than in Aguilera. Although there are no *tientos de falsas* by Correa, the style of many of his interludes is similarly tranquil, often displaying little or no imitative counterpoint. Others foreshadow the entry of a solo subject in loose imitation, but rarely in all voices like the opening. Still others involve imitation of a subject that is altogether different from the solo to follow (Nos. 27, 48).

The melodic nature of the solos readily distinguishes Correa's *tientos de medio registro* from those of the Aragonese school. After the solo voice has faithfully imitated the subject introduced in the accompanying voices, it takes off on a melismatic free flight that hardly resembles the chain of sequential figurations typical of Aguilera and his colleagues. Is it too farfetched to suppose that residual Moorish influence in the southern region of Andalusia left its impact on Correa's music?

A superb illustration of such melismatic writing is provided in the *Tiento de medio registro de tiple de décimo tono* (No. 36; see Ill. 6.5). The treble solo, following a dark, austere introduction near the bottom of the keyboard, soon develops into a flowing, serpentine *glosa* (Ex. 6.14). After a nonimitative interlude the subject enters again as a solo, but up a fourth. The third solo entry brings in a new subject whose introductory

EXAMPLE 6.14. Correa, *Tiento de medio registro de tiple* (No. 36), mm. 15–23

TIENTO DE MEDIO

REGISTRO DE TIPLE DE DECIMO TONO, O ASSI

mifmo de primero tono alto, efto es: fenecido irregularmente en el, la, de delafolrre, del genero femicromatico blando. En algunas partes de eftos dif curfos (y en particular en efte, en el compas 80.) donde ay corchea con pun tillo, y de neceſsidad fe a de feguir femicorchea, la dexo de poner, por la di cha razó, y por no cargar de figuras efta obra. Efte tiento, aunque de a diez y feys, es facil para difcipulos del fegundo curfo, y es de mis principios.

ILLUSTRATION 6.5. Tiento No. 36 (f. 48r) from Correa's *Facultad orgánica* (1626) in Spanish numerical tablature. Each of the four horizontal lines on the staff represents one polyphonic voice, while the numbers 1–7 indicate pitches (beginning at F); any rhythmic ambiguities are clarified above the staff.

long notes soon give way to a concatenation of triplets. The fourth and fifth solos also do not recapitulate the original subject—in fact, they seem to involve barely any thematic material at all, but rather suggest continuations of the previous melismas. A touch of sequential figuration in the final *glosas* does not disrupt their improvisatory character and in any case never descends to the self-indulgent repetition at numerous levels that sometimes afflicts tientos of the eastern school.

A similar ethos pervades the tientos with a solo in the bass *(baxón)*, the left-hand subjects usually dissolving into somewhat less complex *glosas* than solos in the treble *(tiple)*, but still avoiding the Aragonese repertoire of sequential figures. Correa's *Tiento de medio registro de baxón de primero tono* (No. 34) is a rather compact example, more unified and tightly constructed than several other *medio registro* pieces. Until the final section there is basically a single subject, the three main solo entries appearing at tonic and dominant levels (I–V–V). The brevity of this particular work limits the number of episodes to two, but the second is notable for its introduction of a lively secondary subject in imitation. The importance of the augmented triad in Correa's harmonic language is illustrated most prominently in a deceptive resolution at m. 52, and his fondness for the jarring cross-relation *(punto intenso contra remisso)* is evident in the two preceding measures (Ex. 6.15).

The remarkable final section introduces a new subject in running eighth notes concluded by a brief coda in *falsas* style, but what strikes the listener as truly extraordinary is the septuple meter! In the *Facultad orgánica* Correa mentions his use of irregular rhythmic divisions, among other novelties, and this passage is one of several among the tientos involving quintuplets or septuplets. According to his instructions, the half notes in the accompaniment must be assimilated in a 4 + 3 division (Ex. 6.16)[13]

Issues of performance practice such as ornamentation, rhythmic alteration, and fingering are handled in the text of Correa's treatise. The prevailing ethos behind his approach to ornamentation is similar to that of his predecessors: the consonant main note generally falls on the beat, longer ornaments *(redobles)* are attached to longer note values, and short ornaments *(quiebros)* fall on shorter notes. The dissonant upper auxiliary note is emphasized only in certain written-out cadential trills (like traditional sixteenth-century Italian *groppi*). Several points warrant mention:

EXAMPLE 6.15. Correa, *Tiento de medio registro de baxón* (No. 34), mm. 50–53

EXAMPLE 6.16. Correa, *Tiento de medio registro de baxón* (No. 34), mm. 108–12

(1) for the first time in Iberian keyboard music a symbol is used to represent an embellishment in the score—*R* for *redoble*—although Correa often writes out the entire ornament (with or without the *R*); (2) both simple and complex *redobles* are preceded by prefixes *before* the beat; (3) there is no precise number of repercussions in a *redoble*; (4) an optional suffix is possible at the end of a *redoble*; (5) the *redoble* sounds best on a note whose upper auxiliary lies a semitone above, such as a leading tone; and (6) a distinction is made between the organ and clavichord regarding the length and type of embellishment. Correa offers descriptions or abstract models for four basic ornaments, transcribed in Example 6.17 (with an asterisk above the main note). In actual practice, his tientos often include variants of these paradigms fully written out in different contexts.

Other than Santa María, Correa de Arauxo is the only Spaniard to mention the practice of subtle rhythmic inflection. Correa's remarks do not concern pairs of notes or groups of four, however; rather, he describes a manner of playing groups of three notes (e.g., triplets) in which the first note of each group is held a bit longer than the other two. This practice he terms *ayrecillo de proporción menor*, ostensibly used by many of Correa's eminent colleagues and predecessors; it is indicated in the tablature by a *3* placed above the staff (with return to equality signified by a *2*). In the preface to the *Flores de música*, Coelho offers the interesting—and possibly contradictory—advice that the player should "not dwell on one key longer than the other, [but must] give equality to the half notes, quarters, and eighths." Whether Coelho's statement constitutes a proscription against rhythmic alteration or merely sound advice for untrained amateurs is hard to determine.

EXAMPLE 6.17. Correa's ornaments

Correa scatters his suggestions for organ registration among the prefatory notes to the musical works rather than in the text of the *Facultad orgánica,* and he is the first Iberian writer to broach this aspect of performance practice.[14] Most of his advice concerns the *medio registro* pieces, for which he prescribes the *flautado* for the accompanying voices, a *lleno* (principal chorus) or a *mixtura* (combination of several flue stops) for the treble solo, and the *lleno* or a *trompeta* for bass solos. One particularly intriguing suggestion is to remove the lowest stop (*flautado* or *bordón)* from a combination when the pitch of the organ is low and the resulting sound murky or indistinct. (In practice, this works best in the bass part—accompaniment or solo—when it is widely separated from the treble component.) Similarly, he advises that certain pieces with rapid *glosas* are more successfully performed on *realejos* (small chamber organs based on 4' pitch) than on large organs.

Cabanilles (1644–1712)

During the second half of the seventeenth century, the eastern Spanish school established in Aragon by the early 1600s expanded to embrace Catalonia and Valencia as well. Names like Baseya, Bernabé Menalt, Perandreu, Sebastián, Serrano (Sinxano), Puxol, and Xarava (y Bruna) have survived in manuscripts, but none of these was to approach the stature of Juan Bautista José Cabanilles. Born in Algemesí (near Valencia), Cabanilles remained in that area during his years of training and assumed his first position as second organist of Valencia Cathedral in 1665. He quickly advanced to the post of first organist by the following year and although he retained that position until he died, his experience was by no means provincial. After all, Valencia was a cosmopolitan port city with connections to foreign countries, especially Italy, and Cabanilles sometimes traveled to France, where he is reported to have played in several important churches.

The works of Cabanilles are estimated to comprise more than half of the seventeenth-century keyboard literature by known Spanish composers (calculated by the number of measures); even when the anonymous pieces are taken into consideration, his output exceeds 35 percent of the total. In view of these statistics, it is easy to see why a substantial portion of Cabanilles's oeuvre has remained unpublished. None was printed during his lifetime, and not a single autograph survives among extant manuscripts of his keyboard music. In addition to 231 tientos there are 26 miscellaneous pieces (including variations), 56 hymns, and nearly 1,000 separate *versos* (Lloréns Cisteró 1981; for a different count, see the introduction to Cabanilles 1999, vi).

The diversity that characterizes the tientos by Cabanilles may be said to "recapitulate the evolution" of the genre, by this time encompassing a broad spectrum of subgenres. Ranging from modest pieces recalling the venerable Cabezonian style to types previously unexplored in Iberia, they display a mixture of elements old and new, both native and imported.[15] The numerous tientos for full register *(lleno, de todas manos, ple)*[16] are supplemented by dozens more for divided register *(partido, partit)*. The *tientos partidos* may feature a right-hand solo *(tiple, mano derecha, má dreta)*; a left-hand solo *(baixo, mano izquierda, má esquerra)*; or two solo voices *(dos tiples, dos baixos, or dos tiples i dos baixos)*. Beyond the two broad categories defined by *lleno* and *partido* registrations lies a curious mixture of styles. The serene, mystical *tientos de falsas*, for example, continue the tradition established by Aguilera, while the boisterous *tientos de batalla* reflect the growing fascination with the organ as a sound-effects machine (with new and exotic features like horizontal trumpets). The *tientos de contras*, featuring long pedal points in the bass, have no precedent in Iberian keyboard music; in fact, they are the first pieces to indicate any specific use of the pedals.

The bulk of Cabanilles's tientos can be seen as "extended fantasies," in that he tends to avoid tight formal structure or any consistently predictable format. A substantial majority consist of several fairly clear-cut sections, usually signaled by a change of meter; these larger sections, particularly the initial one, are often a composite of smaller subsections. Imitative passages and freer textures may alternate, as in many Italian and German toccatas, or may be combined within the same section. Most begin with traditional imitation of a subject in *stile antico* (as in No. 13)[17] or in a more active "instrumental" style (No. 23). A few have no real subject (as in No. 50, marked *sin passo*, or "without subject"), despite passages with transient motives in imitation. Although four-voice texture is still the rule for *tientos llenos*, there may be passages for three voices or even extended duos. Endings also vary widely, from abrupt and unexpected cadences to elaborate codas in free style.

Even though not many of the tientos are monothematic in the strictest sense, most are held together by a main subject from which others are derived. Cabanilles spins out many of the longer ones not only by transformation of the principal subject but also by introducing new motives or subjects in imitation. Quite often new sections in different meters—especially the $\frac{12}{8}$ passages that frequently appear somewhere between the midpoint and the end—are generated by new rhythmic motives unrelated to the original subject. Sections are usually extended by modulatory passages in which an entire phrase is repeated either precisely or with some modification in a succession of different tonal levels, most often by fourths or fifths. Within each may occur sequential repetition of rhythmic or melodic motives on a smaller scale as well. This technique was often abused among other composers of the eastern school, and Cabanilles himself sometimes pushed it beyond judicious limits.

One of the less prolix and more engaging works is the *Tiento por A la mi re* (No. 23). It opens with an energetic subject suggesting a sharpened canzona rhythm (Ex. 6.18a). Presented *inverso* as well as *recto* in the first part, the subject is rhythmically transformed into $\frac{6}{4}$ meter in the second section (Ex. 6.18b), but not without the occasional suggestion of $\frac{3}{2}$. The third section (also in $\frac{6}{4}$) introduces a rhythmic variant of the original subject counterpointed against its own inversion (Ex. 6.18c). The strong dactylic rhythm continues to dance all the way to the last real section, wherein the first subject returns in simple augmentation (Ex. 6.18d). Finally, the counterpoint dissolves into a scintillating free coda befitting one of Cabanilles's most attractive and effective works.[18]

Encroaching Italian and south German influences can be sensed most readily in the *tientos llenos* that not only contain internal toccata-like

EXAMPLE 6.18. Cabanilles, *Tiento por A la mi re* (No. 23)
(a) mm. 1–4

(b) mm. 44–46

(c) mm. 71–74

(d) mm. 113–17

passages but also begin in a style associated with toccatas. Instead of the expected imitative counterpoint, several of Cabanilles's tientos open with a plain chordal texture (Ex. 6.19a); a highly embellished chordal texture, sometimes with imitation (Ex. 6.19b); rapid scales accompanied by long chords, reminiscent of early Venetian toccatas (Ex. 6.19c); or a brief introduction in *falsas* style followed by scalar figuration (Ex. 6.19d).

The tientos by Cabanilles for divided stops *(registros partidos)* continue an established Iberian tradition, but they do not obey Correa's dictum that the accompanying texture must consist of three voices. Nearly all involve only two voices plus the solo(s), thus freeing up the accompanying hand for a far more active role than in Correa's *medio registro* pieces. In some cases there is a noticeably wide gap between the two hands, possibly implying a 4′ registration for the left hand (as Correa had suggested).

As a rule the *tientos partidos* follow the same opening format already seen in Correa: (1) contrapuntal introduction with preimitation of the first subject; (2) solo entry in one or two voices; (3) interlude; and (4) second solo entry transposed a fourth or fifth. Beyond this point, as in Correa and others, the initial subject may reappear or even disappear. Most often, however, Cabanilles's *partido* subjects simply undergo rhythmic transformation, and a handful of his tientos are nearly monothematic (such as No. 36). Interludes tend to be brief or nearly nonexistent, often providing some type of preimitation before a solo entry, especially toward the beginning of the tiento. Solo passages, on the other hand, can be very long, extended by sequential repetition or florid *glosas*. The overall structure is rather open-ended and no more predictable than that of the *tientos llenos*.

Cabanilles's three-voice *tientos partidos* with a single solo voice (treble or bass) far outnumber the four-voice type (one pair per hand). The solos, especially for the right hand, sometimes become freely melismatic like Correa's, spinning out a breathless string of sixteenth notes (as in No. 36). More usual, particularly in bass solos, is a chain of motives strung together in sequence and extended by longer modulatory passages, as in many Aragonese tientos (No. 39). The generic motives typical of the left-hand solos by Aguilera and his successors are to be found at times in Cabanilles as well, but far less regularly. It is fair to say that most of his tientos with divided registers combine both techniques to generate solo lines that in sheer length surpass the earlier types. Moreover, one finds a rhythmic and polyphonic independence absent from the older four-part *medio registro* settings.

The predominant texture of the tientos for "two trebles and two basses" is more restricted and usually resembles that of the four-voice *llenos*. But when each hand is expected to execute more active and independent two-voice textures, the performer may encounter passages of unusual technical difficulty (Ex. 6.20).

EXAMPLE 6.19.
(a) Cabanilles, *Tiento de 1º tono* (No. 55), mm. 1–4

(b) Cabanilles, *Tiento de 2º tono* (No. 37), mm. 1–2

(c) Cabanilles, *Tiento de 5º tono* (No. 18), mm. 1–5

(d) Cabanilles, *Tiento de 1º tono* (No. 3), mm. 1–7

EXAMPLE 6.20. Cabanilles, *Tiento de 2º tono* (No. 60), mm. 74–77

Cabanilles also composed a number of keyboard pieces other than tientos or liturgical works. Most of these are in the form of continuous variations, demonstrating that the art of the *diferencia* had not yet disappeared even in the late seventeenth century. The *pasacalles* and the *paseos* are rather conservative in character, set in a four-part contrapuntal framework, most of them in duple meter. The figuration is often restrained and "organistic," relying heavily on imitation of motives. With the exception of *Pasacalles IV*, all these *diferencias* are based on a repeated 4-measure harmonic pattern: I–I–IV–V (Ex. 6.21).

The lone *Xácara* also crystallizes into a 4-bar skeleton, but based on the characteristically Spanish descending tetrachord; like the *gallardas*, it is more inclined toward the extroverted figuration associated with stringed keyboard instruments. Rather than 4-measure patterns, the five *gallardas* are based on longer harmonic schemes of 8, 10, 14, or 16 measures, some of them actual subjects introduced in the bass. Unlike most traditional *galliards*, these pieces are all in duple meter. *Gallardas I*, possibly the most powerful and stirring of all Cabanilles's variation sets, is based on an 8-bar phrase in D minor.[19] Each of the 12 variations is to be repeated, some with first and second endings, but slight adjustments are necessary in a few spots to smooth out awkward repeats, as in variation 6. The first variation begins somewhat languorously with arpeggiated figures more idiomatic to the harpsichord than to the organ (Ex. 6.22), but the rhythmic momentum builds with succeeding variations, unrelenting to the end.

Of the miscellaneous pieces other than variations, the six tocatas are in a class by themselves. The title tocata, used by Cabanilles for the first

EXAMPLE 6.21. Cabanilles, *Pasacalles II*, mm. 1–4

EXAMPLE 6.22. Cabanilles, *Gallardas I*, mm. 1–5

time in Iberian keyboard literature, does not imply that these half-dozen pieces are equivalent to some species of Italian or German toccata, or even that they closely resemble each other. Despite their modest proportions most are sectional, the last two *tocatas* subdivided by meter changes. *Tocatas V* and *VI* are similar to many of the tientos, with each discrete section (marked *discurs*) introducing a rhythmic variant of the original subject, but the other four are less contrapuntal. The first develops into a *medio registro* texture (with undivided stops), while the second actually specifies a left-hand solo. *Tocata III* and *Tocata IV* are highly unusual, the former opening with a mini-etude exploiting long trills, the latter involving similar material in rapid repeated notes.[20]

Although not yet published in its entirety, the portion of Cabanilles's organ music expressly intended for liturgical use is considerable, constituting in total number of measures nearly a third of his known output. Most of his hymn settings are based on the *Sacris solemniis* (15) and, as one might expect, the ubiquitous *Pange lingua* (60!). The latter are cast in the traditional mold—three voices and triple meter—with the cantus firmus in one voice. The myriad *versos*, some intended for masses but most for the divine offices (especially vespers), are typically arranged in sets (*juegos*) according to mode. When the versets are based on a *canto llano* (plainchant tune), the structural division is often clearly marked by the word *mediación*. Virtually every technique, device, or style used in the tientos can be found in these *versos* as well (including divided stops, although not always indicated). A few of Cabanilles's psalm and Magnificat settings still reflect the solemn austerity of Cabezón's liturgical pieces, but the majority of them signal the dawn of the next century.

The works of Juan Cabanilles clearly represent the culmination of an epoch in Iberian keyboard music, and his astounding range of styles and techniques affords a kind of retrospective view of Spanish keyboard literature before 1700. Moreover, in sheer quantity of production he exceeded any of his predecessors, and in quality of workmanship he had no equals among his contemporaries. Cabanilles's celebrated pupil José Elías once inscribed the verse: "The world will surely meet its demise/ Before a second Cabanilles may arise." With the death of his master a venerable musical era had come to a close—on the heels of a transfer of political power from the Hapsburg dynasty to the Bourbons—and the influx of Italian music and musicians into the eighteenth-century Spanish court was just around the corner.

Guide to Literature and Editions

Secondary literature on the early keyboard music of Spain and Portugal is not abundant, for a common perception that the keyboard works of Iberian composers are peripheral to other schools has limited the number of publications outside of the Peninsula. In recent years, however, this area has attracted attention as more students of keyboard literature seek to continue the pioneering efforts of Higinio Anglés, Willi Apel, and Macario Santiago Kastner.

Studies of individual composers and their works include Kastner 1977 on the Cabezóns, Jacobs 1973 on Correa de Arauxo, and García Ferreras 1973 on Cabanilles. More up-to-date biographical data on Correa plus a full translation of the *Facultad orgánica* can be found in Holland 1985. Portuguese composers Carreira, Coelho, and Araújo are the subject of Kastner 1979; much of it is available in English as prefatory material to the pertinent volumes in *Portugaliae musica*.

Among the few monographs treating specific genres in Iberian keyboard music are Esses 1992–94 on instrumental *diferencias* and Sutton 1975 on the organ *batalla*. For a general history of the keyboard tiento, see Kastner 1973.

A relatively uncomplicated but somewhat subjective introduction to the subject of performance practice is Kastner 1987; for coverage of seventeenth-century practices in greater depth, see Hoag 1980. See Parkins for detailed discussions on ornamentation (1980) and fingering (1983), Bernal Ripoll 1998–99 for embellishments in Cabanilles.

The most useful general history of the early Spanish organ and aspects of its literature remains Wyly 1964, although more recent significant contributions to the study of the organs are Jambou 1988, and Lama 1995. Specifications and descriptions of many Spanish instruments (some still extant) are provided in Reuter 1986. For an introduction to organs in Portugal, see Jordan's series of articles in *The Organ* (1983, 1986, 1987); also important as well as meticulously documented is Doderer 1978.

The proceedings of the *I Congreso Nacional de Musicología* (1981) include a number of essays by leading Spanish scholars and organ builders on the Spanish organ, keyboard literature, and performance practice. Among them is Lloréns Cisteró's invaluable "Literatura organística del siglo XVII," an exhaustive and detailed checklist of seventeenth-century composers, keyboard works, sources, and modern editions.

Modern Editions

The general lack of familiarity with Iberian keyboard music is attributable, at least in part, to the limited availability of published editions. Until 20 or 30 years ago a sizable portion of this literature was still untranscribed. Playing editions were confined largely to a handful of unreliable anthologies or collected editions that were difficult or at times impossible to obtain. The situation is much improved now, but even today a substantial number of pieces, especially those by lesser composers, remain unpublished.

Venegas's *Libro de cifra nueva* was edited by Anglés in 1944 with extensive critical notes and prefatory information, reprinted in its entirety in 1985. More recently, the musical portion of the text has been reprinted in four volumes by Masters Music Pubications (Boca Raton, FL: The Well-Tempered Press, n.d.); also available from the same publisher are reprinted editions of Cabezón (in six volumes) and Correa de Arauxo (in eight volumes). Inexpensive reprints of the handful of pieces by Bermudo and Santa Maria in the Schola Cantorum series are obtainable from Belwin Mills (formerly Kalmus).

The first reliable modern edition of Antonio de Cabezón's *Obras de música* was also edited by Anglés (1966), a revision of Felipe Pedrell's late nineteenth-century transcription, and it remains the preferred playing edition despite the omission of the intabulations. These *glosados* were finally edited and published by Ester Sala (1974). The only competing edition of Cabezón's works is by Jacobs (1967–86); although his set has the virtue of including pieces outside the *Obras de música* (e.g., those in Venegas plus a few found in Coimbra 242), it features only incipits of the *glosados*. A major drawback in Jacobs's edition is the problematic reduction of original note values, which not only gives a false visual impression of the music but also creates unnecessary difficulties in studying various aspects of performance practice.

The relatively few Spanish pieces surviving from the era between Cabezón and Correa have been published by Apel in *Spanish Organ Masters* (CEKM, 14). The lion's share of these 26 pieces belongs to Aguilera, with 17 works. Two more recent editions of Aguilera's *obras,* including one additional piece, are those of Siemens-Hernandez (1978) and Gay (1979–80); the last, with the exception of one short *Pange lingua*, avoids reducing note values. Editions of the complete works of later Aragonese composers include Jiménez (1975), comprising 22 pieces, and Bruna (1979, 1993), with more than 30.

The most important modern source of Portuguese keyboard music is the series Portugaliae musica (PM hereafter). Coelho's *Flores de música* is published in two volumes edited by Kastner (PM A/1, 3); a facsimile reprint of the 1620 edition is available from Minkoff (1986). Keyboard works of later seventeenth-century Portuguese composers appear in three further volumes: Costa de Lisboa's *Tenção* (PM A/7) includes a selection of 34 pieces from Oporto 1576, most attributed to Gaspar dos Reis; Roque da Conceição's *Livro de obras de órgão* (PM A/11) contains 67 works from Oporto 1607, including several by Araújo; and *Obras selectas para orgão* (PM A/25) is a selection of 74 pieces from Braga 964, mostly anonymous, but including a substantial number of works from the *Flores de música* of Coelho. Music by sixteenth-century composers, especially Carreira, is contained in *Antologia de organistas do século XVI* (PM A/19).

Correa's *Facultad orgánica* and *Libro de tientos* have long been available in two volumes of the series Monumentos de la música española (1948, 1952). A two-volume reprint of the *Libro de tientos* (1974) is accompanied by a revised errata sheet that still does not correct all the errors. However, the conscientious performer can easily check a facsimile of the 1626 edition from Minkoff (1981).

Also available for many years have been four volumes of organ music by Cabanilles in the *Opera omnia* (1927–56), more recently reprinted by Kalmus. Several years elapsed before vols. 5–7 appeared (1986, 1989, 1992). Some tientos not yet included in the *Opera omnia* are available in *Música de tecla valenciana* (1986–94). Cabanilles's enormous output of liturgical versets remains largely unpublished, although the first in a two-volume selection has appeared as *Versos para órgano* (1986)–but not without numerous errors. Nelson Lee's edition (CEKM, 1999–) of the *versos* plus some tientos and miscellaneous pieces—519 in all, including a few by other composers, mostly anonymous—from the Felanitx manuscripts provides a more accurate transcription, judging by the initial volume of 162 pieces (with four volumes to follow).

Modern anthologies can be frustrating when searching for an edition of a particular work or the works of a single composer, but they are helpful to those surveying a relatively unfamiliar literature. Selected keyboard works by most of the previously mentioned Spanish composers, particularly of the eastern school, are still available in *Antología de organistas españoles del siglo XVII* (1965–68), the second volume reprinted by Kalmus as *Anthology of Spanish Organists of the 17th Century*. Works by mostly lesser-known eastern composers, transcribed from a manuscript in Astorga Cathedral, are included in the anthology *Colección de obras de órgano de organistas españoles del siglo XVII* (1976). Among other collections are the seven volumes in *Nueva biblioteca española de música de teclado* (1978–84), but nearly all of the pre-eighteenth-century music is obtainable in modern editions elsewhere. Also worthy of mention are the nine volumes of *Organa Hispanica* (1971–84)—vols. 1, 3, 4, 5, and 9 include pre-eighteenth-century music. Calvert Johnson's *Historical Organ Techniques* (1994) is notable in that it serves both as a performance practice tutor and as an anthology.

A set that should be cited as a model for scholarly playing editions is *Early Spanish Keyboard Music* (1986), vols. 1 and 2 of which contain only pre-eighteenth-century pieces. Maintaining the highest standards of editorial scholarship, the editors have provided critical notes plus a substantial introduction with historical information and reliable notes on performance practice. Not quite as thorough but also to be recommended are the *Spain and Portugal* volumes of the *Faber Early Organ Series* (1987).

Selected works from Antonio Martín y Coll's five-volume manuscript collection, one of which consists of his own music, have also been published in recent years. Editor Sagasta Galdós has chosen mostly unattributed works for the three volumes of *Tonos de palacio y canciones comunes* (1984–86). *Seventeenth- Century Spanish Organ Music* (1986–87) is a selection of 10 anonymous pieces (vol. 2) and 11 works by identified composers (vol. 1), the latter generally available in other editions.

Notes

1. For example, Pablo Nassarre's discussions on keyboard fingering and ornamentation in his *Escuela música* (Saragossa, 1723–24) are not at variance with sixteenth-century sources.

2. The largest and most significant collection of (mostly) anonymous seventeenth-century Spanish keyboard pieces–some 1,850 pieces in manuscript–was compiled by Antonio Martin y Coll between 1706 and 1709 (Madrid 1357–1360).

3. Alejandro Luis Iglesias has recently discovered a copy of the long-lost *Arte novamente inventada pera aprender a tanger,* a collection of simple keyboard intabulations of polyphonic vocal music notated in letter tablature. Compiled by the Spaniard Gonzalo de Baena and published in Lisbon in 1540, it now represents the earliest surviving print of Iberian keyboard music.

4. Of lesser musical significance but of some historical interest are two curiosities in this volume: an intabulation of Crecquillon's *Belle sans paire* in 12 parts, designated for two keyboard instruments, and a short, innocuous piece by the nun Gracia Baptista, quite possibly the only Iberian keyboard work ascribed to a woman before the eighteenth century.

5. Six additional pieces attributed to Cabezón are found in Coimbra 242 (published in Portugaliae musica 19*),* two of which are in Venegas as well. Madrid 1358 contains unidentified works in the style of Cabezón and his circle.

6. A presumably earlier work by Bernardo Clavijo del Castillo (c. 1550–1626) could be regarded as a forerunner of Aguilera's *falsas.* The *Tiento de 2⁰ tono (por gesolreut),* Clavijo's only surviving work, may very well have been inspired by a similar *durezze e ligature* style encountered during his years spent in Palermo.

7. This particular scheme, probably derived from folk rhythms, still survives in Latin American popular dance music. The Afro-Cuban *cinquillo* (♩♪♩♪) and tresillo (♩·♩·♩) are common background rhythms for familiar dances like the rumba. Even more than the 3 + 3 + 2 pattern, the alternating ³⁄₄:⁶⁄₈ meter remains common in Iberian and Latin American folk music.

8. Even more than the 3 + 3 + 2 pattern, the alternating ³⁄₄:⁶⁄₈ meter remains common in Iberian and Latin American folk music.

9. Correa de Arauxo's *Tiento de 6⁰ tono* (No. 23 in Kastner's 1974 edition), based "on the first part of the Batalla by Morales" (now lost), could probably be considered the first of this genre in Spain.

10. There are three main sources: the *Tenção* of João da Costa de Lisboa (Oporto 1576); *O livro de orgão do Mosteiro do Bouro* (Braga 964); and the *Livro de obras de orgão* of Roque da Conceição (Oporto 1607, dated 1695).

11. The handful of pieces not qualifying as tientos consists of two extremely ornate intabulations, two cantus firmus settings (in *Fabordón* style), and three variation sets.

12. The earliest surviving tiento to specify this novelty is a *Medio registro alto* (that, is, for half register with a solo in the treble) attributed to Francisco Peraza (1564–98), organist at Seville Cathedral. See Fernández de la Cuesta 2001, however, for a recently discovered challenge to this distinction.

13. Correa's irregular subdivisions are not entirely unprecedented in Spanish keyboard music—the quintuplets in Antonio de Cabezón's *Fabordón del sexto tono* and in Hernando's *Dulce memoria* are but two examples. In Example 6.16 the d′ in the solo bass line (indicated by an asterisk), although present in the original edition, is doubtless an error. Any note above c′ would lie within the territory of the accompaniment.

14. The well-known registration lists from San Juan de las Abadesas (1613) and Lérida (1624) are also worth examining in detail as contemporary documents, but their relevance to practice outside Catalonia is questionable. Perhaps more pertinent are four somewhat older Sevillian lists (the earliest dated 1584); see Ayarra Jarne 1979, 1981 and Cea Galán 1993.

15. A curious relic in the old style is his *Tiento ple sobre ut re mi fa sol la* (No. 46), undoubtedly one of the last keyboard works based on the hexachord either in Spain or elsewhere.

16. Modern editions of Cabanilles sometimes use Catalan as well as Spanish terminology; both are given here.

17. Tiento numbers correspond to the continuous numbering in the Cabanilles *Opera omma,* unless otherwise stated.

18. The written-out trills in mm. 146–47 are typical examples of Cabanilles's myriad embellishments, always carefully notated in full.

19. The *tono* designation for this piece (mode I) is a reminder that traces of the modal system still linger, even in ostensibly secular tonal works.

20. The otherwise inexplicable left-hand shifts in register toward the c′/c′♯ division in *Tocata IV* (mm. 15 and 20) leave little doubt that the organ was the intended instrument.

Selected Bibliography

EDITIONS

Aguilera de Heredia, Sebastián. *L'oeuvre d'orgue.* 2 vols. Ed. Dom Claude Gay. La Flèche, 1979–80.

———. *Obras para órgano.* Ed. Lothar Siemens Hernández. Madrid, 1978.

Antologia de organistas do século XVI. Ed. Cremilde Rosado Fernandes. PM, A/19. Lisbon, 1969.

Antología de organistas españoles del siglo XVII. 4 vols. Ed. Higinio Anglés. Barcelona, 1965–68.

Bermudo, Juan. *Oeuvres d'orgue.* Ed. Pierre Froidebise. Orgue et Liturgie, 47. Paris, 1960.

Bruna, Pablo. *Obras completas para órgano*. Ed. Carlo Stella. Saragossa, 1993.

——. *Obras completas para órgano*. Ed. Julián Sagasta Galdós. Saragossa, 1979.

Cabanilles, Juan. *Keyboard Music from the Felanitx Manuscripts: Juan Cabanilles and His Contemporaries., I*. Ed. Nelson Lee, CEKM 48, I. 1999.

——. *Musica de tecla valenciana*. 5 vols. to date. Ed. Julián Sagasta Galdós. Valencia, 1986–98.

——. *Opera omnia: musici organici Johannis Cabanilles*. 4 vols. Ed. Higinio Anglés. Barcelona, 1927, 1933, 1936, 1956. Vols. 5–7, ed. José Climent. Barcelona, 1986, 1989, 1992.

——. *Versos para órgano*. Vol. 1. Ed. José María Lloréns Cisteró and Julián Sagasta Galdós. Barcelona, 1986.

Cabezón, Antonio de. *Collected Works*. 5 vols. Ed. Charles Jacobs. New York, 1967–86.

——. *Glosados del libro "Obras de música para tecla, arpa y vihuela."* Ed. María A. Ester Sala. Madrid, 1974.

——. *Obras de música para tecla, arpa y vihuela*. Ed. Higinio Anglés (rev. after Felipe Pedrell). Monumentos de la música española, 27–29. Barcelona, 1966.

Coelho, Manuel Rodrigues. *Flores de música pera o instrumento de tecla & harpa* (Lisbon, 1620). Ed. M. S. Kastner. Portugaliae musica, A/1, 3. Lisbon, 1959, 1961.

——. *Flores de música pera o instrumento de tecla & harpa* (Lisbon, 1620). Facsimile edition. Geneva, 1986.

Colección de obras de órgano de organistas españoles del siglo XVII Ed. José Maria Alvarez. Madrid, 1976.

Composizioni inedite dai "Flores de múisica" de Antonio Martín y Coll. Ed. Carlo Stella, and Vittorio Vinay. Milan, 1979.

Conceição, Fr. Roque da. *Livro de obras de órgão*. Ed. Klaus Speer. PM, A/11. Lisbon, 1967.

Correa de Arauxo, Francisco. *Libro de tientos y discursos de música práctica y theórica de órgano intitulado Facultad orgánica* (Alcalá, 1626). Ed. M. S. Kastner. Monumentos de la música española, 6, 12. Barcelona, 1948, 1952. Reprint. Madrid, 1974.

——. *Libro de tientos y discursos de música práctica y theórica de órgano intitulado Facultad orgánica* (Alcalá, 1626). Facsimile edition. Geneva, 1981.

Costa de Lisboa, João da. *Tenção*. Ed. Cremilde Rosado Fernandes. PM, A/7. Lisbon, 1963.

Early Spanish Keyboard Music. 3 vols. Ed. Barry Ife and Roy Truby. Oxford, 1986.

Faber Early Organ Series: Spain and Portugal. 3 vols. Ed. James Dalton. London, 1987.

Jiménez [Ximénez], José. *Collected Organ Compositions*. Ed. Willi Apel. CEKM, 31, 1975.

Johnson, Calvert, ed. *Historical Organ Techniques and Repertoire*. Vol. 1: *Spain 1550–1830*. Greensboro, NC, 1994.

Martín y Coll, Antonio. *Tonos de palacio y canciones comunes*. 3 vols. Ed. Julián Sagasta Galdós. Madrid, 1984–86.

Nueva biblioleca española de música de teclado. Siglos XVI al XVIII. 7 vols. Ed. Antonio Baciero. Madrid, 1978–84.

Obras selectas para orgão: Ms 964 da Biblioteca Pública de Braga. Ed. Gerhard Doderer. PM, A/25. Lisbon, 1974.

Organa Hispanica: Iberische Musik des 16., 17. und 18. Jahrhunderts für Tasteninstrumente. 9 vols. to date. Ed. Gerhard Doderer. Heidelberg, 1971–.

PM. *Portugaliae musica.* Lisbon, 1959–.

Santa María, Fray Tomás de. *Oeuvres transcrites de l'Arte de tañer fantasía.* Ed. Pierre Froidebise. Orgue et Liturgie, 49. Paris, 1961.

Seventeenth-Century Spanish Organ Music from "Huerto ameno de varias flores de música." 2 vols. Ed. Sally Fortino. Vienna, 1986–87.

Silva Iberica de música para tecla de los siglos XVI, XVII y XVIII. 2 vols. Ed. Macario Santiago Kastner. Mainz, 1954, 1965.

Spanish Organ Masters After Antonio de Cabezón. Ed. Willi Apel. CEKM, 14, 1971.

Venegas de Henestrosa, Luis. *Libro de cifra nueva para tecla, harpa y vihuela.* Ed. Higinio Anglés. Monumentos de la música española, 2. Barcelona, 1944.

LITERATURE

Ayarra Jarne, José Enrique. *Francisco Correa de Arauxo, organista sevillano del siglo XVII.* Seville, Diputación Provincial, 1986.

——. "Un documento de excepcional interés para la historia de los órganos catedralicios de Sevilla." *Revista de Musicología* 2 (1979): 299–306; 4 (1981): 159–70.

Bernal Ripoll, Miguel. "La ornamentación en las obras de Cabanilles." *Anuario musical* 53 (1998): 111–64.

——. "La ornamentación en las obras de Cabanilles II: tabla de ornamentos empleados por Cabanilles." *Anuario musical* 54 (1999); 149–54.

——. "Las contras de los órganos barrocos del país valenciano: reflexiones sobre su empleo en la música de Cabanilles." *Revista de musicología* 19 (1996): 133–52.

——. "Una nueva contribución a la técnica de la música de tecla antigua ibérica: unas digitaciones para órgano de 1649." *Anuario Musical* 55 (2000): 87–98.

Beurmann, Andreas E. "Iberian discoveries: six Spanish 17th-century harpsichords." *Early Music* 27, 2 (1999): 183–208.

Bovet, Guy. "Essai d'un résumé des principales règles d'interprétation de la musique d'orgue espagnole et de leur utilisation sur un orgue moderne." *La Tribune de l'Orgue* 30 (September 1978): 1–9; 31 (March 1979): 10–15; 31 (June 1979): 1–7; 31 (September 1979): 3–7; 31 (December 1979): 4–9.

Bradshaw, Murray. "Juan Cabanilles: The Toccatas and Tientos." *Musical Quarterly* 59 (1973): 285–301.

Calahorra Martinez, Pedro. *La música en Zaragoza en los siglos XVI-XVII: I. Organistas, organeros y órganos.* Saragossa, 1977.

Cea Galán, Andrés. "El ayrecillo de proporción menor en la Facultad Orgánica de Francisco Correa de Arauxo." *Nassarre* 6, 2 (1990): 9–23.

——. "El libro de órgano de Maese Jorge Flamenco: unas memorias de registros y misturas olvidadas en el archivo catedralicio de Sevilla." *Nassarre* 9, 1 (1993): 33–77.

——. "Pablo Bruna según fray Pedro de San Lorenzo: perspectivas para la interpretación de la música de los organistas aragoneses el siglo XVII." *Nassarre* 16 (2000): 9–34.

Climent, José. "Cabanilles, una vía al clasicismo." In *De musica hispana et aliis: Miscelánea en honor al Prof. Dr. Josí López-Calo en su 65⁰ cumpleaños,* ed. Emilio Casares and Carlos Villanueva, vol. 1, 489–500. Santiago de Compostela, 1990.

Corry, Mary Jane. "The Keyboard Music of Juan Cabanilles: A Stylistic Analysis of the Published Works." Ph.D. dissertation, Stanford University, 1966.

Doderer, Gerhard. *Orgelmusik und Orgelbau im Portugal des 17. Jahrhunderts: Untersuchungen an Hand des Ms 964 der Biblioteca Púiblica in Braga.* Tutzing, 1978.

Esses, Maurice I. *Dance and Instrumental* Diferencias *in Spain During the 17th and Early 18th Centuries.* 3 vols. Stuyvesant, NY, 1992–94.

Ester Sala, María A. "La ornamentación en la música de tecla del siglo XVII." In *I Congreso Nacional de Musicología,* 179–96. Saragossa, 1981.

———. *La ornamentación en la música de tecla ibérica del siglo XVI.* Madrid, 1980.

Ferguson, Howard. "Corrupt Passages in 'Diferencias' by Cabezón." *Music & Letters* 52 (1971): 402–06.

Fernández de la Cuesta, Ismael. "Un tiento de Peraza entre papeles de San Zoilo de Carrión." *Anuario Musical* 56 (2001): 33–45.

García, Juan Alfonso. "Errores de edición y sugerencias para la interpretación de las obras de Pablo Bruna." In *I Congreso Nacional de Musicología,* 309–18. Saragossa, 1981.

García-Ferreras, Arsenio. *Juan Bautista Cabanilles: Sein Leben und Werk (Die Tientos für Orgel).* Regensburg, 1973.

Göllner, Marie Louise. "The Intabulations of Hernando de Cabezón." In *De musica hispana et aliis: Miscelánea en honor al Prof. Dr. José López-Calo en su 65º cumpleaños,* Ed. Emilio Casares and Carlos Villanueva, vol. 1, 275–90. Santiago de Compostela, 1990.

Hoag, Barbara Brewster. "The Performance Practice of Iberian Keyboard Music of the Seventeenth Century." Ph.D. dissertation, New York University, 1980.

Holland, Jon. "Francisco Correa de Arauxo: Organist, Priest, Author." *The Diapason* 78 (April 1987): 14–16.

———. "Francisco Correa de Arauxo's *Facultad orgánica:* A Translation and Study of its Theoretical and Pedagogical Aspects." D.M.A. dissertation, University of Oregon, 1985.

———. "Performance Practice and Correa de Arauxo's *Facultad orgánica.*" *The Diapason* 78 (May 1987): 15–18; 78 (June 1987): 14–16.

Howell, Almonte C., Jr. "Cabezón: An Essay in Structural Analysis." *Musical Quarterly* 50 (1964): 18–30.

———. "Paired Imitation in 16th-Century Spanish Keyboard Music." *Musical Quarterly* 53 (1967): 377–96.

Jacobs, Charles. *Francisco Correa de Arauxo.* The Hague, 1973.

———. "The Performance Practice of Spanish Renaissance Keyboard Music." 2 vols. Ph.D. dissertation, New York University, 1962.

Jambou, Louis. *Evolucíon del órgano español: Siglos XVI-XVIII.* 2 vols. Oviedo, 1988.

Johnson, Calvert. "Rhythmic Alteration in Renaissance Spain." *The Diapason* 67 (July 1976): 4, 6–7.

Jordan, Wesley D. "A Brief Investigation of Organbuilding Traditions in Portugal during the 16th, 17th and 18th Centuries." *The Organ* 62 (1983): 51–77.

———. "The Organ in Portugal: Brief Comments Concerning Its Design, Construction and Use within the Iberian Liturgy in the 17th Century." *The Organ* 65 (1986): 163–85; 66 (1987): 25–29.

Kastner, Macario Santiago. *Antonio und Hernando de Cabezón: Eine Chronik dargestellt am Leben zweier Generationen von Organisten.* Tutzing, 1977.

———. *The Interpretation of 16th- and 17th-Century Iberian Keyboard Music.* Trans. Bernard Brauchli. Stuyvesant, NY, 1987.

———. "Orígenes y evolución del tiento para instrumentos de tecla." *Anuario Musical* 28 (1973): 11–86.

———. "Randbemerkungen zu Cabanilles' Claviersatz." *Anuario Musical* 17 (1962): 73–97.

——. "Semitonia-Probleme in der Iberischen Claviermusik des 16. and 17. Jahrhunderts." *Anuario Musical* 23 (1968): 3–33.

——. "Sobre las diferencias de Antonio de Cabezón contenidas en las 'Obras' de 1578." *Revista de Musicologia* 4 (1981): 213– 35.

——. *Três compositores lusitanos para instrumentos de tecla: Séculos XVI e XVII (António Carreira, Manuel Rodrigues Coelho, Pedro de Araújo).* Lisbon, 1979.

Kenyon de Pascual, Beryl. "*Clavicordios* and Clavichords in 16th-Century Spain." *Early Music* 20 (1992): 611–30.

Lama, Jesús Angel de la. *El órgano barroco español.* 2 vols. in 3 [another vol. to follow]. Valladolid: Junta de Castilla y Léon, 1995.

Lash, André. "Beyond the Preface: Some Thoughts on the Application of Ornaments in the Organ *Tientos* of Francisco Correa de Arauxo." *Early Keyboard Journal* 12 (1994): 95–112.

Lloréns Cisteró, José María. "Literatura organística del siglo XVII: Fuentes, concordancias, autores, transcripciones musicales, estudios, comentarios y síntesis." In *I Congreso Nacional de Musicología,* 29–131. Saragossa, 1981.

Müller-Lancé, Karl H. "Juan Bautista Cabanilles, 1644–1712: Beitrag zu den Kompositionsarten der Verse und ihrer Anordnung in der Handschrift." *Anuario Musical* 47 (1992): 133–51.

Nelson, Bernadette. "Alternatim Practice in 17th-Century Spain: the integration of organ versets and plainchant in psalms and canticles." *Early Music* 22 (1994): 239–57.

——. "The Integration of Spanish and Portuguese Organ Music Within the Liturgy from the Latter Half of the Sixteenth to the Eighteenth Century." Ph.D. dissertation, University of Oxford, 1986.

Olson, Greta J. "Required Early Seventeenth-Century Performance Practices at the Colegio-Seminario de Corpus Christi, Valencia." *Studies in Music* 21, (1987): 10–38.

Parkins, Robert. "Cabezón to Cabanilles: Ornamentation in Spanish Keyboard Music." *The Organ Yearbook* 11 (1980): 5–16.

——. "Keyboard Fingering in Early Spanish Sources." *Early Music* 11 (1983): 323–31.

Powell, Linton E. "Organ Works Based on the Spanish *Pange lingua.*" *The American Organist* 31 (1997): 66–70.

Ree Bernard, Nelly van. *Interpretation of 16th-Century Iberian Music on the Clavichord.* Buren (The Netherlands), 1989.

Reuter, Rudolf *Orgeln in Spanien.* Kassel, 1986.

Roig-Francolí, Miguel A. "En torno a la figura y la obra de Tomás de Santa Maria: aclaraciones, evaluaciones y relación con la música de Cabezón." *Revista de Musicología* 15 (1992): 55–85.

Santa María, Fray Tomás de. *The Art of Playing the Fantasia.* Trans., transcription, commentary Almonte C. Howell, Jr., and Warren E. Hultberg. Pittsburgh, 1991.

Speer, Klaus. "The Organ *Verso* in Iberian Music to 1700." *Journal of the American Musicological Society* 11 (1958): 189–99.

——. "Tonus Designations in the Tientos of Juan Cabanilles." *Anuario Musical* 17 (1962): 31–36.

Stevenson, Robert. *Juan Bermudo.* The Hague, 1960.

Sutton, Mary Ellen. "A Study of the 17th-Century Iberian Organ Batalla: Historical Development, Musical Characteristics, and Performance Considerations." D.M.A. dissertation, University of Kansas, 1975.

Torrent, Montserrat. "Registración de la música de tecla del siglo XVII." In *I Congreso Nacional de Musicología*, 197–222. Saragossa, 1981.

Wyly, James. "Historical Notes on Spanish Façade Trumpets." *The Organ Yearbook* 8 (1977): 41–55.

——. "The Pre-Romantic Spanish Organ: Its Structure, Literature, and Use in Performance." D.M.A. dissertation, University of Missouri at Kansas City, 1964.

——. "Registration of the Organ Works of Francisco Correa de Arauxo." *Art of the Organ* 1 (December 1971): 9–23.

MANUSCRIPT SHORT TITLES

Braga 964	*P-BRp* MS 964
Coimbra 242	*P-C* MS 242
Madrid 1357–1360	*E-Mn* MSS 1357–1360
Oporto 1576	*P-Pm* MS 1576, Col. B/5
Oporto 1607	*P-Pm* MS 1607

CHAPTER SEVEN

Performance Practice

Alexander Silbiger

This chapter presents a general introduction to performance practices on the keyboard for the pre-1700 era. Specific national or regional traditions have already been dealt with in earlier chapters.[1] We begin by asking why, for this period in particular, there developed among modern keyboard players such an interest in performance practice; what did they hope to gain from its study? After a brief historical review we discuss how today's musicians best approach the subject and what pitfalls they should avoid. We shall also note a special aspect of performance practice on keyboard instruments: the attention given to coaxing expression from these comparatively inflexible instruments.

Our treatment is divided between topics that concern the instruments, including how to play them regardless of whether improvising or performing solo or ensemble literature, and those that concern specifically the interpretation of notated music. The former topics include the principal instrument types and their appropriateness to different repertories; questions of registration, pitch, and tuning; body and hand positions; fingering; and articulation. Performance practice topics associated with notated compositions (for the most part, really aspects of early keyboard notation) include accidentals; meter and tempo; rubato; rhythmic alterations; handling of repeats; and various forms of embellishment and other liberties taken with the notated text. Our discussion will concern the performance of solo repertory; for continued practice we refer to specialized guide books (e.g., Williams 1970).[2]

Why Study Performance Practice? A Brief History

The revival of early music, beginning in the late nineteenth century and gaining momentum through much of the twentieth, came out of the resurgence of interest in two kinds of historical artifacts: surviving musical instruments and surviving musical scores. Most often interest in the scores came first, which led to a curiosity about the instruments for which the music had been written, although in some instances an interest in an instrument may have led to a search for appropriate music.

Playing early keyboard music in the form in which it appeared in the old scores proved to be not as straightforward as playing more recent music. The overlay of interpretive markings on which modern musicians had come to rely for phrasing, dynamics, tempo, pedaling, and fingering was altogether missing. The precise meaning of what appeared to be meter and ornament signs was often unclear. Some aspects of these early compositions, for example, the thick encrustation of ornaments, and sometimes overly thin, or on the contrary, overly dense textures (e.g., thick chords in the bass register), were unattractive when played on a piano and, in the case of heavily ornamented works, nearly impossible to render with clarity. Many of these last problems were solved when performers turned to period instruments or reconstructions, but this introduced new quandaries. The means for achieving expression to which pianists had been accustomed, such as dynamic inflection and use of the sustaining pedal, were not available on harpsichords and historical organs. Such problems quite naturally led to a search for information on how this music had been performed in its own time, and that search eventually gave rise to the discipline now commonly called performance practice.

The search proved fruitful. An abundance of instruction books and related materials was discovered, from which it became evident that the relationship between notation and execution was rather different from what it had become in modern practice. Early musicians apparently were expected to bring to their performances both a command of numerous unwritten conventions as well as a creative participation in the form of improvised additions and alterations. This strengthened the belief in the importance of studying performance practice. The initial enthusiasm over the newly discovered precepts also led to their often indiscriminate wholesale application, without much thought as to where, when, to what, and to whom those precepts might have applied. However, that is a matter that the discipline in its subsequent development has been trying to sort out.

If the initial purpose of performance practice had been simply—and somewhat naively—to restore the original practices, its aims roughly a century later have become considerably more complex. First of all, we have come to realize what with hindsight should have been obvious all along: performing practices were never uniform and fixed, and second, the manner of performing a specific body of works continued to evolve as long as those works continued to be played.[3] But also, as this music was being revived, performing practices once again began to evolve as the result not only of the accumulation of historical knowledge and experience with the repertory, but also of changing tastes and fashions, in turn often reflecting larger artistic and social trends. Thanks to recording technology we can now look back (or rather, listen back) to the ever changing fads documenting this earnest performance-practice undertaking, including the "objective" ideal of the 1950s with a faithful literal reading of the text and an unbendable rhythm; the imposition of a swinging, jazz- or even rock-inspired, dance beat during the 1960s, along with the breaking up of the once prized expressive legato line by rhetorical articulations; and, more recently, a kind of new Romanticism with an attempt to restore expression by introducing greater interpretive freedom. Each new fad did not entirely negate the one that preceded it; there was a cumulative effect, and by the beginning of the twenty-first century a distinct manner of interpreting early music has developed that now is taught and practiced widely. At the same time, this manner too continues to evolve, as artists continue to question the historical foundations of specific practices and substitute modifications that they believe to be a closer reflection of earlier performances. As long as that evolution continues (regardless of whether it brings us closer to the "original" practice—which we shall never know), the performance of early music, with its associated discipline of performance practice, continues to be a living tradition.

Adding Expression

When early twentieth-century pianists first tried out a harpsichord, they were frustrated by their inability to play it expressively. (They might have done slightly better on the clavichord, but that humble instrument was, and to this day remains, on the margins of the early keyboard revival.) To many it confirmed their belief that those instruments represented an immature stage of development, and, after having satisfied their curiosity, they turned their backs to those quaint artifacts. Others embraced this apparent shortcoming, taking the modernist position that early music should be performed "objectively" rather than expressively or "romantically," but for most musicians that stance was not satisfactory. Besides, it was contradicted by much early pedagogical writing in which an expressive, "vocal" performance was held up as an ideal.

Several attempts were made to transfer the central tool of pianistic expression, dynamic differentiation, to the harpsichord; in retrospect most such attempts appear misguided. Many early twentieth-century players relied on constantly changing registrations by shifting manuals and fancy footwork, made possible by the elaborate stop dispositions and multiple pedal arrangements of early twentieth-century instruments.[4] Another recourse was the use of leather plectra, which, although producing a dull sound and requiring frequent regulation, allowed more dynamic inflection than the original quills. But during the 1960s, along with the introduction of delrin as a viable substitute for the original crow quill,[5] a technique developed that was effective in achieving expression, while at the same time reflecting the prescriptions of early pedagogical writings.

This new (or, one likes to think, revived old) technique involves the subtle combination of two ingredients that largely took the place of dynamic inflection: flexibility of the rhythmic placement of each note (or rubato) and variation of the spaces between successive notes (or articulation). Further intensification of expression can be provided by embellishments, and a final, arguably essential, ingredient is the instrument itself; on a modern piano or on an organ not built according to historical principles, the technique is ineffective. The details of this newly revived technique are difficult to describe in words and are best learned by study with those who have mastered it or by listening to their performances. But without it (and one still hears plenty of playing without it, especially from recent converts from the piano or modern organ), other aspects of performance practice such as fingering, ornamentation, registration, and temperament, are like so much icing without a cake.

How to Use (and How Not to Use) Evidence from the Past

Performance practice is based on the interpretation of various types of historical evidence gathered from instruction manuals and other writings, visual representations, surviving instruments, and the music itself. Three important points must be made regarding this process.

1. Historical evidence (except for sound recordings) can never tell us precisely how a work was performed at a particular time and place; at best it can provide a range of possibilities, which are almost always surrounded by vast areas of uncertainty. Furthermore, it often is difficult, impractical, or even impossible to recreate certain conditions of the original performances, which nevertheless may strongly have affected their impact, such as the acoustics of the performing spaces or the original state of the instruments (wind supply of organs, composition of harpsichord strings and plectra).

2. When we learn about a particular practice from the report of a performance or a treatise, we often don't know how commonly and widely it was applied. During much of the twentieth century musicians operated under a principle of "guilty until proven innocent": if a given practice was described (or prescribed) in one place at one time, it is assumed also to have been used at other places and at other times until contrary evidence is discovered. Needless to say, this is a precarious principle, and it becomes more so the further a work is removed from the place and time in which the practice was described. Prescriptions or recommendations by the writers of treatises offer a further problem: did those "rules" represent contemporary practice, or, on the contrary, something that performers usually were not doing but—in view of the authors—ought to be doing? One is left with the justification that often we have nothing better to go on, and that following such a prescription may at least be closer to the mark (or in any case, more interesting) than doing nothing, meaning, just playing the way concert musicians have traditionally been playing.

3. One further point must not be overlooked. In our approach to performance of early keyboard music we start at the other end from where musicians of the time ordinarily would have begun. We usually begin with wanting to play a specific piece of music. We have a score of the piece in front of us, and now ask: how do we play it, what is the appropriate instrument to play it on, what is the appropriate setting to play it in? The sixteenth-century or seventeenth-century musician more likely began with facing not a score but an instrument and a situation in which she was expected to produce some music, for example, a religious service or a social gathering. Her problem would be how to accomplish that, which is precisely the situation addressed by most instruction books of the period. The indicated solution generally is not: go and buy some scores and play some of the pieces you find in them, observing such and such performance-practice rules. In fact, how to play ready-made pieces rarely is addressed directly in the early treatises, even if they may include advice that could be applied usefully to that purpose. Instead, most instrumental tutors were oriented toward creating music on one's instrument either based on a well-known song, a sacred hymn, or a polyphonic composition for voices or instrumental ensemble, or, most challenging, made entirely from scratch.

Today we would call such approaches to performance improvising, although the music may not always have been created newly on the spot. Several methods for producing music on one's instrument without recourse to scores are presented in the pedagogical literature, from the fifteenth-century *Fundamenta* onward, along with numerous examples.[6] Creating counterpoint in one or more voices against a chant, hymn, or other melody had always been a basic technique, taught to almost every music student (see, for example, Diruta 1984, 2: 32–59). Learning how to transfer a polyphonic ensemble composition to the keyboard, adjusting inner voices for the sake of playability and adding embellishments to compensate for the expressive limitations of keyboard instruments, i.e., the art of intabulation, was taken up especially in sixteenth-century treatises (see Diruta 1984, 2: 3–31). Even improvising a brief composition by working through a point of imitation, "creating a fantasy," is addressed in at least one keyboard treatise.[7]

Creating a brief fantasy or setting a cantus firmus were skills organists drew upon for one of the most common tasks they faced when accompanying a church service: the production of versets for *alternatim* performance with the choir. This practice was used during both mass and liturgical offices and accounts for the large quantity of versets contained in early keyboard manuscripts. While some of the published versets, such as those by Frescobaldi, may have been intended either as pedagogical examples or even as material for the organist who lacked the skill to create his own, the many modest anonymous examples in the manuscripts probably are exercises by students who were trying to perfect their skill or assembling a repertory collection to meet their needs.

Nevertheless, even if the performance of ready-made music by others was mostly the province of students and amateurs and much of the surviving music was created to serve their needs, I do not believe that we are wrong in focusing our performance-practice studies on how to play the written compositions of the period; it will enable us to bring back to life the large quantity of wonderful music that has been preserved from the past. Perhaps a few musicians with exceptionally creative gifts will enjoy learning to improvise in the style of Byrd or Buxtehude, but most of those who have the urge to improvise prefer to do so in a more current idiom. Since this book is devoted principally to the existing musical literature, the emphasis in this chapter will be on the performance of that literature rather than on how to create your own music in pre-1700 styles.

Some final advice: The study of early treatises, and modern writings on performance practice such as this chapter, should be supplemented by listening to, or better still, working with musicians who specialize in the practice of "historically informed performance" (or HIP)—see also the earlier remarks on expressive playing.[8] Their interpretations are the fruit of the research, hands-on testing, insights, and intuition of several generations of artists, and one would do well to benefit from their accumulated experience. Some of their practices have been—rightly or wrongly—criticized as lacking solid historical validation and as being probably more reflective of the performer's own time than of the original practices. Those objections can be countered by pointing out that the original practices are inherently unknowable and that following the educated, historically informed intuitions of the outstanding specialists in the performance of a given repertory on appropriate instruments is surely one of the most effective ways of doing justice to both the music and the instrument in our own time.

The Instruments and How to Play Them

In the traditional classical concert world only two types of keyboard instruments are generally recognized: piano and organ. Their repertories are entirely distinct, as are, for the most part, their players. The pianos themselves have become largely homogenized to a single standard: the concert grand. However, for daily practice the majority of pianists do not have concert grands at their disposal; they play on a variety of other models, from smaller, "baby" versions to uprights and those abominable "spinet pianos" (not to mention various electronic surrogates). Classical pianists usually play such instruments by necessity rather than by choice; the smaller instruments simply are less space-consuming and more affordable substitutes for the real thing. There is no repertory associated with upright pianos, even if much fine music may have been conceived at and first performed on them.

A fundamentally different situation prevailed in preindustrial Europe. To begin with, instrument manufacture was not standardized. Even if at a given time and place there were common types, those might change dramatically within a generation. The considerable differences between national styles of instrument manufacture have for many years been taken into account in their modern revival.[9] Instruments were not mass-produced but constructed, often to order, in small workshops in a great variety of models, including one-of-a-kinds and cross-breeds such as the *Lautenwerk* and *Geigenwerk* (see, for example, p. 243). Virginals and spinets were not considered poor cousins of harpsichords; in fact, some of the small instruments were exquisitely and expensively made for wealthy patrons. The popularity of the English virginal is evident, for instance, from its portrayal on the title pages of *Parthenia . . . the first Musicke that ever was printed for the Virginalls* from 1612/1613 (see p. 27) and *The Second Part of Musick's Hand-maid . . . Set for Virginals, Harpsichord, and Spinet* from 1689 (see p. 73, Ill. 2.6).[10] Payment records for performances in seventeenth-century Rome sometimes include entries for players on both the *cembalo* and on the *spinetta* (as well as on the organ); *spinetta* playing, in fact, seems to have been a specialty of certain artists, and the instrument is specified in some ensemble compositions.[11] A number of recent recordings suggest that there is once again recognition of the special affinity of virginals and spinets for selected repertories.[12]

Church organs have always been one-of-a-kind instruments, even if constructed within national and regional traditions; the rediscovery of the rich, infinitely varied qualities of the surviving European instruments has formed an important part of the excitement brought by the twentieth-century organ revival. Among modern organs built according to historical principles, there has been a distinct change from "versatile," all-purpose instruments to organs adhering to distinct regional styles (especially North-European), and performers, perhaps more than with any other instrument, make considerable effort to match the repertory to the instrument they are using. Indeed, many organists would argue that there is no way one can do full justice to a Spanish seventeenth-century composition on a French organ or vice versa.

On the other hand, in the old days, organists often had to prepare for their church performances at home on a harpsichord, or, very commonly, a clavichord; some even possessed pedal instruments for this purpose. In fact, the comparatively easy-to-build clavichord often seems to have functioned primarily as an inexpensive practice instrument, somewhat comparable to the modern upright piano. It was praised as being especially valuable for developing a fine touch and enjoyed continued popularity in Spain and Germany, but after 1600 it seems not to have been used much in England, France, and Italy. No music specifically designated for clavichord survives from before the eighteenth century, when musicians (again, especially in Germany) began to value its capability for adding dynamic nuance.

Selecting the Appropriate Instrument.

Few areas of performance practice are as much in need of a strong dose of common sense as that of the appropriate choice of instrument for performing a given composition. It is necessary to reject two extreme positions: that only an exact simulacrum of the instrument for which the composer intended a work (or on which it was first performed) could do it justice, or, alternatively, that the choice of instrument was a matter of indifference, and that performers played on whatever was conveniently at hand.

There are several problems, both theoretical and practical, with the notion of trying to perform on the instrument the composer had intended. Often he did not bother to make his intention known (assuming that he had a well-defined intention), and we have no information on which type of instrument the work was first played. But even if we happen to know that a work was intended or performed, say, on an organ, and if we are so lucky as to know on which organ, and even if, miraculously, this particular organ still survives, chances are that that instrument has not remained in its original state from several centuries ago. The problem of performing on the appropriate instrument is compounded when playing a recital of varied repertory, although the use of different harpsichords or even organs for successive pieces is no longer unheard of.[13]

Advocates of the other, "anything goes," extreme will point to publications designated either as suitable "for any kind of keyboard instruments" (Andrea Gabrieli, *Ricercate* I, 1595), or for "organs, harpsichords, clavichords and similar instruments" (Attaingnant, *Quatorze gaillardes*, 1531), or that do not specify any instrument at all (e.g., Frescobaldi, *Capricci*, 1624).[14] In addition they will point to well-known instances (usually chosen from the works of J. S. Bach) in which a composition written for one medium was subsequently adapted to another medium, although that merely shows that the composer decided the work in question could be tweaked to work with a different instrumentation. On the other hand, there is no lack of publications that are quite specific in assigning instruments, and while some of those designations might be understood generically (e.g., "organi" for keyboard instruments), others are no doubt meant to be taken literally. It is evident that in France the harpsichord and organ repertories had become pretty much distinct by the second half of the seventeenth century, witness the *Livres de clavecin* and the *Livres d'orgue* and the quite different natures of their contents.

No doubt most compositions trace their origins to the need to provide music for a specific occasion or situation, whether it be a church service, a social entertainment, a lesson, or solo practice. Each of these situations is likely to have involved a particular instrument, and the composer probably was thinking of that instrument as he was writing out his score. He may have taken advantage of certain qualities of its sound and individual character, such as the attack and decay or the balance of high and low registers.

As a result the piece may sound more effective when played on a similar instrument, although that need not always be the case. Thus, if an Italian elevation toccata (see p. 246) works better on an organ and a French free prelude (see p. 129) better on a harpsichord, this may be not only because of their intended functions and contexts, but also because of the way they were written. Nevertheless, we must not automatically assign clearly secular music to the harpsichord and clearly sacred music to the organ; chamber organs graced many an affluent home, especially in England, and harpsichords were sometimes heard in the church, in addition to or instead of organs.[15] In conclusion, it is probably true that people played whatever they wished on whatever instrument they had at their disposal, and there is no reason why we cannot do the same, but nevertheless, the early instrument revival has taught us that great insights and aesthetic rewards are to be reaped by making the effort to match composition and instrument as closely as is practical.

Registration and Other Instrument Issues

ORGAN

Few areas of performance practice have brought as rich rewards as the attempt to match the music with the instruments, but with the organ there remains a further quest: how to make the best of this instrument's wealth of resources. How was the music allocated to its several manuals and pedals; which stops were drawn on each? With some notable exceptions, the original scores provide rather few answers. One looks in vain for the unambiguous guide maps provided by recent organ editions: the three staves representing the two hands—each possibly on its own manual—and feet, often with registrations specified for each staff. When early scores do use staff notation (as opposed to letter or number tablature), they generally provide only two staves, with the pedal part (if any) incorporated into the lower staff. Some organ music was notated in four-part open score, and tablatures also often were laid out in separate voices, but this served more to display the contrapuntal voicing than to guide the hands and feet.

Until the later fifteenth century, all ranks of pipes sounded together, and the earliest method of obtaining different sound colors was to have separate manuals and pedal board, each with its own set of pipes. Only when distinct registers could be accessed from a single manual (which seems to have first happened on Italian instruments) did it become necessary to make decisions as to which stops would work best for certain kinds of music. Nevertheless, before the seventeenth century the only indications encountered in scores were directions to take certain notes or voices on the pedals. These were found mainly in German tablatures (see pp. 148, 156), no doubt because in the Germanic regions pedal divisions and associated techniques reached a high state of development quite early on.

From the later sixteenth century onward organ design develops more and more along distinctively national lines, and, not surprisingly, the differences in the instruments' resources are reflected in markedly distinct registration practices. The first scores with directions for using separate manuals, such as *Auf 2 Clavier, f(orte)* and *p(iano),* or *O(berwerk)* and *R(ückpositiv)* come from Germany, with its history of fondness for complex, multiple-division instruments; the division between the manuals generally serves to create echo effects (see pp. 178–79) or to highlight a cantus firmus. There is also an occasional instruction to engage the *plenum* or *das volle Werk,* but almost never a call upon a specific stop or combination, notwithstanding the enormous range of choices offered by the large North-European instruments.

Italian instruments were, and largely remained, much simpler than their northern counterparts, often with just a single manual and rarely offering a wide range of colorful timbres. Pedals, when present at all, usually were merely pull-downs of manual keys. Pedal indications were therefore confined to sustained notes or slowly moving bass parts, and no other registration directions are found in Italian organ scores. The picture in England was not altogether different; most instruments were small and limited to one or two manuals; independent pedal divisions never really gained a foothold until fairly recent times. There exists, however, a fine seventeenth-century repertory of fantasies or voluntaries for the "double" organ, which exploit—sometimes quite dramatically—the contrast between different divisions of the instrument (see pp. 58, 72, and 80–81). Spain went its own way with organ construction, as with many other areas of musical practice; the wide array of colorful dispositions made possible by the unique resources of the Spanish instruments, in particular their divided registers, are often reflected in titles of the many *tientos* (see pp. 336–49). Nevertheless, it was the organ repertory of late seventeenth-century France that first prescribed specific registrations with some consistency, a practice made feasible by the fairly standardized "classical" organ design that was developed during the reign of Louis XIV (see pp. 314–16).

Fortunately, the rather limited information on registration provided by the music is supplemented by an abundance of evidence provided by other sources. Much of it concerns primarily the dispositions of the instruments (knowledge of which is, of course, a precondition for "historically informed" registration decisions), but it is not unusual for stop listings or descriptions to be accompanied by at least some recommendations for their use. The most directly applicable advice is found in prefaces to publications of organ music and pedagogical treatises, and such works have been drawn upon throughout this volume (e.g., see pp. 110–12 and 267). Also useful are books on organ building such as Arnolt Schlick's *Spiegel der Orgelmacher* (1511) and Costanzo Antegnati's *L'arte organica* (1608), and the encyclopedic coverage of instruments in comprehensive musical treatises such as Michael Praetorius's *Syntagma musicum* (1618) and Marin Mersenne's

Harmonie universelle (1636). In addition, a great deal has been learned from many other kinds of documents, including builders' and musicians' contracts and payment records (which may incorporate instrument designs and descriptions and even registration advice), court inventories, and liturgical service books. When few instruments are extant, such documents can sometimes fill in a surprising amount of detail; see, for example, pp. 24–27 for fifteenth- and sixteenth-century England.

Nevertheless, the most important evidence is undoubtedly provided by the surviving instruments themselves. Their number is not nearly as large as one might wish for, and most of those that do survive have been rebuilt or altered repeatedly during their long history. Still, throughout Europe, but particularly in the Netherlands, northwest Germany, France, Spain, and north-central Italy, many fine specimens are preserved in sufficiently original state to continue to inform and inspire musicians and modern builders, and devotees of early organ music would do well to seek them out.

HARPSICHORD

Harpsichordists are in a less fortunate situation: recommendations for harpsichord registration, whether in scores or in other writings, are not to be found before 1700 and continue to be scarce after that. Changing registers must not have been an important aspect of harpsichord playing; but then, possibilities on pre–eighteenth-century instruments were rather limited. Most instruments had only a single manual with two sets of strings, or at most two manuals with three sets of strings, which in principle could be played in various combinations.[16] In practice, however, on many instruments it was difficult to change registers during a performance because the physical means for doing so were not within reach of the player. The introduction of a second manual during the early seventeenth century at first did not serve for changing registers but to facilitate transposition.

Evidence from the eighteenth century suggests that by that time harpsichordists in France ordinarily used the lower manual with all three stops engaged (8', 8', and 4'), and switched to the upper manual (with a single 8') for echoes and other special effects (see Fuller 2001). We have no way of determining whether that practice was also followed in earlier periods and in other countries. Harpsichordists today shy away from the continual, kaleidoscopic registration changes fashionable during the earlier twentieth century, but they generally feel free to change when there is a definite break in the musical texture, at the beginning of a new movement or section, or for a repeat. There now is a similar reluctance to using both manuals at the same time in works written before 1700, except when voices can be divided consistently between the two hands. That mostly is the case in certain pieces primarily conceived for organ such as chorale variations and cantus firmus settings; in typical harpsichord textures voices tend to move continually between the hands.

Short Octave and Broken Octave

The newcomer to the early repertory must be alerted to a feature found on certain historical keyboards—more often on originals than on modern reconstructions—the *short octave*. Since in keyboard music from before c. 1650, certain chromatic notes like C sharp, F sharp, and G sharp are almost never called for in the lowest bass register (they are only likely to appear in little-used "remote" tonalities), the corresponding keys can be diverted to extend the compass to more useful notes. For instance, with the common C/E short octave, the lowest key appears to be E, but in fact, this E is tuned down to C, F sharp is tuned to D, and G sharp to E. When the two lower accidentals began to be missed, they were accommodated by the *broken octave*, in which the F-sharp and G-sharp keys were split, with the front portion providing the D and E and the back portion the accidental. Apart from the economical advantage of shortening the width of the keyboard, short and broken octaves facilitate the performance of certain large intervals. For example, in the passage from Peter Philips's *Dolorosa Pavan*, Ex. 2.18 (p. 56), the alternating octaves and tenths in mm. 104–106 and m. 111 would be played simply as if they were a series of parallel chromatic octaves from F to A. Numerous similar examples can be found in the early literature, and the modern player, if not equipped with large hands, will need to decide whether to retune to a short octave or to modify the passage.

Pitch Standards

Today most of us grow up believing that the pitch we call and notate as "A" is fixed in nature and that it corresponds to a frequency of exactly 440 cycles per second (or some octave thereof), although it sometimes is taken a little higher ("tuning sharp") or lower ("tuning flat"). Without this notion of a universal pitch standard, the concept of "absolute pitch," and the debate about whether it is inborn or learned, hardly makes sense.[17] But before the nineteenth century there was no assumption of a fixed correspondence between a specific pitch and a note name independent of the particular instrument or locality. The pitch representing "A" might depend on what part of Europe you found yourself, and furthermore, the type of instrument you were playing or on the setting, whether church, chamber, outdoors, etc. Some lute methods advise players to tune their strings up to just below the breaking point (which is where they are supposed to sound their best).[18] Organs were tuned high because that meant shorter pipes, saving the church money. That consequently the pitches of different instruments disagreed and transposed parts were required, was as much a fact of musical life as the transpositions that are required today of many orchestral instruments, except that the latter are considered to be "transposing instruments," whereas the former were merely adhering to different pitch standards (e.g., *Cammerton, Cornet-Ton, Ton de la chapelle,* or *Tuono corista*). Of course, in any one locality the different pitches had to be precisely a whole number of semitones apart to make transposition feasible, which indeed seems to have been the case.[19]

Through measurements on large numbers of surviving instruments, particularly on winds and also on organs (although those are more likely to have been retuned at various stages of their existence) and by combining the resulting data with observations by various writers on comparative pitch levels, estimates of pitches used in various localities for various purposes has been emerging slowly. For the pitch a' these estimates range over more than a perfect fourth, from below current f' sharp to above current b'. (I will indicate here pitch levels in terms of the approximate equivalence to an equal-tempered scale with a' at 440 Hz.) The following very brief summary of a highly complex situation will largely be confined to pitches likely to have been used during the seventeenth century for organs and harpsichords.[20]

In England, the early seventeenth-century common pitch for church organs and choirs was quite high, slightly above b' flat. Harpsichords and chamber organs seem to have been tuned a minor third lower, somewhat above g'. After the Restoration, most organs were tuned down by as much as a tone, to slightly above g' sharp; the chamber pitch remained a semitone below that. In seventeenth-century France a low pitch around g' was prevalent until near the end of the century, when the pitch at court was raised approximately a quarter tone, to c. 404 Hz. This higher pitch, effectively the same as the English chamber pitch of the same period, was adopted by most instruments, including harpsichords. Many French church organs, however, remained at the lower pitch. In Germany, a double standard also had prevailed from at least the beginning of the century, with organs being tuned a whole tone above the pitch used by choirs and other instruments. Some organs even late in the century were tuned quite high, at b' (for example Buxtehude's organ at the Marienkirche in Lübeck), although b' flat was more common; chamber instruments continued to be tuned a whole tone lower, at g' sharp. The situation in Italy varied strongly by region. In Rome, during the late sixteenth century, organs had been pitched around g' sharp, but at the beginning of the seventeenth century they were lowered appreciably to a quarter tone below g' (presumably to favor the castrati), where they remained in some cases through the nineteenth century. Elsewhere in Italy, most organs were tuned high, at a' sharp, although a' was not uncommon; in chamber settings a low pitch of g' sharp prevailed.

Clearly it would not be practical to retune our harpsichord to the appropriate pitch for each composition we play, assuming that this pitch could even be securely determined. Nowadays in "historically informed" performances instruments most often tune a' at g' sharp or 415 Hz, an equal-tempered semitone below 440, which was commonly used in eighteenth-century Germany, and many reproductions of period instruments are currently manufactured at that pitch. Harpsichords and even some organs are made now with moveable keyboards, allowing an instant switch down a semi-tone and sometimes also down a whole tone to g' ("French pitch"), and many musicians, especially string players, believe their instruments are favored by those deeper pitch levels. They may be right, but nevertheless, those pitches are not necessarily the ones at which the music originally sounded, as should be evident from the preceding summary. A further complication with shifting a keyboard up or down a semitone is that such a shift generally is not compatible with historical, unequal temperaments (without retuning the instrument).

Tuning and Temperament

An appropriate temperament no doubt makes a more crucial contribution to the effective performance of an early work than a lower (or higher) pitch standard. Nevertheless, it should not be thought that the various historic temperaments correspond to as many exotic colorings, each singularly appropriate to add its special charm to specific compositions. There is nothing mysterious about historic temperaments; they merely correspond to alternative procedures to maximize the "in-tuneness" of a performance. On a keyboard instrument, perfect intonation cannot be achieved for all pitches of a composition, and a tuning must be chosen that will do the least damage to a particular repertory. This usually involves a trade-off: the better the intonation, the fewer keys are usable. Since these days an understanding of tuning is not as universal as one might wish, probably because it is neglected in many music curricula, we provide here a brief, non-mathematical introduction to this important subject; the theory is best grasped, however, from the practice of tuning a keyboard instrument oneself. Our treatment, as that of several other topics in this chapter, by necessity simplifies a complicated history and glosses over a great number of details.[21]

Each of the musical consonances, whether octaves, perfect fifths, major and minor thirds, or their derivatives (inversions and duplications at the octave), can be tuned to a point at which it sounds at it purest and smoothest—at which all roughness and beating is minimized. When it reaches that point, it agrees with the corresponding interval in the overtone series and is called "just." There is, however, no way of tuning the twelve pitches of the chromatic keyboard so that every consonant interval is just, as anyone who tries to tune a keyboard soon discovers. This is because of two problems, both inherent in the mathematical relationships of the overtone series: the lack of closure of a cycle of just fifths and the incompatibility of just fifths and just thirds. The first of these problems can be explained as follows: if starting from C, you try to tune the twelve chromatic pitches by means of a series of just perfect fifths (for convenience substituting the equivalent fourths to stay within an octave range) you will not return to where you started, as would be the case with equal-tempered fifths. Eventually you reach what really is E sharp, and if you check that pitch against your starting C, you discover that it does not form a just fifth (or fourth) but is appreciably and unpleasantly sharp (by approximately a quarter of a semitone—the Pythagorean comma—a small but quite noticeable difference). Hence this E sharp cannot function satisfactorily as an F. We encounter a similar problem when we try to use an enharmonic equivalent for any of our chromatic pitches (B flat for A sharp, etc.). Thus our tuning sets a limit to the chromatic pitches that can be used without retuning.

Compounding this problem is the incompatibility of thirds and fifths. The major third C-to-E obtained by tuning four just fifths C-G-D-A-E will not be just, but appreciably larger (by slightly over one-fifth of a semitone—the Syntonic comma). To make it just, at least one of those fifths needs to be tuned flat by this comma, enough to make it sound badly out of tune, which will still leave us with a lot of other sharp thirds. Furthermore, just thirds are also incompatible with just octaves: if you tune a series of three just thirds: C-E-G sharp-B sharp, that B sharp will not be at the same pitch as the C; three just major thirds do not add up to a just octave. This is similar to the result of tuning twelve just fifths, except that rather than being higher, this B sharp will be considerably (nearly a quarter tone!) lower. In short, there is simply no way of having either all major thirds or all perfect fifths just. Some kind of compromise is called for, and a multitude of temperaments were designed to provide one. Many of the temperaments described by early writers are, however, merely theoretical constructs, since they are impossible to set accurately without a modern electronic device.

Issues of tuning occupied a much larger place in musical thinking in earlier centuries than in more recent times (more or less since the advent of the piano). Several interrelated factors account for that: the sound ideal of the period, the character of the instruments (which both reflected the sound ideal and contributed to it) and the nature of the music itself. A harpsichord produces a very focused sound that is rich in pure overtones; by comparison the piano sound is rather fuzzy, with weaker and less pure overtones. Several factors contribute to this difference, including the thickness of the piano strings, the way they are set in vibration, and the practice of modern piano tuners to mistune the three unison strings with respect to each other to produce a more "vibrant" sound. Similar differences can be heard between the sound of early and later organs and other instruments. On string and wind instruments, early playing styles, such as restraint in the use of vibrato, will draw additional attention to intonation. It is likely that such differences also existed in vocal production and choral sound of singers working within the early "sound culture," with the small size of both early vocal and instrumental ensembles further contributing to the effect. As a result, the effect of deviations from just intonation, heard for instance, in equal-tempered major thirds, will be much more pronounced and unattractive than in modern practice. The harmonic idiom of sixteenth- and seventeenth-century music, with its predominance of root-position triads is another important factor; see the also discussion of quarter-comma mean-tone temperament below.

We shall briefly describe the main categories of temperaments that were of practical significance.

Pythagorean Tuning

In medieval music there was little need to deviate from the tuning based on perfect fifths or Pythagorean tuning. Generally speaking, in this period imperfect consonances held an intermediate position between dissonance and consonance, rarely being used at significant points of closure or rest. Thus their rough quality in this tuning would not have been considered so disturbing. Neither would the lack of enharmonic equivalence have been a problem because music rarely strayed to the more remote chromatic regions.

Quarter-Comma Meantone Temperament

For the increasingly triadic idiom of the Renaissance, the roughness of the large major thirds of Pythagorean tuning became more disturbing, espe-cially when keyboard players desired to emulate the smooth and rich har-monic sound of sixteenth-century choral singing. Smaller thirds require smaller fifths; we recall that four just fifths produce a third that is larger than a just third by the interval of a Syntonic comma, and therefore, if we flatten all fifths by a quarter of that amount, all major thirds will be just. This gives us the quarter-comma meantone temperament; meantone refers to the fact that the major just third (C-E) is divided into two equal major seconds (C-D and D-E); similarly, the major ninth C-D is divided into two equal, although not just, perfect fifths (C-G and G-D).

For the triadic sixteenth-century idiom, which derived much of its momentum from dissonant suspensions and their consonant resolutions, meantone temperament was highly effective, since it enhanced the disso-nance-consonance contrast. Not only are consonances like thirds and sixths purer, more consonant than, say, in Pythagorean or equal temperament, but dissonances like major seconds, minor sevenths, and augmented fourths are more dissonant. The contrast is given additional emphasis, and hence the momentum further strength, by the pure, focused sonorities of instruments of the period discussed earlier.

Meantone has, however, the same limitation as Pythagorean tuning: for all practical purposes enharmonic equivalents are not usable. In this tempera-ment, G sharp is nearly a quartertone *below* (not above!) A flat, and the aug-mented third from E flat to G sharp cannot decently pass for a perfect fourth; in fact, because of its howling quality it is appropriately called the "wolf." Other diminished and augmented intervals, such as diminished fourth and augmented seconds, also shed their disguises as major and minor thirds, and reveal their true character as nasty dissonances.[22]

Meantone temperament, which is relatively easy to set, enjoyed a widespread and long-lasting popularity. Since most sixteenth-century keyboard music, and, indeed, much of the seventeenth-century repertory, does not cross the "enharmonic barrier," the limitation to a range of twelve chromatic pitches did not present a problem. For example, Michelangelo Rossi's toccatas (c. 1630), despite their often extravagant chromaticism, never venture in the sharp direction beyond G sharp or in the flat direction beyond E flat, and thus can be played effectively in meantone. To be sure, there were much earlier keyboard pieces that called for an A flat and even occasionally for a D sharp, and several solutions were available. One could retune the instrument (easier on a harpsichord than on an organ); a key signature with a flat would be a clear indication that A flats were more likely to show up than G sharps and that raising all G sharps would be prudent. One could also simply put up with the sour pitch or bury it under an ornament. Clearly another, more satisfactory solution was needed for pieces that included both G sharp and A flat or other harmonic equivalents.

Microtonal Tunings

One way of solving the problem, if expensive and challenging to the player, was to extend the division of the octave to more than twelve intervals by means of additional keys (and pipes or strings). Split accidentals, with the front and the back portions of keys producing the enharmonic equivalent flat or sharp pitches, were already present on some fifteenth-century organs. Most commonly, these were provided for G sharp/A flat, C sharp/D flat, and E flat/D sharp. In the later sixteenth century, when keyboard players desired to expand into the more remote chromatic regions explored in contemporary madrigals, instruments were constructed that included even more keys, and it became necessary to accommodate these on additional manuals. These *archicembali*, or *cembali cromatici* and *enharmonici*, made available increasingly finer divisions of the octave, enabling the desired chromatic extensions of the temperament, but because of the many keys, the instruments also became increasingly difficult to play. Despite reports of the virtuoso mastery by the likes of Luzzasco Luzzaschi, they soon became curiosities that no one quite knew what to do with (see pp. 243–44 and Ills. 5.6 and 5.7).

Other Meantone Temperaments

In a second, more practical kind of solution, entailing a compromise between the desire for just thirds and for increasing the chromatic range, all the fifths, and consequently the major thirds, were widened until the wolf and other diminished and augmented intervals became tolerable, even if still a bit harsh. Popular temperaments of this type were the fifth- and sixth-comma temperaments; since with these the major third continued to be divided into equal whole steps, they are still regarded as forms of meantone.

When the fifths are widened to the point that they equal the wolf interval, the diminished sixth, we have reached equal temperament, to be discussed shortly; in this temperament the thirds will have become nearly as wide as those of Pythagorean tuning.

Unequal, Cyclic Temperaments

All the tunings considered thus far were based on a chain of fifths of equal size. As a result, all other intervals of the same type will also be of the same size as long as they do not use enharmonic equivalents. The widely held belief that in meantone, unlike in equal temperament, different keys sound different is mistaken; all chords and scales of a certain type are constituted of identical pitch relationships unless they have to substitute enharmonic equivalents, in which case they are not musically usable. This misunderstanding is the result of confusion with yet another category of temperaments in which the fifths are no longer tuned equal but varied in such a fashion that the diatonic keys sound nearly like meantone, but the more remote keys become gradually rougher without sounding altogether intolerable. The more successful of such temperaments allow performance in all keys and the use of enharmonic equivalents without retuning. Since these temperaments make possible modulations around the circle of fifths, they are called cyclic temperaments, and no doubt by the later seventeenth century represented the most common form of tunings.[23] The change in quality from the smoothness of diatonic keys like C or G major to the rougher sound of E flat or B major was in fact praised by some writers and cited as an advantage over equal temperament. Cyclic temperaments that enjoy current popularity, mostly dating from the eighteenth century, include Werckmeister 3, Kirnberger 3, Young, and Vallotti; each appears to have its ardent advocates.

The theoretical possibility of equal temperament was certainly well understood at least by the late sixteenth century; in fact, lutes and other fretted instruments were tuned to something close to it. Although equal temperament may occasionally have been introduced on keyboards, it was not widely used until the middle of the eighteenth century, and even then not universally. Originally this temperament was rejected because of its large major thirds, almost as large as Pythagorean thirds. Later on, one heard the added objection that, unlike cyclic temperaments, it made all keys sound the same and thus made each lose its special character. However, during a period in which many players customarily tuned their own instruments, the greatest barrier to its acceptance most likely was that before the introduction of electronic tuning devices, equal temperament was an extremely difficult temperament to set accurately, almost beyond the capabilities of anyone but a professionally trained tuner.

Body and Hand Positions

We now turn from the instrument to the player. Advice on the most effective physical engagement with the keyboard—how to sit, how to move, which fingers to use—is relatively scarce and comes to us from widely scattered places and times: Buchner (c. 1540), Santa María (1565), Diruta (1593), Nivers (1665), and Couperin (1717) among others (see the Guide to Literature section below). Some of these authors had a specific type of keyboard instrument in mind; nevertheless common elements run through the advice they offer, which often differs markedly from what we were taught by our piano teachers. There is a good reason for that.

To set a harpsichord string in vibration merely requires a determined, well-timed descent of the finger, with no more pressure than needed to overcome the string resistance to the quill, which on a well-regulated instrument should be minimal. A similar, if not quite identical action is required on a tracker organ to open the pallet and allow air to enter the pipe, or on a clavichord to press the tangent against the string and start it vibrating. The task of depressing a key falls essentially to the finger, and the role of the rest of the body is mainly to allow the finger to accomplish its task as efficiently as possible. On a modern piano, however, the player must impart an appreciable, well-controlled momentum—a combination of force and speed—to the key, so that the hammer can reach the string with sufficient impact to produce the desired sound. A finger can almost only achieve this momentum with the help of other parts of the body; hands, wrists, and forearms, sometimes also the elbows, shoulders, and even the entire torso must be marshaled. Furthermore, the required momentum needs to be delivered promptly, and simultaneously by both hands, at constantly varying locations over a more than seven-octave (4 feet) wide keyboard, and to accomplish this, pianists have been trained since childhood to execute intricate body choreography, with subtle motions of the feet on the pedals contributing further to shape the sound and musical line.

On early keyboards pianists have to "unlearn" this complex and refined body skill in order to do something much simpler and more natural: let the fingers do the playing.[24] Of course, for the fingers to be able to do their job unimpeded, the hands need to be in the right place at the right time, and this in turn requires efficient cooperation of the other linkages to the torso: the wrists, arms, elbows, and shoulders. All these links should "hang loose," but nevertheless, be well supported to allow swift, easy movement of the hands to wherever the fingers require them to be; proper seat height is also crucial to this. The torso ordinarily does not take part in the movement, but maintains an erect, well-poised position. Facial grimaces are universally condemned; they are signs of tension, but another unspoken reason no doubt is that a gentleman, and even more so, a lady, should at all times maintain a pleasant appearance appropriate to his or her station.

Most authorities agreed that the fingers function best if they maintain a curved position, with their tips on the keys near the edges (to obtain the best leverage with the often comparatively short keys), and the back of the hand, wrists, and forearms all in a plane parallel to that of the keyboard. Only when the hand has to stretch for chords or octaves, do the fingers need to straighten a bit. In music before 1700, in which hand crossings are almost never called for, there is rarely a need for the fingers to leave the surface of the keys or for the hands and forearms to leave their plane. In the writings of a few authors one encounters exceptions to the preceding guidelines; thus Tomás de Santa María recommends a low hand position with arched fingers, "like a cat's paw," for playing the clavichord, and according to Diruta, dance-playing harpsichordists, for whom he barely restrains his contempt, strike their keys from some distance to overcome the resistance of the quills.

Articulation

The art of articulation, the subtle control of endings and beginnings of notes, is central to expressive performance on early keyboard instruments, and makes up for limited or absent dynamic differentiation. As mentioned earlier, it is an art difficult to describe in words. During the early nineteenth century, the favored playing mode on the piano became more and more a continuous legato, in which the notes follow each other seamlessly, the pressing of one key coinciding with the release of the next. Contrasting episodes might employ a staccato in which the notes are systematically and audibly separated.[25] On early keyboard instruments, the prevalent playing style rather seems to have been (and is again today) one in which the release precedes the attack by a slight but continually varying amount of separation. True legato is reserved for brief groupings and ornamental figures that use adjacent or nearby keys; on the harpsichord such figures may even be played with some overlap, a kind of *faux* pedaling. Holding keys beyond their notated length is also often practiced in arpeggio figures.

The technique of leaving such tiny gaps between notes should not be thought of as performing with a continuous staccato. When managed skillfully, taking into account the properties of the instrument and the ambient acoustics, these finely graduated, often infinitesimal separations will not be perceived as interruptions of the sound, but create the illusion of a flowing, vibrant, and articulate vocal line. In fact, they function much like clearly enunciated consonants in singing or speech. At the same time, they provide a tool for introducing clear rhythmic accentuation indispensable for a medium that cannot depend on dynamic contrasts. Without this technique, organ and harpsichord playing tends to sound lifeless and incoherent. An additional factor, no doubt contributing to the origin of the articulate playing style and to some extent indispensable to its effectiveness, was the long reverberation time of many old churches and chambers with high ceilings.

Finally, harpsichords, especially old ones, don't dampen as abruptly as modern pianos, but tend to have a certain ring, even in dry acoustics.

Markings for these articulations in the form of slurs or dots are rarely found before 1700, probably because it would be impossible to indicate the subtle shades of separation, and because it was considered part of normal expressive playing, requiring no special marking. The only exceptions are slurs indicating an occasional brief grouping (usually just a pair of notes), to be executed with a smooth, if not overlapping, connection (see above) and a shortening of the final note. Such slurs are most likely to appear in a melodic passage emulating a melismatic vocal line, or, as in the case of some passages in Scheidt's *Tabulatura nova* explicitly marked "in imitatio violinistica," emulating a slurred passage on a bowed string instrument. Scheidt's marking implies that that style was not the norm on keyboard instruments. The harpsichord more likely emulated the lute and the organ a chorus of voices or wind instruments (on the latter during this period most notes were individually articulated with the tongue), even if for all instruments of the period imitation of the rhetoric of gesture and speech formed the ultimate goal.

Fingering

The number of early keyboard scores that are provided with fingerings is surprisingly large, considering the scarcity if not complete absence of other information that might have been useful for the player, such as markings for articulation, tempo, or registration. Appropriate fingering must have been deemed important for proper performance and by no means self-evident. Most fingerings appear in manuscripts rather than in printed editions and ordinarily should not be assumed to stem from the composer; more likely they were inserted by a player or his teacher, although the latter could of course have been the composer. For some unexplained reason, these fingerings appear only in North-European (English, German, Dutch) manuscripts, although the southerners (e.g., Santa María, Diruta, Banchieri, Nivers) do provide discussions and examples of fingerings in their treatises.

The fingered pieces and the pedagogical literature show both chronological developments and regional differences, but nevertheless, a basic approach to fingering is discernible that differs in several respects from that of later centuries. Anyone trying out early fingerings needs to realize that the fingerings are not only intimately connected to the instruments and to the type of music played on them, but are also part of a total performance-practice package, including the generally non-legato playing style discussed earlier. The fingerings often will not make sense without the other elements of that package; thus, they will not work well on a modern piano, even when applied to early music, and they will not be very effective on early instruments if used in the context of an otherwise anachronistic playing style.

Early fingerings favor the central three fingers, and call upon the thumb and fifth fingers less often than in later practice, although they are, of course, indispensable for large intervals and chords. This avoidance should probably be understood in the context of the playing technique described above; the off-center thumb and fifth finger, when played by themselves tend to unbalance the hand and are more likely to cause tension (although not so much when both play simultaneously). For the left hand, the thumb, index, and middle fingers tend to be favored instead, probably because of its notoriously weak fourth finger; this might indicate a slight counter-clockwise pronation, shifting the central axis of the hand from the third to the second finger. The hand maintains as much as possible a closed, rounded position, with the fingers on adjacent keys. To reach more remote keys, the hand, contrary to modern practice, often was shifted rather than extended; finger substitution seems not to have been used before the eighteenth century.

Early twentieth-century writers were especially fascinated, if not horrified, by early scale fingerings, which usually make no use of the "thumb-under" technique and require an alternation of two adjacent fingers like 3434 or 3232 (see, for example, p. 76, Ill. 2.7; p. 169, Ill. 4.3; and p. 319). Such fingering did not necessarily imply a literal crossing of the third finger over the fourth or second, nor did it necessarily result in a slurring of notes two-by-two. The latter articulation would be especially unlikely with Diruta's scale fingerings, in which the third finger is placed off-beat. Nevertheless, a more or less unavoidable, and, indeed, desirable consequence of the paired fingering is an audible pattern, comparable to the back-and-forth bowing on string instruments and double tonguing on winds; such fingering would, furthermore, facilitate the execution of various types of *notes inégales* described by authors throughout the period.[26] Even patterns that resemble modern thumb-under fingering, such as 1234 1234, already encountered with Santa María, were probably not played in that manner, but rather as musical groupings of four. Thumb-under technique, as much as we take it for granted due to our early piano training, is a difficult, sophisticated technique that had to wait for the middle years of the eighteenth century.

We now turn to performance-practice questions associated with the interpretation of notated music, with, as elsewhere in this chapter, the emphasis on solo keyboard music. Various aspects of early keyboard notation, such as accidentals, meter, and note values, were briefly touched upon in our introductory chapter (pp. 8–9); here we supplement that discussion by examining associated performance issues in greater depth.

Accidentals

When using a modern edition, the performer should begin by determining whether the placement of the accidentals corresponds to that in the source (in which ordinarily sharps and flats would have applied only to the notes with which they appeared—see pp. 8–9), or whether the modern practice, in which an accidental also applies to all subsequent notes of the same pitch up to the next barline, was followed. Editions following the first policy are less troublesome; one merely needs to be careful not to follow old habits and extend the application of an accidental beyond the first note. Often the editor has inserted a helpful warning in the form of a cautionary accidental, which should not be interpreted as an optional, *musica ficta* suggestion (see below). When, however, the accidental placements have been altered to follow modern practice, the performer has to exercise more care, and ascertain whether an accidental should indeed be applied to another note that follows later in the measure, or whether the editor has failed to insert the necessary natural sign (that would not have appeared in the source but would be called for when following modern notation practice). Without recourse to the original, one will have to make an educated guess, based on general familiarity with the style.

Such familiarity will also be called upon when the source itself was careless with accidentals—still quite common in early seventeenth-century manuscripts—and the editor did not intervene by providing what anachronistically is often called *musica ficta*.[27] Some general rules of thumb may be helpful, for example:

1. The accidentals within a passage often are more determined by the local harmony (i.e., the underlying chord or progression) than by the overall tonality or key area (somewhat like the practice followed in jazz improvisation).

2. Pieces in "high" genres, such as toccatas and ricercares, are more likely to be governed by modal scales than those in "low" genres like dances and popular song settings. Thus, when the underlying harmony is F major or D minor, the pitch B natural more likely needs to be altered to B flat in the latter than in the former; however, this "rule" needs to be applied very loosely.

3. When the bass (or root) of an underlying progression descends by a fifth, as in a V-I cadence formula, the first chord should almost always be a major chord (often requiring raising the third of the bass by a semitone).

4. If the final chord of a movement or major segment (such as the A or B section of a dance) contains a minor third with the bass, it should be raised to a major third.

Tempo

Early musicians had essentially three means for determining the intended or appropriate tempo of a notated composition: verbal indications in the score such as "allegro" and "adagio"; knowledge of the tempo, or range of tempos, conventionally associated with the genre or style of the work; and aspects of the work's notation such as its time (or mensural and proportional) signatures and note values. Verbal tempo indications remain rare until the later seventeenth century, so for most early music, the performer has to rely on the second or third method, or, quite often, in fact, on a combination of the two. We shall discuss these three methods in reverse order, commencing with the complex and somewhat controversial topic, already touched upon in the Introduction (pp. 9–10) of the interrelationships between tempo, meter, and notation.

The situation of metric notation during the seventeenth century was not only very complicated—perhaps "confusing," or even "chaotic," might describe it better—and strongly dependent on time, locality, and the composer of the work, but, despite a great deal of historical research, it is not yet fully understood. Within these pages we can do no more that make some very general, if nevertheless helpful (we hope) observations. Our readers are urged to supplement this summary discussion by their own study of the practices associated with particular repertories, as well as consultation of more comprehensive treatments recommended in the Guide to Literature at the end of this chapter. Those treatments will also provide more background in mensural theory, another messy subject from which, to the extent possible, we try to keep our distance here.

Mensural Signatures

In the Introduction (p. 10) we mentioned the many different combinations of mensural and proportional signatures and metric note-value patterns found in keyboard music from the late sixteenth century onward; often several of these appear in successive segments of a single composition. Each signature typically consists of a mensuration sign followed by a number; either the sign or the number may also appear by itself. By the early seventeenth century the mensuration signs still in use are O with or without a slash (vertical or diagonal stroke) and C (sometimes backwards) with or without a dot or a slash. The chief purpose of these vestiges of the ancient mensural system was to indicate the metric pattern, but by the early seventeenth century all except for the two duple-meter signs C and ¢ were well on their way toward extinction.

In theory ¢ signified either a shift of the beat to longer note values (usually from minims to semibreves) or a faster tempo than C. In practice, however, the two signs rarely appeared in the same repertory or in works by the same composer, at least before the later seventeenth century. In the sixteenth century ¢ was used almost exclusively, and the English virginalists as well as Scheidt continue to employ it, whereas Frescobaldi and Froberger stick to C with hardly an exception. Presumably, none of these composers saw a musically useful distinction between the two signs that would have impelled them to use both. However, later French composers such as d'Anglebert in his *Pièces de clavecin* not only uses both C and ¢, but also a third duple sign, 2, the three signs corresponding to duple meters at three successively faster tempo levels. Similarly, in Locke's *Melothesia* (1673) we encounter C, ¢, and 𝕾, with this last sign, like the French 2, indicating the fastest tempo.

Two mensural triple meter signs were still in use: O and C, signifying metric patterns of three semibreves and three minims, respectively.[28] Either sign is almost invariably accompanied by a triple proportion or numeral sign (see below), and in that case may itself be replaced by C or ¢, or even omitted, without discernible change of meaning. In fact, the two triple signs survive mainly in the works of Frescobaldi and a few other Italians, while the English hold on for a while to just C ; the Germans and French largely dispense with both. No special mensural signs existed for triple patterns of semiminims because such patterns did not form part of the mensural system; as they became common, they were indicated by C3, just 3, or as triplets with a "3" above each group.

Proportions

The number that follows the mensural sign (or appears by itself) is either a ratio like $\frac{3}{2}$ or just a numeral (ordinarily 3). A ratio, at least in theory (but not always in practice, as we shall see shortly), indicates a proportional tempo relationship. Thus $\frac{3}{2}$ did not imply a meter of three minims,[29] but merely signified that three beats (which could be three minims but just as well three semibreves) are equivalent to two beats of the preceding section. The very commonly encountered numeral 3 could, however, have several different meanings: it could be equivalent to the ratio 3/1, hence a triple proportion, but it also could signify instead the proportion 3/2, or it could merely indicate a triple meter of some sort. The use of 3 with this last broad meaning is in fact very common, and often it functions precisely like a modern $\frac{3}{4}$ signature.

There are many situations in which a signature with a numerical ratio cannot or should not be interpreted as a proportional relationship, for example, when it appears at the beginning of a composition, so that there is nothing to relate to. It has been proposed that in such a case the proportion relates to a kind of imaginary fixed standard beat or tactus, and therefore the signature does suggest a tempo, but for this period the notion of a uniform tempo standard is now regarded as untenable.[30] When the proportion sign appears at the beginning of a section in a multisectional work, a tempo relationship to a preceding section does deserve consideration, especially when it leads to reasonable tempi before and after the transition. The case becomes less compelling when there is a marked break between the sections, especially when the break is preceded by a strong cadential termination including florid passages that more or less dissolve the preceding tempo and meter. The performer's taste and judgment will be called upon in such situations, as well as when dealing with distinct movements, such as sets of dances or variations. Sixteenth-century dances often concluded with a variation in triple time (sometimes even called *tripla* or *proportz*), which no doubt was played with a proportional relationship. For an English pavan/galliard pair a *sesquialtera* relationship (3 minims of the galliard being equivalent to 2 minims of the pavan) often works well, although we don't know that such a relationship was mandatory. Proportional relationships have been proposed for the successive movements of dance suites, sonatas, and variations, and often are quite effective, although, again, there is no evidence that they were expected.

We mentioned earlier that it is not always clear whether the numeral 3 signifies a 3/1 or a 3/2 proportion or merely indicates a triple-meter pattern. But even when the sign is a ratio, it is not always clear which note values are governed by a proportional relationship. For example, when a section in duple time with a beat that seems to fall on the minim, is followed by a pattern of three semibreves introduced by ³⁄₂, the equivalence of three semibreves to two semibreves often yields too slow a tempo, and equating the three semibreve beats to two minim beats provides a more satisfactory result. Another not uncommon transition is one from a pattern of three minims governed by a ³⁄₂ signature to six semiminims (or two dotted minims) governed by ⁶⁄₄. In such a case the 6/4 proportion probably does not relate the semiminims of the second section to the semiminims of the first, but both proportions relate to a (real or imaginary) earlier section in duple meter, resulting in a rhythmic regrouping or shift of accentuation rather than in a change in the speed of note values. There are transitions from duple to triple meter at which a similar relationship, that is, changing the metric grouping but keeping the minim pulse constant, may well have been practiced, but such a shift was not recognized in theoretical writings because it did not fit with mensural theory.

Metric Note-Value Patterns

There was another notational tool besides mensural signatures to prescribe or suggest tempo: the type of note values that formed the metric patterns. When composers prepared or had prepared collections of their keyboard music, for example Byrd's "My Lady Nevells Booke" (1591), Frescobaldi's various publications (1608–37), Scheidt's *Tabulatura nova* (1624), and Froberger's imperial dedication autographs (1649–58), they usually included not only works in different genres, but also made a point of featuring a variety of metric patterns, such as triple or sextuple patterns of semibreves, minims, semiminims, and even shorter note values, as well as of blackened semibreves and minims, and triplet semiminims. Most composers did not use many different signatures for these patterns and often were satisfied to mark the majority simply by 3. Frescobaldi was quite exceptional in that he used an astonishing variety of combinations of mensural and numerical signs, often employing several different ones for identical note-value patterns.

What was the point of notating triple patterns with so many different note values, and including in the same composition, sections with both semibreve patterns and minim patterns? Our intuitive answer would probably be that, everything else being equal, the shorter note values no doubt are meant to be taken faster, and this is precisely what some seventeenth-century musicians ask for. The best-known example appears in the preface to Frescobaldi's *Capricci* (1624), in which the composer states that semibreves preceded by $\frac{3}{1}$ or $\frac{3}{2}$ should be taken slowly; minims preceded by $\frac{3}{1}$ or $\frac{3}{2}$ somewhat faster; a pattern of three semiminims still faster; and a $\frac{6}{4}$ pattern (usually of six semiminims) quite fast.[31] Although this does not cover every pattern he uses, it provides the broad principle that the triple patterns with smaller note values should be taken at a faster tempo. Similar guidelines are offered by Mersenne, Ban, Carissimi, Reincken, and Purcell.[32]

Frescobaldi's guidelines are as important for what they do not say as for what they say. He does not relate the tempos in any mathematically precise way, such as prescribing that the minim beats should be twice as fast as the semibreves, but uses vague and relative terms like "slowly" and "faster." Furthermore, he does not relate the tempos in a proportional manner to a preceding section according to the signature; in fact, he implies that his tempo directions apply equally to $\frac{3}{1}$ or $\frac{3}{2}$. It may very well be that his guidelines concern only situations where the tempo was not unambiguously determined by a proportional relationship, and hence, in which it would not be obvious what to do. Nevertheless, his "rules" imply that for him, neither note values nor signatures by themselves prescribe a tempo in any absolute sense. We stated earlier that he liked to use a great variety of mensural signatures, and it has been proposed that these convey different tempos. In fact, some scholars have constructed elaborate and ingenious systems to relate the tempos of various sections of multisectional works like the *Cento partite sopra passacagli* and some of the *Capricci*. There is, however, little evidence that the composer had anything in mind along the lines of those clever schemes, which require the performer to engage every few measures in mental gymnastics in order to calculate the appropriate tempo. The composer's broad tempo guidelines discussed earlier provide no support for them; one probably should not attach too much importance to the proliferation of signatures in his works, which often are used with great inconsistency.[33]

During the later seventeenth century metric notation gradually began to assume more familiar aspects, although this was by no means a uniform evolution, and some residues of mensural principles, such as "cut time," persist. Measures of four and three semiminim beats became ubiquitous, as did metrical signatures like $\frac{3}{4}$, $\frac{2}{4}$, $\frac{6}{8}$, and $\frac{3}{8}$, and their meaning was largely what it is today. However, although these signatures generally did not function as proportions, they did sometimes have tempo implications, especially in France (see Houle 1987, 27–28 and 336–38).

Genre and Tempo

We have seen that notation provides only limited, and mostly relative guidance for tempo decisions. For the most part, performers relied—as they always have—on their familiarity with the conventions associated with particular genres and styles. For instance, musicians would have had an instant sense of a suitable tempo for a popular dance type, which they might have danced since childhood. This obviously places us at a disadvantage, and, furthermore, we must be careful when drawing on experiences with more familiar later music. For example, we may have acquired ideas of appropriate tempos for certain dance types from our familiarity with the music of J.S. Bach, but tempos of seventeenth-century antecedents sometimes differed significantly. Thus, in the seventeenth century, sarabandes were considerably faster, and allemandes also were generally somewhat faster, than those of Bach.

Tempo and mood were also, to a certain extent, implied with non-dance genres; thus a canzona would call for a lively tempo, whereas a ricercare invited a more restrained rendition. But as the new seventeenth-century styles evolved, composers evidently began to have less confidence in traditional cues such as notation and genre, and started to add verbal tempo descriptions to their scores or to provide guidelines in the prefaces to their editions. For Frescobaldi, communicating the proper tempo seems to have been a primary concern; several compositions in his *Fiori musicali* (1634) have sections marked *adagio* and *allegro*, and much of the advice offered in his prefaces concern choice of tempo. As mentioned earlier, his recommendations usually are not couched in absolute terms; indeed, most are along the lines of urging the player to select a tempo in accordance with the character of the music (as opposed to, one assumes, according to some theoretical rule). Verbal tempo instructions become more frequent during the later seventeenth century, especially in France, although not nearly as frequent as in ensemble music, presumably because it is essential that all members of an ensemble are aware of a new tempo.

Rubato

This applies even more to the slowing down and resumption or quickening of the pulse, frequently marked in ensemble music as *adagio* and *allegro*, or in English ensemble sources with vivid descriptiveness as "drag" and "away." Such expressive liberties had become fashionable in the performance of late sixteenth-century madrigals, where they were introduced in response to the text, and early seventeenth-century instrumentalists evidently sought to imitate this manner even in the absence of text. Verbal instructions for tempo deviations are less often found in solo keyboard music, although there are occasional examples in the early seventeenth-century Italian repertory.[34] Nevertheless, it is clear from the recommendations provided in Frescobaldi's prefaces that even in the absence of such indications, performers were expected to take similar liberties in response to changes of mood in the music, at least within certain types of works in the newer styles.

One type of instrumental solo music that seems to have been performed with rhythmic freedom from its traceable beginnings was the improvised prelude (or written-out imitation thereof). German examples go back to the amorphous *praeambula* in fifteenth-century organ tablatures, often including extended passages lacking regular metric groupings over sustained pedal notes. Well-known later examples include the toccatas of the Italian and German composers and the free preludes of the *clavecinistes* (see p. 128) as well as the later seventeenth-century German organ preludes. Another group of pieces that calls for a free interpretation are the laments and *tombeaux*. Several of those by Froberger are marked "Se joue lentement avec discrétion" (to be played slowly with discretion) or something along those lines.

Rhythmic Alterations, Notes Inégales

The framework of a regular, even beat still allows a flexibility with respect to its subdivisions, and while some unevenness, such as prolonging the first of a pair or group of notes, is common in the performance practices of many kinds of music, in certain styles the systematic rhythmic inflection of shorter note values was carried quite far and sometimes even codified. In sixteenth-century Spain the first in pairs of quarter or eighth notes was either lengthened or shortened, and similarly one in a group of four notes could be prolonged. In Louis XIV's France the practice of lengthening the first of each pair of notes was legalized into a well-regulated system, that of *notes inégales*, described at length in numerous sources (Hefling, 1993). The inequality was most commonly applied to strings of short note values, usually eighths or sixteenths, that proceeded by scale step in moderate tempo. The amount of lengthening continues to be a topic of debate; it clearly went beyond slight expressive stretching and probably was applied with some variation. One imagines this manner of playing to have some resemblance to the "swing" interpretation of evenly notated notes in jazz performances, and, when executed effectively, it can indeed lend the performance a swinging quality. To what extent the *inégales* practice infected performances outside France is another hotly argued issue. There is some evidence that it was considered primarily a French practice, but that it might occasionally be adopted by foreigners performing "in stile francese."

We shall pass by here the related issue of overdotting in the French overture style (see Helfing, 1993), since, notwithstanding a few exceptional instances like d'Anglebert's harpsichord arrangements of Lully overtures, French overtures don't really enter into the keyboard repertory until the eighteenth century. The habit of some scholars to declare any slow piece with dotted rhythms to be in French overture style, and hence calling for an overdotted style, can hardly be justified.

Repeats and First and Second Endings

Today when encountering repeat signs, we expect to have our course of action unambiguously specified, with clear indications of what should be repeated, as well as how to handle first and second endings. Early performers, on the other hand, were expected to take some initiative or at least to exercise musical common sense. Single-sided repeat signs were not yet in use; repeats were indicated in several ways, including a double bar with dots on both sides (often more than two), dots between the two bars of a double bar (see p. 186, Ill. 4.10), or sometimes no dots at all (see p. 66, Ill. 2.4). Since the signs are symmetrical, the performer must decide to which side (if not both) of the double bar they apply. For example, when a repeat sign separates a rather brief first section from a very long second one, preference may be just to repeat the former.

During most of our period, distinct first and second endings are generally not provided; if they are needed, the player will have to make them up. During the later seventeenth century composers, particularly in France, start writing out first endings, usually as what looks like an extra measure with a slur over it, which must be skipped during the second pass. A similar situation may be encountered with the French *rondeaux*, in which the refrain, although written out only once at the beginning, must be inserted between all couplets, with the improvisation of appropriate bridges if not supplied. The performer may also need to decide whether to repeat the refrain (each time, or first and last time only?) and/or the couplets. Also in French *doubles*, choices must be made between several possible alternative routes (see pp. 18 and 127).[35]

Ornamentation

As was discussed in the Introduction (pp. 11–14), and elsewhere throughout this book, musicians frequently made up their own music rather than playing pieces notated in scores. However, even when playing a piece composed by someone else, they were in the habit of changing and elaborating or sometimes simplifying them according to their own whims. Manuscript copies often (in fact, nearly always) show such changes (see also pp. 16–19 and 123–26), and treatises such as those by Santa María and Diruta frequently provide guidance on how and where to introduce variations and embellishments (see pp. 267 and 318–19).

Keyboard scores often included signs telling a performer where embellishments should be added. Such signs are already present in the earliest sources, probably because keyboard players have always recognized that embellishments provided a means of overcoming the limitations of their instruments and emulating the varieties of attack and tone production commanded by singers and players of melodic instruments. At first, the explanations of how to execute the embellishments represented by those signs were rather vague, if provided at all. Only during the seventeenth century, as the number of different signs multiplied, did composers occasionally provide more detailed instructions for their realization, sometimes in the form of tables of ornaments. However, even when such explanations were present, the signs allowed a fair amount of freedom in their execution, for example, regarding such matters as how fast a trill should be played and how long it should continue. Indeed, that freedom is essential to the role of these ornaments as an expressive tool in the hands of the performer.

The proper execution of ornaments, whether indicated in the score or not, has generated a huge amount of attention—and heat—in the modern performance-practice literature, and debate on such questions as whether a trill should start on the main note or the upper second, and whether before or on the beat, seems to continue without an end in sight. How then is the poor player to go about realizing the ornaments of a particular composition he wishes to perform? Obviously, he should consult the guidelines most likely to be pertinent to the repertory and guard against inappropriate application of late French ornamentation to earlier, non-French music. But it is equally important to consider the expressive (or rhetorical) function of the ornament in its musical context: does it serve to accent a note, to prolong it, to simulate an exclamation, a swell, or a diminuendo? Each of these situations will require different handling of the chosen figure. For example, Diruta's *tremolo* can enrich a note (Ex. 7a), and a quick *tremoletto* can accent either a "good" or a "bad" one (Ex. 7b), whereas a *groppo* serves well at a cadence, essentially enhancing the 4–3 suspension and its resolution (Ex. 7c). Analogous ornaments, although differing in detail, can be found in most other repertories, as can be seen by comparing the examples on pp. 48–49, 77, 141, 215, 319, and 341.

EXAMPLE 7.1. Girolamo Diruta, *Il Transilvano* (Venice, 1593)

(a) *Tremolo*

(b) *Tremoletto*

(c) *Groppo*

Guide to Literature

Although there exists no book devoted specifically to performance practice on early keyboard music, several recent general texts include chapter-length surveys that provide good introductions to the performance practice of the sixteenth century (Ashworth 1994), of the seventeenth century (Kroll 1997), the organ (Marshall 1998); and of the harpsichord (Moroney 2002). Each is written by a noted artist-scholar who brings his or her own perspective, and each can be profitably applied well beyond the indicated repertories. For those who prefer to consult the original sources, most important treatises and prefaces are now available in facsimile (e.g., Banchieri, Nivers), and many as well in English translations (e.g., Diruta, Santa María, Frescobaldi[36]); in addition, the indefatigable facsimile publisher Fuzeau has brought out a comprehensive anthology of French harpsichord methods and treatises (Lescat and Saint-Arroman 2002). These ancient texts often provide surprisingly helpful insights as well as—at times—quite entertaining reading. We also highly recommend François Couperin, *L'art de toucher le clavecin*, which, although published in the eighteenth century, includes much that applies to earlier music (after all, Couperin was born in 1668) and to harpsichord playing in general. In fact, one finds in all these writings many concise, lucid, and genuinely helpful observations on several topics covered in this chapter.

For many performance-practice topics, the corresponding articles in NG 2001 are as authoritative, comprehensive, and up to date as any reference one could cite. We have already referred to the articles on *musica ficta*, registration, and temperament, and could add those on fingering, *notes iné-gales*, ornaments, and several others. We will mention here a few other useful studies on special topics. A very thorough exposition on fingering by Harald Vogel (1999) is buried in an appendix to vol. 2 of the new edition of Scheidt's *Tabulatura nova*; while its focus is on early seventeenth-century German practice, much of it is applicable to early keyboard music in general. Vogel includes a discussion of the connection between fingering and articulation; for an analysis of the fine details of organ articulation (much of it also applicable to the harpsichord), we also recommend Marshall 1998, 98–103. For a clear and well-organized introduction to the complex subject of organ registration we recommend Owen 1997, and for both organological and performance issues regarding the clavichord Brauchli 1998 is the reference of choice. Finally we shall suggest a few good guides for those who want to venture farther into the marshes of the notation, meter, and tempo relationships; none of these is limited to keyboard music. Houle 1987 presents a broad overview, oriented toward exploring the intellectual backgrounds; his "Meter and Tempo" chapter (1997) is a more succinct summary, limited to the seventeenth century. Kurtzman 1999, while ostensibly a chapter in a monograph on Monteverdi's Vespers of 1610, is one of the best-researched and most penetrating analyses of the subject for the early seventeenth century and beyond. Also extremely detailed and comprehensive is the treatment in Wolf 1992 of this and many other performance-practice topics, despite its focus on the printed Italian repertory during the years 1570 to 1630 (one would welcome an English translation!).

Notes

1. Information on performance practice in various countries can easily be located through the Index by looking under "performance practice" or under specific topics, such as "*alternatim* performance" or "improvisation."

2. For literature on topics discussed in the text, see the Guide to Literature section at the end of this chapter.

3. A dramatic, well-documented example is the changing fashion of ornamenting the slow movements of Corelli's violin sonatas; see Robert E. Seletsky, "18th-Century Variations for Corelli's Sonatas op. 5 ," *Early Music* 24 (1996): 119–30.

4. Some players proudly displayed their skill at distributing the fingers of one hand over two manuals; see for example the photographs of the artist's hands in Eta Harich-Schneider, *Die Kunst des Cembalo-Spiels* (Kassel, 1958), Tafel IV, after p. 33.

5. Delrin is a tough plastic, more durable than leather, easy to obtain, and closer in sound to the real thing. We should add though that while delrin plectra are used almost universally today, they are not nearly as touch-sensitive as real crow quills.

6. On the *Fundamenta*, see pp. 147–55.

7. Tomás de Santa María, *Libro llamado Arte de tañer fantasía* (Valladolid, 1565); for an English translation, see Santa María 1991.

8. The acronym HIP was defined by John Butt in an interesting and informative essay: "Bach Recordings since 1980: A Mirror of Historical Performance," *Bach Perspectives* 4. (Lincoln, NE, 1999), 181–98.

9. For discussions of some of the main national traditions, see under the specific instrument type (clavichord, harpsichord, organ) in the Index.

10. Note, however, that in early English usage "virginals" could refer to any type of harpsichord; see p. 27.

11. See Alexander Silbiger, "The Roman Frescobaldi Tradition: 1640–1670," *Journal of the American Musicological Society* 33 (1980): 52–87, especially 59–60.

12. For example, Davitt Moroney, in his recording *William Byrd: The Complete Keyboard Music* (Hyperion CD A66551/7, 1999) chooses to perform selected works on a muselar virginal.

13. The Duke University Chapel boasts three pipe organs in three different styles (early seventeenth-century Italian, eighteenth-century North-European, and early twentieth-century American), and it is not unusual for organists to move to different instruments for parts of their recital, with the audience moving along to the areas of the chapel where the instruments are located.

14. For additional examples of instrument specifications in publication titles, see Table 4 in Alexander Silbiger, *Italian Manuscript Sources of 17th Century Keyboard Music* (Ann Arbor, 1980), 27. Published collections that name both harpsichord and organ as performance options are surprisingly rare, although they include such important publications as Frescobaldi's two *Libri di toccate* (1637). However, for

those collections, which include a very diverse repertory, it is not clear whether the options apply to every piece in the collection or merely indicate that both harpsichord and organ pieces are included. In fact, some pieces in those Frescobaldi volumes are specifically designated for organ, and the first (1615) edition of the first book, which does not include all the works published in 1637, specifies only harpsichord on the title page.

15. See Silbiger, "Roman Frescobaldi Tradition," 46.

16. This represents the norm, but as with other aspects of instrument construction, there was much variability, with all kinds of exceptional dispositions; see Fuller 2001.

17. Some instruments perform from transposed parts, but a clarinetist knows that when he plays what looks like an A in a part for his B-flat instrument it is "really" a G.

18. It seems, nevertheless, that in various countries there were distinct pitches to which lutenists used to tune; see Haynes 2002, 22–24.

19. Haynes 2002, 64.

20. For more details, see Haynes 2002.

21. For a more technical discussion and historical sources, see Lindley 2001.

22. The Spanish exploited this sound in their *tientos de falsas*; see p. 327.

23. Pieces like John Bull's *Hexachord Fantasia*, which because of their enharmonic transformations were thought to point to the early use of equal temperament, more likely were intended for such a cyclic temperament.

24. Needless to say, the player of a large church organ has, if anything, to perform an even more complex body dance than the pianist, but on such an organ it is more a matter of ensuring that the fingers are ready to go on the proper manual and the feet on the right pedal keys than imparting a momentum.

25. This characterization is of course rather oversimplified; one finds subtle articulations marked throughout the scores of composers like Chopin, even if these all too often are disregarded.

26. The pairing was often described as an alternation of "good" and "bad" notes, with the good notes corresponding to the metrically strong positions; see also the section *Rhythmic Alterations, Notes inégales*, below.

27. Twentieth-century musicologists used *musica ficta* to refer to chromatic alterations that were not present in the score but that players were expected to add in performance according to certain rules. The original meaning of the term was somewhat different; also, by the seventeenth century the practice of adding unwritten accidentals in performance was rapidly becoming obsolete (see Margaret Bent "Musica ficta," NG 2001, 17:441 and Alexander Silbiger, "Musica ficta 5: After 1600," NG 2001, 17: 449–51).

28. In their original mensural setting there was more to these signs than their metric pattern, but almost none of it affecting their seventeenth-century usage.

29. In our further discussion we shall employ the English terminology of the period—still used by the British—when referring to note values: semibreves for whole notes, minims for half notes, and semiminims for quarter notes.

30. For a discussion of the *tactus* see Kurtzman 1999, 434–35.

31. "And in the triplas or sesquialteras, if they are major they must be taken adagio, if minor a bit more allegro, if three semiminims, [still] more allegro and if six for four, make them go with a rapid beat"; see Kurtzman 1999, 453 n.78 for the Italian original.

32. For Mersenne and Ban, see Paul Brainard, "Proportional Notation in the Music of Schütz and His Contemporaries," *Current Musicology* 50 (1992): 29–30; for Carissimi, see Houle 1987, 26; for Reincken, see Jan Pieterszoon Sweelinck, *Werken* vol 10, ed. Hermann Gehrmann (s'Gravenhage, 1901), 56–58; for Purcell, see Kroll 1997, 214.

33. For example, in a set of four *correnti* in Frescobaldi's *Toccate* (1615), the first two have a C 3 signature, the third has C$\frac{3}{2}$, and the fourth C3; yet all four are very similar in style, with three semiminims to the bar. It is hard to imagine how the different signatures might prescribe differences in interpretation.

34. The prescription "allarga la battuta" (broaden the beat) is found in several versets in Trabaci's *Secondo libro de ricercate* (1615) and *adagio* and *allegro* markings are found with passages throughout Frescobaldi's *Fiori musicali*.

35. For more on French repetition practices, including the *petite reprise*, see p. 127; some of the special practices described there may not have been confined to France.

36. The texts of all of Frescobaldi's prefaces, along with excellent translations, are available in Frederick Hammond, *Girolamo Frescobaldi: A Guide to Research*, Garland Composers Resource Manuals 9, (New York, 1988), 83–106.

Selected Bibliography

Ashworth, Jack. "Keyboard Instruments." In *A Performer's Guide to Sixteenth-Century Music*, ed. Jeffery Kite-Powell, 173–88. New York, 1994.

Banchieri, Adriano. *L'organo suonarino . . . Quinto registro*. Venice, 1611. Reprint, Amsterdam, 1969.

Brauchli, Bernhard. *The Clavichord*. Cambridge, 1998.

Buchner, Hans. *Sämtliche Orgelwerke*. Ed. Jost Harro Schmidt. Das Erbe deutscher Musik, 54–55. Frankfurt, 1974.

Carter, Stewart, ed. *A Performer's Guide to Seventeenth-Century Music*. New York, 1997.

Couperin, François. *L'art de toucher le clavecin / The Art of Playing the Harpsichord*. Ed. and trans. Margery Halford. New York, 1974.

Diruta, Girolamo. *The Transylvanian (Il Transilvano)*. 2 vols. Trans. Murray C. Bradshaw and Edward J. Soehnlen. Henryville, 1984.

Fuller, David. "Gigault's dots, or, *Notes inégales* 'wie sie eigentlich gewesen'[*sic*]." In *The Organist as Scholar: Essays in Memory of Russell Saunders*, ed. Kerala J. Snyder. Stuyvesant, NY, 1994.

——. "Registration II: Harpsichord." In NG 2001, 21: 113–17.

Haynes, Bruce. *A History of Performing Pitch: The Story of A*. Lanham, MD, 2002.

Hefling, Stephen. *Rhythmic Alteration in Seventeenth- and Eighteenth-Century Music: Notes inégales and Overdotting*. New York, 1993.

Houle, George. "Meter and Tempo." In *A Performer's Guide to Seventeenth-Century Music*, ed. Stewart Carter, 297–317. New York, 1997.

——. *Meter in Music, 1600–1800: Performance, Perception, and Notation*. Bloomington, IN, 1987.

Kroll, Mark. "Keyboard Instruments." In *A Performer's Guide to Seventeenth-Century Music*, ed. Stewart Carter, 198–222. New York, 1997.

Kurtzman, Jeffrey G. "Metre and Tempo." In *The Monteverdi Vespers of 1610: Music*,

Context, Performance, 433–66. Oxford, 1999.

Lescat Philippe and Jean Saint-Arroman, eds. *Clavecin: Méthodes, traités, dictionaires et encyclopédies, ouvrages généraux.* Méthodes & traités 12. Série I, France, 1600–1800. Courlay, 2002.

Lindley, Mark. "Temperament." In NG 2001, 25: 248–68.

——, and Maria Boxall. *Early Keyboard Fingerings: A Comprehensive Guide.* Mainz, 1992.

——, and Maria Boxall. *Early Keyboard Fingerings: An Anthology.* Mainz, 1982.

Marshall, Kimberly. "The Fundamentals of Organ Playing" and "A Survey of Historical Performance Practices." In *The Cambridge Companion to the Organ,* ed. Nicholas Thistlethwaite and Geoffrey Webber, 93–129. Cambridge, 1998.

Moroney, Davitt. "Keyboard." In *A Performer's Guide to Music in the Baroque Period,* 67–84. London, 2002.

Nivers, Guillaume-Gabriel. *Premier Livre d'orgue.* Paris, 1665. Reprint, Paris, 1987.

Owen, Barbara. *The Registration of Baroque Organ Music.* Bloomington, IN, 1997.

Rowland, David. *Early Keyboard Instruments: A Practical Guide.* Cambridge, 2001.

Santa María, Tomás de. *The Art of Playing the Fantasia.* Trans. Almonte C. Howell Jr. and Warren E. Hultberg. Pittsburgh, 1991.

Vogel, Harald. "Keyboard Playing Techniques around 1600." In Samuel Scheidt, *Tabulatura nova,* ed. Harald Vogel, vol. 2, 145–80. Wiesbaden, 1999.

Williams, Peter. *Figured Bass Accompaniment.* Edinburgh, 1970

Wolf, Uwe. *Notation und Aufführungspraxis: Studien zum Wandel von Notenschrift und Notenbild in italienischen Musikdrucken der Jahre 1571–1630,* 2 vols. Kassel, 1992.

Index

Note: references to musical examples and illustrations are printed in boldface; references to extended discussions are in italics. Manuscripts are listed by their common designations or short titles under the entry "Manuscripts"; for most manuscripts the corresponding RISM sigla are given in the tables at the end of chapters (for page references to those tables, see the entry "Manuscript short titles"). All compositions quoted in musical examples or facsimile reproductions are entered by title under the composer or, if anonymous, under the manuscript.